Dr. S. Fritz Forkel
د. سليمان فريتس فوركل
ד״ר שלמה פריץ פורקל
Skén:nen Rón:nis

Hebrew in Ashkenaz

Hebrew in Ashkenaz
A LANGUAGE IN EXILE

EDITED BY

Lewis Glinert
School of Oriental & African Studies
London University

New York   Oxford
OXFORD UNIVERSITY PRESS
1993

Oxford University Press

Oxford New York Toronto
Delhi Bombay Calcutta Madras Karachi
Kuala Lumpur Singapore Hong Kong Tokyo
Nairobi Dar es Salaam Cape Town
Melbourne Auckland Madrid

and associated companies in
Berlin Ibadan

Copyright © 1993 by Oxford University Press, Inc.

Published by Oxford University Press, Inc.
200 Madison Avenue, New York, NY 10016

Oxford is a registered trademark of Oxford University Press

All rights reserved. No part of this publication may be reproduced,
stored in a retrieval system, or transmitted, in any form or by any means,
electronic, mechanical, photocopying, recording or otherwise,
without the prior permission of the publisher.

Library of Congress Cataloging-in-Publication Data
Hebrew in Ashkenaz : a language in exile / edited by Lewis Glinert.
p. cm.
Includes bibliographical references.
ISBN 0-19-506222-1
1. Hebrew language—Europe—History. 2. Hebrew language—Social
aspects. 3. Hebrew language—Revival. I. Glinert, Lewis.
PJ4515.H44 1993
306.4'4'08992404—dc20   92-2831

London Borough
of Enfield
Arts And Libraries

2 4 6 8 10 9 7 5 3 1

Printed in the United States of America
on acid-free paper

For Chaim Rabin,
who first ploughed these fields

Preface

"Hebrew in Ashkenaz." Try as I may, the words evoke swarms of sacred letters and swaying figures, Chagallesque, even a trifle burlesque, something too "ethnic" for words.

Is this perhaps, at root, the reason why the role and nature of the Hebrew language in Ashkenazi Europe was for so long virtually ignored by Jewish secular scholarship—itself, ironically, largely Ashkenazi?

So much Ashkenazic writing seemed, in A. Halkin's words, to "lack grace of style or even the rudiments of grammar," in turn an incontrovertible mark of a lack of worldly culture. Medieval Ashkenaz, as even so sympathetic a scholar as Zimmels conceded, combined piety and all-consuming devotion to traditional learning with a "deep scar" of introversion, guilt, and asceticism born of constant persecution. It was the Sephardim that appeared to have had the "correct" accent and the sophistication for framing the rules for Hebrew and the polish and flair for enshrining them in poetry, philosophy, and the rest. And this perceived Sephardi "cultural supremacy" has translated itself, as Ismar Schorsch has so penetratingly observed, into the linguistic and cultural values of our own day—into the choice of synagogue accent by Reform temples in the U.S.A. and the U.K., into the rules of "schoolbook" grammar in Israel, and into the very pronunciation norms of the Israeli-in-the-street.

If the Hebrew of Ashkenaz did attract attention, this generally began with the Haskalah—the late eighteenth-century German-Jewish "Enlightenment," embodying the first phase in the rapid secularization and modernization of Ashkenazi Jewish culture. And out of the Haskalah was born a new Ashkenazi Hebrew, drawing mightily on non-Ashkenazi and non-Jewish linguistic and literary models but still *nolens volens* distinctively Ashkenazi in major linguistic and sociolinguistic senses. This would soon lay the foundations for a radically new Hebrew culture seeking a total rupture with Diaspora continuity—in Europe, for a tragically brief few years, but above all in Eretz-Israel.

Of this New Hebrew in Ashkenaz, of its outpourings and aspirations, much has been written. But what of the Old Hebrew that continued to exist side-by-side, and that still lives on, unextinguished, in the writings (and readings) of that survival of the Ashkenazi past, the "Yeshivah World"? Despite the acknowledged intellectual achievements of sixteenth and seventeenth century Central European Jewry in education, language study, and critical method, despite the remarkable fact that down the centuries it was the medieval Ashkenazim who insisted on using Hebrew, intensively, in all their vast outpouring of prose—rather than resorting to the language of the Gentiles, as did the Jews of Arab lands—the sad fact is that little of this traditional Hebrew usage has been documented.

What of the histories of literature, the anthologies, the cultural companions? Typically dedicated to the imaginative as the sole legitimate concept of the esthetic, and to belles lettres (and perhaps folk tales) as its sole expression, they have generally found little room for anything not belonging to the Haskalah or proceeding therefrom: for the wealth of Ashkenazic literature, moral or philosophical prose, religious poetry—elegiac, enigmatic, didactic, panegyric—that refuses to comply with general Western criteria for literature. Indeed, the two most cited Hebrew literary historians, Lachower and Klausner, made no bones about defining their subject matter philosophically rather than just esthetically. The new modern creative secularism was their yardstick.

A generation has passed. But Judaic studies, it is increasingly being realized, have still to shake off the shadow of the Jewish Enlightenment.

Running even deeper, perhaps, in the Israeli perspective on Ashkenaz has been the drive to be free of the memory of the Diaspora and its ghettos, a drive that lay at the core of classical Zionism. Here, another language, Yiddish, has been—and still is—a potent force. At the very root of the Jewish bid for "enlightenment" and modernization lay a set of neuroses about the Yiddish language, not just for its being a low-function folk vernacular but also and especially for its being so uncomfortably close to the language that symbolized enlightenment, German. And just as the desire to revitalize Hebrew has ubiquitously been bound up with the desire to be rid of Yiddish, so too it has sought to reject the "old-style" Hebrew of Ashkenaz, its sound and words—and the knowledge of it.

Hebrew in Ashkenaz seeks to confront these linguistic neuroses head-on. The essays gathered here are perforce a small window on the fabric and function of Hebrew in Ashkenazi life. But the window looks out on a field far broader than the linguistics and literature that one expects to find when there is talk of Hebrew. This volume brings together sociologists, linguists, philosophers, and historians of literature and ideas, to share the question "What was (and is) Hebrew in Ashkenazi life?"

The universe of the contemporary linguistic sciences is vast and still expanding; as I endeavor to suggest in my introductory essay, the workings of any language and its interaction with society and culture are a truly vast field of research. So too with Hebrew in Ashkenaz, never a mother tongue but so much more than a "mere" vernacular. Its full implications for the Judaic humanities and social sciences have still to be grasped.

London L.G.
February 1992

Contents

1. Hebrew in Ashkenaz: Setting an Agenda   3
   LEWIS GLINERT

2. The Ashkenazi Hasidic Concept of Language   11
   JOSEPH DAN

3. The Grammatical Literature of Medieval Ashkenazi Jewry   26
   ILAN ELDAR

4. The Phonology of Ashkenazic   46
   DOVID KATZ

5. Confronting the Hebrew of Responsa: Intensifiers in the Syntax of Rabbi Me'ir of Rothenburg   88
   MENAHEM ZEVI KADDARI

6. On the Role of *Melitzah* in the Literature of Hebrew Enlightenment   99
   MOSHE PELLI

7. A Duty Too Heavy to Bear: Hebrew in the Berlin Haskalah, 1783–1819: Between Classic, Modern, and Romantic   111
   YAACOV SHAVIT

8. What Did "Knowing Hebrew" Mean in Eastern Europe?   129
   SHAUL STAMPFER

9. From Traditional Bilingualism to National Monolingualism   141
   ISRAEL BARTAL

10. Cartoons about Language: Hebrew, Yiddish, and the Visual Representation of Sociolinguistic Attitudes   151
    JOSHUA A. FISHMAN

11. Hebrew and the Habad Communication Ethos   167
    NAFTALI LOEWENTHAL

12. Why Did Ben-Yehuda Suggest the Revival of Spoken Hebrew?   193
    GEORGE MANDEL

13. The Emergence of Modern Hebrew: Some Sociolinguistic
    Perspectives   208
    SHELOMO MORAG

14. Hebrew as a Holy Tongue: Franz Rosenzweig and the Renewal of
    Hebrew   222
    PAUL MENDES-FLOHR

15. The Status of Hebrew in Soviet Russia from the Revolution to the
    Gorbachev Thaw   242
    AVRAHAM GREENBAUM

16. Language as Quasilect: Hebrew in Contemporary Anglo-Jewry   249
    LEWIS GLINERT

Hebrew in Ashkenaz

It gives me such fiendish pleasure to see myself in the beloved twenty-two letters that nothing else seems to matter.
Franz Rosenzweig, July 14, 1929

1

Hebrew in Ashkenaz: Setting an Agenda

LEWIS GLINERT

Until recent years, students of Diaspora Hebrew had good reason to feel under a cloud. Linguistics, burgeoning as a rigorous scientific discipline (in its various forms: structuralist, generative, and so on) in the mid-twentieth century, saw fit to give primacy to language in its native spoken form, and in terms of data as sharp and as mathematical looking as possible. Diaspora Hebrew, essentially a written language (or nonvernacular language, to be precise), lay outside this domain. How it had functioned, for whom and for what, was of little consequence. It should have been of some consequence to social scientists or to historians—except that here there was no particular interest in language factors per se. And so interest in the Hebrew of the Diaspora remained the province of the literary historian and the traditional grammarian—with Hebrew in Ashkenaz coming off decidedly the worst. (See Preface.)

The 1960s and 1970s saw a sudden broadening of linguistics, to embrace the interface of language with behavior (sociolinguistics, linguistic ethnography, sociology of language), language with knowledge (psycholinguistics, philosophy of language), language with art (poetics, stylistics). Scholars such as Uriel Weinreich, Dell Hymes, William Labov, Joshua Fishman, John Gumperz, Charles Ferguson, and Einar Haugen have been at the forefront of the rigorous exploration of language as a system of variant forms and variant languages, pulled this way and that by social forces, which in turn can be rigorously characterized and quantified. Common among such linguistic systems are multilingual systems—particularly those described by Ferguson as "diglossic," involving a "low-status language" for vernacular functions and a "high-status language" for certain other functions.

Ashkenazic Hebrew was, and still contrives to be, part of just such a multilingual system (a "polysystem"). And the growing focus on such complex sociolinguistic situations invites new interest in Ashkenazic Hebrew, both as part of a broader linguistic-cultural system and as a linguistic system (albeit a nonvernacular one) in itself. Far from being a marginal curiosity—as post-Enlightenment and Zionist-oriented Judaic scholarship, as well as mid-century linguistics, has tended to see it—Hebrew in Ashkenaz must now be ranked as a fairly typical linguistic phenomenon, and one that invites a multifaceted, indeed a *multidisciplinary* approach.

Pointing the way, in the seventies, to a multi-disciplinary approach to language as a social science is the work of the sociologist Basil Bernstein and the linguist and semiotician Michael Halliday. Bernstein's theory of the social system and cultural transmission across the generations assigns to language a central role in the process of socialization and the perpetuation of the social system. Halliday, for his part, has explored the notion of language as part of a more general social system of signs or semiotic: "the concept of the culture as a system of meaning, with language as one of its realizations." In the same way, an understanding of the form and functions of Ashkenazic Hebrew promises to make a significant contribution to the expanding field of Ashkenazic social studies—sociology of literature, ethnography of religion, social history, and so on—as well as to other branches of the humanities, such as political history and literary analysis.

Figure 1.1 represents Halliday's (1978: 11) useful attempt at a scheme for the linguistic sciences.

The triangle at the heart of this scheme is what is commonly considered "core linguistics": The sound system (phonology), grammar (morphology and syntax), vocabulary, and the semantics that they support. Also regarded as core subjects, but represented here as three broad projections from the triangle, are:

1. *Varieties within* a given language (geographical and social "dialects," and the genres, situations, and role relationships that create various "registers")
2. *Changes* undergone by a language
3. Phonetics

Outside the agreed core are several other dimensions:

1. The "idiolect," i.e., the language of the individual (often called "style")

and, relating to other disciplines:

2. Language as behavior: sociolinguistics, sociology of language, linguistic anthropology, etc.
3. Language as knowledge: psycholinguistics, philosophy of language, etc.
4. Language as literature (just one "metaphorical" use of language, but a particularly notable one): poetics, literary stylistics, etc.

Also alluded to in figure 1.1 are a number of other disciplines to which linguistics relates, such as education and pathology.

The very words "Hebrew" and "Ashkenaz" take on a special sense in the light of this global approach to language. "Hebrew" is of interest not just as the multipurpose medium of written communication, intensive textual study, and sacred or mystic symbolic value that it was—and still is—in traditionalist religious society but also in its much-reduced function, so widespread today in secular Jewish circles, of a micro-system or "quasilect," with a value more symbolic than linguistic. And this conception of Hebrew allows us to use a broad definition of "Ashkenaz": initially the domain of Franco-German Jewry, from the emergence of a distinct sociocultural Ashkenazic identity in the tenth and eleventh centuries, and then—from

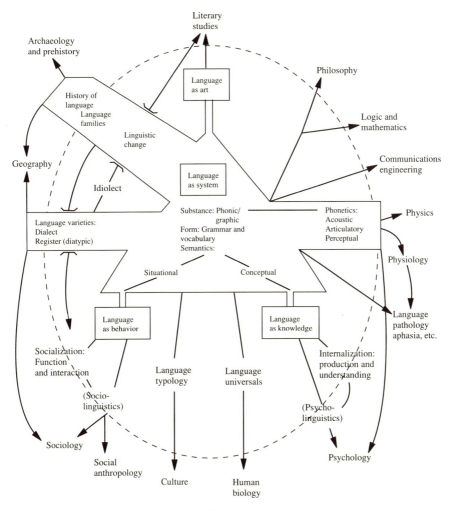

Fig. 1.1.

Figure 1.1 is reprinted with the permission of the publisher, from *Language as a Social Semiotic* by Michael A. K. Halliday (1978), published by Edward Arnold (Publishers) Limited.

the sixteenth century on—spreading to include Eastern European Jewry that saw itself as heir to this culture (Zimmels 1958, M. Weinreich 1967, Bartal 1985, Kirshenblatt-Gimblett forthcoming), and extending to the emigrants from these lands and their descendants. Where these descendants are "Ashkenazi" Israelis, whose linguistic system has been turned inside out or "normalized" (Fishman 1979), the notion of Hebrew in Ashkenaz is of course almost certainly vacuous. But British Jewry and American Jewry, sociolinguistically and in many other ways too, still bear the hallmark of "Ashkenaz"; for this reason I have included an essay on the role of Hebrew in Anglo-Jewish religious life, suggestive, I hope, of the fact that any account of Hebrew in Ashkenaz must be set in the present and future tense as well as the past historic.

Now given that Hebrew in Ashkenaz has essentially been a written-and-read, not a spoken, language—and thus arguably a secondary rather than a primary language (though the notions "primary" and "secondary" are far from uncontroversial)—one may ask if a scheme like that in figure 1.1 is relevant in its entirety or even in its major part to our purposes.

In principle, the answer is "yes." To be sure, there will be nothing of mother-tongue acquisition nor of speech acquisition in general—until one arrives at the modern-Hebrew-as-second-language movement in pre-War Europe. Nor will there be anything of the "creative" childhood functions of language. And yet the general scheme still remains an appropriate one. Hebrew in Ashkenaz has had its grammar, phonology, phonetics, etc; its array of social and anthropological functions; its psychological and philosophical dimensions; its literary applications, and so on and so forth. Quite possibly, case studies even exist of the Hebrew reading problems of dyslexics or the written Hebrew syntactic decoding disabilities of aphasics.

Without doubt, the workings and functions of such a language are different, in principle, from those of mother tongues or secondary vernaculars. But that does not make it any less worthy of attention per se, nor any less significant for a general theory of language structure or language use.

The contributors to this volume have explored Hebrew structure, uses, and attitudes from a broad range of perspectives. Introducing them in a thematic rather than chronological order, conceptions of Hebrew on the *religious plane* have ranged between the rational and the mystic, relating now to the Hebrew of the classical sources and now to Hebrew as an open-ended sacred medium. Two papers in this volume explore the mystic conception in some of its earliest and most recent major embodiments—the Hasidim of twelfth- and thirteenth-century Germany (Joseph Dan) and modern Eastern European Habad Hasidim (Naftali Loewenthal). The worldview depicted by Dan, wedded to tradition and Scripture, is intent on elaborating the ancient scriptural hermeneutics into a "radical and far-reaching semiotic statement." As enunciated in the *Sefer Ha-Hokhmah* of Rabbi Eleazar of Worms, the biblical letters and language provide seventy-three esoteric gates to a numinous experience of the Divine, through the shapes of the letters, their ornamentations, the numeric value of words, the combination of first or last letters and so on; as for the literal meaning of the text, it is just one among the myriad other messages that the divine author is conveying. The traditional prayers were subjected to similar contemplation.

A remarkable transmutation of the medieval Hasidic philosophy of Hebrew in response to modernity is described by Loewenthal. In seeking to communicate the esoteric to the masses, through the medium of the charismatic *zaddik,* nineteenth- and twentieth-century Habad-Lubavitch Hasidism has interpreted ancient midrashic notions of the sacred sparks within foreign tongues to legitimize and promote the translation of sacred texts into Yiddish and utterly non-Jewish languages—thus also coming to terms with the rise of modern secular Hebrew. The contrast and conflict between this philosophy—that the divine word "is beyond limitations, and can and even must reach the *anokhi* of the most foreign of tongues"—and the linguistic enclavism of many other sectors of Ultraorthodoxy has still to be explored.

The philosophy of Hebrew of the great twentieth-century philosopher Franz Rosenzweig is the subject of Paul Mendes-Flohr's essay. German Judaism, for Rosenzweig, had lost God; it had also lost any emotional sense of Judaism as a "world unto its own." Hebrew was the lifeline—the language of the original revelation and hence the divine language, animated by a breath of eternity and vessel of the Jewish soul. Hebrew had something linguistically special about it too: a tense system oriented to "flow of time" rather than "point of time," hence the Jewish emphasis on the historical rather than the natural, with the future not a static "somewhere" but a "not yet to be." Hebrew, in Rosenzweig's thought, is thus uniquely able to project a messianic future. And meanwhile, in exile, Hebrew is achieving its dialectical fullness: freed from mundane tasks and devoted to the spirit, it creates an estrangement from the workaday world—while yet continuing to evolve and nourish the Jewish vernacular. What, then, of modern, everyday Hebrew? Hebrew is now faced with ultimate death, like any language; and yet.... Flohr quotes Scholem's words, "God will not remain silent in the language in which He affirmed our life a thousand times and more."

The salience and vitality of language within culture can differ widely (as can all "core values"), to the point of having purely symbolic, non-communicative functions; at any rate, subjective and objective salience and vitality can be two very different things; so too the situation among the elite and the masses. Indeed, even within traditional, religious Ashkenaz, the salience of Hebrew as a component of religious values and identity is no easy matter to assess and may have varied widely; the danger in "talking up" those spheres in which language has been an issue, while ignoring all others, is self-evident. The essay by Lewis Glinert addresses one angle of this problem in a role-study of Hebrew in contemporary Anglo-Judaism—one of the major surviving loci of Ashkenazidom. Hebrew there is primarily a "quasi-lect," with functions such as the Bar-Mitzvah boy's "trial by language" that have little to do with linguistic communication but are still highly valued in Jewish society, as they are in several others.

Secularization of Hebrew in the nineteenth century represented a highly complex shift in values. Yaacov Shavit's paper shows how the German Haskalah (Enlightenment) promoted a "pure" classical Hebrew as a vehicle for a rationalistic, humanistic form of Judaism, untainted by Ashkenazi "atavism," and as a medium for a new, "modern" secular poetry and science. This was not just the cultivation of Hebrew for the sake of its literature but the Romantic notion of a language as "a mirror of the state of the nation."

The far-reaching fallout from these ideas, particularly on the Ashkenazi grass roots, cries out for a comprehensive assessment. Israel Bartal draws a parodoxical parallel between the linguistic goals of the Haskalah and those of nineteenth- and twentieth-century Orthodoxy: the maintenance of a diglossic state of affairs, in the one case introducing a modern Gentile substitute for Yiddish, in the other desperately seeking to maintain the Jewish vernacular—and pitted against them, Zionism, Yiddishism, and other nationalisms committed to a stark monolingualism.

A radical twist to secular Hebraism occurred with Eliezer Ben-Yehuda. As George Mandel demonstrates, Ben-Yehuda's celebrated article of 1879, *She'elah Nikhbadah,* was nothing less than a proto-Zionist call for a Jewish state; a state was the only hope for Hebrew to be "revived." Initially, however, for Ben-Yehuda as for Maskilim throughout the nineteenth century, "revival" meant a *literary* revival. It was only subsequently that his famous idea of "Native Spoken Hebrew" dawned on him: the modern educational system, he realized, would never have room for Hebrew literature unless Hebrew became a spoken language in a Jewish state. Thus the "birth" of the concept of spoken Hebrew was not as smooth as commonly fancied.

Some dimensions of Hebrew have gained sharpness by sheer differentiation from Yiddish: Hebrew as "eternal," "alive," "universal," "noble," and "beautiful" (Yiddish as transient, moribund, parochial, base, and ugly)—or conversely, with the rise of Zionism and Bundism, "unworldly" and "reactionary" (Yiddish as pragmatic and liberal); the scattered Hebrew literary circles as a substitute homeland. Another dimension was Hebrew's sheer irrelevance.

In evaluating such complex attitudes, visual signals can say as much as verbal ones—if not more. Joshua Fishman's paper signals the potential for language-attitude theory in general, and Hebrew studies in particular, of the work of cartoonists depicting the rocky relationship between Hebrew and Yiddish—from the turn-of-the-century image of the author Sokolov sharing his arm between the elegant "daughter of heaven" (Hebrew) and the buxom "maidservant" (Yiddish) through to the servant girl's liberation and the adoption, in modern Eretz-Israel, of more masculine and altogether more threatening postures by Hebrew. Hebrew in Ashkenaz gains a sharper perspective from consideration of Hebrew *outside* Ashkenaz.

Gentile attitudes to Hebrew—governmental, clerical, academic, popular—are a major topic in themselves. Avraham Greenbaum assesses the brutal repression of Hebrew in the former Soviet Union up to the Gorbachev era, suggesting that the Zionism of many Hebrew activists played into the hands of Communists who depicted the whole language as a vehicle of Zionism, clericalism, and counter-revolution—although religious Jewish circles did continue substantive publishing throughout the twenties. One prays that the dizzy revival of the Jewish-Hebrew spirit under *perestroika* and de-sovietization will not end as tragically as the "Hebrew Spring" of 1917.

What have been the social functions of Hebrew in Ashkenaz? Was it a "speech community"? Did it aid socialization or indicate group-belonging (e.g., via dialect or sociolect?) As a language of scholarship, did it constitute a "language of power"—and did secularization produce a "language of solidarity"? Shaul Stampfer's essay explores the social function of traditional and secularized Hebrew literacy in Eastern Europe. He argues that the relative failure of the *ḥeder* to impart Hebrew proficiency actually suited the religious elite, though neither they nor the masses realized it; they alone were able to spend their time in study in the communal study hall—unconsciously demonstrating, as it were, a "posture of ease." And meanwhile, Torah traditions were largely maintained by imitation and word of mouth; this was "in many respects a profoundly oral society."

The common view (e.g., Bendavid 1967: 1: chap. 23) that Hebrew in Ashkenaz was a linguistic jungle—most of it weeds—is not one based on substantive analysis; if anything, it has been prejudicial to the conduct of such analysis. For all of this, a combination of careful vignettes and broad quantitative sweeps—using, e.g., the

Bar-Ilan Responsa Database (whose potential is described here by M. Z. Kaddari)—will be mandatory.

On Ashkenazi Hebrew phonology in general, Dovid Katz provides a comprehensive picture—in which the sound patterns of the Hebraisms within Yiddish are first shown to be quite distinct from Ashkenazi Hebrew itself (e.g., *kál*ᵉ "bride" vs. *kalú*), be this the "Formal Ashkenazic" of Torah recitation or the "Popular Ashkenazic" of a Torah quotation tossed into everyday chit-chat or any of the important sociolinguistic gradations in between. Katz then maps out a synchronic and a historical phonology of the Ashkenazic vowel and consonant system, backed up by transcriptions from recitations of Megilas Esther. Phonetically, this Hebrew was much like Yiddish; but *phonologically,* it has shown "a substantial measure of independence resulting both from generation to generation language transmission . . . and from the phonologically retentive power of the hallowed system of vocalization signs."

M. Zvi Kaddari uses the Bar Ilan University database to explore intensifier adverbs (e.g., *kol kakh* "so," *me'od* "very") in the writings of the great jurist Rabbi Me'ir of Rothenburg (thirteenth century), a writer whose Hebrew has never before been the subject of linguistic analysis. He finds an eclectic mix of biblical, mishnaic, and Babylonian talmudic intensifiers—and comes up with the striking stylistic finding that—unlike the Bible, Mishnah, or Talmud—Rabbi Me'ir's writing does not allow any one intensifier to predominate: a datum with potential implications for the overall stylistic and syntactic shape of this rabbinic genre.

Controversy has raged around the *melitzah* or *shibutz* ("euphuistic" or "biblical-quotation") style so closely associated with the fiction of the Haskalah. Moshe Pelli's paper conducts a word-by-word exploration of a purple passage of Haskalah travelogue—to demonstrate how the Tanakhic linguistic routine, "though it may be full of generalities, ill-designed for self-expression and unsuited to relaying personal experiences, enjoys the great advantage of rousing the reader to an involvement in the events described." The imaginative welding of biblical "off-cuts" (Pelli rejects the term "shreds of verses") served to create a bond between author and reader through the intellectual game of "spotting the source," and through the aesthetic game of observing how it had been refashioned—games in which the modern reader is unlikely to be a player: today's Tanakh and midrash cognoscienti tend not to favor secular literature—and verily, this type of literature was "a reflection of all that is problematic in the duality of Jewish existence in the modern, secular world."

A major dimension of Ashkenaz Hebrew metalinguistics has been the work of grammarians and lexicographers, generally seeking to "purify" Hebrew usage or (which is often harder) to determine what the "correct" usage should be—and more recently, to expand or guide the language in some way or other.

It was the Sephardi world that wrote the grammars and the dictionaries—conventional wisdom would have it—until the Enlightenment. However, Ilan Eldar lifts the wraps off a virtually unknown world of intellectual-religious endeavor, the Ashkenaz circle of grammarians, which emerged in twelfth-century northern France, Germany, and England—reaching its peak between 1250 and 1300. Although grammar does not generally connote romance or adventure, there is a touch of both in the fact that just eight works have come down to us fully in manuscript, while we know of ten Ashkenazi grammarians whose work has been lost—evocative names like Rabbi Moshe ha-Nakdan of Londres and Rabbi Shimshon of Soissons. True, these scholars "never matched the scientific quality of the Spanish scholars writing in Arabic." And yet one must acknowledge their importance in their time and place. In lieu of the image of the Talmud-obsessed early Ashkenazi scholar, Eldar depicts a scholarly circle producing (and consuming) "a full and comprehensive picture of the rules of Hebrew as embodied in the Biblical text."

Hebrew in Ashkenaz still exists, in much reduced form. Meanwhile, the focus of Hebrew has shifted massively from Ashkenaz to the Land and State of Israel—and in many senses, from exile to return. What of the transition? Shelomo Morag assesses the "Full Return" sociolinguistically and asks how the encounter of two linguistic cultures, the Ashkenazi and the Sephardi—each with its own version of a Classical Hebrew Corpus and an Integrated Hebrew Corpus (integrated into Yiddish, Arabic etc)—was so rapidly and smoothly resolved. In fact, Morag shows, it was the Hebrew of the Sephardim that served as input for the Full Return, for reasons linguistic, ideological and aesthetic. "Its rules . . . all ran roughly along the lines of biblical Hebrew, grammatically at that time the overriding objective of the Return." And more important: for the European immigrants, Ashkenazi Hebrew "formed part of the semiotic system that portrayed the Old World from which they sought to escape." The result, however, has been nothing like pure "Sephardi."

Time will show whether the history of Ashkenazi Hebrew has now really entered a final phase.

References

BARTAL, ISRAEL. "The Image of Germany and German Jewry in Eastern European Jewish Society During the Nineteenth Century." In Isadore Twersky, ed. *Danzig, Between East and West: Aspects of Modern Jewish History.* Cambridge: Harvard University Press, 1985, pp. 3–17.

BENDAVID, ABBA. *Leshon Mikra u-Leshon Hakhamim* (Biblical and Mishnaic Hebrew). Tel Aviv: Dvir, 1967.

FISHMAN, JOSHUA A. "The Sociolinguistic 'Normalization' of the Jewish People." In E. Polome, ed. *Archibald Hill Festschrift.* Vol. 3. The Hague: Mouton, 1979.

HALLIDAY, MICHAEL A. K. *Language as Social Semiotic.* London: Edward Arnold, 1978.

KIRSHENBLATT-GIMBLETT, BARBARA. *Ashkenaz: Essays in the Intellectual History of Jewish Folklore and Ethnography.* Bloomington: Indiana University Press. Forthcoming.

WEINREICH, MAX. "The Reality of Jewishness versus the Ghetto Myth: The Sociolinguistic Roots." In *To Honor Roman Jakobson.* The Hague: Mouton, 1967, pp. 2191–2211.

ZIMMELS, H. J. *Ashkenazim and Sephardim.* London: Oxford University Press, 1958.

2

The Ashkenazi Hasidic Concept of Language

JOSEPH DAN

In the religious culture of the Ashkenazi Hasidic movement in the second half of the twelfth and the thirteenth century, language had become the main—and probably the only—avenue by which the pietist, the esoteric thinker, and the mystic might attain any kind of contact with God. The only source of divine revelation which was available was the ancient record of the revelations to Moses, the prophets, the talmudic sages and the early Jewish mystics—and this divine revelation was coined in letters, words, and sentences. Any attempt to reach out toward heaven, to satisfy the deep religious craving for contact with God, had to start by the pietist immersing himself in the language of the old divine revelations.

Unlike their contemporaries among the Jewish philosophers in the sphere of influence of Islamic civilization, the Ashkenazi Hasidim did not accept the notion that human logic, and therefore rational contemplation of divine truth, can serve as a way to achieve religious meaning. Their opposition to the "dialectics" of the rationalists was vehement,[1] and while Jewish-Spanish culture tried to build a religious culture on the twin pillars of tradition and [rational] wisdom, the Ashkenazi Hasidim recognized tradition alone as the source of religious truth. The other contemporaneous Jewish religious movement which began its development at the end of the twelfth century—the Kabbalah—while officially admitting only tradition as a source of truth, actually added to it the experiential stratum of a mystical contact with the Divine (often achieved through the use of ancient texts and their interpretation). The Ashkenazi Hasidim, as far as we know, saw in tradition alone their way to achieve spiritual goals, including mystical experiences.

Tradition, in this sense, is completely identical with language. There is little doubt that the Ashkenazi Hasidim preserved very old oral traditions, which were passed from father to son, from rabbi to disciple, during many generations. But even this oral tradition was always formulated in language. Even more than that, as will be shown below, it is very probable that a major segment of these oral traditions was directly related to method rather than content, to the ways by which one can interpret the word of God, rather than any specific content. Oral or written, tradition for the Ashkenazi Hasidim was the language of scripture and the methods of its interpretation. Religious experience and the craft of the commentator became identified. There is no surprise, therefore, that the considerable body of esoteric religious thought which the Ashkenazi Hasidim produced is almost exclusively hermeneutical.

Some further observations about the nature of the union between religion and hermeneutics will be presented below. This study, however, will concentrate on one document, which is unique in Ashkenazi Hasidic literature for its reflective character. It is a conscious presentation of the ways by which this union is achieved, expressing an attempt to formulate and systematize the attitude of the Ashkenazi-Hasidic theologian and mystic toward his sources, thus revealing, more than any other, the concept of language which enabled the medieval Jewish pietists in Germany to use the Hebrew letters, words, and books as a vehicle to achieve a fully religious, numinous experience of the Divine.

The two main sources which present the Ashkenazi Hasidic concept of the esoteric meaning of the Hebrew language are, first, Rabbi Eleazar of Worms's commentary on the letters of the alphabet, which constitutes the first treatise in the author's magnum opus of esoteric theology, *Sodei Razaya.* The second is the same author's explanation of the seventy-three "Gates of Wisdom," the methods of investigation of the esoteric meaning of the biblical verses. This paper is dedicated to the second work and represents an attempt to investigate the concept of language in Ashkenazi Hasidic theology according to their treatment of the words of the sacred biblical text.

The main textual basis for the following analysis is Rabbi Eleazar of Worms's ספר החכמה *(Sefer Ha-Ḥokhmah)* "The Book of Wisdom," which is found in two manuscripts in the Bodleian Library, Oxford,[2] and in a different version in two other manuscripts in the same library.[3] Part of this book has recently been printed,[4] and the book has received some scholarly attention.[5] The linguistic concepts of the book have not been studied as yet, and I believe that such an analysis is meaningful not only to the understanding of the esoteric theology of the Ashkenazi Hasidim, but also to the understanding of Hebrew hermeneutics in the ancient Midrash and the medieval Kabbalah.

The circumstances in which this book was written and the message it is intended to present are important to the understanding of its structure and contents. In this case Rabbi Eleazar was extremely helpful and opened the work with an interesting, uncharacteristic preface, which explains his reasons for writing it. This preface, which I published and analyzed twenty-five years ago,[6] states clearly the date of the writing—the only Ashkenazi Hasidic work which does so clearly. It was the year 1217, the year in which Rabbi Judah ben Samuel ben Kalonymus, "The Pious," died. Rabbi Eleazar mourned his great teacher's death and described his situation after this event as one of complete loneliness: he has no son or student to whom he can transmit the "Wisdom"; the long chain of misfortunes which began with the great catastrophe of 1096, the massacres by the Crusaders, has caused the decline of the esoteric tradition; and after the death of Rabbi Judah all hope of keeping it alive, so he seems to be saying, has been lost. It is his duty, therefore, to write down the secrets of the esoteric traditions which he received from his ancestors and his teacher, because otherwise they will be completely lost.

The tone of this preface clearly indicates that this book was the first work on the esoteric traditions of his school that Rabbi Eleazar wrote, and it serves as an introduction to them and as a justification for their writing. Rabbi Eleazar wrote before that time an extensive commentary on the prayers, possibly in several versions,[7] and also his halakhic work, ספר הרקח *(Sefer Ha-Rokeah),* but no treatise dealing specifically with esoteric wisdom. His large collection of works on this subject, the סודי רזייא *(Sodei Razaya),* was written after "The Book of Wisdom," and it is possible that this work was intended to present the methodological basis for the later, more detailed work.

The main subject presented in *Sefer Ha-Hokhmah* is the list of the seventy-three שערי החכמה, "The Gates of Wisdom," and the detailed exposition of most of them. The number of these "gates" is determined by the numerical value of the Hebrew word for wisdom, חכמה *(hokhmah),* thus expressing Rabbi Eleazar's belief that the number of these "gates" is no accident, but inherent in the concept of "wisdom" itself. It seems that Rabbi Eleazar sincerely believed that he was not presenting an artificial system, but that he was actually listing the intrinsic components of divine wisdom itself. To prove this, he devoted the major part of the "Book of Wisdom" to a detailed demonstration, in which he presented examples of the hermeneutical interpretation of most of these seventy-three "gates" when applied to one and the same biblical verse—the first one in the book of Genesis. This choice proves that he believed that the whole Torah can be interpreted in these seventy-three ways; the complete "wisdom" is therefore seventy-three commentaries on the Torah, each exhausting the methodology incorporated in each of these "gates." These methods, therefore, are not alternatives, as are, for instance, the talmudic מידות שהתורה נדרשת בהן *(middot she-ha-Torah nidreshet bahen),* each of which should be used in the appropriate place, one at a time: when קל וחומר *(kal vahomer)* is used, גזירה שוה *(gezerah shavah)* is not. Here, all the seventy-three methods are applicable and relevant for every letter and every word in every verse, and thus the Torah should be interpreted by each of them; none is ever superfluous or unnecessary. There can be no contradictions or "true" or "false" interpretations; if the method is valid, the hermeneutical conclusion is valid as well, and all the various conclusions, whatever their content, are regarded as complementary. The notion that they may be conflicting, and that a choice has to be made, does not appear either in this book or in any other Ashkenazi Hasidic work of speculative esoteric teachings. The confidence that the tradition of interpretation by these methods can lead the commentator only to true, valid conclusions is complete.

The seventy-three "gates" are presented by Rabbi Eleazar without any obvious order or sequence, though in some sections of the list related subjects are grouped together. In the various versions of the list we have actually seventy-eight "gates," which can be divided by us into three major types. Most of them are clearly methodological; some are speculative subjects, and a few are texts to be interpreted. It is evident that this, or a similar, list supplied the authors of the esoteric works of the Ashkenazi Hasidic circle with titles to their books, in an inverse relationship to the proportions of the list: among the titles, commentaries of texts come first, followed by monographs on subjects, and only a small minority of the Ashkenazi Hasidic literature which has reached us is dedicated to the exposition of methodological principles.

The list of texts, which is the most problematical element in this system, includes: *Sefer Yezirah, Pirkei Avot* or *Pirkei Abraham;* Mishnah, Talmud and Midrash, and the Prayers. Among these, the most popular among the Ashkenazi Hasidim was the *Sefer Yezirah;* it is doubtful whether there was even one Ashkenazi Hasidic writer who did not try his hand at producing a commentary to this text.[8] We do not know of the Ashkenazi Hasidim as writers of commentaries on the Mishnah, Talmud and Midrash. The possible conceptual basis of this list will be discussed below.

The theological subjects in this list include: Shaar Ha-Emet ("The Gate of Truth"), Shaar Ha-Shem ("The Gate of Name," i.e., the holy name, the tetragrammaton), Shaar Ha-Shemot ("The Gate of Names," i.e., other holy names), Shaar Ha-Merkavah ("The Gate of the Holy Chariot"), Shaar Maase Bereshit ("The Gate of the Work of Genesis"), Shaar Ha-Kavod ("The Gate of the Divine Glory"), Shaar Ha-Nefesh ("The Gate of the Soul"), Shaar Ha-Mitzvot ("The Gate of the Religious Commandments"), Shaar Ha-Malakhim ("The Gate of the Angels"), Shaar Ahavah ("The Gate of the Love of God"), Shaar Yir'ah ("The Gate of the Fear of God"), Shaar Anavah ("The Gate of Humbleness"), Shaar Hasidut ("The Gate of Piety"), Shaar Shalom ("The Gate of Peace"), Shaar Ha-Sod ("The Gate of Esoteric Truth"), Shaar Emunah ("The Gate of Faith"), and the last—Shaar Ha-Hokhmah ("The Gate of Wisdom"). Of these seventeen subjects, at least fourteen are to be found as titles to works or chapters of works by Rabbi Judah the Pious and Rabbi Eleazar of Worms.[9] It is evident, therefore, that this was no theoretical list; it was the general system, and every book and every chapter in a book written by these authors was intended to be a part within the great whole represented by this concept of the totality of wisdom. It is also obvious that in this list the otherwise meaningful separation between the Ashkenazi Hasidic teachings in the realm of ethics and that of esoteric theology is completely disregarded. The main subjects of their teachings in the realm of pietistic behavior, spiritual or practical, are listed here as an integral part of the esoteric wisdom; indeed, Rabbi Eleazar expressed this notion clearly when he began his magnum opus, the *Sodei Razaya,* a collection of esoteric theological works, with an introduction dedicated mainly to the ethical subjects listed here—Love, Fear, Piety, and Humility.[10]

The examples Rabbi Eleazar provides following this list leave no doubt concerning the meaning of this segment of the general framework he presents: every biblical verse can be interpreted to deal with any of these subjects. The first verse in the book of Genesis can be used in order to glean some religious truth concerning the divine glory, the Holy Chariot, the human soul, the divine name, as well as to demonstrate piety or the love of God. This is true, because of the introductory nature of this work, concerning every other biblical verse, for what is presented here is only an example. If so, the whole Torah is a detailed, inexhaustible treatise on the human soul, the divine name or the fear of God. A commentary on the Torah, following one such subject, will be a monograph on that subject as well as a biblical commentary. This seems to be a most radical expression of the belief that the words of the Torah include a vast source of religious truth on any subject of religious wisdom in an equal manner. The Torah does not dedicate this verse or that to a specific subject; the first verse does not deal with the problem of creation any more than with the Holy Chariot or the meaning of the commandments. Even though this is a list of specific subjects, it is not related to special portions of the Scriptures dedicated to it, because every verse, disregarding its simple, literal meaning, is equally relevant to every other subject. This concept makes the literal meaning of the biblical verses of secondary importance if not less. If a verse dealing with the geographical borders of the tribes of Israel in the book of Joshua is as relevant to the understanding of the "work of Genesis" as is the first verse of the book of Genesis, the individual meaning of every verse becomes immaterial. The divine nature of the Scriptures, so it seems, makes it impossible to dedicate any divine utterance to one subject only. Every such verse includes divine truths concerning all the subjects listed here. While on the one hand this attitude strengthens and fortifies the importance of the religious message included in the verses of the Bible, on the other hand it deprives them of any specific, literal meaning. They can be interpreted to reveal divine truth concerning any subject, be it completely remote in content from any actual word included in it. On the one hand, the message of the language of the Torah is inexhaustible, but on the other any specific message loses its exclusivity.

The more profound concept of language expressed in this document is found in the analysis of the list of methodological "gates." We know of six treatises written by Rabbi Judah the Pious, the titles of which are included in this list: The now lost *Book of Gematria,* of which several quotations are to be found in medieval literature,[11] and five monographs which are included in the second half of the Oxford manuscript of the works of Rabbi Judah:[12] *Sefer Ha-Ne'elam, Sefer Tagi, Shaar Semuchim, Shaar Ha-Kolot* and *Sefer Pesaq.* These monographs deal, according to the same order, with the letters "missing" *(ne'elam)* in biblical verses: the decorations of the Hebrew letters when used to write Torah scrolls *(tagim);* the proximity of verses to each other *(semuchim);* the "sounds" *(kolot)* of the Hebrew vowels and vocalization marks, and the endings of verses *(pesaq).* It is evident from these treatises that the methodologies to which they are dedicated can be used throughout the Scriptures and can reveal divine truths concerning any subject. They are relevant wherever the particular linguistic phenomenon with which they deal is present, which, in most cases, is almost everywhere in the Bible. Rabbi Judah's testimony thus joins that of Rabbi Eleazar in clarifying the nature of the fifty-five methodologies present in the list: each of them can and should be used constantly, without conflicting with any other and without making any other superfluous. The *tagim* and the signs representing the endings of verses, as well as the grouping of verses, join letters which are mentioned in the verse and those which are not mentioned, and the sounds of the Hebrew syllables, in conveying the divine message to the esoteric scholar and the mystic.

Some of the "gates" included by Rabbi Eleazar in the list and discussed in the following pages of the *Sefer Ha-Ḥokhmah* represent well-established and traditional methodologies of Jewish hermeneutics. The use of *gematria, notaricon,* and *temurah* has a long tradition in Jewish study of the Scriptures before the Ashkenazi Hasidim. Indeed, it seems to me that it is no accident that it is difficult to find in Rabbi Eleazar's list any fundamentally new element; I believe that he intended to present the list of methodologies as an exhaustive one and not as an innovative one. He believed that he had collected the old, traditional methods of Biblical interpretation but did not seek any new additions. Sometimes he elaborated traditional methods and included their details as independent "gates": Shaar Aḥadim, Shaar Kaful, Shaar Meshulash, Shaar Meruba, and Shaar Meḥumash probably relate to one and the same simple principle—the counting of the appearance of a certain term in a verse or paragraph in the Bible (most often, a certain divine name), once, twice, thrice, four, or five times. The general principle of the counting of the appearance of terms in biblical sections is represented by Shaar Ha-Mispar and Shaar Ḥeshbonot. On the other hand, in the case of *temurah,* the permutation of letters between one sequence and another, he included the general term and one example—Shaar Etbash, when, if he so wished, he could list dozens of different examples.

The use of the Aramaic translation of the Bible as a vehicle for interpretation of many verses is a traditional one, which the Ashkenazi Hasidim employed like other medieval commentators and hermeneutics. Yet there is a certain emphasis in this list on another aspect—the external characteristics of the biblical text, beginning with the Mesorah, the traditional counting of words and letters, the "small and large letters" of the text, the differences between what is written and what is read, additional letters or those which are omitted in the tradition of the Scriptures, etc.—these are undoubtedly a part of the Jewish hermeneutical tradition since the classical Midrash, yet they seem to be emphasized in Rabbi Eleazar's system. On the other hand, the inclusion of some of the old rabbinic hermeneutical methods, like *gezerah shavah,* while most of them were not included, is surprising. It is possible that Rabbi Eleazar wanted, deliberately, to distance this system from the usual ways in which halakhah is decided, but if so, why include *gezerah shavah?*

If we try to summarize in a systematic manner the hermeneutical system which is expressed in Rabbi Eleazar's list, following his own purpose in the *Sefer Ha-Ḥokhmah* as a methodological introduction to the hermeneutical analysis of a biblical verse, using modern terminology rather than his own, it seems to me that we will reach the following conclusions.

1. On the level of content, each biblical verse should be viewed as a key to more than twenty conceptual subjects.[13] Every such verse is, by its nature as a record of divine revelation, a repository of truth concerning the creation of the earthly world and the structure of the divine realm, the names of the angels and archangels, and the name of God himself, the Holy Chariot and the divine glory. Within it are hidden directives for human behavior, for ethical conduct between man and God and between individuals, directives which will lead the commentator to the true pietistic way of life. It also contains keys to the understanding of other sacred texts. Interpreted correctly, every biblical verse can open new vistas in the understanding of the Mishnah and the Talmud, the Midrash and the halakhah, the prayers and the *Sefer Yeẓirah.* According to this system, it is not the specific wording of this or that verse which enables one to use it for the understanding of the divine glory, love of God or a passage in the *Sefer Yeẓirah.* It is the very fact that it is a verse written in the Bible which makes it, by nature, a key to one and all of these secrets. The connection may be obvious or may be completely obscure on the literal level, but if God chose to include this group of letters in His holy scriptures, there can be no doubt that it bears a relevance to every one of these subjects, independent of the first impression conveyed by its literal meaning.

Beyond the stratum of the content, every biblical verse should be studied in the following ways, each focusing on one of the characteristics of the ways in which it appears in the Torah:

2. The shape of the letters of the alphabet conveys divine secrets. Rabbi Eleazar's cosmogony and cosmology are based, to a very large extent, on this type of analysis, following the ancient traditions of the mystics of the Talmudic and Geonic periods, incorporated, for instance, in the *Otiot de-Rabbi Akibah*.[14] The letter is not an arbitrary, agreed human sign for a certain sound or shape which are just a technical means by which content is conveyed. When God first used it, it had a shape as well as a meaning, and this shape is an inseparable aspect of the divine revelation which occured when the secret of the alphabet was given to man, when the Torah was written with such signs, originating within God before the creation. The shape of a letter, therefore, is no less part of its divine message than is its role in structuring the word in which it figures.

3. In a similar way, the name of the letter is as meaningful as its shape and its other characteristics. The true way to read a word includes the full names of the letters, and reading the word in this way, taking into account all the letters which comprise the name of the original ones, is called מילוי *(milluy)*. This method is often used by Ashkenazi Hasidic commentators, especially concerning the divine names. Sometimes a special position in the commentary is allotted to the "superfluous" letters, i.e., those letters which comprise the name of the letters without being included in the original word (אלף, בית, etc.). Long before modern linguists discovered it, the Jewish hermeneutics knew full well the secret that what is not actually written is no less important than what is clearly visible in a written text.

4. The position of grammar in interpreting a biblical text in the context of this hermeneutical system is quite unusual. According to Rabbi Eleazar, among the "Gates of Wisdom" are included such methods as the "singular and plural" (שער יחיד ורבים, *shaar yaḥid ve-rabbim*) and the "masculine and feminine" (שער זכר ונקבה, *shaar zakhar u-nekevah*). Any commentator, seeking the literal meaning of a text, obviously uses the grammatical form of the sentence he studies. But here Rabbi Eleazar does not deal with the search for the one, literal meaning. He postulates that the study of the grammatical form of a biblical term is an independent way for God to convey esoteric meaning, unconnected with the demands of the laws of grammar. God, when formulating language before the world was created and as a tool for its creation, could give any word any form He wished. The fact that He chose to express this phrase in the singular or the plural, or the masculine or the feminine, is not the result of His bowing to the laws of grammar, which do not exist outside of Him and are completely in His hand to formulate. As natural, physical phenomena in creation are not the expression of God's bowing to the laws of the physics, but express His purpose in creation, so the grammatical form in which a sentence is written in the Torah is a part of the revelation of divine wisdom, and each case should be studied individually, as an expression of some specific divine secret.

5. As the letters of the alphabet, in all their aspects, are regarded in this system as a divine phenomenon, revealed to man but still including within it the totality of divine wisdom, it is impossible for the interpreter to distinguish between "essential" and "nonessential" aspects of them. The *tagin,* for instance, the decorations

of the letters, have been established in rabbinic tradition long before the Ashkenazi Hasidim as meaningful aspects of divine truth. Rabbi Akibah, so the rabbinic tradition states, derived from their analysis great legal secrets and used them to establish profound legal decisions.[15] The Torah was created two thousand years before the world; during the time that elapsed from the Torah's creation (which included, necessarily, the creation of the Hebrew letters) to the creation of the world by it, and then until the time it was given to Moses, God, so a talmudic tradition maintains, occupied Himself by "tying crowns to the letters."[16] The origin of the *tagin,* therefore, is as ancient and as sacred as everything else in the Torah, secondary to none in its divine meaning. An ancient Hebrew writer, the author of the *Sefer Yezirah,* based upon this concept his detailed description of the process by which the letters of the alphabet serve as a source for all worldly existence; according to him, when God was "tying crowns" to the letters He also assigned to each of them a specific role in cosmic existence—within nature, within time, and within man.[17] For him, the "tying of crowns," i.e., the *tagin,* was the process by which each letter received a specific potency to "govern" and control one of the aspects of existence. When Rabbi Eleazar included several "gates of wisdom" in his list which pertain to the external appearance of the letters, he was not describing a secondary or an auxiliary aspect which could be used by the commentator; these "gates" are as central and as meaningful as any other "gate" in the list. These include, besides the *tagin,* the gate of "small and large letters," referring to the several occurences of letters which are written in a larger or smaller script than the others in the Bible; the signs of vocalization which are included in the total picture, as well as the meaning, of the Hebrew letters; the occurences of differences between the way a word is read from the way it is written (שער כתבן ולא קרין, שער קרין ולא כתבן, *shaar katvan velo karyan, shaar karyan velo katvan*), thus achieving a system in which all the aspects of the form of the written word are taken into consideration by the hermeneutical process.

6. The order of the letters in a sentence, the most essential element in literal understanding of a text, is regarded by this system as one of many possibilities, each as legitimate and meaningful as any other. A sentence, a verse, or a paragraph in the Bible include infinite layers of meaning, some of which can be exposed by reading these letters in a different order or a different selection. The clearest examples of this are the שער פנים ואחור, שער התחלת או סופי תיבות (*shaar panim veahor, shaar hathalat o sofei teivot*). In its simplest form, this method is represented by the acronym, when the word arrived at by the initial letters of the phrase or verse carries as much meaning as any other segment of Scripture. But according to Rabbi Eleazar, this is only an example of a much wider field of hermeneutical possibilities. He does not differentiate between using the first letters or the last ones (a practice found in the classical Midrash),[18] nor even changing the order of the letters and reading them from the end to the beginning. In principle, these methods convey the concept that the letters of the Torah can be reassembled in any form the commentator wishes; the letters represent a vast potentiality of infinite meanings, and can be rearranged and the new result, which includes words not actually found in the Bible, interpreted on an equal basis with words which are present in the literal form of the verse.[19]

7. The previous method, represented by the acronym or *notaricon,* deals with

the creation of nonexistent words from letters which are present in the verse. The *temurah* expresses the belief that nonexistent letters are as meaningful a part of a verse as those which are. Again, this classical midrashic (and even biblical[20]) concept was carried to the extreme by the Ashkenazi Hasidim. Not only the substitution of one letter for the other by the classical אתב"ש, but all the other possibilities of permutation of letters were used. It seems that the *Sefer Yeẓirah* was the source from which they derived the legitimacy of this system, which actually enables the commentator to substitute every letter for every other one, and therefore every word by every other one. They did not hesitate to use different *temurah* sequences in the interpretation of the same word or phrase, thus actually rewriting the verse and changing radically all its words and letters. While *notaricon*, in its wider sense, represents the concept that the letters are constant while their order can be changed, here we find the opposite notion—the order is constant, but the letters themselves can be changed. The text of the Bible, in this system, is therefore one "accidental" assemblage of letters and words from among an infinite number of possibilities.

When modern scientists debate the problem of probability, a frequent example used is that of a monkey arbitrarily typing letters on a typewriter; what is the probability of his producing, accidentally, the complete text of Shakespeare's plays? Here Rabbi Eleazar seems to be saying: The present literal words and sentences of the Torah are just one "accident," arbitrarily selected by God when he gave the Torah to the people of Israel, but intrinsically the text carries all the possible permutations that such a hypothetical monkey could type. Every other assemblage of letters will be as sacred and as meaningful as the present one. The "Shakespearean" text, to continue the analogy, is no more meaningful than the myriad "attempts" by the unknowing monkey to produce it. The theological basis of this concept is, that while Shakespeare's poetry is a human achievement arrived at by the use of human language, the language of the Torah is *ab initio* sacred and contains infinite truth, which is present in all the possible manifestations. The commentator does not "transmute" or change the letters and their order; he is just unearthing a different layer which existed deep within the divine text long before the world and man were created.

8. שער הנעלם *(shaar ha-ne'elam)* represents another variation of this concept. When a certain verse presents its literal meaning and order, it is based on a selection among the letters of the alphabet; some are used and some are not. Thus, in fact, two groupings of letters come into being: the one which is present in Scripture, and the one which has been selected, in an identical divine process, not to be present. The "nonexistent" group, therefore, is a reflection of divine wisdom in an identical manner to the one obvious to the reader. In order to exhaust the full meaning of the divine selection, the "missing" letters have to be taken into account, as well as the obvious ones. Indeed, in Ashkenazi Hasidic hermeneutics, quite often this system is used: why is this or that letter "missing" *(ne'elam)* in this verse? The theology hidden behind this method is one which expects a complete representation of the whole alphabet in every divine expression. Only the totality of the linguistic divine instrument can convey the totality of divine truth. God informs His pietistic commentator of His divine meaning by the omission of certain letters as well as by presenting them.

9. The use of the Aramaic translation as one of the "gates of wisdom" should be discussed briefly. This "gate" is on the borderline between contents and form. It represents the belief that the Aramaic translations were divinely inspired, and that the work of translation can be regarded as an endeavor to reveal one more layer of divine meaning within the sacred text. The Ashkenazi Hasidim do not use the Aramaic translation as if it were an early, authoritative commentary to the Scriptures; it is as if they regard it as an independent layer of revelation, adding more meaning rather than choosing from the various Hebrew meanings the one to be rendered into Aramaic. Hebrew and Aramaic were not regarded as separate languages; God did use Aramaic in his revelation, to Daniel, for instance. Therefore, the text of the Aramaic translation supplements the hermeneutical process like every other aspect presented in the list of seventy-three gates.

10. The largest group of methodological "gates of wisdom" is devoted to those which are based on numbers. The Ashkenazi Hasidim were the most intensive users of the method of *gematria* among early medieval Jewish commentators, and it seems that they had an impact on subsequent Jewish mystical writers in later centuries. It should be noted that neither Hekhalot mysticism nor the *Sefer Yezirah* ever used this method. Though it is known in rabbinic midrashic hermeneutics, it was never a central one before the Ashkenazi Hasidim. They cannot be regarded as its innovators, but they certainly represent a new intensity in its use. Rabbi Judah the Pious and Rabbi Eleazar of Worms not only used *gematria* for words and phrases, but quite often transformed whole verses into lists of harmonized numbers. It seems that when they looked at a page of Scripture (or prayers) they did not see only words and letters; they immediately perceived also the long lists of numbers which these words and letters represent.

Jewish mysticism is described quite often as a system which bases its biblical hermeneutics on "numerology." This is basically incorrect: many central works, from *Sefer Yezirah* to the Zohar, neglect it or almost ignore it. Throughout the ages, there were Jewish mystics who were inclined to use the method of *gematria,* and others who were not interested. It should be remembered that there is nothing mystical in rendering Hebrew letters into numbers: until the last few generations, Hebrew did not have any alternative but to use letters for numbers. The use of special signs as numerals, which reached Europe from the east in the early Middle Ages, did not penetrate into Jewish culture until modern times. Therefore, every Hebrew word or letter could legitimately be read either as word or number—as was the case in ancient Greece, and partially in Latin, the latter custom surviving in our day and age. The basic fact that it is possible to "play around" with the numerical value of words and letters is inherent in Jewish culture and does not denote any particularly mystical inclination.

Within the framework of Rabbi Eleazar's "Gates of Wisdom" this aspect is put, I believe, in its proper perspective in Jewish mysticism and hermeneutics. *Gematria* is just one more aspect of the variety of ways in which letters convey divine meaning. It is no better and no worse than the method of counting missing letters, or interpreting the full name of letters or their shapes and decorations. One of the many levels of meaning is conveyed by the numerical value of words, phrases, and verses, and it also should be used among the seventy-three "gates of wisdom." The

Ashkenazi Hasidim were inclined to use *gematria,* and they intensified its presence in the Jewish hermeneutical endeavor beyond anything known before them, but they did not impose on it a new dimension of meaning or see in it a major key unlocking divine secrets hidden in the Bible, any more than the other methodologies used by them and present on this list.

11. While the previous paragraph seems to diminish the importance of the *gematria* in Ashkenazi Hasidic hermeneutics, it should be emphasized that the concept of numbers and their intrinsic harmony was central, and innovative, in their system. *Gematria* is but one among the many "gates" which seem to be concerned with numbers. Others, like שער אחדים, שער כפול, שער משולש, שער מרובע, שער מחומש, שער מספר, שער חשבונות *(shaar ahadim, shaar kaful, shaar meshulash, shaar meruba, shaar mehumash, shaar mispar, shaar heshbonot),* are concerned with the number of times that a certain linguistic element appears in a verse or a biblical paragraph. The clearest example of that is the holy name, the tetragrammaton, and the other divine names: much of Ashkenazi Hasidic hermeneutics is based on the counting of such appearances. This is not confined to sacred names; Rabbi Judah the Pious started his treatise on the angels with a long list of the forty verses in Psalms in which the term "hasid" is present, deducing from that the number of angels accompanying and guarding each pious Jew,[21] and there are many such examples. Beyond *gematria,* the Ashkenazi Hasidim believed (following several examples in the classical Midrash) that as any other part of Scripture is not accidental, so the number of times that a certain linguistic element appears in a biblical section cannot be accidental. It must convey a specific meaning. But what kind of meaning?

In this case, another important source of Ashkenazi Hasidic hermeneutics presents a clear answer to the question. It is the great *Commentary on the Prayers* by Rabbi Eleazar of Worms, and even more than that, the now lost *Commentary on the Prayers* by Rabbi Judah the Pious. Rabbi Judah's commentary was probably the first comprehensive commentary on the prayers to be written (while Rabbi Eleazar's is the earliest one which has reached us). The question, why did Rabbi Judah write such an unprecedented work, is therefore a legitimate one. The quotations we have from Rabbi Judah's commentary (collected in the treatise *Sodot ha-Tefilah,* "The Secrets of the Prayers," by one of his disciples)[22] give a clear answer to the question. Rabbi Judah was horrified by small variations in the text of the prayers as said by the Jews of France and England and wrote his extensive commentary in order to demonstrate that they were wrong and that the only correct version of the prayers was the one practiced by the Kalonymus tradition in Germany.

Using the text of the "Secrets of the Prayers" and the parallels found in Rabbi Eleazar of Worms's *Commentary on the Prayers,* we can get a clear picture of the methods used by Rabbi Judah the Pious to prove the veracity of his version of the prayers to the exclusion of any variation. These methods are purely numerical ones. Rabbi Judah states that the structure of the prayers is a fabric in which everything has numerical meaning: the number of words, the number of letters, the number of divine names in each section of the prayers is meaningful, and this meaning can be understood when compared to biblical sections, or events, in which the same numbers are interwoven.[23] The comparison between the numerical structure of the prayer under discussion and the meaning of that number in other sections of Jewish sacred tradition proves that no change is possible, because the addition of even one letter destroys the intrinsic numerical harmony.

In conclusion, we arrive at a rather radical and far-reaching semiotic statement, probably unequaled in the very long history of Hebrew commentaries on the Bible, yet, surprisingly, one which is not ideologically innovative; it is surprisingly similar to the hermeneutical message of the classical Midrash, the basis of all Jewish hermeneutical traditions.

Rabbi Eleazar clearly claims in this list, speaking for other Ashkenazi Hasidic scholars: When one is studying a biblical verse, one should interpret it taking into account the following: the shape of the letters of the alphabet, the external image they present; the shape of the decorations with which they are adorned; the shape and sound of the musical signs which accompany the syllables; the shape and sound of the vocalization marks which are added to every syllable; the fact that some letters are sometimes written in a larger or smaller fashion than the rest; the fact that some letters may be pronounced differently than they are written; the number of times each letter is mentioned, and the number of letters which are absent from this biblical section; the number of holy names and other terms, the many possible permutations of every group of letters, the numerical value of the letters, the combinations of first and last letters, and all the other methodological "gates of wisdom." Besides that, one should be aware of the fact that every biblical verse or phrase, disregarding its literal meaning, conveys deep truth concerning two dozen subjects, theological and ethical, and a verse has not exhausted its message until its possible relevance to all these subjects has been elucidated. In other words: every biblical verse is, at one and the same time, nothing and everything. Its literal meaning may be regarded as an accidental one among the myriad other messages incorporated in it by its divine author.

Language, according to this concept, is indeed the only and the perfect vehicle to bring man into touch with divine truth, provided that one completely rejects its limitations as a human means of communication. As long as the scholar and mystic is bound by the concept of a literal meaning—or even believes it has but a few midrashic or esoteric ones—one cannot approach the infinite, divine nature of the religious ladder leading man out of the realm of the earthly and the literal and into the depth of the infinite, divine truth.[24]

Notes

1. The term "dialectics" is found in *Sefer Ḥasidim,* Wistenzki-Freimann edition (Parma ms.), Frankfurt-am-Main 1924, par. 752, p. 191; and in Rabbi Eleazar of Worms's *Ḥokhmat Ha-Nefesh,* Lvov 1876, p. 7b.

2. Ms. Oxford, Bodleian Library, Neubauer 1568, 1912. A shorter version of the book is found also in mss. 1566 and 1567 in the same library; see the following note.

3. The two mss., 1566 and 1567 (the latter is probably a copy of the former, both from the Oppenheim collection), contain a series of treatises by Rabbi Judah the Pious. See J. Dan,

Iyyunim be-Sifrut Hasidei Ashkenaz (Ramat Gan: Massada Publishing House, 1975), pp. 134–47. To this compilation was added at the end a shorter version of the Sefer Ha-Hokhmah; it contains only forty-eight gates and a selection of examples of their use.

4. The short version of the *Sefer Ha-Hokhmah* was printed in the beginning of "Perush ha-Torah le-Rabbi Eleazar mi-Germaiza," 3 vols. (Beney-Brak) 1979–1981, serving as an "introduction" to the body of the book, which was printed from ms. Oxford 268. There was some justification to this combination, because the Torah commentary in this ms. is organized according to this system of the "Gates of Wisdom." The author, however, is not Rabbi Eleazar, and I described the commentary in my paper, "The Ashkenazi Hasidic 'Gates of Wisdom',": *Hommage à Georges Vajda*. ed. G. Nahon and C. Touati (Louvain) 1980, pp. 183–89. This commentary, which seems to be independent of Rabbi Judah the Pious and Rabbi Eleazar, serves as proof that the system was one which was known and accepted in Ashkenazi Jewry, and not only by one specific group of writers. See J. Dan, "Perush ha-Torah le-Rabbi Eleazar of Worms," *Kiryat Sefer* 59 (1984): 644.

5. Scholarly interest was concentrated on a few passages in the *Sefer Ha-Hokhmah* which describe the prayer in terms closely reminiscent of kabbalistic terminology; I called it "proto-Bahiric" terminology. See G. Scholem, *Reshit ha-Kabbalah* (Jerusalem and Tel Aviv: Schocken, 1948), pp. 51, 60; idem, *Ursprung und Anfange der Kabbala,* Berlin: Walter de Gruyter, 1962, pp. 162–66; idem, *The Origins of the Kabbalah,* transl. A. Arkush, ed. R. J. Zvi Werblowsky (Princeton NJ: The Jewish Publication Society and Princeton University Press, 1988), pp. 184–87; J. Dan, *Torat ha-Sod shel Hasidut Ashkenaz* (Jerusalem: The Bialik Institute, 1968), pp. 117–29; idem, *Hugei ha-Mekubalim ha-Rishonim* (Jerusalem: Academon, 1977), pp. 159–65; idem, "The Emergence of the Mystical Prayer," in J. Dan and F. Talmage, eds:, *Studies in Jewish Mysticism* (Cambridge, MA: Association of Jewish Studies, 1980), pp. 112–15; A. Farber, "The Concept of the Merkavah in 13th-Century Jewish Esotericism" (Ph.D. thesis, Jerusalem 1986), I: 232–44 et passim; M. Idel, *Kabbalah: New Perspectives* (New Haven, CT: Yale University Press, 1988), pp. 191–97.

6. "Sefer ha-Hokhmah le-Rabbi Eleazar mi-Worms," *Zion* 29 (1964): 168–81; reprinted in *Iyyunim be-Sifrut Hasidei Ashkenaz,* pp. 44–57.

7. On the *Commentaries on the Prayers* see my *Torat ha-Sod,* pp. 56, 65; and in "The Emergence of the Mystical Prayer," pp. 85–93; a detailed study of the Ashkenazi Hasidic commentaries on the prayers and *piyyutim* is presented by E. E. Urbach in his introduction to his edition of *Arugat ha-Bosem* by Rabbi Abraham berabi Azriel, vol. 4 (Jerusalem: Mekizey Nirdamim, 1964).

8. Outstanding among the Ashkenazi Hasidim in this realm was Rabbi Elhanan ben Yaqar of London, who wrote three such commentaries, one of which was published by G. Vajda in *Kovets Al Yad,* 16 (Jerusalem I 1966), pp. 145–97, and the two others (one of them entitled *Sod ha-Sodot*) in my *Textim be-Torat ha-Elohut shel Hasidei Ashkenaz* (Jerusalem: Academon, 1977). The two best known commentaries are those of Rabbi Eleazar of Worms, printed in Premiszla, 1883; and the anonymous "pseudo-Saadia" commentary, which is found in many manuscripts and a short version of which is printed in the regular editions of the *Sefer Yezirah*. Besides these, Rabbi Judah the Pious, Rabbi Eleazar ha-Darshan and others wrote such commentaries.

9. The list of titles taken from this list and the books written by Rabbi Eleazar and Rabbi Judah according to them is to be found in *Iyyunim,* pp. 55–56.

10. This ethical introduction to *Sodei Razaya* was first printed in *Sefer Raziel* (Amsterdam: 1701), p. 6a.

11. See Freimann in his introduction to *Sefer Hasidim* (Frankfurt am-Main: Wahrman, 1924), pp. 5–6. This book is mentioned by Hayim Yosef David Azulai in his lexicon *Shem*

ha-Gedolim (s.v. Yehudah he-Hasid). See also A. Epstein, *Mi-Kadmoniot ha-Yehudim*, (Jerusalem: Rav Kook Institute, 1956), p. 238. It is not clear whether this is an original work by Rabbi Judah or a compilation edited by his disciples from his works.

12. The first half is devoted to three thematic treatises, on the soul, the angels, and the divine glory; while the second half includes the methodological treatises. See my *Iyyunim*, pp. 134–38.

13. Among such works we should include Rabbi Judah the Pious's *Sefer ha-Kavod* and *Sefer Malachim*, dealing, respectively, with the divine glory and the angels. Rabbi Eleazar's *Sodei Razaya* is based completely on this section of the list, and covers a dozen or more such subjects in the five titles of the books included in it (The Secret of Creation, The Secret of the Merkabah, The Holy Name, The Soul and the Sefer Yeẓirah); The introduction includes the ethical subjects, and others, which are chapters in these books, like the Kavod and Malachim, which are titles within "The Secret of the Chariot."

14. The shape of the letters, which does not play a central part in the cosmogony of the *Sefer Yeẓirah*, is a prominent source of divine truth in the midrashic-mystical collection known as the Alphabet of Rabbi Akibah. See A. Jellinek, *Bet-haMidrash*, (Jerusalem: Wahrman, 1938), 3: 12–64; S. A. Wertheimer, *Batei Midrashot*, (Jerusalem: Rav Kook Institute, 1953), 2: 333–417. It should be noted that it does not serve as a means of mystical knowledge in the literature of the *Yordei ha-Merkabah*, in the works of the Hekhalot, but because of the impact of the Alphabet of Rabbi Akibah it was central in the works of the medieval mystics. Several sections of the *Sefer ha-Bahir*, the earliest work of the Kabbalah written at the end of the twelfth century, contain mystical speculations based on the shape of the letters. Rabbi Eleazar used it in his commentary on the "secret of Genesis." Among later writers, Rabbi Jacob ha-Cohen of Castile wrote a very popular kabbalistic treatise on the subject. See G. Scholem, *Kabbalot Rabbi Yaakov ve-Rabbi Yitzhak,* Madaei ha-Yahadut (Jerusalem: 1928), 2:165–293. The author of the Zohar also devoted to it a section in the magnum opus of the Kabbalah. See M. Oron, "The Narrative of the Letters and Its Source: A Study of a Zoharic Midrash on the Letters of the Alphabet," in J. Dan and J. Hacker, ed., *Studies in Jewish Mysticism, Philosophy and Ethical Literature Presented to Isaiah Tishby* (Jerusalem: The Magnes Press, 1986), pp. 97–110.

15. Bavli Menahot 29b ("tag" and "koz" are synonymous in talmudic usage). Several treatises, some of them attributed to Rabbi Akibah, were written in the early Middle Ages presenting such interpretations of the *tagin*. See *Sefer Tagin,* ed. J. J. L. Barges (Paris: 1866); and the detailed introduction of Shneor Zaks (reprinted, Jerusalem, 1975); Wertheimer, Batei Midrashot II, 467–474.

16. Bavli Shabat 89a: When Moses ascended to God, he found Him "tying crowns to the letters." Comp. Menahot 29b.

17. See Peter Hayman, "*Sefer Yetsira* (The Book of Creation)," *Shadow, The Newsletter of the Traditional Cosmology Society,* 3: (1986) 20–38; for instance, section 52 (1) (p. 33): "He (God) made [the letter] **He** rule, and bound to it a crown, and combined one with another, and formed with it Aries in the universe, [the month of] Nisan in the year and the liver in mankind," and similar descriptions concerning all other letters.

18. The best-known talmudic example of this method is the one in Bavli Shabbat 55a: חותמו של הקב"ה אמת *(hotamo shel hakadosh barukh hu emet),* based on the last three letters of the last three words in the story of creation in Genesis 2:3.

19. In his commentary on the first verse of the Bible in *Sefer Ha-Ḥokhmah* Rabbi Eleazar created many new words from the letters of this verse. For instance: the first and last letters of בראשית read בת , which can be read as תורות ב'. The last letters of בראשית and ברא read: את, thus making three such words in the verse; בראשית can be also read as א"ב תשרי, giving the date of the creation, and many other combinations.

20. See Jer. 25:26, and 51:41, where Bavel is called Sheshach, using the system of את״בש.

21. I published this treatise by Rabbi Judah the Pious in *Da'at*, 2–3 (1978–79): 99–120.

22. On this treatise see J. Dan, "On the Historical Personality of Rabbi Judah Hasid," in *Culture and Society in Medieval Jewry, Studies Dedicated to the Memory of Haim Hillel Ben-Sasson,* ed. M. Ben-Sasson, R. Bonfil, J. R. Hacker (Jerusalem: The Historical Society of Israel, 1989), pp. 389–98.

23. "Sodot ha-Tefilah" and traditions included in it have been the subject of scholarly study for a century and a half. See a brief bibliography in *Torat ha-Sod,* pp. 14–15 n. 1. Concerning the concept of the prayers see E. E. Urbach *Arugat ha-Bosem* (Jerusalem 1964) 4; and in my paper, "The Emergence of the Mystical Prayer," pp. 87–93.

24. Most of the elements described in this paper have their parallels both before the appearance of Ashkenazi Hasidism in the twelfth century and later, in the Kabbalah of the late-twelfth and the thirteenth centuries. A comprehensive study of the concept of language in Hebrew midrashic, hermeneutical, and mystical literature will be presented elsewhere.

3

The Grammatical Literature of Medieval Ashkenazi Jewry

ILAN ELDAR

Background

Hebrew linguistic science in medieval Europe was of two schools of thought, one Spanish ("Sephardi") and the other northern European ("Ashkenazi"). The former emerged in mid-tenth century Moslem Spain (Andalusia), reaching its zenith in the first half of the eleventh century in the grammatical and lexicographical works of Yehudah Ḥayyuj, Yonah ibn Janaḥ and Shemu'el Ha-Naggid. Following the destruction of the southern communities in the middle of the eleventh century, the Spanish-Andalusian school continued to exist outside of Spain for some two generations in the hands of Spanish exiles and their offspring: in Italy (Avraham ibn Ezra and Shelomo ibn Parḥon) and in Provence (Yosef Kimḥi and his sons, Moshe and David Kimḥi, and the Tibbon family of translators).

The Ashkenaz school of grammar took shape and solidified in the main centers of early Ashkenaz Jewry in western Europe: northern France, Germany ("Ashkenaz" in the narrow sense), and England. This school first flourished in the generations that followed Rashi (d. 1105), and reached the peak of its development in the second half of the thirteenth century; the decades on either side of 1300 marked its finale. The scholars of Ashkenaz by now, and in particular from the middle of the fourteenth century, already belonged to another age (the *Aharonim*, i.e., "the later scholars") in the history of Ashkenaz Jewry's intellectual and religious scholarship; the center of gravity was meanwhile shifting to eastern Europe.[1]

Unlike its Spanish counterpart, the Ashkenaz school of grammar has aroused scant interest among students of Hebrew linguistic literature, evidently on account of the prevailing view that linguistic studies suffered neglect at the hands of the Ashkenazi Torah scholars of the day, preoccupied as they were with halakhic activity and talmudic exegesis. And there are indeed good grounds for ascribing this neglect to the intrinsically different character and inclination of Jewish culture in Ashkenaz. It would be a fair generalization that the early scholars of Ashkenaz (and their later counterparts likewise) did not develop an attitude of respect and preference for the grammarian's craft, unlike their Spanish counterparts with their disciplinary debt to their Arab neighbors, and were on the whole less *au fait* with the

Hebrew language than Spanish scholars, less adept philologically and less committed to independent linguistic exploration.

The linguistic attainments of the scholars of Ashkenaz, written for a relatively small audience well versed in rabbinic literature but scientifically somewhat naive, never matched the scientific quality of the Spanish scholars writing in Arabic, who embedded their Hebraic linguistic craft within the philosophical and linguistic knowledge of the age, addressing their grammars to a wide and sophisticated public renowned for its intellectual curiosity and philological awareness.

Aside from a few (though not insignificant) displays of innovation and originality—discernible particularly in the work of Rashbam, known for his independent thinking—no fundamental and substantive advances were made by Ashkenaz grammarians that were not due to Spanish influence, nor did they effect any radical changes in the patterns of grammatical thinking about the Hebrew language.

Nonetheless, one cannot gainsay the value of the Ashkenazi grammatical compositions or the importance of their contribution to the study of language in their day and in their localities; though almost totally lacking in theoretical expression of grammatical principles and methodological assumptions, a few of these compositions (meaning those that were already able to exploit the achievements in grammatical research that had been notched up meanwhile in Spain—see directly below) contain a full and comprehensive picture of the rules of Hebrew as embodied in the biblical text with its vocalization and accentuation marks.

Of the grammatical writings of the Ashkenaz school, just eight compositions have been preserved in manuscripts and come down to us in their entirety:

a. *Dayyakot* of Rabbi Shemu'el ben Me'ir (Rashbam)
b. *Hakhra'ot* of Rabbenu Ya'akov Tam
c. *Eyn Ha-Kore* of Rabbi Yekutiel ben Yehudah Ha-Nakdan
d. *Darkhei Ha-Nikkud* of Rabbi Moshe Ha-Nakdan
e. *Sefer Ha-Shoham* of Rabbi Moshe ben Yitzhak
f. *Hibbur Ha-Konim* (also known as *Ha-Shimshoni*) by Rabbi Shimshon Ha-Nakdan
g. *Mafteah Shel Dikduk* of Rabbi Mordekhai Ya'ir
h. An unnamed composition by Rabbi Shene'ur

We also know of the following Ashkenazi grammarians, whose works have been lost:

a. Rabbi Moshe Roti
b. Rabbi Yosef Hazzan of Troyes, author of *Sefer Yedidut*
c. Rabbi Levi ben Yosef, author of *Sefer Semadar*
d. Rabbi Yosef ben Yehotzadak
e. Rabbi Ya'akov Nakdan
f. Rabbi Berakhyah Nakdan ben Natronai
g. Rabbi Shelomo ben Me'ir (grandson of Rashi)
h. Rabbi Yosef Ha-Nakdan (mentor of Yekutiel Ha-Nakdan who penned *Eyn Ha-Kore*, see above)
i. Rabbi Shimshon of Soissons
j. Shimshon of Germany, author of a dictionary of biblical Hebrew[2]

The grammatical activity in the centers of Ashkenazi Jewry followed a number of creative trajectories, gearing grammatical compositions to a particular need and serving a defined aim with its own characteristic features. Let us therefore endeavor to specify the goals of grammatical composition in early Ashkenaz.

Inculcation of the Norms of Masoretic Tiberian Vocalization

The Jews of medieval Ashkenaz (up to around the mid-fourteenth century) had just five vowel qualities in their pronunciation (a, e, i, o, u)—as against the set of symbols in Tiberian vocalization, representing a phonological system of seven vowels (a = *patah*, å = *kamatz*, e = *tzere*, ε = *segol*, i = *hirik*, o = *holam*, u = *shuruk/kubutz*). The Ashkenazi *nakdanim* ("vocalizers"), and particularly those responsible for the vocalization of the prayers and liturgical poems in *mahzorim* ("festival prayer books"), were thus in difficulties over inserting vowel-points in the Tiberian tradition, incompatible as this was with their "Sephardi" pronunciation (with its five vowels), and proceeded to confuse *kamatz* with *patah*, *tzere* with *segol*, and *holam* with *kamatz "katan."* Some *nakdanim*, with finer linguistic awareness and philological skills, searched for ways to remedy this situation; the books they composed were designed to introduce some system and rules into these matters of vocalization. Among such compositions were *Darkhei Ha-Nikkud* of Moshe Ha-Nakdan of London, the large chapter *Sha'arei Nikkud* in *Hibbur Ha-Konim* by Shimshon Ha-Nakdan of Germany, and the nameless composition by Rabbi Shene'ur.

Eradication of Errors in Biblical Reading

The scholars of Ashkenaz themselves testify to the errors committed when reading the Scriptures, and we learn that some errors were due to negligence on the part of scriptural *nakdanim* or insufficient knowledge of the rules for accentuation marks, *ga'ayot*, and *makafim;* while others were due to an insouciance or sheer ignorance on the part of the readers themselves. Yekutiel ben Yehudah Ha-Nakdan, a scholar immersed in the study of superior biblical manuscripts and Masoretic literature, recognized the importance of a correct and meticulous scriptural reading and the superiority of the Tiberian tradition; his response was to compose his own treatise, *Eyn Ha-Kore*.

Providing a Linguistic Basis for Research into the "Simple Sense" of the Scriptural Text

The *peshat* ("simple sense") system of exegesis, which sprang up in northern France at the end of the eleventh century and peaked in the twelfth, liberated the commentator from the fetters of *derash* (with its concern for the meaning of realities that lie beyond the word) and led him to focus on explanations based upon word morphology, sentence syntax, rhetorical and literary devices, and linguistic context.[3] The grammatical compositions of Rashi's grandsons, Rashbam *(Dayyakot)* and Rabbenu Tam *(Hakhra'ot)*, were designed primarily to establish the grammatical norm concerning identification of roots and analysis of weak verb forms (i.e., defective or reduplicative verbs).

Composition of a Comprehensive Descriptive Grammar

Beginning in the mid-thirteenth century, Ashkenaz Jewry was increasingly exposed to the influence of the Spanish school of linguistics. The achievements of the classic Spanish-Jewish grammarians—as concerns both their analytical tools and their concepts and principles—were utilized in the name of a complete and systematic account of biblical grammar and of its morphological system in particular, in the works of Moshe ben Yitzḥak of London *(Sefer Ha-Shoham),* Shimshon Ha-Nakdan *(Ḥibbur Ha-Konim),* and Mordekhai Ya'ir of Friedberg in Germany, the latter's *Mafteaḥ Shel Dikduk* making full use of the morphological method of Shimshon Ha-Nakdan for practical pedagogical purposes and organizing it in paradigms accompanied by efficacious rules of inflection and word formation.

The point of lift-off in the broad evolutionary history of the Ashkenaz school, chronologically speaking, lies in the creative activity along the third of these foregoing trajectories; the school's subsequent development occurs within the first and second and, drawing increasingly on outside influences, it reaches its climax and cadenza in the fourth trajectory of activity.

In what follows I shall survey, as fully and roundly as is feasible, the known grammatical writings of the Ashkenazi school,[4] some of which are as yet confined wholly or partly to manuscripts. (The use of actual specimens of the texts, which might have enriched the survey, has not been possible in the present framework.)

Dayyakot by Rabbi Shemu'el ben Me'ir

Rashbam (Rabbi Shemu'el ben Me'ir), a grandson and student of Rashi, was born and was active in northern France (ca. 1080 to at least 1159). Most familiar is his contribution to biblical exegesis[5] and his work in the field of Halakhah and talmudic commentary. Rashbam's grammatical composition has been preserved in a solitary manuscript in the State Library of Berlin (Or. Qu. 648 [ms. Steinschneider 118], dated to 1440), entitled *Dayyakot* by the copyist.[6]

This composition is in two parts: (a) A grammatical treatise, beginning, "Open your eyes and see, and give your attention and incline your ears to hear and consider and see the history of the Holy Tongue and all its laws and regulations." (b) A grammatical commentary to the Bible, which begins, "And now I wish to elucidate the remaining words and their grammar . . . from Genesis to the end of the twenty-four books of the Bible." (In the manuscript that we possess this commentary goes as far as Genesis 7:5.)

Dayyakot is the first grammar to have been composed by a Jewish scholar in Ashkenaz. Its importance resides particularly in its being a "first," but it has other features besides: it reflects the grammatical understanding of Scripture among hebraists in northern France from the tenth century, and it gives us a bird's-eye view of the scope and content of metalinguistic activity underway among eleventh- and twelfth-century French Jews as part of the *peshat*-based exegesis, built around Rashi's commentary and all the linguistic material included therein.

Rashbam, it would be fair to say, did not intend *Dayyakot* as a full-blown, systematic grammar; the work deals with two central topics: the morphology of the verb (occasionally also embracing the noun) and the study of vocalization. Rashbam's pioneering status—and his inadequate expertise in grammatical categories—is in evidence in the argumentation and organization of the treatise: the organization is far from transparent, the order of presentation is at times confused or repetitive, and the grammatical terminology lacks sufficient clarity and consistency.

I shall not enumerate all the topics dealt with in *Dayyakot*, preferring to highlight a few that reveal Rashbam's penetrating understanding of the scriptural medium, already familiar from his explanations on the Bible:[7]

a. Stress placement as a diagnostic for homographic verb forms
b. The distinction between transitive and intransitive verbs
c. The meaning of *binyan pi'el*
d. The influence of guttural consonants on vocalization
e. The distinction between *dagesh kal* and *dagesh ḥazak*
f. The rules for mobile *sheva* and quiescent *sheva*
g. Changes in vocalization occasioned by *semikhut*
h. The meaning of verbal tenses
i. Connected and pausal forms in the verb

Of special note is Rashbam's distinction between three types of weak verb: "hataphed verbs" (roots with initial *yod* or *nun*, or final *he,* and mixed roots with a combination of these), "biliteral verbs" (roots with middle *vav*), and "verbs with a final reduplicative letter" (*ayin-ayin* verbs). This distinction is anchored of course in our author's conception of the root, but he does not in fact say anything explicit about the nature of the Hebrew root. His terms, his statements, and the formal analyses that form part of his treatise indicate that he was still unfamiliar with the grammatical doctrine of Yehudah Ḥayyuj of Spain and with all that it had to say concerning "hidden quiescent letters" *(naḥ ne'elam)* and the three-letter nature of the root across the whole Hebrew lexicon, including even "middle *vav*" roots. At the same time, he most certainly did not hold to the theory of Menaḥem ben Saruk, the first Spanish-Hebrew grammarian, that weak verbs have two or even just one root consonant.

Closer examination reveals that Rashbam only regarded verbs with a "middle *vav*" as "biliteral verbs," assigning to all other weak verbs as well as strong verbs a triliteral root.

It is a fair assumption that Rashbam arrived at the root of a verb on the basis of what he considered the basic form, i.e., third person masculine singular past tense of *binyan kal*, without regard for the other inflectional forms in which a root letter was liable to disappear (לְהֵיחָטֵף) in writing. Thus forms like נָפַל, יָרַד, בָּנָה, נָטָה, יָדָה representing the "hataphed" root-types and forms like שָׁמַם, סָבַב representing the "reduplicative" root-type have three root letters, whereas a form such as קָם has two letters for a root and is a representative of the "biliteral" root-type in its entirety. Since Rashbam did not know Ḥayyuj's notion of *naḥ ne'elam,* he could not recognize the abstract existence of the middle root letter in forms such as מֵת, קָם.

In this context, it should further be noted that in the "hataphed" root-type with initial *yod,* Rashbam distinguishes between verbs that lose the weak letter, e.g., שֵׁב, אֵשֵׁב, and verbs that retain it, e.g., יִיקַץ, יִיעַץ, or alter it, e.g., נוֹדַע, מוֹרָא.

Hakhra'ot by Rabbenu Ya'akov Tam

Rabbenu Ya'akov Tam (born ca. 1100) is considered the greatest halakhic scholar of northern France, but like his grandfather, Rashi, and his brother, Rashbam, he also took an interest in the study of language. He resided in Ramerupt and learned Torah from his father, Rabbi Me'ir, and his elder brother. Rabbenu Tam was admired and respected both near and far: the scholars of Ashkenaz, Provence, and southern Italy addressed questions to him, and his house of study attracted students from as far afield as Bohemia and Russia.

Rabbenu Tam's grammatical composition, known as *Hakhra'ot* (though early scholars referred to it by the name *Maḥberet*), was intended on the one hand to decide the linguistic controversies between the two early Spanish grammarians, Menaḥem ben Saruk and Dunash ben Labrat, the dominant authorities for all the French biblical exegetes, and on the other hand to seek a compromise for the contradictions between the two. Rabbenu Tam sought to defend Menaḥem against the sharp criticisms of Dunash, and generally came down in favor of the former, though occasionally finding with the latter or concurring with neither.

By the very nature of things, this composition consists for the most part of biblical elucidations (Menaḥem's *Maḥberet* being primarily devoted to ascertaining the meaning of Hebrew roots and the elucidation of biblical words and verses) and here Rabbenu Tam applies the principles of *Peshat* ("plain sense") exegesis practised by the French commentators. At the same time, he finds a little room for brief excursi (unrelated to what Menaḥem or Dunash have to say) on questions of Masorah and vocalization and on issues of grammar. His grammatical discussion centers on the classification of verbs by *gezarot* (verbal classes), and it transpires—without getting enmeshed in details—that Rabbenu Tam's conception of the root was very similar, if not identical, to his brother's. In terms of the overall evolution of Hebrew linguistic thought, Rabbenu Tam and Rashbam both stand midway between Menaḥem ben Saruk (and Rashi) and Yehudah Ḥayyuj: independently of Ḥayyuj in Spain, both grandsons of Rashi recognized the triliteralism of the Hebrew root in most types of weak verb; but failing to recognize the "hidden quiescent letter" (Ḥayyuj's great discovery), they were unable to discover the minimal tripartite formula for those defective verb forms in which "defective" spelling does not exhibit the weak root letter in the third person past (i.e., *ayin vav* verbs), and were forced to draw a line among the "hataphed" triliteral verbs between a stable, undeletable root letter and one that does sometimes undergo deletion.

Eyn Ha-Kore of Yekutiel Ha-Kohen ben Rabbi Yehudah

Two early traditions exist concerning the locale of Yekutiel Ha-Kohen ben Yehudah (or Yitzhak), who styles himself Zalman Ha-Kohen or simply by his initials יהב״י (see Katz in this volume). One tradition, mentioned by a Spanish copyist of *Eyn Ha-Kore,* locates him in Ashkenaz (Germany); the other, of Rabbi Eliyahu Bahur, sees him as based in Prague. Doubt persists, however, as to the reliability of these traditions; it is more likely, particularly in view of external evidence, that Yekutiel Ha-Kohen lived in Northern France. In any event, his patently German name (Zalman) and the pronunciation he considers and condemns in his composition point fairly convincingly to German origin. As for his dates, Zunz, Bacher, and others assumed he could be placed in the second half of the thirteenth century, a view for which Rivka Yarkoni, in her recent edition of the work, has attempted to find internal support from Yekutiel Ha-Kohen's grammatical doctrine, as compared with other contemporary sources. She writes:

> In his linguistic doctrine, as set out in various areas . . . material is embedded which is very reminiscent of Rabbi Moshe Ha-Nakdan's *Darkhei Ha-Nikkud Ve-Ha-Neginot* and Rabbi Shimshon Ha-Nakdan's *Hibbur Ha-Konim,* both of which are dated conventionally to the first half of the 13th century. However, what is displayed in the latter without order or system is set out neatly in *Eyn Ha-Kore,* classified by rule and condition. . . . Logic forbids that these writers' garbled account of stress, the *meteg* and the *dagesh* could have been penned after Yekutiel Ha-Kohen set them out in his *Eyn Ha-Kore.* . . . The conclusion is that *Eyn Ha-Kore* dates from after 1250, and the evidence it provides relates to this period in Ashkenazi life.[8]

As I see it, the balanced and comprehensive rehearsal of certain basic issues must not be taken *ipso facto* as evidence of lateness, nor may a work short on order and system be assumed to be early and pioneering (the sophisticated may after all predate the garbled). How successful a work is depends above all on the talent and erudition of the author, and should not be used as a historical criterion; one cannot, in any event, draw from it far-reaching conclusions for the chronology of our grammatical literature.

Working both from internal and from historical evidence (mentioning Yekutiel son of Yehudah Ha-Kohen as a pupil of Rashbam and Rabbenu Tam martyred in 1171 in the northern French city of Blois), one may safely date Yekutiel Ha-Kohen's activity to the second half of the twelfth century.

Eyn Ha-Kore is a grammatical treatise similar in character to works of the orthoepic genre, and seeks to safeguard the correct and meticulous recital of Scripture in all that concerns letters, vocalization, and accentuation signs. In his introduction, the author informs us of his distress at the nonchalance shown by vocalizers and Masoretes at that time and locale; Yekutiel Ha-Kohen claims that when inserting the diacritics (vowels, *metagim, makafim,* and accentuation signs) in biblical texts, they felt free to disregard "good, decent" model manuscripts and thus led the general public astray in the reading of Scripture. In view of this, Yekutiel Ha-Kohen undertakes the task of redressing the situation, of eradicating errors or preventing their spread, while simultaneously alerting the public to "the art of correct recitation."

The treatise itself is in two parts. The first provides an impressive range of rules concerning the place of stress (correct stress being of course a prerequisite for a correct recitation) and the juncture and phonological rhythm (as marked by the *meteg* and *makaf*). Appended to these rules is a selection of rules (which he labels *azharot*) for the correct realization of consonants, vowels, the *sheva* and the *dagesh*. The second part of the treatise features hundreds of remarks, dealing for the most part with details of the accentuation marks, the *meteg* and the *makaf*, and occasionally with pointing; the remarks relating to verses in the Torah, Esther, and Lamentations and arranged by order of verse are designed to correct faults "wherever I have become aware of a widespread error."

Besides making use of accurate biblical manuscripts from Spain—he reports having six to work from—Yekutiel Ha-Kohen took advantage (as he states in his general introduction to *Eyn Ha-Kore*) of the material of the Masorah (the notes of the Masorah Magna and Masorah Parva, the summary lists, the list of differences between Ben-Asher and Ben-Naftali), the rules of the Masoretes concerning accentuation and vocalization and their mnemonic devices (the "signs of the ancients," as he calls them), the treatise *Horayat Ha-Kore* from Eretz-Israel (a classic of the genre of treatises on scriptural recitation),[9] and the writings of the Spanish grammarians Yehudah Ḥayyuj, Yonah ibn Janaḥ, and Shelomo ibn Parḥon (active in Italy).

In the apparatus of notes to the Pentateuch and Megillot, Yekutiel Ha-Kohen also mentions by name three Ashkenazi scholars: Rabbenu Shemuel (i.e., Rashbam), Rabbenu Tam, and Rabbi Yosef Ha-Nakdan. More than likely, these scholars lie behind the terms "my mentors," "my mentor," "my mentor the vocalizer" used both in the grammatical section of *Eyn Ha-Kore* and in the apparatus of notes. Others mentioned (just once) in the notes are Rabbi Avraham ibn Ezra and Rabbi David Kimḥi, though one suspects that this is a copyist's interpolation.

Besides a general introduction, the grammatical treatise comprises three chapters.

1. On stress. This chapter describes the rules for ultimate *(millera)* and penultimate *(mille'el)* stress in biblical Hebrew words. Like the other chapters, it is arranged following a grammatical criterion. There are three sections: Letters, Verbs, and Nouns.[10] The first is keyed to the final-syllable inflectional letters, the second to verbal classes *(gezarot)*, and the last to noun patterns *(mishkalim)* and to groups of similar words. In a preface to the three sections, the author discusses the importance of knowing the correct stress; a postscript deals briefly with retraction of word stress *(nesigah)*.

2. On the *meteg*.[11] The *meteg* (the early term for which was *ga'aya*) is listed with the accentuation signs, although it is not one strictly speaking (for it has no tune of its own); it indicates a lengthened vowel and a slowing in the reading. Yekutiel Ha-Kohen sees two classes of *meteg*: one light *(kal)*, in an open syllable, and the other heavy *(kaved)*, in a closed syllable, each in turn subdivided into two: simple *(pashut)* before a vowel, and supported *(tamukh)* before a *sheva*. Yekutiel Ha-Kohen sets

out the occurence conditions for each kind of *meteg,* illustrating them according to the associated vowel. He inserts into the chapter some discussions and remarks on the retraction of the *meteg* in a word with a *makaf,* on various ways of symbolizing the light *meteg,* two *metegs* in one word, replacement of the light *meteg* by a conjunctive accent and so on.

3. On the *makaf.*[12] This depicts two groups of *makafim:* (a) *Makafim* dependent on juxtaposition of stresses, i.e., *makafim* in tightly-knit two-word phrases with one stress following on the heels of another (where the first word has final-syllable stress and the second first-syllable stress). Such a *makaf* is of eight types, according to the vowel in the final syllable of the hyphenated word. (b) *Makafim* nondependent on consecutive stresses. This includes phrases in which the second word does not have first-syllable stress.

The Masoretic and grammatical literature prior to Yekutiel Ha-Kohen mentions few rules relating to stress, the *meteg* or the *makaf;* Yekutiel Ha-Kohen is the first scholar systematically and comprehensively to have assembled and described these highly complex rules.

The final chapter of *Eyn Ha-Kore,* called *Azharat Ha-Kore,*[13] comprises a selection of directions and admonitions pertaining in the main to the exact and meticulous phonetic realization of the letters and vowel signs as well as of certain graphic distinctions.

The "Azharot" are as follows: (a) An admonition to leave a gap between two adjacent words, where the consonant that ends the first word is the same (or similar) as that beginning the second word—in other words, to avoid consonantal elision at word boundaries. Among his examples are יֶלֶד זְקוּנִים, אֶת זֵכֶר, כֶּסֶף וְזָהָב. (b) A directive to sound the *dagesh* called "light" in the letters ו, ז, ט, ל, מ, נ, ס, צ, ק, ש as marked in certain Ashkenazi biblical manuscripts from Germany (in forms such as אֲחֶלְמָה, יִשְׁמְעוּ). (c) An admonition not to elide the strong *dagesh* when it comes in letters marked with a *sheva* (e.g., גָּלְתָה, מְצֻוָּה, הַטְּהוֹרָה, זַמְּרוּ). (d) A directive to show especial attention to the phonetic realization of the "final letters" in similar sounding words that differ only in their last consonant (e.g., אַף, אָב). (e) A directive to take care in producing a mobile *sheva* in the first syllable, when followed by א or ע (e.g., וְאִשָּׁה, וְאָמַר), thus avoiding the common error of eliding the consonantal א or ע following a mobile *sheva* and catapulting its vowel to the preceding consonant (i.e., וָמַר rather than וְאָמַר). (f) An admonition to sound the *hataf* with word-initial א and ע, when preceded by a conjunctive ו as in וַאֲמַרְתֶּם. In sounding a warning against slackening the pronunciation of *hatafim,* the author's aim is to stop the whole guttural syllable falling by the wayside, i.e., וַמַרְתֶּם. (g) An admonition to be extracareful about stressing the right syllable when the last syllable of the word is marked with an *etnah* mark.

All but one of these admonitions can arguably be taken as evidence of an existing pronunciation at the time and localities in question, whether among the public at large or in a small circle of the "misguided" or "ignorant" (as Yekutiel Ha-Kohen dubs them). However, one cannot rule out the possibility that at least one admonition, to pronounce the light *dagesh* in most consonants (bar אהח"ע) and not just in בגדכפ"ת, rests upon a consideration that knows no basis in traditional pronunciation—for the light *dagesh* in the letters ו, ז, ט, ל, מ, נ, ס, צ, ק, ש, as marked in certain

Ashkenazi manuscripts of the Bible and of festival prayerbooks with a so-called Palestinian-Tiberian vocalization, is evidently a purely methodological symbol marking the syllable boundary for certain types of syllables and lacking any phonetic significance.

Darkhei Ha-Nikkud by Rabbi Moshe Ha-Nakdan

Rabbi Moshe ben Rabbi Yom-Tov of London (died ca. 1268), scion of one of the most distinguished families of Anglo-Jewry, occupied a leading position among the scholars of the Jewish community before the expulsion of 1290.[14] He was a student or disciple of Rashbam[15] and mentor to Rabbi Moshe ben Yitzhak, author of *Sefer Ha-Shoham* (see analysis below). His *Darkhei Ha-Nikkud* was first published by the grammarian and proofreader Ya'akov ben Ḥayyim ibn Adoniyah of Tunis, on the margins of the Masoretic notes appended to Daniel Bomberg's *Mikra'ot Gedolot* (Venice 1524–25).

The name and identity of the author, Moshe, has occupied many minds. Some have identified Moshe Ha-Nakdan with Rabbi Moshe ben Yitzhak, himself an English Jew, attributing to him the authorship of *Sefer Ha-Shoham*—but without basis. The manuscripts of the work provide ample testimony that only in the case of one manuscript (Berlin 78/2) did the copyist have a tradition as to the author's father and place; he rounds off the manuscript with the words: סליק יסוד הר"מ בה"ר יום טוב מלונטריש ("Here ends the work of Rabbi Moshe son of Rabbi Yom Tov of London"). This name receives confirmation in *Sefer Ha-Shoham* ("and my mentor Rabbi Moshe son of the eminent Rabbi Yom-Tov") and from historical documentation.

Although *Darkhei Ha-Nikkud* has appeared in a scientific edition (Löwinger 1929), we still lack a full, accurate picture of the textual transmission (a relatively large number of manuscripts survive) and of the evolution and stemmatic relationship of the various versions; we thus still await a final answer about the original scope and structure of the treatise and its original title (there is no title at the beginning or in the body of the work).

The Löwinger edition comprises seven chapters, as follows:

1. The rules for the alternation of *kamatz* and *pataḥ*
2. The rules for the alternation of *tzere* and *segol*
3. The rules for the alternation of *ḥolam* and *kamatz "katan"/"ḥatuf"*
4. The rules for the vocalization of *ḥataf pataḥ* and *ḥataf segol*
5. Non-operation of the יהו"א law (i.e., the rules by which *dagesh kal* comes with בג"ד כפ"ת word-initially, when preceded by a word ending in one of the letters יהו"א); this chapter has three brief appendices on kindred topics
6. The rules for the *ga'aya (meteg)*
7. The rules for stress

Löwinger himself doubted whether the three appendices to chapter five or the last two chapters belong to the original work. If not, an appropriate title for the work would clearly be *Darkhei Ha-Nikkud* (as appears in ms. Oxford 2521/4) or *Sefer*

Ha-Nikkud (as in ms. Munich 53/12 and in three manuscripts of the Parma library) rather than *Darkhei Ha-Nikkud Ve-Ha-Neginot,* as it is called in the introduction by Ya'akov ben Ḥayyim in his edition of *Mikra'ot Gedolot* and in Löwinger's edition. Without going into detail, there are two reasons to share Löwinger's doubts about the last two chapters: (a) comparison of the first five chapters with the others reveals discrepancies in grammatical terminology; (b) the first five chapters make passing reference to problems of stress in certain linguistic forms, but nowhere is there so much as a hint at the overall chapter on stress, i.e., chapter seven.

As for the sources of the work, the first and fifth (i.e., the last) chapter are profoundly connected to *Sefer Ta'amei Ha-Mikra.* As the latter—a mere rendition and extended adaptation of the Arabic *Mukhtasar Hidāyat al-Qāri* (an abridgement of *Horayat Ha-Kore*)[16]—predates *Darkhei Ha-Nikkud,* it follows that *Sefer Ta'amei Ha-Mikra* is the source of the work under discussion.

Looking at the type of link between the two works, it emerges that in terms of grammatical approach and basic chapter structure (i.e., the method of presenting the basic rules and their exceptions) Moshe Ha-Nakdan followed what he found before him in *Sefer Ta'amei Ha-Mikra* in the chapters on the law of יהו"א and בג"ד כפ"ת and on the rules for *kamatz* and *pataḥ.* Foremost among his original achievements are: (a) the application of the schema of the various categories of exceptions to the *tzere-segol* and *ḥolam-kamatz "katan"* distinction; (b) the expanded reformulation of the rules for *kamatz* and *pataḥ.*

Moshe Ha-Nakdan cites the following scholars in the original five chapters of his work: Shemuel Ha-Nakdan, i.e., Rashbam; Yehudah Ḥayyuj, the *abir ha-dayekanim* ("prince of grammarians"); Moshe Roti, mentioned also in *Sefer Ha-Shoham;* Yonah ibn Janaḥ; Ba'al Ha-Parḥon, i.e., Shelomo ibn Parḥon; Rashi; Avraham ibn Ezra; Menaḥem and Dunash. The Masorah too is mentioned, as is the Sephardi system of biblical vocalization.

Though not a work of morphology, *Darkhei Ha-Nikkud* makes appreciable reference to morphological categories of the verb. One is left in no doubt that the principles and concepts of Ḥayyuj, including the "quiescent letters" and the across-the-board minimum triliteral root, were perfectly apparent to the author and formed part and parcel of his system. In this sense, it is Moshe Ha-Nakdan—and not, as has been thought, his pupil Moshe ben Yitzḥak, author of *Sefer Ha-Shoham*—who can be considered the first grammarian of the Ashkenaz school to have followed Ḥayyuj of Spain and drawn full conclusions from the linguistic research of the Spanish center.

Ḥibbur Ha-Konim (Ha-Shimshoni) of Rabbi Shimshon Ha-Nakdan

By what title Rabbi Shimshon Ha-Nakdan referred to his composition we do not know—no title appears either before or within the work in any of the manuscripts. It would appear that the author himself gave it no name, which would explain why the redactor of the work ultimately saw fit to give it an etiological name of his own, as he writes in the subscription: "I have called this work *Ḥibbur Ha-Konim,* as it was achieved ["קנו אותו"] by many elders." A further name, *Ha-Shimshoni,* derived from the name of the author, has gained wide currency in the literature through the Masorete and grammarian Eliyahu Baḥur (Levita) Ashkenazi in his *Masoret Ha-Masoret* (Venice 1538).

Who Shimshon Ha-Nakdan was and when he lived are two interrelated questions. Briefly, conventional wisdom would have it that the author of *Ha-Shimshoni* was the grandfather of the vocalizer Rabbi Yosef of Xanten, son of Kalonymos of Neuss,[17] in view of comments by Rabbi Yosef on the margin of a biblical manuscript that he wrote in 1294, making repeated mention of the *nikkud* of "My grandfather and mentor Rabbi Shimshon." If this hypothesis is sound—and we may accept it in the absence of counter-evidence—it would testify that Shimshon Ha-Nakdan was still alive in 1294. (Rabbi Yosef would otherwise have used an honorific term for the deceased.) And as we have just demonstrated that his grandson and pupil was already a well-versed scholar, it seems that the author of *Ha-Shimshoni* was born around 1230. This identification had already led Geiger to state that the author was Ashkenazi and was alive around 1240. His death can be dated between 1294 (the date of the biblical manuscript written by Yosef ben Kalonymos) and 1297. Thus our author must have been active from midway through the thirteenth century.

Thematically and organizationally, *Ha-Shimshoni*[18] divides into two: the first part is devoted to morphology and leans heavily on the linguistic writings of the Spanish school of grammar, while the second part deals with vocalization and accentuation in the spirit of the grammatical tradition of Ashkenaz—with the exception of the opening chapter on vowels, a kind of theoretical introduction to *nikkud* strongly influenced by the vowel theory of Avraham ibn Ezra of Spain.

The chapters are as follows:

Part One
1. One chapter deals with the personal pronouns and pronominal suffixes (the "ten possessors").
2. "Verbs" describes the verb system with its regular and irregular forms under eight verbal classes (regular verbs, פ"נ, פ"י, ע"ו, ל"ה, פ"נ/ל"ה, פ"/ל"ה , ע"ע and the quadriradical class) and eight verbal patterns (the seven familiar *binyanim* plus the quadriradical pattern.) The order of "tenses" for each is past, future, imperative, active and passive participle, infinitive.
3. "Nouns" comprises a limited sketch of the nouns according to their patterns *(mishkalim),* based primarily on Ibn Ezra's *Sefer Tzaḥot.*

Part Two
4. "Vowels" is preceded by a brief discussion of the quiescent (or latent) letters אהו"י in relation to the various Hebrew vowels.
5. *"Nikkud"* has four chapters that paint a connected, integrated picture of vocalization:
    a. rules for the *kamatz* and *pataḥ*
    b. rules for the *tzere* and *segol*
    c. rules for the *ḥolam* and *kamatz "katan" ("ḥatuf")*
    d. rules for *ḥataf pataḥ* and *ḥataf segol.*

6. A chapter on the law for אהו"י and בג"ד כפ"ת
7. A chapter on the *meteg*
8. A chapter on accentuation
9. A chapter on the *dagesh lene ("kal")*

The scholars mentioned in these chapters as direct or indirect sources or references are Ben-Asher and Ben-Naftali, Sa'adyah Gaon, Yehudah Ḥayyuj, Yonah ibn Janaḥ, Shemu'el Ha-Nagid, Moshe Ha-Kohen ben Jikatila, Ya'akov ben Elazar, Shemu'el Ha-Dayyekan (= Rashbam), Avraham ibn Ezra and his books *Tzaḥot, Moznayim, Sefat Yeter, Areshet Ha-Safa,* Shelomo ibn Parḥon, Yosef Kimḥi, David Kimḥi and his book *Mikhlol,* Yosef Ḥazzan of Troyes, and Moshe Roti.

Also mentioned in *Ha-Shimshoni* are the following books: "Spanish books" (meaning vocalized and accentuated Spanish books of the Bible), *Sefer Semadar,* and *Sefer Even Boḥan.*

Of the chapters that make up *Ha-Shimshoni,* we wish to say something of *"Nikkud."* A first attempt in the linguistic literature of Ashkenaz to marshall the rules for vocalization into one body (enabling the theory of vocalization to be taught for its own sake) had already been undertaken in *Sefer Ta'amei Ha-Mikra;*[19] and sure enough, no new theory of vocalization is to be had from the chapter in *Ha-Shimshoni*—Shimshon Ha-Nakdan in fact reiterates the phonological schema proposed in *Sefer Ta'amei Ha-Mikra* and expanded and improved one generation before him by Moshe Ha-Nakdan of London in his *Darkhei Ha-Nikkud* (described above). Rabbi Shimshon does however probe and rework existing material, adding substantial Masoretic material as well as rules and explanations of other grammarians and of his own. Taken together with the other chapters relating to vocalization (6 and 9, and to a lesser extent 7), and with the rules for vocalization embedded in the extensive chapter on the verb and those on pronouns and nouns, the theory of vocalization (in the broad sense) in its Ashkenazi version has crystallized into a rounded, sophisticated system.

If the genesis of vocalization theory took place away from Tiberias, it was because the biblical reading tradition in Tiberias matched the so-called Tiberian system of vocalization (the traditional system of the biblical text) and because the principles of vocalization and the ground rules for vocalizing the Bible were clear and familiar to those in Eretz-Israel using the early grammatical works of the Masoretes of the Tiberian school. To them and their age, the vocalization was self-explanatory.

The serious problem with vocalization arose for those whose actual Hebrew pronunciation was at odds with the pronunciation rules inherent in the Tiberian vocalization and for those who were far removed from the language tradition in which the rules for pointing the biblical text were grounded. Vocalization theory was evolved among grammarians whose community had adopted the sign system of an alien phonetic tradition that had more vowel *signs* than the community possessed vowels. Thus their vocalization theory, first and foremost, addresses the mismatch between linguistic reality and the traditional vocalization with all its sanctity and normative force.

In all probability, vocalization theory was aimed less at methodological ends (i.e., teaching how to insert pointing) than at enlightening Hebrew students as to the relation between the Hebrew pronunciation in their circles and the traditional vocalization of the biblical text (i.e., teaching an understanding of the pointing).

The vocalization theory of Ashkenaz scholarship sought to describe and teach the ground rules of the Tiberian vocalization system for the Bible—representing an ancient reading tradition with seven vowel qualities (a, å, e, ε, i, o, u)—to Hebrew readers (and non-Hebrew speakers) whose actual pronunciation does not distinguish *kamatz* from *patah* and *tzere* from *segol,* nor *holam* from *kamatz "katan,"* and who thus make a phonetic distinction between *kamatz "gadol"* (equivalent to a *patah*) and *kamatz "katan"* (equivalent to a *holam*).

This contradiction had its roots in the reality of medieval Ashkenaz: on the one hand, the traditional Tiberian vocalization system had become accepted and entrenched in Ashkenaz; on the other, the phonetic distinctions practiced within the Tiberian reading tradition failed to put down roots here. As a whole series of researchers has demonstrated (one might mention Yalon, Gumperz, Max Weinreich, Beit-Aryeh, and Eldar), it was a "Sephardi" pronunciation that prevailed among Ashkenaz Jewry in Germany, France, and England up until the mid-fourteenth century or thereabouts, meaning a pronunciation that reflected a linguistic tradition (hailing from Eretz-Israel) of five vowels: a, e, i, o u.

As the Tiberian vocalization system for the Bible, in which graphic symbol is mapped onto vowel, did not correspond to the "Sephardi" pronunciation (or, to be historically accurate, the Palestinian pronunciation) of medieval Ashkenaz, it will be self-evident why Ashkenazi grammarians felt the need to base their *nikkud* theory upon creating a distinction between *kamatz* and *patah, tzere* and *segol, holam* and *kamatz katan* (known by the Ashkenazim as *"kamatz hatuf"* or *"hataf kamatz"*).

The vocalization theory of Moshe Ha-Nakdan in his *Darkhei Ha-Nikkud* and of Shimshon Ha-Nakdan is thus two-edged: methodologically, it rests on the Ashkenaz reality of a Sephardi pronunciation, while it seeks to depict an ideal (Tiberian) pronunciation distinguishing seven vowel qualities alien to its time and place.

Sefer Ha-Shoham of Rabbi Moshe ben Yitzhak

Sefer Ha-Shoham is one of two grammatical works bequeathed to us by pre-expulsion (pre-1290) Anglo-Jewry—the other being Moshe Ha-Nakdan's *Darkhei Ha-Nikkud.* Incontrovertibly, *Sefer Ha-Shoham* is the most outstanding contribution by any scholar in Ashkenaz to the grammar of Hebrew. In terms of the evolution of Ashkenazi linguistic thought, "it is in fact the first work which introduced to northern Europe in a systematic fashion the results of the philological investigations of Spanish Jewry."[20]

Moshe ben Yitzhak ben Ha-Nesi'a (son of the countess or contesse) was the pupil of Moshe ben Yom-Tov of London, author of *Darkhei Ha-Nikkud* (depicted above). As the latter died ca. 1268, it is fair to assume that his pupil, the author of *Sefer Ha-Shoham,* was active around the middle of the thirteenth century.

Shoham ("onyx") is mentioned as the name of the composition in the author's introduction: "And I have called this book *shoham* since my own name lies therein" (*shoham* is an anagram of his first name, Moshe). He further informs us there that in his youth he composed a grammar book entitled *Leshon Limmudim,* which unfortunately has not come down to us nor found a mention in any other source.

Moshe ben Yitzḥak was patently intent on encompassing the whole Hebrew language in his grammar. The theoretical elements underpinning the greater part of the book, and most of the author's opinions, are those of the Spanish school, as expressed in particular in the works of Yehudah Ḥayyuj, *Sefer Ha-Hasaga* of Yonah ibn Janaḥ, *Sefer Ha-Zikkaron* of Yosef Kimḥi, the works of Avraham ibn Ezra, and Shelomo ibn Parḥon's *Maḥberet He-Arukh.*

At second hand, via Ibn Ezra, Yosef and David Kimḥi, and Ibn Parḥon, whose works summarized the attainments of the classical Spanish school, Moshe ben Yitzḥak knew the content of Ibn Janaḥ's *Kitab Al-Tankiḥ,* its grammatical as well as its lexical section (*Sefer Ha-Rikmah* and *Sefer Ha-Shorashim*).

More than once, in the lexical elucidations embedded in the grammatical sections of *Sefer Ha-Shoham,* the author follows the exegesis of Rashi, Ibn Ezra, and David Kimḥi. These scholars apart, *Sefer Ha-Shoham* also refers to Sa'adyah Ga'on, Menaḥem ben Saruk, Rashbam, Berakhyah Ha-Nakdan, Moshe Roti, and the biblical commentators Yosef Kara and Eliezer of Beaugency.

Sefer Ha-Shoham is in three parts.²¹ The first offers introductory chapters to two domains: (a) The study of letters and sounds: the phonetic classification of consonants, consonantal interchange, division of letters into root letters and servile letters (letters which serve as formative elements), the function, meaning and vocalization of the servile letters, assimilation of the seven letters א, ה, ו, י, ל, נ, ת in the *dagesh* of another letter, changes in vocalization due to morphological causes, consonantal change of position. (b) Biblical rhetoric and hermeneutics: missing words (ellipsis), pleonastic words; inverse order ("and sometimes a later event in a verse is really earlier"), the connected and the disconnected ("and sometimes the text abandons all connection with the immediately foregoing and instead harks back to something that appeared way back"), masculine and feminine ("wherever you find masculine and feminine together in one statement, they all become masculine"), word interchange ("sometimes they say one thing and in their heart is another").

Part two, the main body of the book, is devoted to morphology. Hebrew word structure is described under three headings: verb, noun, and particle. (Despite the prevailing view that the noun is prime and the verb secondary, the author leads off with the latter.)

The substantial chapter on the verb is organized like a dictionary, with roots as entries (using the same method as Ḥayyuj in his description of the irregular verb). The dictionary is in nine parts, each devoted to a particular group, i.e., *gizrah,* of roots: strong verbs, פ״י, פ״נ, ע״ו/י, ע״ה, ל״ה, the "forma mixta" פ״י/ל״ה and פ״נ/ל״ה, ע״ע, the quadriradical verbal class.

The discussion for each entry involves identifying the *binyan* of the actual verb-forms yielded by the root in question, illustrated by biblical verses (sometimes in lieu of a discussion), plus grammatical observations where these are particularly needed, e.g., where the vocalization or the grammatical form is abnormal or where the very identification of the root is at issue or where several inflectional alternatives exist. These observations are peppered with references to earlier grammarians (sometimes by way of a "some say . . ."), either as further support or simply as a reference. Biblical words are occasionally elucidated, sometimes by way of comparison with Aramaic, Old French, or post-biblical Hebrew.

Equally impressive in its breadth and comprehensiveness is the chapter dealing with the noun. Arranged by *mishkal* ("noun pattern"), it alphabetically lists all nouns of each *mishkal,* beginning with the unaffixed patterns (*pe'el, pa'al,* etc.); followed by patterns with a prefix (*mif'al, mif'ol,* etc.); feminine patterns (*pe'alah, pe'ilah,* etc.); patterns with a suffix (*pa'alan, pi'alon,* etc.); feminine patterns ending in -*t* (*pa'elet,* etc.); and finally patterns with nouns from defective, reduplicative, or bi-consonantal roots (such as *pa', pol, pil, mafol, mif'eh, pe'ut,* etc.). Discussion is rounded off with a sketch of nouns from four- and five-letter roots. Along the way, the author offers brief grammatical explanations for nouns that pose problems in terms of form or vocalization, with the odd semantic remark thrown in.

The chapter on particles *(millot ha-devek)* treats of prepositions and conjunctions, interrogatives and personal pronouns—again in the form of an alphabetical lexicon, with a further, short chapter on numerals *(Sha'ar Ha-Ḥeshbon).*

The third and final part of *Sefer Ha-Shoham* is about vocalization and accentuation of the Scriptures, involving the following topics: the distinction between long and short vowels; the rules for pronouncing mobile *sheva* and for distinguishing it from quiescent *sheva;* the rules for final and penultimate stress; the rules for *kamatz* and *pataḥ, tzere* and *segol, ḥolam* and *kamatz katan,* the rules for אוי"ה and בג"ד כפ"ת.

The book concludes with what is conceivably a later addition to the whole, a concise lexicon of Aramaic words in the Bible.

Mafteaḥ Shel Dikduk by Rabbi Mordekhai Ya'ir

Mafteaḥ Shel Dikduk is a study guide to the verb, offering a practical learning method: detailed paradigms (arranged in tables), as an aid to memorizing verb forms by *gizrah* and *binyan.* These paradigms, it transpires—and the snappy explanations and grammatical rules of thumb accompanying them—are but a neat and thorough reduction of the detailed picture of the verb in Shimshon Ha-Nakdan's *Ha-Shimshoni* and Yosef Kimḥi's *Sefer Zikkaron.*

It was apparently because of this affinity to *Ha-Shimshoni* that *Mafteaḥ Shel Dikduk* was attributed by one of its copyists to Shimshon Ha-Nakdan. The fact that the two are found side-by-side in some manuscripts led Steinschneider to regard *Mafteaḥ Shel Dikduk* as the first part of *Ha-Shimshoni,* while Margoliouth considered it a separate work of Shimshon Ha-Nakdan.

There is no doubt that *Mafteaḥ Shel Dikduk* is an independent work, but it seems more likely that its author was Mordekhai Ya'ir, the redactor of *Ha-Shimshoni,* who was living in Friedberg, Germany in 1297.

The paradigms, which form the larger and most significant portion of *Mafteaḥ Shel Dikduk,* specify all the verbal classes and patterns and supply all the inflected forms of the verb in past and future tense, active and passive participle, imperative, and infinitive. (The verbs are given without suffixed pronouns.) The author does not display the whole inflectional system through a single model root but through various roots. Rather than limit himself to the verbal forms extant in the Bible, he uses analogy to create all the grammatically possible forms needed to complete his paradigms.

The forms of the verb are enumerated person by person, with each person subdivided for gender and number. In the past tense, the fixed order is 3rd m.s, 3rd f.s, 3rd m.pl, 3rd f.pl, 2nd m.s, 2nd f.s, 2nd m.pl, 2nd f.pl, 1st s, 1st pl. In the future there is no set order, but 1st person is always first, followed by 3rd person. The explanations accompanying the paradigms involve rules of word formation, vocalization of the formative letters, the effect of the guttural letters upon this vocalization, anomalous forms, the patterns of *binyan kal*, the distinction between transitive and intransitive, and more.

Introducing the detailed tables of inflection is a general overview of the verb and its classes *(gezarot)* and patterns *(binyanim)*. Having opened with the customary division of the Holy Tongue into three classes (noun, verb, and particle), the author sets out his method by depicting the verb system: a division of all verb forms into eight *gezarot* (each the subject of a brief description) and a classification of all forms of a *gizrah* into eight *binyanim*.

The *gezarot* enumerated are as follows: The strong verb, ל"ה, פ"נ, פ"י, doubly weak verbs ("forma mixta") פ"י/ל"ה and ע"ו/י פ"נ/ל"ה, ע"ע, quadriliteral and five-letter verbs. The names of the *binyanim* in their set order are *pa'al (kal), nif'al, pi'el, hif'il, meruba* (the quadriradical verbal pattern),[22] *pu'al, huf'al*,[23] *hitpa'el*.

Rabbi Mordekhai divides these *binyanim* (save the *binyan meruba*) into three groups,[24] on a morphological basis but with consideration for semantics (i.e., active versus passive *binyanim*). The three active *binyanim—pa'al, pi'el* (termed *kaved*), and *hif'il* (termed *nosaf*)—are the basic *binyanim* in the system, and are dubbed *avot*. The three passive *binyanim—nif'al* (termed *nif'al kal*), *pu'al* (termed *nif'al ḥazak* or *kaved*), *huf'al* (termed *nif'al nosaf*)—on the one hand, and *hitpa'el* on the other, are adjudged to be derivatives of the active *binyanim* (and called *toladot*): the three passives because they are derived from their active counterparts, either by affixation (in the case of *nif'al*) or by internal modification (in the case of *pu'al* and *huf'al*), and the *hitpa'el* because it is a "complex" *binyan* built out of a combination of formative elements characteristic of the basic *binyanim*, namely *pi'el* (with its *dagesh forte*) and *hif'il* (with its prefix *h*).

Rabbi Shene'ur's Treatise with No Name

A nameless work of grammar has been preserved in a single manuscript. The author gives his own name, Rabbi Shene'ur, four times in the body of the work. Since he cites French scholars (see below), some have assumed that the author himself was French. While it is difficult to accept an assumption resting on such evidence alone, counter-evidence is lacking. From the fact that Rabbi Shene'ur was familiar with the treatises of Moshe Ha-Nakdan (mentioned several times, and once in terms appropriate to the deceased) and of Shimshon Ha-Nakdan, it seems likely that he operated in the last quarter of the thirteenth century, at the earliest.

Our nameless composition cannot be deemed original; it is entirely a compilation adapted from a number of works, as follows: (a) The major part is adapted en bloc from *Darkhei Ha-Nikkud* of Moshe Ha-Nakdan of London, meaning all five original chapters plus the chapter on the *ga'aya* appended in some manuscripts (see section 5). The author follows his source clause by clause, making small alterations in phrasing and form, adding and switching examples and sometimes looking to explanations of his own and of others. This part involves the following chapters: the *ga'aya*, rules for *kamatz* and *patah*, rules for *tzere* and *segol*, rules for *holam* and *kamatz "katan"/"hatuf,"* rules for *hataf patah* and *hataf segol*, the rules for אוי"ה and בג"ד כפ"ת. (b) The opening chapter, dealing with the *gezarot* of the verb (the beginning is missing in the manuscript), is a précis of the theoretical introduction of *Mafteah Shel Dikduk* (discussed above). (c) The final chapter, devoted to the rules of accentuation, is a shortened reworking of the chapter on accentuation in *Sefer Ta'amei Ha-Mikra* or in *Ha-Shimshoni*.

Three short chapters—on types of *sheva*, the pronunciation of the mobile *sheva* and its syllabic status, and the rules for *dagesh* and *rafeh*—do not appear to be an adaptation, though they too reveal Rabbi Shene'ur's general dependence on the grammarians of the Ashkenazi school that predate him.

Notes

1. On the transitionary period (1350–1450) in Rabbinic literature in Ashkenaz, see Dinari 1984: 9–16.

2. Shimshon the Lexicographer is not the same as Shimshon the Punctuator (author of the grammar *Hibbur Ha-Konim/Ha-Shimshoni*). The one manuscript containing his biblical lexicon was still available to A. Geiger before going astray.

3. The efforts of the *Peshat* commentators, above all Rashi, to identify, analyze and formulate the principles of sentence structure, morphology and style as embodied in the biblical text reflect an empirical methodology grounded in the writings of the first Spanish grammarians, Menahem ben Saruk and Dunash ben Labrat, whose works had been written in Hebrew in the mid-tenth century. On the impact of Menahem and Dunash on Rashi and Rashbam, see Poznanski 1913: xvii (Rashi), xlvif (Rashbam); Rosin 1880: 64–65, 128, 133; Melamed 1978: 398–405 (Rashi), 496 (Rashbam); Mirsky 1987; Berger 1982: 211–223.

4. Overviews of the Ashkenazi grammatical literature (whether by way of dedicated studies of the historiography of Hebrew philology or books on the history of medieval Hebrew literature) are weak and fragmentary. The present survey is the first comprehensive one based on a study of the printed editions or manuscripts of the works under review.

5. Rashbam's (definitely identified) commentaries to the Torah, Kohelet and Esther have come down to us; isolated sections of his commentaries to these and other books lie embedded in works of later commentators and in medieval compilations. On his work and exegetical methods see Poznanski 1913: xxxix–l; Melamed 1978: 454–80; Yefet-Salters 1985: 13–54 (and pp. 152–53 of a selected bibliography of Rashbam research).

6. A critical edition (with German introduction but no commentary) is Stein 1923. The identification of "Rabbenu Shemu'el" author of *Dayyakot* with the Bible commentator Rashbam was proved by the editor in his introduction (in view of sections corresponding to

his Commentary to the Torah). Yalon 1942: 28–29 adduced two decisive proofs from the grammatical method used.

7. For grammatical aspects of Rashbam's commentary to the Torah, see Rosin 1880: 128–44; Melamed 1978: 471–78, 496–507.

8. Yarkoni 1985:III; on the date of Yekutiel see ibid: 9–13.

9. *Horayat Ha-Kore* is the name of a Hebrew translation done in Mainz, Germany (in the first half of the twelfth century, it seems) from the abbreviated Arabic version of the Eretz-Israel work *Hidāyat Al-Qāri*. Another translation bears the name *Sefer Ta'amei Ha-Mikra*.

10. It has been published by Eldar 1976 (Introduction; *Sha'ar Ha-Otiyot*); 1977 *(Sha'ar Ha-Pe'ulot)*; 1978: 191–96 *(Sha'ar Ha-Shemot)*; Yarkoni 1985, part 2: 16–83.

11. This was published in Gumperz 1958; Yarkoni, part 2: 83–135.

12. This was published in Yarkoni 1985, part 2: 136–57.

13. This was published in Wolf Heidenheim's Chumash *Me'or Eynayim*, part 1, Roedelheim, 1818, introduction (only some of the *Azharot*); Yarkoni 1985, part 2: 158–88.

14. See Urbach 1968: 10; Roth 1957: 22. On the genealogy of Moshe Ha-Nakdan, documented as stemming from the Rhineland and recorded by a late thirteenth-century scion, see Kaufmann 1891.

15. The scholars of England maintained close ties with their French counterparts, copying their works and espousing their theories.

16. See n. 9.

17. Xanten and Neuss are towns on the Rhine, close to Cologne.

18. *Ha-Shimshoni* has yet to be published in its full form. Recent years have seen scientific publication of three chapters, dealing with vowels (edited by Eldar 1979), with pronouns, and with verbs (edited by Ben-Menahem 1987).

19. See n. 9.

20. Roth 1947: 9; compare Klar 1947: p vii.

21. It was in 1883 that the first part of *Sefer Ha-Shoham* was first published, by the Jewish Hebraist Collins; it was republished in 1947 by Klar with the first three chapters of the second part.

22. The existence of the binyan *po'el* in biblical Hebrew (in such forms as יְסוֹעֵר, יוֹדְעְתִּי, שׁוֹשַׁתִּי) was first established by Ḥayyuj, but Mordekhai Ya'ir also includes in this *binyan* forms derived from *Ayin Vav* (e.g., כּוֹנֵן) and *Ayin Ayin* (e.g., סוֹבֵב).

23. Yosef Kimḥi in his *Sefer Zikkaron* is the first grammarian to give the forms *pu'al* and *huf'al* the status of distinct *binyanim* (just in past and future tense), enumerating eight *binyanim* all told. In his footsteps, our author relates the participles of these passive *binyanim* to their active counterparts.

24. This division is already found in *Ha-Shimshoni*, but Shimshon Ha-Nakdan classifies the quadriliteral *binyan* (יְסוֹעֵר and its ilk) as a compound *binyan* (like *binyan hitpa'el*).

References

BEN-MENAHEM, D. "*Ḥibbur ha-Qonim (ha-Shimshoni)* by R. Shimshon ha-Naqdan." Ph.D. diss., University of California, 1987.

BERGER, M.B. "The Torah Commentary of R. Samuel ben Meir." Ph.D. diss., Harvard University, 1982.

DINARI, Y. A. *Ḥakhmei Ashkenaz be-Shilhei Yemei-ha-Beinayim* (The Rabbis of Germany and Austria at the Close of the Middle Ages). Jerusalem, 1984.

ELDAR, ILAN. "Sha'ar Noaḥ Ha-Tevot mitokh *Eyn Ha-Kore*: Kelalei Milera u-Mile'el le-

Yekutiel ha-Nakdan" (On Word Stress in *Eyn Ha-Kore:* The Penultimate and Ultimate Stress Rules of Yekutiel Ha-Nakdan). *Leshonenu* 40 (1976): 190–210.

———. "Mi-Kitvei Askolat ha-Dikduk ha-Ashkenazit: *Ha-Shimshoni*" (The Writings of the Ashkenazi School of Grammar: *Ha-Shimshoni*). *Leshonenu* 43 (1979): 100–111, 201–10.

GEIGER, ABRAHAM. "Schimschon, ein Lexikograph in Deutschland." *Wissenschaftliche Zeitschrift für jüdische Theologie* 5 (1844): 413–30.

GUMPERZ, YEHIEL. "Sha'ar ha-Metigot le-Yekutiel ha-Nakdan" (On the Classes of Meteg in Eyn Ha-Kore). *Leshonenu* 22 (1958): 36–47, 137–46.

KAUFMANN, D. "Three Centuries of the Genealogy of the Most Eminent Anglo-Jewish Family before 1290." *Jewish Quarterly Review* 3 (1891): 550–66.

KLAR, BINYAMIN, ed. *Sefer ha-Shoham (Sha'arei Dikduk ve-Otzar Milim) le-Rabbi Moshe ben Yitzḥak ben ha-Nesi'ah me-Inglaterra.* Jerusalem, 1947.

LÖWINGER, D. S, ed. *Sefer Darkhei ha-Nikkud ve-ha-Neginot ha-Meyuḥas le-R. Moshe Ha-Nakdan.* Budapest, 1929.

MELAMED, E. Z. *Mefarshei Ha-Mikra: Darkeihem ve-Shitoteihem* (The Bible Commentators: Their Ways and Methods). Jerusalem, 1978.

MIRSKI, A. "Rashi u-Maḥberet Menaḥem" (Rashi and the Mahberet of Menahem). *Sinai* 100 (1987): 579–86

POZNANSKI, S. A. *Perush al Yeḥezke'el u-Trei Asar le-R. Eliezer mi-Beaugency,* with appended introduction *Al Ḥakhmei Tzarfat Mefarshei ha-Mikra.* Warsaw, 1913.

ROSIN, D. R. *Samuel ben Meir als Schrifterklärer.* Breslau, 1880.

ROTH, B. "Toldot Rabbenu Eliyahu Menaḥem" (The History of Rabbenu Eliyahu Menahem). In M. Y. Sacks. *Perush Rabbenu Eliyahu mi-Londres u-Fesakav.* Jerusalem, 1957.

ROTH, CECIL. "Moses ben Isaac Nessiah and his Work The Sefer haShoham." In B. Klar, ed., 1947: 5–16.

STEIN, Y. T. "Shiyurei Yom Tov: Dikduk me-Rabbenu Shemu'el u-Ferusho al ha-Torah al-pi ha-Dikduk." In *Jahrbuch des Traditionstreuen Rabbinerverbandes in der Slowakei.* Tranava, 1923: 33–59, i–vii.

STOKES, H. P. *Studies in Anglo-Jewish History.* Edinburgh, 1913.

URBACH, EFRAYIM. *Ba'alei Ha-Tosafot: Toldoteihem, Ḥibbureihem ve-Shitotam* (The Tosaphists: Their History, Writings and Methods). Jerusalem, 1968.

YALON, HANOKH. *Inyanei Lashon* (Language Matters). Jerusalem, 1942.

YARKONI, R. *"Eyn Ha-Kore le-Yekutiel Ha-Kohen."* Ph.D. diss., Tel Aviv University, 1985.

YEFET (JAPHET), SARAH, AND R. SALTERS, eds. *Perush Rashbam le-Kohelet* (Rashbam's Commentary to Kohelet). Jerusalem, 1985.

4

The Phonology of Ashkenazic

DOVID KATZ

> I rejoice and thank God with all my heart that He made me an Ashkenazic Jew in my pronunciation.
>
> Jacob Emden 1761:§53

The Notion "Ashkenazic"

Ashkenazic Hebrew and Ashkenazic Aramaic

The terms "Ashkenazi(c) Hebrew" and "Ashkenazi(c) pronunciation" are often encountered in reference to the pronunciations of Hebrew deriving from central and eastern Europe. These terms are fine for continued general use but more precision is needed in a study of the subject. For one thing, Ashkenazic Hebrew involves a lot more than pronunciation: it comprises a set of characteristic features in lexicon, semantics, morphology, and syntax (see e.g., Noble 1958). For another, the Ashkenazic sound pattern applies equally to Aramaic. The work at hand calls for a term limited to pronunciation, but encompassing Aramaic as well as Hebrew. I shall use the noun "Ashkenazic" for the phonological system used by traditional Ashkenazim in their pronunciation of Hebrew and Aramaic.

For around a thousand years, Ashkenazic thrived in Ashkenaz, the Jewish culture area that covered much of central and eastern Europe and comprised the geographically and demographically largest speech community in Jewish history. Following the Holocaust, Ashkenazic survives among some of its progeny worldwide, most perfectly so among a number of the more traditional Hasidic and yeshiva-centered communities. In other communities, both in Israel and around the world, its use has diminished sharply, or disappeared, in response to a conscious campaign of discreditation and denigration, the roots of which can be traced, ultimately, to the "Berlin Enlightenment" of the late eighteenth century. Reference to "Ashkenaz," "Ashkenazim," and "Ashkenazic" in this study involves the linguistic state of affairs in pre-war central and eastern Europe, and in traditional communities today around the world.

Internal Jewish Trilingualism in Ashkenaz

In order to fathom the place of Ashkenazic in linguistic and cultural history, we must bear in mind its multilingual environment. In addition to varying degrees of mastery of local non-Jewish languages, Ashkenazim have three distinct Jewish languages, Yiddish, Hebrew, and Aramaic, which participate in a unique trilingualism (see Katz 1985: 98). Yiddish (itself containing a Hebrew and Aramaic component) is the only vernacular in traditional Ashkenazic culture. Hebrew and Aramaic, although nonvernacular, are, in Ashkenaz, very much alive, used in reading, study, prayer, declaiming, singing, and in quoting from classical texts. They are "uttered" in the course of these activities, thus meeting the proposed definition of Ashkenazic as a phonological system. Moreover, Hebrew and Aramaic thrive as literary languages, and the degree to which writers and readers "mentally utter" the phonological representations of these texts is an issue open to study.

In writing, the three Jewish languages of Ashkenaz complemented each other in part. Yiddish dominated popular literature and intimate personal written communication. Hebrew occupied in social terms the broad educated middle ground of communal, rabbinic, and more formal written communication, Bible and Mishnah commentaries, and works on customs and ethics. Aramaic was the principal language of much talmudic and kabbalistic literature. None of the three languages of Ashkenaz was "low-prestige" or "stigmatized" in any modern sense of these terms. Such notions arose later as a consequence of the Enlightenment and its various offshoots. All three had their accepted and unquestioned place in the eyes of the society in question, and those are the eyes that count. An absence of "low prestige" does not imply an absence of "high prestige." Sociological "highness" was clearly linked with knowledge, learning, and creativity and can be charted on an upward curve from the universally known Yiddish to the more select and learned Hebrew through to the most select and learned Aramaic language of the two most profound and esoteric branches of the culture: the jurisprudence of the Talmud and the mysticism of the Kabbalah. Moreover, those parts of the liturgy that are in Aramaic, although a minority, have the greatest psychological sanctity, including the kaddish prayer for the dead, and the *Kol Nidrey* on the Day of Atonement. The often-encountered notion that Hebrew and Aramaic had somehow blended in Ashkenaz into a hodge-podge, sometimes called "Hebrew-Aramaic" ("Hebrew-hyphen-Aramaic"), is mistaken. To be sure, Hebrew has its Aramaic component, and (Jewish) Aramaic its Hebrew component, but never did the twain merge in lexicon, morphology, or grammatical machinery (see Katz 1985: 98), and a monograph would prove this. They did merge phonologically, however, hence the term and the concept "Ashkenazic."

The Work at Hand

I shall propose principles and methodology concerning the structure, origin, and history of Ashkenazic and its relation to both the antecedent Hebrew and Aramaic and to contemporary Yiddish. The ideas offered differ sharply from the views that collectively constitute "standard theory" on the subject (see e.g., Lebensohn 1874: 19–25; Tshemerinski 1913: 61–63; Veynger 1913: 79–81; Yalon 1937–38: 63, 1942: 27; Birnbaum 1934: 28–29; Klar 1951; M. Weinreich 1954: 89–99; 1963–1964; 1973: 2: 20–21, 124, 334, 352–54; Morag 1971; Eldar 1978). Arguments on contentious issues have been put forward elsewhere, and will not be repeated (see Katz 1977; 1979; 1980; 1982; 1983a; 1985; 1986; 1987a; 1991; 1992). For previous treatments of Ashkenazic, see Schreiner 1886; Ember 1903; Idelsohn 1913: 531–32, 697–99; Bauer and Leander 1922: 170–71; Cohen 1923: 56–64; Segal 1928a: 18–19, 29, 50, 75, 90, 137; 1928b; Gumpertz 1953; Assaf 1954: 1: 234; Chomsky 1957: 112–16; Zimmels 1958: 82–90, 308–14; U. Weinreich 1959–1961; Leibel 1965; Altbauer 1977.

Dialectological Framework
Classification of Yiddish Dialects

Nearly all late twentieth-century forms of both Yiddish and Ashkenazic derive from the territory of "Eastern Yiddish," in the Slavonic and Baltic lands. Eastern Yiddish comprises three major dialect areas: (1) Northeastern Yiddish (popularly "Lithuanian") on the territory of ethnographic Lithuania, Latvia, White Russia; (2) Mideastern Yiddish (popularly "Polish") on the territory of ethnographic Poland and parts of Hungary and Czechoslovakia; and (3) Southeastern Yiddish (popularly "Ukrainian") on the territory of ethnographic Ukraine, Bessarabia, and Romania.

The no-longer spoken varieties of "Western Yiddish" may also be subdivided into three major dialect areas: (1) Northwestern Yiddish (Netherlands, northern Germany); (2) Midwestern Yiddish (central Germany); and (3) Southwestern Yiddish (Alsace, Switzerland, southern Germany). There are two major intermediate areas: (1) Northern Transitional Yiddish (East Prussia; see Katz 1988a: 43–53) and Southern Transitional Yiddish (parts of Czechoslovakia and Hungary), also known, after U. Weinreich (1964), as Transcarpathian Yiddish. These classifications follow Katz (1983b).

Coterminous Dialect Areas

The dialect areas of Yiddish and Ashkenazic are coterminous. Thus, Northeastern Yiddish is coterritorial with Northeastern Ashkenazic, Southwestern Yiddish with Southwestern Ashkenazic, and so forth. The identity of the geolinguistic patterning is determined by the identity of the speakers: a Northeastern Yiddish speaker in traditional Ashkenaz is by definition a user of Northeastern Ashkenazic.

The Vowel Systems of Yiddish Dialects
Primacy of Vernacular Phonology

Neither Hebrew nor Aramaic was anybody's native language in Ashkenaz. An abstraction of the phonology of these sacred languages without reference to their users' native language would be folly, firstly because it is spoken language that divulges the true phonology of a speaker, and secondly because, in the society in question, the links between the vernacular and the two sacred languages were profound for virtually the entire population (cf. M. Weinreich 1973: 1:251–320; 3:253–331). The most profound linguistic link is the cooccurrence, in different phonological guise, of thousands of items from the sacred languages in the vernacular.

As a point of departure, therefore, Ashkenazic is best conceived from the perspective of the coterritorial Yiddish dialect, and, especially, the dialect's "Semitic component." The Semitic component in Yiddish, comprising the parts of the language deriving from Hebrew or Aramaic, is synchronically fused with the quantitatively much larger Germanic component. These two Pan-Yiddish components (Eastern Yiddish has, in addition, a prominent Slavonic component) share some phonological features, but each nonetheless maintains a distinct phonological and morphological identity.

Coexisting Phonologies within Yiddish

Documented forms of Ashkenazic cannot, as a rule, have sounds not generally present in the coterritorial Yiddish (one possible exception being the η reflex of historical ʕ in Netherlandic Ashkenazic, which may be a borrowing from local Sephardic usage; see Hirschel 1940: 455). In fact, the vowel inventory of each variety of Ashkenazic constitutes a subset (generally a large subset) of the inventory of the Semitic component of the local dialect of Yiddish. While Ashkenazic has not preserved ancient Semitic sounds, it has preserved phonological patterning that underwent change in Yiddish. Even in Yiddish, change never came close to levelling the phonologies of the two components of the language: they coexist and interact as subphonologies of the supersystem "Phonology of Yiddish."

To cite one pervasive contrast, the Germanic component has root-bound stress and, consequently, fixed full and reduced vowels, e.g., Northeastern Yiddish *lɛb* "(I) live," *lébn̩* "life," *lébədik* "lively", *lébədikə* "(pl.) lively," *lèbədikərhéjt* "during his/her lifetime." Even when the stem loses primary stress in deference to a stressed suffix (as in the last cited item), it retains stress and vowel color vis-à-vis the posttonic vowel which remains both stressless and shewa-like in quality. Semitic component items, by contrast, exhibit penultimate stress. Suffixation results in shift of stress to the newly penultimate syllable and in the transformation of shewa to a full vowel, e.g., Northeastern Yiddish *málbəš* "garment," pl. *malbúšim*. In other words, the synchronic underlying form of **[málbəš]** is in fact |**malbuš**|. Stress is boundary linked, as in classical Hebrew, although penultimate rather than ultimate (cf. Hebrew מַלְבּוּשׁ *malbū́š*, מַלְבּוּשִׁים *malbūšī́m*).

Pan-Yiddish Vocalism

The system of Pan-Yiddish vocalism that follows is based on M. Weinreich's (1960) but reduces his twenty correspondences to the sixteen that can be reconstructed from Yiddish per se, i.e., without reference to the stock languages (see Katz 1983b: 1021–24). Each correspondence represents a diaphoneme. The diaphoneme may be regarded as the conceptual coexistence of all dialect realizations of a single historical vowel (i.e., one occurring consistently in the same positions in the same words).

The sixteen diaphonemes are assigned numbers, facilitating discussion of any historical vowel or group of vowels (see Herzog 1965: 228 n. 1; Katz 1983b: 1021–24). The first digit represents the broad proto-quality posited by Max Weinreich, according to the code $1 = a, 2 = e, 3 = i, 4 = o$ and $5 = u$. The second is a code for historical status, by which series 1 = short, series 2 = long, series 3 = short subject to early lengthening, and series 4 = diphthong. Series 1 and 2 have five vowels each, series 3 has two vowels, and series 4 has four vowels, making for a total of sixteen historical vowels. In any given variety of Yiddish, splits and new acquisitions from neighbouring languages increase the number, while mergers decrease it. The "magic number sixteen" is a unit of comparative Yiddish linguistics, and irrelevant to the synchronic analysis of any single dialect.

For example, Yiddish dialectologists may discuss notions such as "Northeastern Yiddish $ej_{22/24/42/44}$," a formulation encompassing a mass of ideas and information, including "the Northeastern Yiddish synchronic vowel phenome /ej/ which represents a merger of protovowels $*\bar{e}, *\partial j, *\bar{o}$, and $*\partial u$"; or, perhaps, "the Northeastern ej cognate with Northwestern $\varepsilon j, a$, or ∂u"; or "the Northeastern vowel usually corresponding to classical Hebrew ṣere or ḥolem and to Middle High German $ê, ei, ô$, or ou"; or any number of other potential statements of correspondence. Circularity is averted by the firm anchorage of each vowel number to an empirically real set of consistently corresponding realizations, in the same lexical items, amply documented in the dialects of the modern language.

It is not necessary to accept Max Weinreich's or anybody else's proposed phonetic protovalues to use the system. Vowel 12, for example, *exists,* in thousands of lexical items, and one can still refer to it as "vowel 12" even if one disagrees, as I do, with Max Weinreich's reconstruction of the a quality which provides the first digit of "12" (I opt for open $ɔ$, and thanks to the numbering system, historical interrelationships can be constructively discussed independently of any one phonetic reconstruction).

Two vowels in the system are not protovowels. They are the two Series 3 vowels (anomalously comprising 13 and 25, see Katz 1983b: 1024). They derive from 11 and 21, subjected to a lengthening that occurred very early in the history of the language, and one that has had repercussions throughout the phonological history of the language. For these reasons, they are included among the diaphonemes. A stricter protolanguage construction would eliminate them and regard 13 and 25 as the results of the splits effected by Open Syllable Lengthening on 11 and 21, respectively (see below for examples).

Table 4.1 provides an illustrative corpus of three items each from the Germanic component (GC) and Semitic component (SC) of Yiddish, except for those vowels which are usually exclusively Germanic (e.g., 24/44) or where fusions with Semitic component words are restricted to only portions of the Yiddish territory (see below). Major dialect reflexes of each vowel are provided, but for brevity illustrative words appear in their Standard Yiddish (StY) form.

Table 4.1. Diaphonemic Systematization of Pan-Yiddish Vocalism
GC = Germanic Component; SC = Semitic Component

Series 1 (originally short):

Vowel 11:
Pan-Yiddish a (but SEY ɔ ~ a)

GC: *gas* "street," *hant* "hand," *vant* "wall"
SC: *aváda* "certainly," *dáſkə* "as a matter of fact," *prat* "detail"

Vowel 21:
Pan-Yiddish ɛ

GC: *bésər* "better," *hélfn̩* "help," *vɛn* "when"
SC: *éfšər* "maybe," *éməs* "true," *šɛd* "ghost"

Vowel 31:
Pan-Yiddish i (but ɛ in some NWY)

GC: *fiš* "fish," *nídərik* "low," *zílbər* "silver"
SC: *bris* "circumcision," *ínjən* "matter," *šíkər* "drunk"

Vowel 41:
Pan-Yiddish ɔ

GC: *gɔt* "God," *lɔx* "hole," *vɔx* "week"
SC: *kɔl* "voice," *kɔ́rbn̩* "sacrifice," *xɔ́xmə* "wisdom"

Vowel 51:
NWY ö || MWY, SWY, NEY, StY u || MEY, SEY i

GC: *frum* "religious" [Jewish]," *hunt* "dog," *kúmən* "come"
SC: *gúzmə* "exaggeration," *štus* "nonsense," *xúpə* "wedding canopy"

Series 2 (originally long):

Vowel 12:
NWY ō || MWY ō / ū || SWY ō / ɔu || NEY, StY ɔ || MEY, SEY ū ~ u

GC: *blɔ́zn̩* "blow," *nɔ́dl̩* "needle," *šlɔ́fn̩* "sleep"
SC: *ləvónə* "moon," *mišpóxə* "family," *xɔ́ləm* "dream"

Vowel 22:
NWY ɛj || MWY ē || SWY ɛj || NEY, StY ɛj || MEY aj || SEY ej

GC: *bejz* "angry," *lejb* "lion," *šejn* "beautiful"
SC: *bréjrə* "choice," *maxašéjfə* "witch," *séjxl̩* "common sense"

Vowel 32:
Pan-Yiddish ī (but isochronic NEY, StY i)

GC: *briv* "letter," *grin* "green," *štivl̩* "boots"
SC: *mevínəs* "expertise," *nəvíim* "prophets," *tfísə* "jail"

Vowel 42:
NWY ɔu || MWY ō || SWY ɔu || NEY ej || MEY, SEY, StY ɔj

GC: *brɔjt* "bread," *grɔjs* "large," *vɔjnən* "live [= "dwell"]"
SC: *gɔ́jləm* "golem," *šɔ́jtə* "fool," *xɔ́jdəš* "month"

Vowel 52:
NWY, MWY, SWY ū || NEY, StY u || MEY, SEY ī

GC: *bux* "book," *fus* "foot," *šul* "synagogue"
SC: *bsúlə* "virgin," *malbúšim* "clothing," *rəfúə* "remedy"

Series 3 (series 1 vowels subject to early lengthening):

Vowel 13:
NWY ō || MWY, SWY ā || NEY, StY ɔ || MEY, SEY ū ~ u

GC: grɔz "grass," nɔ́mən "name," tɔg "day"

Vowel 25:
NWY ē || MWY ī || SWY ē || NEY, StY ɛ || MEY ej || SEY ej (older ī/i)

GC: bétn "request," lébədik "lively," štétl̩ "village"
SC: régə "minute," tévə "habit," xésəd "act of kindness"

Series 4 (original diphthong):

Vowel 24:
NWY, MWY, SWY ā || NEY, StY ej || MEY aj || SEY ej

GC: gléjb "(I) believe," klejd "dress," zéjgər "clock"

Vowel 34:
NWY ɛj || MWY, SWY aj || NEY, StY aj || MEY ā || SEY a

GC: bašájmperlax "obvious," lájləx "sheet," vajs "white"

Vowel 44:
NWY, MWY, SWY ā || NEY, StY ej || MEY, SEY, StY ɔj

GC: bɔjm "tree," ɔjg "eye," tɔjb "deaf"

Vowel 54:
NWY, MWY, SWY ɔu || NEY, StY ɔj || MEY ōu, ō || SEY ou/u

GC: hɔjz "house," mɔjl "mouth," tɔjb "pigeon," "dove"

Construction of Synchronic Systems

Systematization of these geographically differentiated reflexes of common historic sources allows for the construction of a synchronic system for a given variety. Thus, the system may be used to construct the actual stressed vocalism of Northeastern Yiddish, which is illustrated in Table 4.2, and to compare it with that of Mideastern Yiddish (Table 4.3) or Northwestern Yiddish (Table 4.4), a variety no longer spoken. Where possible, a sample word is provided from the Semitic component. Where the vowel is limited to the Germanic component, the sample is drawn from that component. Glosses are provided at the relevant point in Table 4.1.

Table 4.2. Stressed Vowel System of Northeastern Yiddish

$i_{31/32}$ *(šíkər, tfísə)*	$u_{51/52}$ *(gúzmə, bsúlə)*
$ej_{22/24/42/44}$ *(bréjrə, glejb, géjləm, bejm)*	$ɔj_{54}$ *(hɔjz)*
$ɛ_{21/25}$ *(éfšər, régə)*	$ɔ_{12/13/41}$ *(ləvɔ́nə, nɔ́mən, xɔ́xmə)*
	aj_{34} *(lájlax)*
	a_{11} *(avádə)*

Table 4.3 Stressed Vowel System of Mideastern Yiddish

ī$_{32/52}$ *(tfísə, bsílə)*	u$_{12/13}$ *(ləvúnə, númən)*
i$_{31/51}$ *(šíkər, gízmə)*	
ej$_{25}$ *(réjgə)*	ōu$_{54}$ *(hōus)*
	ɔj$_{42/44}$ *(gɔ́jləm, bɔjm)*
ɛ$_{21}$ *(éfšər)*	ɔ$_{41}$ *(xɔ́xmə)*
aj$_{22/24}$ *(brājrə, glajp)*	
ā$_{34}$ *(lālax)*	
a$_{11}$ *(avádə)*	

Origins of the Vowel System of the Semitic Component in Yiddish

Sources of the Semitic Component's Vowel System

The vowel system of the Semitic component in Yiddish derives directly from a Northwest Semitic vowel system akin to that known as "Tiberian." Tiberian is a highly sophisticated system of diacritic marks (comprising vowel signs and stress marks), codified on the western shores of Lake Tiberias (the Sea of Galilee) in the late first millennium CE. Both the Tiberian system and its specific phonological version of the text of the Hebrew Bible have been standard for many centuries. There are two principal phonological interpretations of the system. One postulates seven vowel qualities (*i, e, ɛ, a, ɔ, o, u*). Another, formulated by the Kimchis, a prominent family of philologists of the twelfth and thirteenth centuries, posits a ten-vowel system comprising five tense vowels distinguished from five lax vowels (see M. Kimchi [1509–1518]: [11]; D. Kimchi 1545: 48). The graphemic system can be constructed to support either, but metrical evidence supports the Kimchis (see Ben-David 1958). The Semitic component in Yiddish unambiguously derives from a Kimchian-like system comprising ten protovowels. Arguments that have been put forward linking Yiddish to another system, the five-vowel Palestinian system, are unsustainable (see Katz 1977; 1979; §§10–14; 1982: §9; 1987a: 50–57).

In Table 4.5, Tiberian graphemes are confronted with their cognates in the Pan-Yiddish system, yielding the following basic correspondences. Yiddish samples are

Table 4.4. Stressed Vowel System of Northwestern Yiddish

ī$_{32}$ *(tfísə)*	ū$_{52}$ *(bəsū́lə)*
i$_{31}$ *(šíkər)*	ŏ$_{52}$ *(gózmə)*
ē$_{25}$ *(rēgə)*	ō$_{12/13}$ *(ləvṓnə, nṓmən)*
ɛj$_{22/34}$ *(bréjrə, léjliš)*	ou$_{42/54}$ *(góuləm, hous)*
ɛ$_{21}$ *(éfšər)*	ɔ$_{41}$ *(xɔ́xmə)*
ā$_{24/44}$ *(glāp, bām)*	
a$_{11}$ *(avádə)*	

Table 4.5. Yiddish Cognates of Tiberian Vowels

Series 1:

Vowel 11

NEY	MEY	NWY	gloss	Tiberian
a) closed syllabic pathaḥ:				
cad	cad	cad	"side (of family or dispute)"	צַד [ṣað]
b) originally closed syllabic pathaḥ:				
kálə	kálə	kálə	"bride"	כַּלָה [kalló]
c) ḥatef pathaḥ:				
xázər	xázər	xázər	"pig"	חֲזִיר [ḥăzír]
d) closed syllabic qameṣ:				
jam	jam	jam	"sea"	יָם [jɔ̄m]

Vowel 21

NEY	MEY	NWY	gloss	Tiberian
a) closed syllabic segol:				
éstər	éstər	éstər	"Esther"	אֶסְתֵּר [ʔestḗr]
b) originally closed syllabic segol:				
hétər	hétər	hétər	"legal permission"	הֶתֵּר [hettḗr]
c) ḥatef segol:				
έməs	έməs	έməs	"true"	אֱמֶת [ʔĕméθ]
d) closed syllabic ṣere:				
šɛd	šɛd	šɛd	"ghost"	שֵׁד [šēð]

Vowel 31

NEY	MEY	NWY	gloss	Tiberian
a) unstressed closed syllabic ḥireq:				
mídbər	mídbər	mídbər	"desert"	מִדְבָּר [miðbɔ̄r]
b) originally unstressed closed syllabic ḥireq:				
xídəš	xídəš	xídəš	"surprise"	חִדּוּשׁ [hiddū́š]
c) stressed closed syllabic (long) ḥireq				
din	din	din	"law"	דִין [dīn]

Vowel 41

NEY	MEY	NWY	gloss	Tiberian
a) unstressed closed syllabic qameṣ (qameṣ qatan):				
kɔ́rbn̩	kɔ́rbn̩	kɔ́rbən	"sacrifice"	קָרְבָּן [qɔrbɔ̄́n]
b) closed syllabic ḥolem:				
sɔd	sɔt	sɔt	"secret"	סוֹד [sōð]

Vowel 51

NEY	MEY	NWY	gloss	Tiberian
a) unstressed closed syllabic qibbuṣ:				
xúcpə	xícpə	xŏ́cpə	"chutzpah"	חֻצְפָּה [ḥuṣpɔ́]

b) originally unstressed closed syllabic qibbuṣ:
šútəf   šítəf   šṓtəf   "partner"   שֻׁתָּף [šuttɔ́f]

c) closed syllabic shureq:
zxus   zxis   zəxṓs   "merit"   זְכוּת [zɔxū́θ]

Series 2:

	Vowel 12		
NEY	MEY	NWY	gloss	Tiberian

a) open syllabic qameṣ:
lɔvónə   ləvū́nə   lɔvṓnə   "moon"   לְבָנָה [lɔvɔnɔ́]

	Vowel 22		
NEY	MEY	NWY	gloss	Tiberian

a) open syllabic ṣere:
xéjlək   xájlək   xéjlək   "part"   חֵלֶק [ḥḗlɛq]

	Vowel 32		
NEY	MEY	NWY	gloss	Tiberian

a) open syllabic ḥireq:
šxítə   šxítə   šəxítə   "slaughter"   שְׁחִיטָה [šəḥiṭɔ́]

	Vowel 42		
NEY	MEY	NWY	gloss	Tiberian

a) open syllabic ḥolem:
séjdəs   sójdəs   sóudes   "secrets"   סוֹדוֹת [sōðṓθ]

	Vowel 52		
NEY	MEY	NWY	gloss	Tiberian

a) open syllabic shureq:
búšə   bíšə   búšə   "shame"   בּוּשָׁה [būšɔ́]

Series 3:

	Vowel 13b		
NEY	MEY	NWY	gloss	Tiberian

a) stressed open syllabic pathaḥ:
páxət   pā́xət   pā́xət   "fear"   פַּחַד [páḥað]

	Vowel 25		
NEY	MEY	NWY	gloss	Tiberian

a) stressed open syllabic segol:
régə   réjgə   rḗgə   "moment"   רֶגַע [réɣaʕ]

provided in Northeastern Yiddish (NEY) and Mideastern Yiddish (MEY), the two modern dialects that collectively provide a maximal set of oppositions, as well as Northwestern Yiddish (NWY), to represent the former dialects of the West. Transcriptions of Tiberian follow each example, using the following equivalents: qameṣ ⟨ ָ ⟩ = ɔ̄; ṣere ⟨ ֵ ⟩ = ē; long ḥireq ⟨(ִי)⟩ = ī; ḥolem ⟨וֹ⟩, ⟨ ֹ ⟩ = ō; (long) shureq ⟨וּ⟩ =

ū; pathaḥ ⟨ ָ ⟩ = a; segol ⟨ ֶ ⟩ = ɛ; short ḥireq ⟨ ִ ⟩ = i; unstressed closed syllabic qameṣ (qameṣ qatan) ⟨ ָ ⟩ = ɔ; (short) qibbuṣ ⟨ ֻ ⟩ = u; hatef pathaḥ ⟨ ֲ ⟩ = ă; hatef segol ⟨ ֱ ⟩ = ĕ; hatef qameṣ ⟨ ֳ ⟩ = ɔ̆; mobile shewa ⟨ ְ ⟩ = ə. Glosses provide usage in Yiddish.

Primary and Secondary Fusion

"Primary Fusion" is the fusion between the Semitic and Germanic components of Yiddish immediately upon the settlement in Germanic-speaking lands of the Jews who were, retrospectively taken, the first Ashkenazim. This primary fusion encompassed the ten vowels of series 1 and 2. Each of these ten Yiddish protovowels came into existence by way of the fusion of a given Semitic with a given Germanic vowel into a unitary new Yiddish vowel.

"Secondary Fusion," on the other hand, refers to joinings of Germanic and Semitic some time during the history of Yiddish. Consonantal loss and its phonetic effects are a prime catalyst of secondary fusion. Loss of ʔ (א) and ʕ (ע), for example, gave rise to hiatus which was variously resolved (cf. below). The hiatus merged with vowel 34 in Eastern Yiddish, e.g., NEY *dájgə* "worry," *tájnə* "complaint" || MEY *dãgə, tãnə* || SEY *dágə, tánə* (cf. Tiberian דְּאָגָה *dəʔɔγɔ́*, טַעֲנָה *taʕănɔ́*). Thus, from the viewpoint of Eastern Yiddish alone (and some parts of Western Yiddish), Semitic component 34 could be added to vowel 34 (see Table 4.1, Series 4). In other parts of Western Yiddish, however, hiatus gives *ā*, part of the local realization of merged 24/44 (in Southern Western Yiddish 13/24/44).

Finally, there are isolated cases where a Semitic component form has "gone astray" into a usually strictly Germanic vowel, e.g., (some) Mideastern Yiddish *gō*, *gou* "gentile" with vowel 54, for expected *gɔj,* "Christian" (cf. Tiberian גוֹי *gōj*). The diphthong in the Hebrew-derived word fused in the dialect with the local realization of 54, apparently at a point in time when local 54 was /ɔj/. The conspicuous rarity of such exceptions serves to highlight the remarkable overall consistency in the Yiddish realizations through time and space, clearly pointing toward the derivation of Yiddish, and its Semitic component, from a protolanguage formed when primary fusion transpired (see Katz 1970; 1988c).

The Distinct Phonology of Ashkenazic

The Notion "Formal Ashkenazic"

Contrary to much popular belief, the sound patterns of Ashkenazic are not those of Yiddish. Every traditional Ashkenazi commands two distinct Semitic phonologies, one for the Semitic component in his or her Yiddish, the other for Ashkenazic. There is, moreover, a sociolinguistically determined continuum between the fixed pole of Yiddish, and the variable pole of Ashkenazic: from its most formal through a range of varieties ultimately approaching Yiddish. These varieties of Ashkenazic are discussed below. The forms cited for purposes of illustration will reflect "Formal Ashkenazic," the variety used, for instance, in reading from the Torah. This variety is chosen for examples cited because it provides an opposing conceptual pole to the phonology of Yiddish, facilitating comparison between two maximally different objects. That is not to gainsay the far more widespread usage of "Popular Ashkenazic". In some instances, penultimately stressed Popular Ashkenazic variants are provided alongside their Formal counterparts.

Major Differences between Ashkenazic and Yiddish

Ashkenazic is phonologically distinguished from the Semitic component of Yiddish in two fundamental ways, one prehistoric (from the viewpoint of Ashkenaz), the other historic. Prehistorically, the Hebrew and Aramaic pronunciation that became Ashkenazic was never processed by an across-the-board rule of Closed Syllable Shortening (or "Laxing") which did process the Hebrew and Aramaic that became the Semitic component in Yiddish. In the Semitic component, Closed Syllable Shortening results in the systematic morphophonemic alternations 22 (proto *ē) ~ 21 (*ε); 12 (*ɔ̄) ~ 11 (*a); and 42 (*ō) ~ 41 (*ɔ). In each of the alternations the syllable boundary is the conditioning factor: closed syllables trigger Shortening. Hence the Tiberian pairs שֵׁדִים šēðı̄m "ghosts," sg. שֵׁד šēð; כְּלָלִים kəlɔ̄lı̄m "rules," sg. כְּלָל kəlɔ̄l "general rule," "generality"; סוֹפֵר sōfēr "scribe," pl. סוֹפְרִים sōfərı̄m "scribes," each of which has identical vowels, give Semitic component alternating pairs, e.g., Northeastern Yiddish šéjdim (22) ~ šɛd (21), klólim (12) ~ klal (11), séjfər (42) ~ sófrim (41); Mideastern Yiddish šájdəm (22) ~ šɛd (21), klúləm (12) ~ klal (11), sójfər (42) ~ sófrəm (41). Note that in cases such as classical סוֹפְרִים sōfərı̄m, syllabification was obviously sōf|rı̄m, with no mobile shewa, at the point in history when Shortening occurred.

Dialects preserving length distinctions among the high vowels also alternate 32 ~ 31 and 52 ~ 51, or preserve vestiges of these alternations, e.g., (some) Mideastern Yiddish dínəm (32) "laws" ~ din (31), gífə (52) "itself" ~ gif (51) "body." Cf. Tiberian cognates דִּינִים dīnı̄m, s.g. דִּין dīn; גּוּפָא gūfɔ̄ גּוּף gūf.

The Ashkenazic of each area, however, preserves long vowels in closed syllables as in open ones, except in the case of vowel 12, where Ashkenazic too shortens in closed syllables, not to 11 (a) as in Yiddish, but to 41 (ɔ). This Ashkenazic alternation is obscured in Northeastern Ashkenazic where 11 and 41 are merged (as unitary ɔ), but evident in other dialects. Classical אָדָם ʔɔ̄ðɔ̄m "man," "human," for example, turns up as Mideastern and Southeastern Ashkenazic udóm / údəm and Western Ashkenazic ōdóm / óðəm. The two Mideastern Ashkenazic types of qameṣ are distinguished in modern Hasidic alphabet primers by explicit exercises (e.g., Birnhak 1976: 95; Fried 1983: 141–42; cf. below).

Table 4.6 contrasts Semitic component alternation with Ashkenazic nonalternation (differing alternation in the case of qameṣ) for the three pairs of vowels which consistently alternate in all varieties of Yiddish. The contrasts are illustrated in Northeastern, Mideastern, and Northwestern Ashkenazic. Stress is left unmarked in Ashkenazic forms to allow for both more formal variants (with ultimate stress) and less formal variants (with penultimate stress).

The second series of differences between the Semitic component in Yiddish and Ashkenazic results from the resistance of Formal Ashkenazic to some of the phonological changes that have transpired during the history of Yiddish, most promi-

Table 4.6. Alternation in Yiddish vs No (or other) Alternation in Ashkenazic

Northeastern Yiddish	Northeastern Ashkenazic
šéjdim ~ šɛd	šejdim, šejd
klɔ́lim ~ klal	kəlɔlim, k(ə)lɔl
séjfər ~ sɔ́frim	sejfejr, sejf(ə)rim
Mideastern Yiddish	Mideastern Ashkenazic
šájdəm ~ šɛt	šajdim, šajd
klúləm ~ klal	kəlulim, k(ə)lɔl
sɔ́jfər ~ sɔ́frəm	sɔjfajr, sɔjf(ə)rim
Northwestern Yiddish	Northwestern Ashkenazic
šέjdəm ~ šɛt	šɛjdīm, šɛjd
kəlṓləm ~ klal	kəlōlīm, k(ə)lɔl
sóufər ~ sóufrəm	soufajr, souf(ə)rīm

nently Stress Shift (to penultimate accentuation) and Posttonic Reduction (reduction of full vowels to a unitary shewa-like vowel after word-stress). The contrast is illustrated in Table 4.7 for the same three dialects. The three sample items are, in Tiberian, גַּנָּב *gannṓv* "thief," יִשְׂרָאֵל *jiśrɔ́ʔēl* "Israel," כַּלָּה *kallṓ* "bride."

Closed Syllable Shortening, Stress Shift, and Posttonic Reduction all conspire to make for numerous differences in the phonological representations of historically identical lexical items. The correspondences characterizing the Yiddish-Ashkenazic phonological relationship are illustrated in Table 4.8. Oppositions levelled in Yiddish by Closed Syllable Shortening are preserved in Ashkenazic. Stress Shift results in Tiberian pretonic vowels bearing word stress, while Posttonic Reduction

Table 4.7. Yiddish Stress Shift and Posttonic Reduction vs Unshifted, Unreduced Ashkenazic

Northeastern Yiddish	Northeastern Ashkenazic
ganəv	ganɔ́v
jisrɔ́əl	jisrɔéjl
kálə	kalɔ́
Mideastern Yiddish	Mideastern Ashkenazic
gánəf	ganɔ́v
jisrúəl	jisruájl
kálə	kalú
Northwestern Yiddish	Northwestern Ashkenazic
gánəf	ganɔ́v
jisrṓəl	jisrōéjl
kálə	kalṓ

Table 4.8. Yiddish-Ashkenazic Vowel Correspondences

Yiddish	Ashkenazic	Tiberian
11	11, 41	Pathaḥ, closed syllabic qameṣ
NEY: *sam* "poison," *jɔm* "ocean" MEY: *sam, jɔm* NWY: *sam, jɔm*	*sam, jɔm* *sam, jɔm* *sam, jɔm*	סַם *sam*, יָם *jɔ́m*
21	21, 22	segol, ṣere
NEY: *éfšər* "maybe," *ger* "proselyte" MEY: *éfšər, ger* NWY: *éfšər, ger*	*ɛfšɔr, gejr* *ɛfšɔr, gajr* *ɛfšɔr, gejr*	אֶפְשָׁר *ɛfšɔ́r*, גֵּר *gēr*
41	41, 42	unstressed closed syllabic qameṣ, ḥolem
NEY: *kɔ́rbn̩* "sacrifice," *sɔf* "end" MEY: *kɔ́rbn̩, sɔf* NWY: *kɔ́rbən, sɔf*	*kɔrbɔn, sejf* *kɔrbɔn, sɔjf* *kɔrbɔn, sɔuf*	קָרְבָּן *qɔrbɔ́n*, סוֹף *sōf*
ə	11	pathaḥ
NEY: *kárpəs* "celery [at Passover]" MEY: *kárpəs* NWY: *kárpəs*	*karpas* *karpas* *karpas*	כַּרְפַּס *karpás*
ə	21	segol
NEY: *xéjšəx* "darkness" MEY: *xɔ́jšəx* NWY: *xɔ́ušəx*	*xejšex* *xɔjšex* *xoušex*	חֹשֶׁךְ *ḥṓšex*
ə	31	ḥireq
NEY: *jájən* "(ritual) wine" MEY: *jájən* NWY: *jájən*	*jájin* *jájin* *jájin*	יַיִן *jájin*
ə	41	qameṣ
NEY: *bátiən* "lazy fellow" MEY: *bátlən* NWY: *bátlən*	*batlɔn* *batlɔn* *batlɔn*	בַּטְלָן *baṭlɔ́n*
ə	12	qameṣ
NEY *halóxə* "Jewish law" MEY *halúxə* NWY *halóxə*	*halɔxɔ* *halūxū* *halōxō*	הֲלָכָה *halɔ̄xɔ́*
ə	22	ṣere
NEY: *téjvəs* "(month of) Teveth" MEY: *tájvəs* NWY: *téjvəs*	*tejvejs* *tajvajs* *tɛjvɛjs*	טֵבֵת *tēvḗθ*
ə	32 (~ 31)	ḥireq
NEY *jɔ́xəd* "individual" MEY *júxət* NWY *jṓxet*	*jɔxid* *juxīd/juxid* *jōxīd*	יָחִיד *jɔ̄ḥīð*
ə	42	ḥolem
NEY *xaléjməs* "dreams" MEY *xalɔ́jməs* "dreams" NWY *xalóuməs* "dreams"	*xalejmejs* *xalɔjmɔjs* *xaloumous*	חֲלוֹמוֹת *ḥălōmṓθ*
ə	52	shureq
NEY *xɔ́šəv* "important" MEY *xū́šəf* "important" NWY *xṓšəf* "important"	*xɔšuv* *xūšiv* *xōšūv*	חָשׁוּב *ḥɔ̄šū́v*

renders stressed Tiberian vowels both stressless and reduced. Yiddish shewa is therefore cognate with a whole range of full vowels in the Ashkenazic of the same speakers.

In the sample items provided in Table 4.8, stress is left unmarked in Ashkenazic forms to allow for comparison between Yiddish and various styles of Ashkenazic (see below). Thus, for example, in the final contrast cited, Northeastern Yiddish ə in *xɔ́šəv* is cognate with Northeastern Ashkenazic *u* in *xɔšuv*, whether it is *xɔšúv* (Formal Ashkenazic) or *xɔ́šuv* (Popular Ashkenazic). Items penultimately stressed in Tiberian retain penultimate stress in all forms of Yiddish and Ashkenazic.

Resistance of Ashkenazic to Yiddish Sound Change

Sacred Language Resistance to Vernacular Sound Shift

Speakers would not, a priori, in any given generation, hasten to incorporate in their sacred languages the latest vogue in pronunciation to take hold in the vernacular. There is potential in the evidence of sacred languages for better understanding the nature of sound shift in general. Is there a difference in principle, or a predictable difference, between "imperceptible gradual shift" and "abrupt shift"? One might perhaps predict that "low-level phonetic shift" would go unnoticed and permeate the sacred language, while higher level phonological shift not entailing "phonetic difficulty" in undoing a fait accompli sound shift would be more "resistible" in the sacred language. Alternatively, one might postulate a sociolinguistic condition: perhaps as long as a sound shift remains a variable, the population will shun it in the sacred language, but once the old form disappears, it is "goodbye Charlie" in the sacred language every bit as much as in the vernacular.

As in political history, it is often the case in the social history of language that one cannot necessarily predict what will become an issue and what won't. At the end of the day, it may boil down to the linguistic background and views of those in positions of authority and influence who make a fuss of some incorporations of sound shift into the sacred language, and let others go unnoticed. Moreover, scholars of a Dialect A which did not undergo a certain shift would be predisposed to object to incorporation of a Dialect B sound shift in the sacred language used even by Dialect B speakers. Ashkenazic studies can provide a wealth of material for students of theoretical linguistics and sociolinguistics.

Final Devoicing

Modern Standard Yiddish, following Northeastern and Southeastern usage, does not have the rule of Final Devoicing, but Mideastern Yiddish does, and all of Western Yiddish had it. Many modern Mideastern Yiddish speakers who have Final Devoicing in their Yiddish do not have it in their Ashkenazic, producing such pairs as Mideastern Yiddish *kúrəf* "relative (n.)," *mín(h)ək* "custom," *dúvət* "David," contrasting with Mideastern Ashkenazic *kurɔ́jv* / *kúrɔjv* "close"; *minhɔ́g* / *mínhɔg*; *duvíd* / *dúvid*; (cf. Tiberian קָרוֹב *qɔ̄rōv*, מִנְהָג *minhɔ́ɣ*, דָּוִד *dɔ̄wíð*). Hebrew primers for Hasidic children have special exercises dedicated to the preservation of word final voicing distinctions (e.g. Fried 1983: 93–114).

The battle against Final Devoicing in Ashkenazic is at least seven hundred years old on the evidence of Yekusiel of Prague (whether he was indeed from Prague is not at all certain). Dated by Zunz (1845: 115) to the late thirteenth century and by Gumpertz (1957: 36–37) to the early part of that century, he is also known as Yah(a)bi (acronym of Yekusiel Hakoyheyn ben Yehudo). Amongst Ashkenazim he was known as Zalmen Hanakdn "Zalmen the Vocalizer [i.e., expert on the Hebrew vowel pointing system]" (see Elye Bokher 1538: 77). Defending the phonological integrity of the reading of sacred Hebrew and Aramaic texts, Zalmen Hanakdn stormed against the word-final collapse of [d] and [t], and of [v] and [f] in Hebrew reading amongst the Ashkenazim, citing such minimal pairs as אַב ʔav "father (construct)," אַף ʔaf "also." He complains of "people who ruin many words on account of the letters at their end, pronouncing them as other letters" (Yekusiel 1395: [189a]). (See Eldar in this volume.)

Fronting of the Old u Vowels

The Battle of Final Devoicing continues to be fought in the education of today's Mideastern Yiddish speaking Hasidic schoolchildren. Other battles were fought by individuals but resolved by language history centuries ago. It is often acquiescence, not resistance, that has prevailed. A case in point is application of the fronting and unrounding of all old *u* vowels to *i* in Southern Eastern Yiddish (comprising Mideastern and Southeastern Yiddish), whereby *ū* ⟩ *ī* and *u* ⟩ *i*, e.g., מְלוּכָה *məlūxɔ́* ⟩ *m(ə)líxə* "kingdom," "country," חֻצְפָּה *ḥuspɔ́* ⟩ *xícpə* "insolence," "chutzpah."

There is evidence that in older Yiddish, short *u* shifted before long *ū*; at first to *ü*, before its unrounding to *i* which led to merger with old *i*. A large body of evidence was assembled by Birnbaum (1934). Christian Hebraists from Reuchlin onward sometimes distinguish *ü* = qibbuṣ from *u* = shureq, notwithstanding their overall predilection for Sephardic variants (e.g., Reuchlin 1506: 12, 14, 16, 19, 20).

Shabse Soyfer of Pshemishl (Shabbethai Sofer of Przemysl, ca. 1565–1635), a grammarian and specialist on Hebrew pointing, writing of Ashkenazic on Mideastern Yiddish territory, warned against pronouncing *i* for *u* (see Reif 1979: 37, 94). He is echoed by Yekhiel-Mikhl Epshteyn (d. 1706), well-known German rabbi, educationalist, and popular kabbalist, who warned against pronouncing qibbuṣ as ḥireq (i.e., as *i*), insisting that it be pronounced as *shureq,* in other words, that the classical *u* quality be preserved (Yekhiel-Mikhl Epshteyn 1697: 49a–49b; 1714: 20b–21a). In Yekhiel-Mikhl's variety of Ashkenazic, historical short *u* had shifted to *i*, but historical long *ū* remained unshifted. It can be inferred that in seventeenth-century varieties of Ashkenazic known to these scholars, some people succeeded in blocking the application of vernacular sound shift to the sacred language.

Incidentally, these and other traditional Ashkenazic authors use the traditional Ashkenazic terms for these vowels: Ashkenazim's *shureq* = qibbuṣ ⟨ֻ⟩ and Ashkenazim's *melupum* (⟨ Aramaic *məlō pūm* "full mouth") = shureq ⟨וּ⟩. The pronunciation of the vowel names varies according to dialect, hence Northeastern *šúrək, məlúpm̥*, Mideastern *šírək, m(ə)lípm̥*, and so forth.

Among those on the other side of the debate was no less a figure than the Maharal of Prague (Yudo Leyb ben Betsalel ca. 1525–1609), known in folklore as the creator of the Golem. He went to great lengths to defend his *ü* pronunciation of qibbuṣ. The following is an excerpt from a discourse in which he invokes arguments from (a) proposed interrelationships between the shapes of the vowel graphemes and their phonetic realizations, (b) kabbalistic interpretations of the graphic shapes and their relative positions, and (c) the force of tradition and his belief in its sanctity:

> I have seen people accuse the Ashkenazim of changing the vowel system—the vowels which are [symbolically] the People of Israel— . . . saying . . . that the shureq that is in the letter [וּ] and the three dots [ֻ] have a single reading, for they have so read in the works of the grammarians. And in order that the rest of the people who are not experts in the grammar of the language not fall into error and think this thing to be true and bring about the ruin of the language, a matter of great importance to Torah sages, I will here demonstrate with reliable evidence that the reading of the Ashkenazim is a proper reading. In fact, you will not find a true way other than the reading of the Ashkenazim. . . .
>
> They [the grammarians] wrote that the qibbuṣ sefathayim (that we call shureq) [ֻ] and the shureq (that we call melupum) [וּ] should be read identically, which the Ashkenazim do not do. . . . Now according to the reading of the Ashkenazim, all the vowel signs have shapes demonstrating their vowel quality. . . . [Here follows an explanation of the graphic shape of each vowel sign as an indication of the shape of the mouth when uttering the vowel it represents.] And so it is with the three dots . . . and the dot in the letter *vov*. . . . Here too we read each one according to what the vowel points show us: . . . the three dots under each other [apparently his *ü*] because we extend the voice of three dots fully and it is like the extending of the three continuous dots; . . . one dot in the letter [apparently his *u*], according to which the extending . . . is in the middle, not above nor below, but in the middle just as the dot is in the middle. But in qibbuṣ sefathayim the extending of the voice is downward like the three dots which are extended from the top downward. And it is not possible for there to be three extended dots without a middle one which is always the essence of the vowel.
>
> You may understand something great and wonderful, for no other vowel has what is in the shureq. For all the other vowels have their vowel point under the letter or upon the letter, but in the case of shureq a self-contained *vov* was established, and in it the shureq [וּ]. This teaches us something vital on the seven vowels [תְּנוּעוֹת] of the pointing system, which reflects the movements [תְּנוּעוֹת] of the Seven Sides. For one vowel sign is always to one side: above, or below, or to the right, or to the left, or in front, or in back, or in the middle, and therefore they are seven vowels [here follows a discussion of the human qualities kabbalistically represented by each of the vowel signs and their positions] reflecting the Seven Voices at the Giving of the Torah, . . . and the Middle was set apart unto itself, . . . and because the shureq reflects the Middle, it was given a vov unto itself. . . . From this alone you will understand the differentiation that exists between the shureq and the three dots [נְקֻדּוֹת = "dots," "points," "the traditional vowel points"]: that the shureq reflects the middle that is set apart unto itself, and it is the middle point that has no width or length at all, only a single point. Therefore the shureq was given one dot in a letter unto itself, reflecting the Middle which is a single point unto itself. But the three dots comprising the qibbuṣ sefathayim reflect the Middle that is not a point alone, as it is impossible to create a middle without three, for the one that is between the other two is the middle. And the explanation is, that when three dots are placed in such a shape, extended diagonally as such ֻ, the middle dot has the judgment of the Middle that does not go out of the realm of balance and justice. For the upper one tends to the right and the

lower to the left and the middle one tends neither to right nor left, but stands in the middle and in the justice of the middle judgment, and is thereby set apart unto itself as is the case with every middle, but it is not totally set apart as is the dot in the vov [ ]. . . . Qibbuṣ sefathayim refects the movements [/vowels] of the Middle, but does not reflect the Middle that is set apart unto itself, for that which is set apart unto itself has greater virtue. But the qibbuṣ sefathayim reflects the Middle that is not fully distinguished, and therefore no instance of these three dots has a vowel [letter] unto itself. . . . [Arguments are presented in favour of the Ashkenazic pronunciation of shewa as ə, and against the *a* realization preferred by some Sephardi grammarians].

We have not come here to argue other than to maintain the reading that is in our hands from our forefathers of old, to not change, God forbid, anything in it, because of that which is found in the books of the later Sephardi grammarians, who are themselves not of one opinion. It is therefore incumbent upon us to stand for our tradition and our custom of old. For even if a wise man wrote in his work certain things, they did not come down to him by tradition, but according to his hypothesis (and Ibn Ezra [b. Tudela, Spain 1089, d. 1164] himself noted that these things did not come down to him via tradition), and how are his views contradicted by the custom in our hands and the tradition unto us from our forefathers. All the more so bearing in mind that we have explained that our custom has the appearance of wisdom and good taste and knowledge, and if we err, will not our forefathers intercede in our favour? And He, blessed be He, will place His Torah in our hearts to bestow upon us from His wisdom, Amen.

(Maharal of Prague 1599: 58b–59b)

The Maharal's defense of Ashkenazic $ü_{qibbus}$ was echoed by his contemporary, the talmudic luminary Mordekhay Yafe (Mordechai Jaffe), known as *der Levush* "the Levush" (ca. 1535–1612), who was, incidentally, a teacher of Shabse Soyfer (who, as noted above, took the opposite theoretical viewpoint, albeit on the *i* rather than the *ü* realization of qibbuṣ). The Levush starts off with the force of tradition, and proceeds to a structural linguistic argument drawing analogies from the qameṣ (ɔ) vs. pathaḥ (*a*) and ṣere (historically *ē*) vs. segol (ε) oppositions which are distinguished qualitatively in Ashkenazic (e.g., Northeastern Mideastern ɔ vs. *a*, *ej* vs. ε; Mideastern *u/ɔ* vs. *a*, *aj* vs. ε, Western *ō/ɔ* vs. *a*, *ej* vs. ε). By way of analogy, he infers that the shureq vs. qibbuṣ opposition must also be qualitative, presumably shureq = *u* (or *ū*) vs. qibbuṣ = *ü*. He invokes the homiletic argument that the sacred and complete Torah could not be bereft of any vowel, and proceeds to offer phonological arguments derived from the graphemes of Tiberian Hebrew:

For I have seen recently that some people who consider themselves wise in their own eyes in the science of grammar have come forward to the point of leading astray some students, who err following them, and have made themselves like remnants of the generation of the Tower of Babel whose language was confounded, and they have invented and thought up a new language, and have gotten themselves and their students used to reading our vowel shureq [= qibbuṣ, ֻ , apparently his *ü*] exactly as we read the vowel melupum [= shureq, ֹ, apparently his *ū/u*], and they say that there is no difference between the vowel shureq and the vowel melupum except for lengthening of the breath of the vowel: for the shureq short, and for melupum long, as in the case of our correct [pronunciation of the] vowel ḥireq without yud [ֶ] and ḥireq with yud [ִ] which we correctly differentiate by shortening the breath for the one, and lengthening it for the other. And maybe they were confused because Rashi calls our melupum "qibbuṣ sefathayim," and some grammarians call the shureq "qibbuṣ sefathayim," and therefore thought that they [ו and ֻ] are one vowel.

I have therefore decided to write somewhat at length to demonstrate the nonsense and the error of the people I referred to, and [to demonstrate] that we should not change the vowel which we have received from our forefathers on the grounds of "Forsake not the teaching of thy mother" [Prov. 1:8, 6:20].

And if they have fallen into this error because all agree that our shureq [= qibbuṣ, ֻ] is [phonologically] the short counterpart of the melupum [= shureq, ו], which is a long vowel (like ḥireq without yud and ḥireq with yud, the one being called short, the other long, but alike in their vowel [quality], only one is short and one long; they therefore want to draw an analogy to the vowels shureq and melupum)—if this is their argument, they have no case, for if so, what will they do with pathaḥ and qameṣ, with segol and ṣere, being that the pathaḥ is [phonologically] the short counterpart of the qameṣ, and the segol is [phonologically] the short counterpart of the ṣere, even though their vowel [quality] does not match that of their long-vowel counterpart. So why should we not say this also in the case of shureq and melupum?

Moreover, I propose that from the viewpoint of common sense and a priori logic it is not possible for things to be so, for if, according to their view, the vowel of the melupum and the shureq are identical and there is no difference between them other than in the length of the breath, if that were the case, one vowel that is within the power of human speech would be missing in the vowel system of the Torah, and that is the vowel which we read for our shureq [presumably *ü*]. Heaven forfend that the complete Torah which was given to us to complete within ourselves wholeness in all human knowledge, physical and logical, should lack a vowel that is present and very common in the pronunciation of humans, and that there should not be found one word to be read with that vowel! That is nothing but nonsense and foolishness, for of course all the vowels that a human can with his palate emit from his lips in his pronunciation are included, and especially this vowel, with which we pronounce our shureq, which is common among all and extremely frequent in the pronunciation of most speakers, and how could it be lacking, God forbid, in the vowels of the Torah.

One cannot claim an inconsistency in my view on the grounds that if I am right then *their* [i.e., the grammarians' Sephardi] pronunciation of shureq would be missing from the Torah, for you would be pointing out an inconsistency in your own position, bearing in mind that the vowels qameṣ and ṣere are called "great vowels" [תְּנוּעוֹת גְּדוֹלוֹת], which are long in the breath. Why were signs not also devised for when one wishes to shorten the breath, as was done in the case of ḥireq without yud and ḥireq with yud? To the contrary, you must concede that the tradition came down to the Pointers [i.e., the Masoretes] who were masters of pure language, that in the case of the "great vowels" even if one wants to shorten them one cannot by nature do so to any great extent, to the point that whoever would try to shorten them greatly would have to lengthen them somewhat to spirantize a following *begedkefet* consonant [*b, g, d, k, p, t* spirantize to *v, γ, ð, x, f, θ* in Hebrew and Aramaic via postvocalic spirantization; in Tiberian, short unstressed vowels occur in closed syllables, hence after a short vowel, *begedkefet* geminate stops occur (spirants do not geminate). Cf., e.g., *jab*|*bɔ̄šš̌ɔ̄* "dry land" vs. *jɔ̄*|*vēš* "dry." The Levush is arguing that qameṣ and ṣere are *phonologically* long/tense vowels that cannot be "shortened" to make a short vowel]. Moreover, a shewa that follows [qameṣ or ṣere] is mobile shewa [because a long unstressed vowel always occurs in an open syllable; hence if the next vowel is shewa, it is a mobile shewa initiating the syllable thereafter; thus, e.g., ⟨כָּתְבוּ⟩ is *kɔ̄*|*θə*|*vū́*]. Moreover, even there we find that special signs were made [which bear upon vowel length], the *mappı́q*, and the *mafsı́q* and the *dehı́q* and *ṣ̌ē mērahı́q*.

This being the case, we may here too also in the case of melupum [= shureq: וּ] discern the reason why there is no diacritic to incite shortening of the vowel, because it is like the qameṣ and the ṣere, and unlike the vowel ḥireq which by nature can be shortened greatly, in view of which a special mark was designed to differentiate the short from the long, i.e., the yud [י]. This seems to me obviously to refute the views of those who are in error, and [confirm] that we should introduce no change in the vowel shureq [= qibbuṣ: ֻ]. And, forsake not the teaching of thy mother.

(Levush 1603: 49b)

It is significant that both the Maharal and the Levush offer intellectual defenses for the retention of *ü* in Ashkenazic. It is equally significant that neither relies on this defense alone. Both bring to bear the argument of tradition. The polemic tone is indicative of the passions raised by disputes on the pronunciation of Ashkenazic. Shabse Soyfer and Yekhiel-Mikhl Epshteyn have as their ideal a "correct" Ashkenazic which preserves the historical [u] quality of qibbuṣ and must not be overrun by the *u* ⟩ *ü*, or *u* ⟩ *i* shift common to some Yiddish dialects.

Looking back, it is obvious that the Maharal's and the Levush's views were in concord with the course of history. Modern Mideastern and Southeastern Ashkenazic users have *i* quality realizations in regard to both qibbuṣ *and* shureq. Older *ü* (from original *u*) was unrounded to *i*. It was never unfronted back to *u*. To the contrary, it dragged long *ū*, which was fronted to **ǖ*, then to *ī*. The two ensuing *i* vowels are no longer phonemically opposed in many forms of Mideastern and Southeastern Ashkenazic (see below).

There are, however, attestations of "dipping into history" or dipping into other dialects in certain circumstances, and preserving an *u* quality. One informant, from a village in Romania (Southeastern Yiddish territory), recalls that shureq was consistently *í* in his Ashkenazic, with the exception of the word רוּחַ *rúah* which was read *rúax* in the Bible to avoid the sacrilege of uttering *ríax* in that hallowed context. In the coterritorial Yiddish, *ríax* is a curse word, e.g., *a ríax in zajn tátn̩* "Damn his father" = "Damn him."

In fact, this *i* vowel, like the other vowels of Mideastern Ashkenazic, is for its users a symbol of authenticity and religiosity which proudly sets them aside from modernized and Northeasternized forms of Ashkenazic as well as from Israeli Hebrew. And thus it transpires, as so often in the history of language and culture, that a feature that once symbolized radical "incorrect" usage becomes the banner of "classic" language for a future generation.

One large question looms here for Western Yiddish studies. In view of all of Birnbaum's (1934) philological evidence pointing to *ü*$_{\text{qibbuṣ}}$ in older Western Yiddish, how is it that attestations from the eighteenth century onward generally have *u* in the West? Could it be that Ashkenazic Resistance prevailed in the West? This calls for a monograph.

Ashkenazic Sound Shift Lag

Looking at twentieth-century relationships between Yiddish and Ashkenazic recoverable from native informants, it is obvious that those dialectal features of Yiddish that are most stigmatized are most likely to be kept out of Ashkenazic. One case in point is the variety of Southeastern Yiddish popularly known as *tótə-mómə lúšṇ*, after its rendition of standard *tátə* "father" and *mámə* "mother." In linguistic terms, historical short *a* (vowel 11) merged with historical *ɔ*₄₁ in most environments (see Veynger 1929: 133-35; U. Weinreich 1958: 225, 236). Southeasterners often report that the historical *a* quality was however retained in Ashkenazic, hence Southeastern Ashkenazic *šabós / šábɔs* "Sabbath" vs. Southeastern Yiddish *šóbəs* (cf. Tiberian שַׁבָּת *šabbṍθ*).

There are other examples of "lag in progress" in the attempts of speakers to override their sound shifts. In *sábəsdikər lósṇ*, a folkloristic name for Northeastern Yiddish, *s* is merged with *š*, and *c* (*tˢ*) with *č* (see U. Weinreich 1952). There is evidence from some informants that sibilant merger was less prevalent in Ashkenazic than in Yiddish. Altbauer (1968: 455) notes that some Northeastern Ashkenazic users, who have *ej*₂₂/₂₄/₄₂/₄₄ in their Yiddish, preserve *ɔj*₄₂ in their rendition of ḥolem, thereby undoing the Northeastern merger of 42 and 22 in the sacred language (e.g., some Northeastern Yiddish *tējrə* "Torah" vs. Ashkenazic *tɔjró / tójrɔ*, cf. תּוֹרָה *tōrṍ*). Bin-Nun (1973: 300) describes a variety of Siebenbürgen that has *ej* for ṣere in Ashkenazic, contrasting with the *aj* of the same speakers in Yiddish.

In each instance, the "stigmatized" feature is one rejected by Modern Standard Yiddish. Ashkenazic thereby provides valuable evidence for the societal forces at work in the rise of Standard Yiddish, before and wholly outside the compass of the secular Yiddish scholars who formalized the notion and the features of the standard language (cf. Kerler 1988). This is one of many potential services of Ashkenazic studies to Yiddish linguistics and to sociolinguistics generally.

It is possible, with caution, to extrapolate Ashkenazic lag into situations in the past where documentation may not be readily available. For example, in Northern Transitional Yiddish and in parts of northern Western Yiddish, initial *s*, for historical samekh (ס) and śin (שׂ), was affricatized to *c* (*tˢ*), merging with the reflex of ṣade (tsadik), historical *ṣ* (צ), giving e.g., Northern Transitional *cájfər* "(sacred) book" ⟨ Tiberian סֵפֶר *sḗfer* (see Friedrich 1784: 39; Cohen 1923: 59; Katz 1988a: 50-51). Perhaps some speakers in the area would have had *sájfɛr* in their Ashkenazic contrasting with the *cájfər* of their Yiddish.

Lexicalized Variants of Yiddish-Ashkenazic Cognates

Phonologically differentiated reflexes of the same Hebrew or Aramaic etymon have often undergone centuries of divergent semantic development in Yiddish, contrasting with older meanings surviving in Ashkenazic. This results in such doublets as e.g., Northeastern Yiddish *baləbós* "boss," vs. Ashkenazic *baal habájis* "head of the household" (⟨ בַּעַל הַבַּיִת *báʕal habbájiθ*); *nəkéjvə* "woman of loose morals" vs. Ashkenazic *nəkejvó / nəkéjvɔ* "female," "feminine gender" (⟨ נְקֵבָה *nəqēvṍ*); *ɔs* "letter [of the alphabet]" vs. *ejs* "heavenly omen" (⟨אוֹת *ʔṍθ*); *vajzósə* "fool" vs. *vajzɔsó / vajzósɔ* "name of one of Haman's ten sons" (⟨וַיְזָתָא *wajzṍθɔ*); *xadgádjə* "jail [humorous]" vs. *xad gadjó, xad gádjɔ* "name of the Passover song *Chad gadyo*" (⟨ חַד גַּדְיָא *ḥað gaðjṍ* "one kid"); *xóxmə* "sense of the joke" or "stupid idea passed off as a wise one" vs. *xɔxmó / xóxmɔ* "wisdom" (⟨חָכְמָה *ḥɔxmṍ*). In each pair cited, note that Yiddish forms can be used for either the "Yiddish" or the "Ashkenazic"

Ashkenazic as a Self-Contained Structure

Synchronic Structure

For the foregoing discussion, Ashkenazic has been viewed through the eyes of the Semitic Component in Yiddish, on the grounds of the primacy of native spoken language in phonological analysis. It is, however, equally important to view Ashkenazic as a synchronic linguistic structure capable of description, analysis, and reconstruction. Everybody learning Ashkenazic acquires the pronunciation via the study of the Tiberian system of vowel diacritics. These diacritics (called *nəkúdəs* in Yiddish) are before the eyes of Ashkenazic users for an important part of their use of Ashkenazic (all of it for speakers whose Ashkenazic is limited to prayer and Pentateuch study, both of which entail "pointed texts," i.e., texts with the vowel diacritics included). A synchronic description of Ashkenazic may therefore include reference to the diacritics. The vowel system of each dialect of Ashkenazic may conveniently be mapped out using the Pan-Yiddish vowel correspondence (see above).

The stressed vowel system of present day Northeastern Ashkenazic comprises six phonemes, as illustrated in Table 4.9.

By contrast, the vowel system of Mideastern Ashkenazic, illustrated in Table 4.10, preserves more distinctions than any other modern form of Hebrew (Ashkenazic or non-Ashkenazic). It does not however preserve as many as the Semitic component of Mideastern Yiddish; in the Semitic component, the long vs. short reflexes of ḥireq and shureq are determined by Tiberian phonology. In many forms of Mideastern Ashkenazic the length differentiation seems on the whole to have been reinterpreted allophonically (long in stressed open syllables, short elsewhere), but this point requires further fieldwork. It is almost certain that *ej* and *ɛ* are also complementary and therefore nonphonemic in Formal Ashkenazic. In popular varieties, application of posttonic reduction causes them to appear in the same environment (stressed open syllable), rendering them clearly phonemic, e.g., *xéjsɛd* "kindness" vs. *émɛs* "truth"; cf. formal *xéjsɛd, emés* (Tiberian חֶסֶד *ḥéseð*, אֱמֶת *ʔɛméθ*; cf. below). The theoretical question arises however of whether a nonvernacular language can have "allophones" that are unquestionably "phonemes" in the native language of its users. Are they real or the results of overstructuralism by the linguist? This question, posed by Ashkenazic studies, merits further research.

Table 4.9. The Vowel System of Northeastern Ashkenazic

$i_{\text{ḥireq}}$	$u_{\text{shureq/qibbuṣ}}$
$ej_{\text{ṣere/ḥolem}}$	
$\varepsilon_{\text{segol/ḥatef segol}}$	$ɔ_{\text{qameṣ/ḥatef qameṣ}}$
	$a_{\text{pathaḥ/ḥatef pathaḥ}}$

Table 4.10. The Vowel System of Mideastern Ashkenazic

i̅ₕᵢᵣₑq/shureq/ in stressed open syllables	ū (~ u)_qameṣ in open syllables
iₕᵢᵣₑq/shureq/qibbuṣ in closed syllables, unstressed open syllables	
ej_segol in stressed open syllables	ɔj_ḥolem
ɛ_segol in closed syllables/ḥatef segol	ɔ_qameṣ in closed syllables/ before hey with mappiq/before yud; ḥatef qameṣ
aj_sere	
a_pathaḥ/ḥatef pathaḥ	

Ashkenazic Hebrew Education in Late Twentieth-Century Primary Schools

Children in Hasidic schools rooted in southern (i.e., non-Lithuanian) East European traditions around the world generally learn the Mideastern Ashkenazic system from the outset. In some schools, however, all segols are rendered ɛ when studying the vowel points, and the *ej* realization in stressed open syllables is "picked up" later in primary education, resulting in a child learning e.g., *ɛmés* and *xésɛd,* modified at a later age to *ɛmés* vs. *xéjsɛd.* Whether this is a symptom of declining use of *ej* for stressed open-syllabic segol in Hasidic communities needs to be researched. The two Mideastern Ashkenazic types of qameṣ (ū / u in open syllables, ɔ in closed syllables) are however distinguished in alphabet primers by explicit exercises (e.g., Birnhak 1976: 95; Fried 1983: 141–42).

Historical Phonology of Ashkenazic

Overview

The historical phonology of Ashkenazic is, in short, one of a Tiberian-like system that has undergone phonetic and phonological development over a millennium of European history. Its phonetic history generally follows closely upon that of co-territorial Yiddish dialects, but its phonological history is characterized by a substantial measure of independence resulting both from generation-to-generation language transmission (nonspoken living languages are transmitted this way too) and from the phonologically retentive power of the hallowed system of vocalization signs.

Consonantism

The consonantism of Ashkenazic is a much leaner system than its Tiberian antecedent. Consonants "not supported" by the indigenous central European phonetic scene, ʔ ⟨א⟩, ʕ ⟨ע⟩, w ⟨ו⟩, ḥ ⟨ח⟩, ṭ ⟨ט⟩, q ⟨ק⟩, and ṣ ⟨צ⟩, disappeared. Likewise, of the "begedkefet" spirants, arising from Northwest Semitic postvocalic spirantization (b ⟩ v, g ⟩ γ, d ⟩ ð, k ⟩ x, p ⟩ f, t ⟩ θ), those without European counterparts—

γ, ð, and θ—also disappeared. Phonetic "disappearance" can have diverse structural implications. The following listing covers (a) loss, (b) merger, and (c) phonetic shift retaining phonological distinctiveness. Within each category, the order follows the Jewish alphabet.

(a) Loss

א [ʔ] ⟩ zero, e.g., אָמֵן ʔɔmḗn "amen" ⟩ Northeastern Ashkenazic (NEA) ɔméjn, Mideastern Ashkenazic (MEA) umájn, Western Ashkenazic (WA) ōméjn.

Functionally consonantal ʔ was lost in all positions although [ʔ] does occur phonetically in various environments in Yiddish dialects. Traces of historical ʔ may be recovered from Yiddish (and cautiously extrapolated, with allowance for time lag, to Ashkenazic). Cf. e.g., Northeastern Yiddish sónim "enemies" ~ sg. séjnə, Mideastern sónəm ~ sójnə. The vocalic alternations in all dialects result from the application of Closed Syllable Shortening, demonstrating that aleph was consonantal (at the pre-Ashkenazic time of Shortening), i.e., *sōn|ʔīm ⟩ *sɔn|ʔīm via shortening (hypothetical sōn|nīm would not have processed by Shortening). On the bearing of this evidence on mobile shewa, see below.

ע [ʕ] ⟩ zero, e.g., עוֹלָם ʕōlɔ́m "world" ⟩ NEA ejlɔ́m / éjlɔm, MEA ɔjlɔ́m / ɔ́jlɔm, WA ōlɔ́m / ṓlɔm.

Ayin too has left recoverable traces in Yiddish, which may bear on its presence in early Ashkenazic. Closed Syllable Shortening has processed the Biblical נָע וָנָד nɔ́ʕ wɔnɔ́ð "a fugitive and a wanderer" (Gen. 4:12, 14), giving Yiddish na vənád (zajn) "wander without a home," where the a in na (⟨ נָע nɔ́ʕ) betrays an erstwhile closed syllable (cf. vowel-final monosyllables, e.g., בָּא bɔ́ "comes" ⟩ NEA bɔ, MEA bu, WA bō etc; syllable-final ⟨ א ⟩ and ⟨ ה ⟩ are not consonantal in Tiberian).

There are a number of issues on which the fates of ʔ and ʕ are best treated together. Loss of both resulted in sequences of two successive vowels. In Yiddish, the ensuing hiatus fused with various Germanic component vowels (see above, where this instance is cited to illustrate secondary fusion): with vowel 34 in Eastern Yiddish (hence דְּאָגָה dəʔɔ́γɔ́ ⟩ Northeastern Yiddish dájgə "worry," Mideastern dágə). In some forms of Western Yiddish, merger occurred with Western Yiddish ā₂₄, the local realization of 24/44 or 13/24/44 (see Guggenheim-Grünberg 1973: 40–43).

In Northeastern Yiddish, hiatus was resolved by yotization, e.g., švújəs "(the holiday) Shavuoth" ⟨ שָׁבוּעוֹת šɔvūʕṓθ. These and other Yiddish reactions to hiatus are often absent in Ashkenazic where the two ensuing vowels in succession are simply read in sequence, e.g., Northeastern Ashkenazic dəɔgɔ́ / də́ɔgɔ, šɔvuéjs / šɔ́vuejs.

Yekusiel of Prague warns against such pronunciations as וָמַר wɔmár "and bitter" for וְאָמַר wəʔɔmár "and he said," quipping that such errors are רַע וּמַר בְּעֵינַי raʕ wɔmár bəʕējnáj "evil and bitter in my eyes" (Yekusiel 1395: [186b]). He also bemoans failure to distinguish עוֹר ʕōr "hide (n.)" from אוֹר ʔōr "light" (ibid. [189b]).

It is evident from Yekusiel's samples that by the thirteenth century the old aleph (ʔ) vs. ayin (ʕ) distinction, and the aleph vs. zero and ayin vs. zero distinctions, were all in trouble.

(b) Merger with European-Compatible Consonants

ג [γ] merged with ג [g], e.g., עֵגֶל ʕéγɛl "calf" ⟩ NEA éjgɛl, MEA ájgɛl, WA éjgɛl.

ד [ð], merged with ד [d], e.g., עוֹד ʕōð "yet" "more" ⟩ NEA ejd, MEA ɔjd, WA ɔud.

In names of letters of the Jewish alphabet there is evidence of *s* reflexes in Western Yiddish. Bibliophilus (1742: 3) offers the variant spellings ⟨Jud⟩ and ⟨Jus⟩ for י, ⟨Lamed⟩ and ⟨Lames⟩ for ל. Cf. classical יוד, למד. These forms are also attested in a twentieth-century variety of German in the village of Schopfloch which borrows heavily from Western Yiddish (see Philipp 1983: 43; Shy 1990: 346).

ו [w] merged with ב [v], e.g., וַיִּקְרָא wajjiqrɔ́ "and he called" ⟩ NEA vajikrɔ́ / vajíkrɔ, MEA vajikrú / vajíkru, WA vajikrṓ / vajíkrō.

Yekusiel mourns the collapse of historical אָבִיו ʔɔ́vīw "his father" with אָבִיב ʔɔ́vīv "Spring" (Yekusiel 1395: 189a).

ח [ḥ] merged with כ [x], e.g., חָכָם ḥɔxɔ́m "wise man" ⟩ NEA xɔxɔ́m / xɔ́xɔm, MEA xuxɔ́m / xúxɔm, WA xōxɔ́m / xṓxɔm.

In the medieval Rhineland dialects of the "Children of hes," *ḥ* merged with ה [h] rather than with כ [x] (see M. Weinreich 1958; Katz 1987a: 57; 1988a: 39–42; 1990b; 1991; and below).

ט [ṭ] merged with [t], e.g., טַל ṭal "dew" ⟩ Pan-Ashkenazic tal.

Yekusiel decries merger of שִׁבְתּוֹ šivtṓ "his sojourn" and שִׁבְטוֹ šivṭṓ "his staff," "his tribe" (Yekusiel 1395: 189b).

ק [q] merged with כ [k], e.g., קָדוֹשׁ qɔðṓš "sacred" ⟩ NEA kɔdéjš / kɔ́dejš, MEA kudɔ́jš / kúdɔjš, WA kōdɔ́uš / kṓdɔuš.

Yekusiel cites merger of קַלָּה qallɔ́ "easy (fem.)" with כַּלָּה kallɔ́ "bride" (1395: 189b) as one of the evils resulting from failure to distinguish the two consonants.

ת [θ] merged with ס [s] (שׂ [ś] was itself almost certainly merged with [s] long before the rise of Ashkenaz), e.g., אֶת ʔɛθ "[particle preceding accusative definite noun]" ⟩ Pan-Ashkenazic ɛs.

In the name of the fourth letter of the Jewish alphabet, דלת, final ת appears as plosive *t* (itself usually the reflex of תּ [t] or ט [ṭ]), or as [d], hence *dálət* or *dáləd* in modern Ashkenazic. There is however evidence of older Western Yiddish *s*. Bibliophilus (1742: 3) has ⟨Dalet⟩ alongside ⟨Dales⟩.

(c) Phonemic Preservation Via Phonetic Shift

צ [ṣ] was affricated to [c] ([tˢ]), leaving a distinct phoneme. Probably during the primary fusion characterizing the birth of Yiddish and Ashkenazic, the Semitic *ṣ* fused with medieval German ⟨tz⟩, producing the unitary Yiddish /c/ phoneme which occurs in both components, producing such homonyms as *kac* = "cat" (cf. Middle High German *katze*) and "Katz" (cf. Hebrew כ״ץ).

Vowel System

The vowel system of Ashkenazic derives straightforwardly from a system closely resembling a version of Tiberian vocalism. There are, however, differences: (1) in Proto-Ashkenazic, the three ḥatef or ultrashort vowels (ֱ [ɛ], ֲ [ă], ֳ [ɔ̆]) were not distinguished from their normal-length counterparts (ֶ [ɛ], ַ [a], unstressed closed-syllabic ָ [ɔ]). Secondly, the variant imported to Ashkenaz apparently had short ɔ (corresponding with Yiddish vowel 41) for qameṣ in *all* closed syllables (not only in unstressed closed syllables, as per classical Hebrew grammar). The descriptive environment of that shortening rule includes as consonants [j] and ה with *mappiq* (הּ), which traditional Hebrew grammarians consider to mark the exceptional consonantality of word-final ה. It is morphologized in third-person possessives ending in ה. The Proto-Ashkenazic qameṣ shortening apparently inherited from the Near East was therefore of the type qameṣ → [− long] /__C| (where | = syllable boundary). The phonology of the language obviously treated /j/ and /H/ (where H = ה) as consonantal.

The effects of this pre-Ashkenazic shortening are evident in modern dialects of Ashkenazic which distinguish vowel 12 (Proto-Ashkenazic *ɔ̄, corresponding with qameṣ) from 41 (Proto-Ashkenazic *ɔ, corresponding with stressed open-syllabic qameṣ and ḥatef qameṣ). Thus, for example, in modern Mideastern Ashkenazic, where open-syllabic qameṣ is realized as *u* (often [ū] but there is no phonemic length opposition for this vowel, hence the unitary transcription *u*), closed-syllabic qameṣ and qameṣ before *j* and mappiq are realized as ɔ, e.g., *purón* "(Wilderness of) Paran" ⟨ פָּארָן; *bizɔjójn* "disgrace" ⟨ בִּזָּיוֹן *bizzɔ̄jṓn*; *íšɔ́* "her husband" ⟨ אִשָּׁה *ʔíšɔH* (cf. *išū́* "woman" ⟨ אִשָּׁה *ʔiššɔ̄*). Mappiq forms often retain ultimate stress even in Popular Ashkenazic, accentuating such contrasts as *íšu* "woman" vs. *íšɔ́* "her husband."

The Proto-Ashkenazic Vowel System

The proposed system of Proto-Ashkenazic vocalism is illustrated in Table 4.11. Yiddish vowel numbers are added to denote the fusion with vernacular vowels which took place at the theoretical linguistic starting point of Ashkenaz.

Table 4.11. Proto-Ashkenazic Vocalism

*ī$_{\text{long ḥireq / 32}}$	*ū$_{\text{(long) shureq / 52}}$
*i$_{\text{short ḥireq / 31}}$	*u$_{\text{(short) qibbuṣ / 51}}$
*ē$_{\text{ṣere / 22}}$	*ō$_{\text{ḥolem / 42}}$
*ɛ$_{\text{segol, ḥatef segol / 21}}$	*ɔ̄$_{\text{open syllabic qameṣ / 12}}$
	*ɔ$_{\text{closed syllabic qameṣ, ḥatef qameṣ / 41}}$
*a$_{\text{pathaḥ, ḥatef pathaḥ / 11}}$	

Summary of Sound Changes

(1) Assorted Consonantal Shifts (See Above)

Loss of ʔ and ʕ; Merger of γ with g; ð with d; w with v; ḥ with x; ṭ with t; q with k; θ with s; shift of ṣ to c (tˢ).

(2) Lengthening

Lengthening, inspired by the analogous German development, processed short vowels in stressed open syllables at an early point in the history of Ashkenaz. Only two Tiberian vowels met the structural description of the rule: pathaḥ and segol in stressed open syllables, hence *xésɛd ⟩ *xḗsɛd "kindness, mercy," páxad ⟩ *pā́xad "fear." In terms of Pan-Yiddish vocalism, proto 21 (*ɛ, e.g., *xésɛd, *ɛmés "truth") split into unlengthened 21 (*ɛmés) vs. lengthened 25 (*xḗsɛd). Proto 11 (*a, e.g., xajjɔ́ "animal," páxað) split into unlengthened 11 (*xajjɔ́) vs. lengthened 13 (*pā́xað) with dialectological consequences parallel to those in the Semitic component of Yiddish (see above). Wherever a Tiberian form did not meet the structural description (the conditions, so to speak) of the sound shift, it escaped Lengthening. In the samples cited, the first ɛ in ɛmɛs escaped because it was not stressed (there is no evidence that ḥatef vowels differed in Proto-Ashkenazic from their non-ḥatef variants). The a of xajjɔ́ was originally in a closed syllable (opened only later by Degemination, no. 3). Cf. the Tiberian cognates חֶסֶד ḥésɛð, אֱמֶת ɛ̆mέθ, חַיָּה ḥajjɔ́, פַּחַד páḥað.

(3) Degemination

By C¹ C¹ → C¹, consonantal length was lost, e.g., *bammɔkɔ́m "in the place" ⟩ *bamɔkɔ́m, *gibbór "mighty (man)" ⟩ *gibór, *jittén "(he) will give" ⟩ *jitén, *mǝnaššé "Manasseh" ⟩ *mǝnašé, *šuttɔ́f "partner" ⟩ *šutɔ́f, *uzzí "my strength" ⟩ *uzí. Cf. Tiberian cognates בַּמָּקוֹם bammɔqóm, גִּבּוֹר gibbór, יִתֵּן jittén, מְנַשֶּׁה mǝnaššé, שֻׁתָּף šuttɔ́f, עֻזִּי ʕuzzí.

(4) Stress Shift

Formal Ashkenazic was never processed by Stress Shift, but many forms of Popular Ashkenazic were, in varying degrees, under the impact of the Semitic component in Yiddish (cf. Katz 1980; and above). Stress Shift entailed the collapse of ultimate and penultimate stress to a unitary pattern of penultimate accentuation, e.g., *axašvērɔ́š "[King] Ahasuerus" ⟩ *axašvḗrɔs, *rɔ́š haššɔnɔ́ "New Year" ⟩ *rɔ́š haššɔ́nɔ, *šɔlɔ́x "(he) sent" ⟩ *šɔ́lax (cf. Tiberian cognates אֲחַשְׁוֵרוֹשׁ ʔăḥašwērɔ́š, רֹאשׁ הַשָּׁנָה rɔ́š haššɔnɔ́, שָׁלַח šɔlάḥ).

There are a number of categories of exceptions. In morphology, articles and particles do not generally accept stress, hence monosyllables preceded by these retain stress, e.g., *hɔ́ʔíš "the man" (⟨ הָאִישׁ hɔʔíš) never became · hɔ́ʔíš (the black dot · distinguishes spurious forms from asterisked reconstructions, which are at any rate not meant to be spurious). In semantics, particularly sacred terms, notably names of

God, retained ultimate stress, e.g., *elōhím "God" did not usually undergo Stress Shift to ·elóhīm (cf. אֱלֹהִים ʔĕlōhím). In phonology, if the penultimate and antepenultimate syllable vowels are both long, stress *may* move back to the antepenult, e.g., Northeastern géjrəšin, Mideastern gájrəšin "laws of divorces" (cf. גְּרוּשִׁין gērūšín), cf. Leibel 1965.

(5) Great Yiddish Vowel Shift

Ashkenazic was fully processed by the Great Yiddish Vowel Shift, which paved the way for it to follow the major events in the ensuing phonological history of the various Yiddish dialects. The Great Shift included raising of $*\bar{\varepsilon}_{25} \rangle \bar{e}_{25}$ and $*\bar{\jmath}_{12} \rangle \bar{o}_{12}$; lowering and diphthongization of old $*\bar{e}_{22}$ to εj_{22} and old $*\bar{o}_{42}$ to ou_{42} (for a more detailed survey, see Katz 1982: 77–81).

By the Great Vowel Shift, then, $*x\acute{\bar{\varepsilon}}sed \rangle x\acute{e}sed$, $*d\acute{\bar{\jmath}}vid \rangle d\bar{o}vid$, $*x\acute{\bar{e}}lek \rangle x\acute{e}jlek$, $*\bar{o}l\acute{o}m \rangle oul\acute{o}m$. These processed forms are amply attested in Western Yiddish. In Eastern Ashkenazic dialects, further phonological development gave the characteristic modern forms (Northeastern xésɛd, dɔvíd, xéjlek, ejlóm; Mideastern xéjsɛd, dūvíd, xájlek, ɔjlóm).

Questions of Relative and Absolute Chronology

Consonantal shifts and the Great Vowel Shift can, from a structural point of view, be ordered anywhere. Consonantal shifts are tentatively assigned to (1) because of the speed with which Semitic sounds would have a priori disappeared among a population shifting to a central European base of articulation (cf. above). The Great Vowel Shift results in vowels largely preserved in Western Yiddish, and the similarity of its results to a documented near-modern variety might augur for a late relative dating.

The internal ordering of Lengthening and Degemination cannot be determined because their environments are mutually exclusive: stressed open-syllabic short vowels are in Tiberian phonology never followed by a geminate consonant. Indeed, geminate consonants invariably close the preceding syllable.

What is certain is that Lengthening preceded Stress Shift. This is evident from forms such as Popular Mideastern Ashkenazic élul "(month of) Elul," émɛs "true." One of the conditions for Lengthening is stress. At the time of Lengthening, these items were still ultimately stressed (*emés, *elúl), hence their escape, whereas items such as *xésɛd "kindness" and *réga "moment," both historically penultimate, were duly processed by Lengthening, hence modern (Popular) Mideastern Ashkenazic élul, émɛs vs xéjsɛd, réjga (cf. Tiberian אֱלוּל ʔĕlúl, אֱמֶת ʔĕmɛ́θ, חֶסֶד ḥésɛð, רֶגַע réyaʕ). By virtue of Stress Shift, the effects of Lengthening, originally allophonic, became phonemicized (é and éj both occur in stressed open-syllabic position).

It is extremely probable that Degemination also preceded Stress Shift. Circumstantial evidence comes from forms such as Popular Mideastern Ashkenazic hékajš "(type of) analogy," šábɔs "Sabbath." At the time of Lengthening, these items were still in closed syllables (*hɛk|kéš, *šab|bɔ́θ), hence their escape, whereas items such as *hévɛl "vanity" and *jáḥaθ "together," historically in open syllables, were duly processed by Lengthening, hence modern (Popular) Mideastern Ashkenazic hékajš vs. héjvɛl, šábɔs vs. jáxad (cf. Tiberian הֶקֵּשׁ heqqḗš, הֶבֶל hévɛl; šabbɔ́θ "Sabbath," יַחַד jáxaθ). Note that ā forms such as jáxad occur only in the more conservative Southwestern portions of Mideastern Ashkenazic (e.g., Stencl 1978). In many varieties of Mideastern Ashkenazic, these forms have been shortened to a. The evidence here is "circumstantial" because stresslessness can also explain nonlengthening of historical ɛ and a in such forms as hékajs and šábɔs. In other words, lack of stress can itself explain all the unlengthened forms, whereas erstwhile presence of geminate consonants (closing the preceding syllable, thereby blocking lengthening) can explain only some of them.

The absolute chronology of Degemination is assisted by Yekusiel of Prague. He notes that dagesh forte (= *dagesh ḥazaq*, the diacritic marking gemination) was pronounced for *w, z, ṭ, l, m, n, s, ṣ, q, š* "by most people of our land," but moans that "the younger readers were in the habit of not pronouncing dagesh forte in these letters when shewa occurs under the letter with the dagesh [i.e., when the relevant consonant is followed by shewa]." A bit later in the same discussion, Yekusiel's characterization of those who fail to geminate sours a bit, proceeding from youth to boorishness. He notes that "for the letters *w, z, ṭ, l, m, n, s, ṣ, q, š*, the boors miss out on their dagesh, as we said, when shewa occurs under the letter with the dagesh" (Yekusiel 1395: [187b]).

Mobile Shewa

The fate of mobile shewa in Ashkenazic, like so many of the issues touched upon, needs to be the object of a monograph. In the most formal style of reading by trained readers, mobile shewa will appear as a shewa vowel (locally [ə], [ɨ], [I], [ɜ], etc.). In Popular Ashkenazic, however, historical mobile shewa underwent various fates. It was reduced to zero in phonetic environments where Yiddish tolerates consonant clusters, e.g., Northeastern Ashkenazic *krejvó* "close" ⟨ *qərōvɔ́*, *gvul* "border" ⟨ *gəvúl, holxó* "she went" ⟨ *hɔ́ləxɔ́*. Contextual loss of mobile shewa may result in wholesale remake of the classical Tiberian CV(C) syllabic structure, e.g., the last cited example, where CV|CV|CV → CVC|CV. There is, however, conflicting evidence from Closed Syllable Shortening that some graphic shewas which classical Hebrew grammar regards as mobile were in fact silent long before Ashkenaz Cf., e.g., Mideastern *sófrəm* "scribes," *sónəm* "enemies" where the short vowel betrays a pre-Ashkenazic closed syllable. The Yiddish forms cannot derive from *sō̍ | nə | ʔīm, sō̍ | fə | rīm*.

Possibly as a hypercorrection introduced to combat shewa loss, and possibly as a normal sound shift buttressed by penultimate stress in popular renditions of Ashkenazic (and maybe even both), shewas that do survive have been known in many forms of Ashkenazic to be "exaggerated" to vowel 22, i.e., to merge with the local realization of ṣere (see, e.g., Emden 1745: 4a; Wessely 1827: 204). In many variants of Yiddish, in fact, the name of the shewa vowel has itself shifted to 22, e.g., (some) Mideastern Yiddish *šájvə*, (some) Southeastern, Northeastern *šéjvə*, both alongside expected *švu, švɔ* respectively (cf. שְׁוָא *šəwɔ́*).

Old East and Old West Ashkenaz

Two Kinds of Ashkenazim

Ashkenaz, in its early history, comprised two culturally distinct groups. The most famous, in the Rhineland, was centered in the cities of Speyer, Worms, and Mainz (collectively known as *Shum,* from the Hebrew acronym שו״ם). The second grouping lay further eastward on the banks of the Danube and the surrounding areas, centered in Regensburg, Rothenburg, Nuremberg, and also Prague. That is the area that was the Eastern Ashkenaz of those days. In later centuries, of course, it along with the Rhineland became the new Western Ashkenaz, in contradistinction to the later and modern Eastern Ashkenaz of the Slavonic and Baltic lands (see Katz 1987a: 54–55; 1990; 1991; 1992).

Two Distinct Languages

The western communities, in the Rhineland, spoke a Germanic-based Jewish language that was not Yiddish, and used a liturgical form of Hebrew and Aramaic that was not at all like any known variety of Ashkenazic. Both the Semitic component of the Rhineland Jewish language and its speakers' pronunciations of Hebrew and Aramaic had a five-vowel system very much like the vocalism of Sephardic Hebrew, in which qameṣ and pathaḥ were merged as unitary *a*, ṣere and segol as unitary *ɛ*, ḥolem and qameṣ qatan as unitary *ɔ*, long and short ḥireq as unitary *i*, long and short shureq as *u*. This is betrayed in medieval manuscripts by massive promiscuous confounding of qameṣ with pathaḥ and ṣere with segol (see Katz 1987a: 56).

Moreover classical [ḥ], represented by the Hebrew letter ח (classical חֵית *ḥēθ*), had merged with [h] among the old Rhinelanders, rather than with [x] (cf. M. Weinreich 1958; Katz 1987a: 57; 1988a: 39–42; 1990b; 1991; 1992). In fact, this isogloss provided the names of the two groups. In Old Ashkenazic folklore, the westerners were known as בני הית *bnej hɛs* "Children of *hɛs*," i.e., "those who pronounce '*hɛs*' for ח," the easterners as *bnej xɛs* "those who pronounce '*xɛs*' for ח. The fictitious letter הית *(hɛs)* was coined to poke fun at the westerners. Westerners occasionally used the spelling כית to refer to the [x] pronunciation of the easterners. These names invoke a humorous reference to the biblical Children of Heth of Genesis 23 (see Katz 1991, 1992).

This shibboleth refers to the two groups in all sorts of legal, cultural, and folkloristic contexts. For example, in his responsa, the Maharil (acronym of Moyreynu Horav Yankev Haleyvi, also known as Mahari Segal; Yankev Segal; Mahari Molin; Yankev ben Moyshe Haleyvi Moellin/Mollin, ca. 1360–1427) notes a difference in custom concerning the *tfiln* (phylacteries) donned during weekday morning prayer. The question concerns the positioning of the box of the *tfiln shel yad* ("hand phylactery"), whether it should be placed with the *maabarto* (aperture at one end of the box through which the strap passes) at top or at bottom. The easterners positioned the box so that the end with the *maabarto* and strap are at bottom, closer to the hand. By contrast, the western tradition placed the side with the *maabarto* at the top, closer to the head (both descriptions assume the arm is at rest at one's side).

The Maharil put it this way:

> Tfiln shel yad: bnej ɛstrajkh ["the Children of Austria"] and all the regions of the *bnej ḥɛs* position the *maabarto* toward the hand; and we, the Children of the Rhine and all the *bnej hɛs,* position the *maabarto* toward the body, as with the head phylactery.
>
> (Maharil 1556: 6a)

Added to their five-vowel system and their *h* realization of ח, the Rhinelanders had a third major linguistic feature. Yekusiel of Prague noted that:

> We also know that there are some Ashkenazim who pronounce ה [hē? = h] and ח [ḥēθ = ḥ] as one and likewise שׂ [śīn = š] and שׁ [šīn = s].
>
> (Yekusiel 1395: [189b])

In pointed Hebrew and Aramaic texts, ⟨שׂ⟩ marked by the diacritic to the left denotes an [s] rather than an [š] pronunciation (the letter is known as *sin, śin smɔl,* or *dɛr smɔl* in Yiddish). Transcribed [ś] by Semitists to distinguish it from *samekh* ⟨ ס⟩, it was nevertheless merged with *samekh* long before the European period in Jewish history, and attempts to prove otherwise have not succeeded (see Faber 1982: 86). On the fate of Hebrew sibilants in medieval Europe, see Gumpertz (1942; 1953: 33–50), M. Weinreich (1973: 2:36–38, 4:51–55) and Faber (1982; 1987: 18).

By the early thirteenth century, then, it was known to Yekusiel of Prague that the subgroup of Ashkenazim who had merged [ḥ] with [h], i.e., the *bnej hɛs,* had also merged [š] and [s]. Unlike [ḥ], which is limited to the Semitic component, [š] and [s] are well represented in the Germanic component, and so in a stroke Yekusiel solves for us the old question of why a single grapheme, ⟨שׂ⟩, is used almost exclusively for both historical [š] and [s] in old Yiddish texts (see, e.g., Shtif 1928: 143–46; Timm 1987: 272–73; Kerler 1988: 227–28).

Destinies of the Two Branches of Old Ashkenaz

Both the vernacular of the early Rhineland Jews, and their Hebrew and Aramaic phonology, became extinct many centuries ago, although not without leaving traces in both Yiddish and Ashkenazic. The language of Danube Jewry—*Yiddish*—and its Hebrew and Aramaic phonology—*Ashkenazic*—spread to the four corners of Ashkenaz, and, via migration in recent centuries, to many parts of the world.

Social and Contextual Dialects

Formal vs. Popular Ashkenazic

Ashkenazic shares with natural languages social and contextual variation. Nearly all that variation can be measured on a scale extending from the pole of "Formal Ashkenazic" to a variety incorporating features of the coterritorial Semitic component in Yiddish, principally: Closed Syllable Shortening, Penultimate Stress Assignment, and Posttonic Reduction (see above). Varieties incorporating one or more of these Yiddish features may collectively be called "Popular Ashkenazic."

The Ashkenazic Continuum

One might a priori postulate that social prestige necessarily slips downward from Formal Ashkenazic to the forms processed by Closed Syllable Shortening, Penultimate Stress Assignment and Posttonic Reduction. One would be misguided. It all depends on what is being uttered, by whom, and in what context. As it happens, Popular Ashkenazic is used in the highest academic endeavours of Ashkenazic society, Talmud and Kabbalah, which are studied from unpointed texts. The same scholar who will read *dɔm* "blood" in the Bible, or in reciting the ten plagues at Passover *seyder,* will use *dam,* with Closed Syllable Shortening, in Talmud study (cf. Tiberian *dɔm*). On the other hand, in synagogue reading from the Pentateuch and weekly portions from the Prophets, Formal Ashkenazic would be the variety aspired to (with the advent of possible interference from varieties of Popular Ashkenazic, or, in other words, interference from the phonology of the vernacular). Use of Popular Ashkenazic in Torah reading might well be taken as a sign of ignorance and lack of education. Khayim ben Moyshe Lifshitz summed up the differential this way in his *Seyfer derekh khayim* ("Book of the Way of Life"):

> A man should be careful to read with the Accents [i.e. the Tiberian stress marks] everything that is from the Torah, the Prophets and the Hagiographa [i.e. anything from the Hebrew Bible]; analogously, [a man should be careful to read] Mishna and Gemara [= the Talmud] with the [traditional] melody.
> (Lifshitz 1703: 20b, no. 28.9)

Jacob Emden allowed rather more leeway:

> One should be careful with *mileyl* ['penultimate stress'] and *milra* ['final stress'], for whom it is possible and knows these things. But for the man who did not acquire this habit in his youth, it is impossible to bother him with placing of the accents for this would trouble him so and make his speech weary, and his loss is greater than his reward.
> (Emden 1745: 4a–4b)

Between the poles of Formal Ashkenazic for biblical readings in synagogue and Popular Ashkenazic for Talmud, Kabbalah, and an array of informal and semiformal uses of phrases and formulas, there is a huge middle ground with considerable variation. Much of that middle ground is occupied by the daily and festival liturgy, and by Torah study (as opposed to formal synagogue reading). The first two words of most blessings, classical בָּרוּךְ אַתָּה *bɔrúx ʔattɔ́* "Blessed art Thou," and the first two words of the Bible, בְּרֵאשִׁית בָּרָא *bərēšíθ bɔrɔ́* "In the beginning created," occur inter alia in variants illustrated in Table 4.12. Note the appearance of pretonic reduction (no. 2).

The complex phonological and sociological interplay of stress pattern and vowel reduction merits a monograph. The same Northeasterner, say, who might have *bərejšís bɔrɔ́* for Torah reading in synagogue, might utter *brejšís bɔrɔ́* when reading the text more rapidly at home, *bréjšis bɔ́rɔ* in a more comfortable setting of study, and *bréjšəs bɔ́rə* when citing the Hebrew passage in a Yiddish conversation. Like many generalizations, these can serve for orientation but cannot do justice to the complexity of real life. In one and the same genre, considerable sociolinguistic

Table 4.12. The Ashkenazic Continuum: Realizations of
בָּרוּךְ אַתָּה bɔrúx ʔattɔ́ and בְּרֵאשִׁית בָּרָא bərēšīθ bɔ́rɔ́

	Northeastern	Mideastern
1. Formal Ashkenazic:	bɔrúx atɔ́ bərejšís bɔrɔ́	burix atú bərajšís burú
2. With Pretonic Reduction:	brúx ətɔ́ brejšís bərɔ́	brix ətú brajšís bərú
3. With Stress Shift:	bɔ́rux átɔ bréjšis bɔ́rɔ	búrix átu brájšis búru
4. With Stress Shift and Posttonic Reduction:	bɔ́rəx átə bréjšəs bɔ́rə	búrəx átə brájšəs búrə

variation can be observed. Appendix 1 provides two renditions of the first chapter of the Book of Esther (traditionally read twice in synagogue during the festival of Purim). The first approaches Formal Ashkenazic (with some incursions by Penultimate Stress Assignment). The second is in a variety of Popular Ashkenazic (with mixed stress patterns and several hypercorrections).

In some cases, a semantic distinction is supported by pronunciations taken from different rungs on the Ashkenazic continuum. The same Northeasterner, say, who might have bɔɔl(ə)mɔ́ or bɔɔ́l(ə)mɔ "in the world" in the hallowed kaddish prayer, will say bəálmə "generally," "with no specific intention," in equally hallowed Talmud study (cf. Tiberian בְּעָלְמָא bəʕɔ́ləmɔ́). The sociophonological differentiation within Ashkenazic represents a treasure of research possibilities in the study of exotic forms of multilingualism.

Modern Standard Ashkenazic

In the nineteenth and twentieth century, various versions of Standard Ashkenazic arose. The classic variety of standard literary Ashkenazic follows Standard Yiddish in its vowel system, characterized as "Northeastern Yiddish except that vowel 42/44 is realized ɔj as in the other Eastern Yiddish dialects, not ej as in Northeastern." As it happens, Standard Ashkenazic adopts penultimate stress, but not, on the whole, posttonic reduction. It is in this variety that some of the greatest modern Hebrew poetry was written. Israeli literary scholars, while Sephardicizing the vowels (merging qameṣ and pathaḥ in a, ṣere and segol in ɛ, ḥolem and qameṣ qatan in ɔ), retain penultimate stress to preserve the rhythm of the poetry.

Standard Ashkenazic renditions of H. N. Bialik's *Loy bayoym veloy balaylo* ("Not by day and not by night," Israeli Hebrew *Lo bayom velo balayla*) and of the original first verses of N. H. Imber's *Hatikvah* appear in Appendix 2. With the final two lines rewritten after the author's death, these verses became the Israeli national anthem. Note from these transcriptions that standard literary Ashkenazic does not spirantize across word boundaries (hence *lɔj bajɔjm*, not *lɔj vajɔjm*); it does not generally preserve pausal forms (*balájlɔ,* not *balɔ́jlɔ*); it often omits mobile shewa (*pɔ́jsrɔ*, not *pɔ́jsərɔ*).

A variant of standard Ashkenazic developed in the United States has *ōu* (or other local American reflexes of "long o" as in *home*) for ḥolem. In the 1960s, it was used as the spoken language in the classroom for Jewish studies classes in New York City in a number of Hebrew day schools, including Etz Chaim, Rambam and RJJ (Rabbi Jacob Joseph Yeshiva). The *ōu* for ḥolem came to signify a Hebrew-speaking, Orthodox, pro-Zionist, Ashkenazic social setting. It was to the cultural "left" of those (Hasidim and "yeshiva circles") using the East European *ɔj*. Ashkenazic in the British Isles similarly uses local reflexes of *ou* (as in *home*), or in circles consisting now mainly of older people *au* ("ou" as in *round*), for ḥolem, variants possibly derived from older German Jewish practice. London Yiddish *ɔ* for historical *a* (*šɔ́bəs* for *šábəs*) seems not to have made many inroads into local Ashkenazic (which usually has expected *šabɔ́s* or *šábɔs*). Here again, as throughout the field of Ashkenazic studies, rewarding fieldwork awaits the researcher.

Epilogue

Sadly, the prejudices and misconceptions concerning Ashkenazic have, as is so often the case, affected scholars as much as others. Of necessity, much of twenty-first century Hebrew historical linguistics will concentrate on the Ashkenazic Hebrew and the Ashkenazic Aramaic that the twentieth century failed to study in depth. There are still many Ashkenazim born before World War II who use exotic and uncharted forms of Ashkenazic, and a rapidly dwindling few born before the First World War. There is still time to capture this invaluable linguistic data and still time to conserve this great Hebrew and Aramaic heritage, one of the most splendid and creative in the history of those languages.

Appendix 1. Two Versions of *Esther,* Chapter 1 in Varieties of Mideastern Ashkenazic

NOTE: These transcriptions aim at phonemic accuracy. In view of both informants' chanting the text according to traditional Ashkenazic muscial realizations of the Tiberian stress marks (which double as musical notes), there are instances where it is difficult to distinguish lexical from musical stress. Some ambiguities also arise concerning vowel length amongst the high vowels, $\bar{\imath}/i$ and $\bar{u}/u$. In the transcription that follows, *i* and *ī* are distinguished because they are distinguished in the native Yiddish of the readers. Longer and shorter renditions of /u/, on the other hand, are strictly contextual variants in both Mideastern Yiddish and Ashkenazic, and are not distinguished in the transcription. Realization of /u/ is longest in stressed open syllables.

Informants' texts are retained intact, even where they diverge from the accepted standard versions.

A: As chanted in synagogue, in London, on Purim of 1984 by Mr. Shimen Mandel, born 1951 in Antwerp. Mr. Mandel is a member of the Belz Hasidic community whose parents were born between 1925 and 1930 in central Galicia between Lancut and Belz.

1: vajəhī́ bimáj axašvajrɔ́jš hī́ axašvajrɔ́jš hamɔjlájx majhɔ́jdī vəád kíš šéjva vəɛsrím imáju mədīnú:

2: bajumím huhájm kəšéjvɛs haméjlɛx axašvajrɔ́jš al kisáj malxisɔ́j ašér bəšīšán habīrú:

3: bišnas šulɔ́jš ləmɔlxɔ́j usú mištéj lɔxɔ́l surɔ́v vaavudɔ́v xajl purás imudáj hapartəmím vəsuráj haməḏīnɔ́js ləfunɔ́v:

4: bəharɔjsɔ́j ɛs ɔ́jšɛr kəvɔ́jd malxisɔ́j vəɛ́s jəkɔ́r tiféjrɛs gədilusɔ́j jumím rabím šmɔjním iməás jɔ́jm:

5: ivimlɔjɔ́js hajumím huájlɛ usu haméjlɛx ləxɔ́l huɔ́m hanimcéim bəšišán habīrú ləmigudɔ́jl vəád kutɔ́n mištéj šivás jumím baxacár gínas bísan haméjlɛx:

6: xīr karpás isxájlɛs uxíz bəxavláj bic vəargumɔ́n al gəlílaj xéjsɛf vəamī́daj šájiš mītɔ́js zuhɔ́v vuxéjsɛf al rícpas báhat vūšájš vədár vəsɔjxúrɛs:

7: vəhaškɔ́js bixláj zuhɔ́v vəxájlim mikájlim šɔ́jnim vəjájin malxís rɔ́v kəjád haméjlɛx:

8: vəhaššíju xadɔ́s ájn ɔjnájs kī́ xajn jīsád haméjlɛx al kɔl rav bajsɔ́j laasɔ́js kīrcɔ́jn iš vuíš:

9: gam vaštī́ hamalkú ɔsəsú mištáj nuším bajs hamalxís ašér laméjlɛx axašvájrɔjš:

10: bajɔ́jm hašvīī́ kətɔ́jv lajv haméjlɛx bajɔ́jin umár liməhímɔn bízəsū xarvɔ́jnu bígsu vaavagsú zajsár vəxarkás šivás hasurisím haməšɔ́rəsím ɛs pənáj haméjlɛx axašvájrɔš:

11: ləhuvī́ ɛs vaštī́ hamalkú lifnáj haméjlɛx bəxéjsɛr málxis ləharɔ́js huámim vəhasúrim ɛs jɔfjɔ́ kī tɔjvás márej hī:

12: vatəmuájn hamalkú vaštī́ luvɔ́j bidvár haméjlɛx ašér bəjád hasurísim vajikcɔ́jf haméjlɛx məɔ́jd vaxamusɔ́j buárū vɔj:

13: vajɔ́jmɛr haméjlɛx laxaxumím jɔjdáj huítim kī xajn dvar haméjlɛx lifnáj kɔl jɔ́jdaj dɔs vudín:

14: vəhakurɔ́jv ajlɔ́v karšənú šajsɔ́r admúsu saršíš méjrɛs mársənu məmī́xɔn šivás suráj purás imudáj rɔjáj
pənáj haméjlɛx hajɔ́jšvim rīšɔ́jnu bamálxis:

15: kədɔ́s ma laasɔ́js bamalkú vaštī́ al ašér lɔj ɔsəsú ɛs maamár haméjlɛx axašvajrɔ́jš bəjád hasurísim:

16: vajójmɛr məmīxɔ́n lifnáj haméjlɛx vəhasurím lɔj
al haméjlɛx ləvádɔj ɔvsú vaští hamalkú kī al kɔl
hasurím vəál kɔl huamím ašér bəxɔ́l mədīnɔ́js haméjlɛx
axašvájrɔjš:

17: kī jajcáj dvar hamalkú al kɔl hanuším ləhavzɔ́js
baalajhén bəajnajhén bəɔmrɔ́m haméjlɛx axašvajrɔ́jš
umár ləhuvī́ ɛs vaští hamalkú ləfunɔ́v vəlɔ́j vúu:

18: vəhajójm hazéj tɔjmárnū surɔ́js purás imudáj ašér
šumī́ ɛs dvar hamalkú ləxɔ́jl suráj haméjlɛx ixədáj
bizɔ́jɔjn vukúcɔf:

19: im al haméjlɛx tɔjv jajcáj dvar málxis mīlfunɔ́v
vəjikusájv bədusáj purás imudáj vəlɔ́j jaavɔ́jr ašér lɔj
suvɔ́j vaští lifnáj haméjlɛx axašvajrɔ́jš imalxīsɔ́ jitájn
haméjlɛx lirīsɔ́ hatɔ́jvu miménu:

20: vənišmá pisgɔ́m haméjlɛx ašér jaaséj bəxɔ́l
malxisɔ́j kī rabú hī vəxɔ́l hanúšim jitnī́ jəkɔ́r
ləbaalajhén ləmigudɔ́jl vəád kutɔ́n:

21: vajītáv haduvɔ́r bəajnáj haméjlɛx vəhasúrim
vajáas haméjlɛx kidvár məmíxɔn:

22: vajišláx səfurím ɛl kɔl mədīnɔ́js haméjlɛx ɛl
mədīnú imədīnú kixsuvɔ́ vəél am vuɔ́m kilšɔjnɔ́j lihijɔ́js
kɔl iš sɔjrájr bəvajsɔ́j imədabájr kilšɔ́jn amɔ́j:

B: As chanted at home, in London, by Majer Bogdanski, born 1912 in Piotrkow, Poland (Yiddish *Pyeterkov*), as per his memory of Piotrkow practice in his youth.

1: vajəhī́ bimáj axašvájrɔjš hī́ axašvajrɔ́jš hamɔ́jlajx
majhɔ́jdī vəád kiš šéjva vəɛsrím imajú mədīnú:

2: bəjumím huhájm kəšéjvɛs haméjlɛx axašvájrɔjš al
kisáj malxísɔj ášer bəšíšan habíru:

3: bišnás šulɔ́jš ləmɔlxɔ́j úsu míštɛ ləxɔ́l súrɔv
vaavúdɔv xajl purás imudáj hapártəmim vəsúraj
haməd̄ínɔ́js ləfúnɔv:

4: bəharɔjsɔ́j ɛs ɔ́jšɛr kəvɔ́jd malxisɔ́j vəés jəkɔ́r
tiféjrɛs gədilúsɔj júmim rábim šmɔ́jnim iməás
jɔjm:

5: ivimlɔ́jɔjs hajúmim huajléj úsu haméjlɛx ləxɔ́l
huɔ́m hanímceim bəšíšan habíru ləmigúdɔjl vəád kútɔn
míštej šívas júmim báxcar gínas bítan haméjlɛx:

6: xīr karpás isxájlɛs úxiz bəxávlaj vic vəargúmim al
gəlílaj kéjsɛf vəamídaj šájiš mátɔjs zúhɔv vəxéjsɛf al
rícpas bahát vūšájš vədár vəsɔjxúrɛs:

7: vəhaškɔ́js bixláj zúhɔv vəxájlim mikájlim šɔ́jnim
vəjájin malxís rav kəjád haméjlɛx:

8: vəhaššíju kadós ajn ɔjnájs kī xajn jisád haméjlɛx
al kɔl rav bájsɔj láasɔjs kīrcɔ́jn iš vuíš:

9: gam váštī hamálku ɔ́səsu mištéj núšim bəbájs
mélɛx ášɛr laméjlɛx axašvájrɔjš:

10: bajɔ́jm haš͡vīī kətɔ́jv lajv haméjlɛx bajɔ́jin umár
liməhímɔn bízəsu xarvɔ́jnu bígsu vaavágsu zájsar
vəxárkas šívas hasur͡ísim hamšɔ́rsim ɛs pnáj haméjlɛx
axašvájrɔš:

11: ləhúvī ɛs váštī hamalkú lifnáj haméjlɛx bəxéjsɛr
málxis ləharɔ́js huámim vəhasúrim ɛs jɔfjíjɔ kī tɔ́jvas
maréj hī:

12: vatmuájn hamálku vašt͡ī luvɔ́j bidvár haméjlɛx
ašɛ́r bəjád hasurísim vaj͡īkcɔjf haméjlɛx məɔ́jd
vaxmúsɔj buáru bɔj:

13: vajɔ́jmɛr haméjlɛx laxaxúmim jɔ́jdaj huítim kī
xajn dəvar haméjlɛx lífnaj kɔl jɔ́daj das vudín:

14: vəhakurɔ́jv ajlɔ́v káršənu šájsɔr admúsu táršiš
méjrɛs mársənu məm͡īxɔn šívas súraj púras imúdaj
rɔ́jaj
pənáj haméjlɛx hajɔ́jšvim rīšɔ́jnu bamalxís:

15: kədɔ́s ma lasɔ́js bamalkú vašt͡ī al ašɛ́r lɔj ɔ́səsu ɛs
maamár haméjlɛx axašvájrɔjš bəjád hasur͡ísim:

16: vajɔ́jmɛr məm͡īxɔn lífnaj haméjlɛx vəhasúrim lɔj
al haméjlɛx ləvádɔj ɔvzəsú váštī hamálku kī al kɔl
hasúrim vəál kɔl huámım ašɛ́r bəxɔ́l məd͡īnɔjs haméjlɛx
axašvájrɔjš:

17: kī jájcaj dəvár hamalkú al kɔl hanúšim ləhávzɔjs
baalájhɛn bəajnájhɛn bəɔ́mrɔm haméjlɛx axašvájrɔjš
úmar ləhúvi ɛs vášti hamálku ləfúnɔv vəlɔ́j vúu:

18: vəhajɔ́jm hazéj tɔjmarnú súrɔs púras imud͡ā ašɛ́r
šɔ́mī ɛs dəvar hamálku ləxɔ́jl súraj haméjlɛx ixdáj
bizújɔjn vukúcɛv:

19: im al haméjlɛx tɔjv jájcaj dəvár málxis milfúnɔv
vəjikúsajv bədúsaj purás imud͡ā vəlɔ́j jáavɔjr ášɛr lɔj
túvɔj váštī lifnáj haméjlɛx axašvájrɔjš umalxísɔ jitájn
haméjlɛx lirīsɔ́ hatɔ́jvu mimɛnú:

20: venišma pisgɔ́m haméjlɛx ášɛr jáasɛ bəxɔ́l
malxísɔj kī rabú hī vəxɔ́l hanúšim jífnī jəkɔ́r
ləbaalájhɛn ləmigudɔ́jl vəád kutɔ́n:

21: vajítav hadúvər bəajnáj hamájlɛx vəhasuŕím
vajáas haméjlɛx kidvár məm͡īxɔn:

22: vəjíšlax səfúrim ɛl kɔl məd͡īnɔjs haméjlɛx ɛl
məd͡īnu vimd͡īnu kixsúvɔ vəél am vuɔ́m kilšɔ́jnɔj lihijɔ́js
kɔl īš sɔ́jrajr bəbájsɔj imdabájr kilšɔ́jn amɔ́j:

Appendix 2. Two Modern Hebrew Poems in Standard Ashkenazic

Sung by Menke Katz (b. Svintsyan, Lithuania 1906) in Spring Glen, New York, 8 October 1990, as remembered from New York in the 1920s. The informant's text is retained intact. Note that in *Hatikvah* (text 2), adaptation of the words to its Bohemiam melody results in most of the final words in each line being ultimately stressed, contrasting with the penultimate stress of the rest. The troche-iamb pattern of each line is a characteristic feature of the song.

1. Bialik's **Loy bayoym veloy balaylo**

lɔj bajójm velɔj balájlɔ
xɛrɛš éjcej li atájlɔ

lɔj bɔhór vɔlɔj babíkɔ
šitɔ ójmdɔ šɔm atíkɔ

vəhašítɔ pójsrɔ xídɔjs
umagídɔ hi asídɔjs

ɛs hašítɔ éšal óni
mi vɔmí jehéj xasóni

umejájin jóvɔj šítɔ
hamipójlin ɔj milítɔ

habmɛrkóvɔ jáavɔjr švílɔj
im bəmáklɔj uvtarmílɔj

uma jóvi li šilúmim
xaruzej pńinim im algúrnim

uma tɔórɔj cax im šóxɔjr
almɔn hu im ójdɔj bóxur

šɛmɔ zókejn šítɔ tójvɔ
ɔz lɔj éšma ɔz lɔj ójvɛ

óymar lɔóvi hamiséjni
uvjad zókejn al titnéjni

ləráglɔv épɔjl vəšókejn
ax lɔj zókejn ax lɔj zókejn.

2. Imber's *Hatikvah (First Stanza and Refrain)*

kɔl ɔjd baléjvɔv pnimó
néfɛš jehúdi hɔjmió
ulfaásej mízrɔx kɔdimó
ájin ləcíɔjn cɔjfió

ɔjd lɔj óvdɔ tikvɔséjnu
hatíkvɔ hanɔjšónɔ
lóšuv ləérɛc avɔjséjnu
ləir bɔ dóvid xɔnó

References

ALTBAUER. M. "Mekhkar hamasoret haivrit haashkenazit vezikato ladialektologia shel hayidish." In *Fourth World Congress of Jewish Studies. Papers,* Jerusalem: World Union of Jewish Studies. 2:455, 1968.

———. "Yesodot shel ivrit ashkenazit betaatik kirili mehamakhatsit harishona shel hamea hashesh-esre." In Werses et al. 1977: 55–65.

ASSAF, SIMCHA. *Mekorot letoledot hakhinukh beyisrael (mitekhilat yemey habenayim ad tekufat hahaskala).* Tel Aviv: Dvir, 1954.

BAUER, HANS, AND PONTUS LEANDER. *Historische Grammatik der hebräischen Sprache des alten Testaments.* Tübingen: Max Niemeyer, 1922.

BEN-DAVID, ABBA. "Minayin hakhaluka litenuot gedolot uketanot?" *Leshonenu* 22 (1958): 7–35, 110–36.

BESCH, W., U. KNOOP, W. PUTSCHKE, AND H. E. WIEGAND, eds. *Dialektologie. Ein Handbuch zur deutschen und allgemeinen Dialektforschung.* Berlin and New York: Walter de Gruyter, 1983.

BIBLIOPHILUS. *Jüdischer Sprach-Meister oder Hebräisch-Teutsches Wörter-Buch.* Frankfurt and Leipzig, 1742.

BIKL, SHLOYME, AND LEYBUSH LEHRER. eds. *Shmuel Niger bukh.* New York: Yivo, 1958.

BIN-NUN, JECHIEL. *Jiddisch und die deutschen Mundarten unter besonderer Berücksichtigung des ostgalizischen Jiddisch.* Tübingen: Max Niemeyer, 1973

BIRNBAUM, SHLOYME [SALOMO/SOLOMON A.]. "Di historye fun di alte u-klangen in yidish." *Yivo bleter* 6 (1934): 25–60.

BIRNHAK, EFRAYIM. *Seyfer alef beys.* Brooklyn, NY: Sefer Lanoar, 1976

BROSI, JOHANNES. "Southwestern Yiddish. A Study in Dialectology, Folklore and Literature." M. Litt. thesis: Oxford University, 1990

BRUGMANS, Hk. AND A. FRANK. eds. *Geschiedenis der joden in Nederland, eerste deel (tot circa 1795).* Amsterdam: Van Holkema & Warendorf N.V, 1940

CATALÁN, DIEGO, ed. *Miscelánea homenaje a André Martinet. Estructuralismo e historia.* 2. La Laguna: Universidad de La Laguna, 1958

CHOMSKY, WILLIAM. *Hebrew: The Eternal Language.* Philadelphia: Jewish Publication Society of America, 1957

COHEN, B. "Die Aussprachegruppen der heutigen Judenheit." In *Jeschurun. Monatsschrift für Lehre und Leben im Judentum* 10 (1923): 56–75.

DAWIDOWICZ, LUCY S., ALEXANDER ERLICH, et al. (Organizing Committee) *For Max Weinreich on his Seventieth Birthday. Studies in Jewish Languages, Literature, and Society.* The Hague: Mouton, 1964

ELDAR, ILAN. *Masoret hakeria hakedam-ashkenazit. Mahuta vehayesodot hameshutafim la ulemasoret sefarad.* Vol. 1. *Inyaney hagaya venikud* [= *Eda velashon. Pirsumey mifal mesorot halashon shel edot yisrael,* ed. Sh. Morag, 4]. Jerusalem: Magnes, 1978

ELYE BOKHER. *Seyfer masoyres hamasoyres.* Venice: Daniel Bomberg, 1538

EMBER, AARON. "Pronunciation of Hebrew among the Russian Jews." *The American Journal of Semitic Languages and Literatures* 19 (1903): 233–34.

EMDEN, JACOB. *Polotin beys eyl hooymeyd al shivo amudey shomayim. Venikro gam oyr shivas hayomim.* Altona: 1745

———. *Seyfer moyr uktsio,* 1. Altona, Author, 1761

FABER, ALICE. "Early Medieval Hebrew Sibilants in the Rhineland, South Central and Eastern Europe." *Hebrew Annual Review* 6 (1982): 81–96.

———. "A Tangled Web: Whole Hebrew and Ashkenazic Origins." In Katz 1987b: 15–22.

FISHMAN, JOSHUA A., ed. *Readings in the Sociology of Jewish Languages.* Leiden: E. J. Brill, 1985

FRIED, CHAIM. *Seyfer alef bino.* Brooklyn, NY: Yeshivah Toldoth Jacob Joseph, 1983
FRIEDRICH, CARL WILHELM. *Unterricht in der Judensprache und Schrift. zum Gebrauch für Gelehrte und Ungelehrte.* Prenzlau: Chr. Gottf. Ragoczy, 1784
GUGGENHEIM-GRÜNBERG, FLORENCE. *Jiddisch auf alemannischem Sprachgebiet. 56 Karten zur Sprach- und Sachgeographie.* Zurich: Juris, 1973
GUMPERTZ, Y. F. "Hashin, tiltuleha vegilguleha." *Tarbiz* 13 (1942): 107–15.
———. *Mivtaey sefatenu. Studies in Historical Phonetics of the Hebrew Language.* Jerusalem: Mosad Harav Kook, 1953
———. "Shaar hametigot lerabi Yahabi." *Leshonenu* 22 (1957): 36–47.
HERZOG, MARVIN I. *The Yiddish Language in Northern Poland. Its Geography and History.* Indiana University Research Center in Anthropology, Folklore, and Linguistics, publication 37 *(International Journal of American Linguistics, 31.2)*. The Hague: Indiana University & Mouton, 1965
HIRSCHEL, L. "Cultuur en volksleven." In Brugmans and Frank 1940: 454–97.
IDELSOHN, A. Z. "Die gegenwärtige Aussprache des Hebräischen bei Juden und Samaritanern." *Monatsschrift für Geschichte und Wissenschaft des Judentums* n.s. 21 (1913): 527–45, 697–721.
KATZ, DOVID. "First Steps in the Reconstruction of the Proto Vocalism of the Semitic Component in Yiddish." Unpublished paper placed before the Seminar in Yiddish Studies, Department of Linguistics, Columbia University, 1977
———. "Der semitisher kheylek in yidish. A yerushe fun kadmoynim. Metodn un meglekhkaytn." Unpublished paper placed before the First International Conference on Research in Yiddish Language and Literature at the Oxford Centre for Postgraduate Hebrew Studies. Oxford, 6–9 August, 1979 [Hebrew version = Katz 1986].
———. "Reconstruction of the Stress System in the Semitic Component of Yiddish." John Marshall Prize essay (unpublished). University College London, 1980.
———. *"Explorations in the History of the Semitic Component in Yiddish."* Ph.D. diss. University of London, 1982.
———. "Yidish in tsvelftn un draytsetn yorhundert: evidents fun hebreyishe un aramische ksavyadn." Unpublished paper placed before the Second International Conference on Research in Yiddish Language and Literature at the Oxford Centre for Postgraduate Hebrew studies, Oxford, 10–15 July, 1983. (1983a)
———. "Dialektologie des Jiddischen." In Besch et al. 1983: 1018–41. (1983) (1983b)
———. "Hebrew, Aramaic and the Rise of Yiddish." In Fishman 1985: 85–103.
———. "Hayesod hashemi beyidish: yerusha mimey kedem." *Hasifrut* n.s. 10.3/4 (35–36) (1986): 228–51.
———. "The Proto Dialectology of Ashkenaz." In Katz 1987b: 47–60. (1987a)
———. Ed. *Origins of the Yiddish Language. Papers from the First Annual Oxford Winter Symposium in Yiddish Language and Literature, 15–17 December 1985* (= Winter Studies in Yiddish). Oxford: Pergamon, 1987. (1987b).
———. "Origins of Yiddish Dialectology." In Katz 1988b: 39–55. (1988a).
———. Ed. *Dialects of the Yiddish Language. Papers from the Second Annual Oxford Winter Symposium in Yiddish Language and Literature, 14–16 December 1986 (= Winter Studies in Yiddish,* 2 Oxford: Pergamon, 1988 (1988b)
———. "Proto Language Theory and the Case of Yiddish." Unpublished paper placed before the Seminar in Linguistics and Philology, University of Oxford, May 1988. (1988c)
———. "Di eltere yidishe leksikografye: Mekoyres un metodn." *Oksforder yidish* 1 (1990): 161–232. (1990a).
———. "The children of Heth and the Ego of linguistics. A story of seven Yiddish mergers" *Transactions of the Philological Society* 89.1 (1991), pp. 95–121.

———. "East and West, Khes and Shin, and the Origin of Yiddish." in *Keminhag ashkenaz u-polin, Festschrift for Chone Shmeruk.* Ed. C. Turniansky et al. Jerusalem: Zalman Shazar Centre, 1992

KERLER, DOV-BER. "The Eighteenth Century Origins of Modern Literary Yiddish." D. Phil. diss. Oxford University. (In press, Oxford University Press), 1988

KIMCHI, DAVID. *Sefer mikhlol.* Venice: Daniel Bomberg, 1545

KIMCHI, MOSHE. *Mahalakh shevile hadaat.* Pesaro: [1509–1518]

KLAR, B. "Letoledot hamivta bimey habenayim." *Leshonenu* 17 (1951): 72–75.

LEBENSOHN, ADAM [AVROM DOV-BER MIKHALISHKER] HAKOYHEYN BEN KHAYIM. "Yisroyn leodom." Subtextual commentary in Yehudo Leyb Ben-Zeeyv, *Seyfer talmud loshoyn ivri.* Vilna: Romm, 1874

LEIBEL, DANIEL. "On Ashkenazic Stress." In U. Weinreich 1965b: 63–72.

LEVUSH [MORDEKHAY YAFE]. *Levush ho'oyro.* Prague, 1603

LIFSHITZ, KHAYIM BEN MOYSHE. *Seyfer derekh khayim.* Sulzbach: Aharon ben Uri Lipman, 1703

MAHARAL OF PRAGUE [YUDO LEYB BEN BETSALEL]. *Seyfer tiferes yisroel.* Venice: Daniel Zanetti, 1599

MAHARIL (YANKEV MOLIN/MÖLIN). *Seyfer sheeloys utshuvoys khibrom hagooyn hamuflog reysh gluso moyreynu horav rav Yaakoyv Segal tehey nishmosoy tsruro bitsroyr hakhayim omeyn keyn yehi rotsoyn.* Cremona: Vincenzo Conti, 1556

MORAG, SHELOMO. "Pronunciations of Hebrew." In *Encyclopaedia Judaica* 13 (1971): 1120–45. Jerusalem and New York: Keter & Macmillan.

NIGER, SH., ed. *Der pinkes. Yorbukh far der geshikhte fun der yidisher literatur un shprakh, far folklor, kritik un biblyografye.* Vol. 1 [No more published]. Vilna: B. A. Kletskin, 1913

NOBLE, SHLOYME. "Yidish in a hebreyishn levush." In Bikl and Lehrer 1958: 158–75.

PHILIPP, K. *Lachoudisch, Geheimsprache Schopflochs.* Dinkelsbühl: C. W. Wenng KG, 1983

REIF, STEFAN C. *Shabbethai Sofer and His Prayer-book,* Cambridge: Cambridge University Press, 1979.

REUCHLIN, JOHANN. *De rudimentis Hebraicis.* Pforzheim: Thom. Anselm, 1506

SCHREINER, MARTIN. "Zur Geschichte der Aussprache des Hebräischen." *Zeitschrift für die alttestamentliche Wissenschaft* 6 (1886): 213–59.

SEGAL, MOSHE TSVI. *Yesodey hafonetika haivrit. Khakira bahibaron haivri vetoledotav.* Jerusalem: J. Junovitch, 1928. (1928a)

———. "Letoledot hamivta shel hakamats." *Leshonenu* 1 (1928): 33–39. 1928b

SHTIF, NOKHEM. "Mikhael Adams dray yidishe bikher." *Filologishe shriftn* 2 (1928): 135–68.

SHY, HADASSAH. "Reshtlakh fun yidish in shopflokh." *Oksforder yidish* 1 (1990): 333–55.

STENCL, AVROM-NOKHEM. Taped interview, Whitechapel, 10 November, 1978

TIMM, ERIKA. *Graphische und phonische Struktur des Westjiddischen unter besonderer Berücksichtigung der Zeit um 1600.* Tübingen: Max Niemeyer, 1987

TSHEMERINSKI, KH. "Di yidishe fonetik." In Sh. Niger 1913: 47–71.

VEYNGER, M. "Hebreyishe klangen in der yidisher shprakh." In Sh. Niger 1913: 79–84.

———. *Yidishe dyalektologye.* Minsk: Vaysrusisher melukhe-farlag, 1929.

WEINREICH, MAX "Prehistory and Early History of Yiddish: Facts and Conceptual Framework." In U. Weinreich 1954: 73–101.

———. "Bney hes un bney khes in ashkenaz: di problem un vos zi lozt undz hern." In Bikl and Lehrer 1958: 101–23.

———. "Di sistem yidishe kadmen-vokaln." *Yidishe shprakh* 20 (1960): 65–71.

———. "Reshit hahavara haashkenazit bezikata lebeayot kerovot shel hayidish veshel haivrit haashkenazit." *Leshonenu* 27–28 (1963–64): 131–47, 230–51, 318–39.

———. *Geshikhte fun der yidisher shprakh. Bagrifn, faktn, metodn.* 4 vols. New York: Yivo, 1973.
WEINREICH, URIEL. "*Sábesdiker losn* in Yiddish: a Problem of Linguistic Affinity." *Word* 8 (1952): 360–77.
———. Ed. *The Field of Yiddish. Studies in Yiddish Language, Folklore, and Literature* 1. Publications of the Linguistic Circle of New York, 3. New York: Linguistic Circle of New York, Columbia University, 1954.
———. "A Retrograde Sound Shift in the Guise of a Survival." In Catalán 1958: 221–67.
———. "Haivrit haashkenazit vehaivrit shebeyidish. Bekhinatan hageografit." *Leshonenu* 24 (1959): 242–52, 25 (1960–61): 57–80, 180–96. Republished in book form as U. Weinreich 1965a.
———. "Western Traits in Transcarpathian Yiddish." In Dawidowicz et al. 1964: 245–64.
———. *Haivrit haashkenazit vehaivrit shebeyidish. Bekhinatan hageografit.* Jerusalem: 1965. (1965a).
———. Ed. *The Field of Yiddish. Studies in Language, Folklore, and Literature. Second Collection.* The Hague: Mouton, 1965. (1965b).
WERSES, SHMUEL, NATAN ROTENSTREICH, and CHONE SHMERUK, eds. *Sefer Dov Sadan,* Tel Aviv: Hakibuts hameukhad, 1977.
WESSELY, NAPHTALI HARTWIG [VIZL, NAFTOLI HIRTS]. *Mikhtovim shoynim* and [in Latin type] *Michtowim*. Vienna: Anton Edlen v. Schmid, 1827.
YALON, H. "Sheviley mivtaim." *Kuntresim leinyaney halashon haivrit* 1 (1937–1938): 62–78.
———. "Hagiya sefaradit betsarefat hatsefonit bedoro shel Rashi uvedorot sheleakharav." *Inyaney lashon* 1 (1942): 16–31.
YEKHIEL-MIKHL EPSHTEYN. *Seyder tfilo derekh yeshoro.* Frankfurt: 1697.
———. *Seyder tfilo derekh yeshoro.* Frankfurt: Johann Kellner, 1714.
YEKUSIEL HAKOYHEYN BEN YEHUDO. MS British Library Add. 19,776 [= Margoliouth 1899: no. 80]. (1395)
ZIMMELS, H. J. *Ashkenazim and Sephardim. Their Relations, Differences, and Problems as Reflected in the Rabbinical Responsa.* London: Oxford University Press, 1958
ZUNZ, [LEOPOLD]. *Zur Geschichte und Literatur,* I. Berlin: Veit und Comp, 1845

Acknowledgments

In preparing this paper, I was generously assisted by the following, none of whom bear responsibility for the contents: Marion Aptroot (Queen Mary and Westfield College, London), Joseph Bar-El (Bar-Ilan University), Majer Bogdanski (London), David Djanogly (London), Lewis Glinert (School of Oriental and African Studies, London), Shmuel Hiley (London), Brad Sabin Hill (British Library, London), Richard Judd (Bodleian Library, Oxford), Dov-Ber Kerler (Oxford Centre for Postgraduate Hebrew Studies), Israel Dov Lerner (Board of Jewish Education, New York), the late I. A. Lisky (London), George Mandel (OCPHS), David Patterson (OCPHS), S. S. Prawer (Queen's College, Oxford), Moyshe-Nosn Rosenfeld (London), Jerry Schwarzbard (Jewish Theological Seminary of America), Nick Thomas (Oxford), Jonathan Webber (OCPHS), Marie Wright (OCPHS), Herbert Zafren (Hebrew Union College, Cincinnati).

5

Confronting the Hebrew of Responsa: Intensifiers in the Syntax of Rabbi Me'ir of Rothenburg

MENAHEM ZEVI KADDARI

It is a sad fact of life that our linguistic picture of written Hebrew as used across large expanses of Jewish history is seriously wanting. In fact, the language of Hebrew texts for the time-span between talmudic times and our own has scarcely been explored. Commonly referred to as "medieval Hebrew," it gives a general impression of little shape or form. We may sense that it is quite rich and variegated, and we learn selectively about a few of its characteristics; of others we have never yet had the faintest of intimations.

We wish to dwell here on one special medieval genre, the "rabbinic responsum," and on appropriate avenues of linguistic research, with particular reference to the responsa of Rabbi Me'ir ("Maharam") of Rothenburg, a leading spiritual light of thirteenth-century Ashkenazi Jewry, whose writings had a decisive influence on subsequent generations[1] and whose language may be assumed to have left its mark too on successive generations of disciples.

After first delineating the language of responsa and examining previous descriptions, we shall proceed to offer a model of this form of Hebrew and then examine the syntax and semantics of one particular sublanguage, the "intensifier," concluding with some thoughts on the evolutionary ("diachronic") description of Hebrew.

Delineating the Field: The Hebrew of the Responsa

We are faced with a language that has served as a written medium and continues to do so as a special register of contemporary Hebrew. To delineate it and distinguish it from other varieties of Hebrew, preceding it or contemporaneous, will involve identifying the literature written in it, the "responsa"—a special branch of rabbinic literature. This literature dates from the Geonic period (mainly the ninth to eleventh centuries) up until the present, and is to be located in any and every center of Jewish culture, from Babylonia to the United States and from Northern Europe to the Yemen. The precise character of this literature, its content and evolution, has

Confronting the Hebrew of Responsa 89

been well documented in research on Hebrew literature and Jewish history—a point of reference outside the study of language proper.

While literary and historical descriptions have had a fair amount to say on the language of responsa, this has been limited to impressions and generalities, such as terms like "rabbinic Hebrew," or "halakhic Hebrew."[2]

If one seeks to go beyond such descriptions, one must look to a systematic presentation of the language using the methods of modern linguistics. Such descriptions will, it is to be hoped, entitle us to treat the language of the special responsum literature as a language variety sui generis.

Previous Characterizations of Responsa Hebrew

Among existing characterizations of responsa Hebrew, certain details stand out: such Hebrew is a continuation of mishnaic Hebrew and regularly indistinguishable from it; it contains Aramaic elements (particularly from the Babylonian Talmud) set within Hebrew sentences, with no clear boundary marker between the two; it gives special place to biblicisms, particularly in its phraseology (referred to sometimes as "rabbinic *melitzah*," i.e., preciosity); it is sometimes also portrayed as tending to neutralize gender and number (and definiteness) agreement within the sentence or between words that would historically have agreed.

These and other generalizations like them confront the analyst of responsa Hebrew with an immediate task: to subject any such characterization to broad and thoroughgoing examination. By way of example, let me take up the claim that responsa Hebrew is the direct continuation of mishnaic Hebrew and hard to distinguish from it. We shall select a number of adverbial phrases originating in mishnaic Hebrew and frequently found in responsa: *mi-kol makom, kol kakh, harbeh yoter* הרבה יותר, כל כך, מכל מקום.[3]

True though it is that these phrases have their origin in mishnaic Hebrew, there is a gulf between their syntactic behavior in mishnaic Hebrew and their use in responsa literature.

(A) *mi-kol makom* מכל מקום "in any case" in mishnaic Hebrew is an adverb of generalization, which always comes after the item it qualifies (a quotation from Scripture or Mishnah), e.g., מי שיש לו אח מכל מקום (*mi she-yesh lo aḥ mi-kol makom*, "he who has a brother on any side." Mishnah Yevamot 2,5, referring to Deut. 25:5). However, in responsa Hebrew it is a concessive expression "nevertheless," introducing the apodosis of the concessive construction, e.g., אע"ג [אף על גב] דאינו כשר לכתחילה ... מ"מ [מכל מקום] לא גרע מכתב ידו (*af al gav de-eyno kasher lekhatehilah . . . mi-kol makom lo gara mi-ketav yado* "although it is not proper from the outset . . . nevertheless it should not count less than his handwriting," Responsum of R. Yizḥaq bar Sheshat).

(B) Mishnaic *kol kakh* כל כך "all that" is an anaphoric noun phrase used in the questions *kol kakh lama?* כל כך למה? and *kol kakh be-yadekha?* כל כך בידיך? harking back in to a preceding statement, e.g., ... אומרים הין ... אומרים הין ... כל כך למה? מפני הביתוסים ... (*omrim hin . . . omrim hin . . . kol kakh lama? mipenei ha-baitusim . . .*, ". . . they say, 'Yes' . . . they say, 'Yes' . . . Why [are they saying] all that? Because of the Boetians . . ." Mishnah Menaḥot 10,3). However, in responsa Hebrew it is an intensifier "so," sometimes preceding the word it qualifies, e.g., מאחר שהמקום אינו רחוק כל כך (*me'aḥar she-ha-makom eyno raḥok kol-kakh,* "since the place is not so distant." Responsum of R. Yosef Kolon).

(C) Late mishnaic (midrashic) *harbeh yoter* הרבה יותר "much more" is made up of the gradating *yoter* יותר qualified by *harbeh* הרבה, e.g., ארץ ישראל שהפסולת שבה משובח חרבה [,] יותר מארץ מצרים (*eretz yisra'el she-ha-pesolet she-bah meshubaḥ harbeh* [,] *yoter me-eretz mitzrayim,* "The Land of Israel, whose low-grade land is excellent, much more than the Land of Egypt." Tanhuma, Warsaw 1875, Shelaḥ 68a). However, in rabbinic Hebrew it is widespread as a quantifier intensified by *harbeh* הרבה, e.g., קונה אותה כשהוא מוצאה בהרבה יותר מדמיו . . . (*koneh otah keshe-hu motze'ah be-harbeh yoter mi-damav,* "He buys it when he can find it, [even] at much more than its value." Rashi on Talmud Bavli, Bava Kama 58b).

Sometimes the shift in the uses of these phrases has already begun in the language of the Gemara; in other cases, it begins only in the language traditions of medieval times, as demonstrated by relatively ancient manuscripts.[4] What such checks reveal is that there is no room for regarding responsa Hebrew as a mere continuation of mishnaic Hebrew, but rather as a language variety in its own right—which warrants separate description. There is similar room for appropriate research to verify the other prelinguistic labels cavalierly given to responsa Hebrew. One might mention here the prevailing view concerning "rabbinic *melitzah*" (preciosity) and its presumed preponderance of biblicisms (to which might be added an equal preponderance of Aramaic and Hebrew talmudisms). It would appear that this linguistic (stylistic) feature can be approached using a criterion of measurement that can make or break the vague claim of "melitzah."

Research along these lines has indeed already appeared: consecutive questioning of a computerized database can yield a distinction between various degrees of adherence to an ancient linguistic source, thereby absolving us of the need to use the catch-all epithet "melitzah."[5]

Researching the Language of the Responsa

The study of the language of the responsa is not an entirely new field, but thoroughgoing discussion has thus far centered on lexical investigations, on the semantic-pragmatic aspects of lexical and phrasal usage, and on some etymologies (such as in loan words and calques from other languages).[6] We wish to point here to the need for a description of language structure in terms of its morphology and syntax, as against its lexicon.[7] Given the paucity of systematic linguistic studies of medieval Hebrew authors,[8] the morphology and syntax of responsa Hebrew is sorely in need of description (this being the dominant language variety throughout the whole of medieval rabbinic writing).

Anyone describing the language of the responsa has at his disposal a powerful tool: a database of hundreds of responsa collections from a variety of times and places (totalling some sixty million words as of 1989), fed into the computer by the Responsa Project of Bar-Ilan University.[9] This database can supply concordances of words and phrases as required for the description of phenomena in the morphological and syntactic system. One must of course also construct the smart and detailed software for retrieving the necessary data from this vast database in such a way that the data will not encumber the researcher.[10] When checking the adverbial phrase *mi-kol makom* מכל מקום, we called up texts featuring this phrase in proximity to one of the phrases *af al pi (she-)* (-אף-על-פי (ש,[11] *af (she-)* (-אף (ש, *hagam (she-)* (-הגם (ש and their ilk (at up to twenty words' remove in either direction), and it was in this way that we found the evidence for the concessive use of *mi-kol makom* מכל מקום; in another check, we called up *nitpa'al* verb forms in proximity to *ein* אין or *hayah* היה, so as to collect *nitpa'al* forms that might be in the participial form. There are many as yet unexplored linguistic questions to which we now have open access by thus gathering data and seeking morphological and syntactic regularities in responsa Hebrew—and these questions deserve to be asked. Here, then, is a serious field of inquiry.[12]

In all of this, the goal is something that goes beyond mere comparison with previous varieties of Hebrew. To be able to give a true picture of the language of this vast literature, even a methodological model of the kind just outlined will not suffice. One will have to weigh up the fundamental advantages of the various methods of linguistic description: is statistic sampling or selection by periods the best or, instead, a mixed method? The main thing is a descriptive method that can uncover the full facts. And the work must not be postponed until such time as we have fuller documentation or until manuscripts or maybe autographs are available. It goes without saying that the task of tackling each linguistic domain here will be a lengthy one; the sooner one starts, the better.

One undertaking recently completed deserves a mention here: the choice of the responsa of the Haskalah period (of the nineteenth century) for a description of aspects of its grammar.[13] In choosing this well-defined genre, which is not restricted to one author, the analyst is automatically confronted by quesions that go beyond the study of an individual author's language. This may appear to be a case of hubris, given that there is not one single previous description—but one has to start somewhere.

Subvarieties of Responsa Hebrew

Are we entitled to view the Hebrew of the responsa as a uniform variety, for all that it extends across Asia, Africa, Europe and America and from the tenth century to the present? Methodologically, despite our anticipated results, it should probably be regarded a priori as a single variety, sparing us from setting up an array of subsystems. In other words, whatever comes up in the responsa concordance is fair game for an all-inclusive description of whichever phenomena we chose to study. Only then can we look at the results—and if these automatically divide up into periods and/or places, we will be entitled to pursue our description by subsystems.

Let me illustrate this working method with results from my study of adverbial phrases: In the initial study of *mi-kol makom* מכל מקום and *be-khol zot* בכל זאת, for example's sake, the concordance generated by the computer database presented a uniform picture: an apparent continuation of mishnaic or biblical usage. But closer inspection of the citations and the way these phrases were employed yielded subdivisions within the responsa.

Once one assembles a number of distinctive features of language subvarieties according to the geographical provenance of the author, one has the "isoglosses" for the subvarieties of responsa Hebrew, amounting to quasi-dialects. Checks carried out so far on these texts raise the prospect of distinguishing the responsa Hebrew of Ashkenaz from that of Sepharad (Spain and the Orient). The distinctive features that stand out are these: for Ashkenazi responsa, a furtherance of the linguistic features of late mishnaic Hebrew; and for Sephardi responsa, a close adherence to a biblical phraseology. Support for this dichotomy comes from checks on other, randomly chosen expressions, such as *le'et atah, lefi sh'ah, mah me'od* מה מאד, לפי שעה, לעת עתה and similar.[14]

However, these provisional conclusions made use of preliminary divisions and classifications fed into the database and based on conventional academic wisdom about the various authors. By this classification, the analyst receives an initial off-the-peg anthology of responsa material according to period (the so-called *Rishonim,* from the tenth to the fifteenth century, the period of the *Shulḥan Arukh,* i.e., the sixteenth century, and the so-called *Aḥaronim,* from the seventeenth and eighteenth century up to the present). And the *Rishonim* period comes with a ready-made geographical division: Sepharad vs. Ashkenaz. As these subdivisions are strictly preliminary, and not content-sensitive, the provisional results must be seen as tentative.

Since the study of the Halakhah and history of the *Rishonim* period has recently thrown up subdistinctions within *Rishonim* literature, we possess finer ideas for a classification by time, place, and school[15] than is so far present in the database. A new improved program is thus an obvious consideration.

We shall seek answers from the data to the questions on our linguistic agenda by a four-way division of *Rishonim:* Sepharad under Islam (mid-tenth to mid-twelfth century), Sepharad in Christendom (end of twelfth to thirteenth and fourteenth century), Provence (eleventh to thirteenth century), and northern France and Germany (eleventh to fourteenth century).[16]

To make these distinctions meaningful, the database has to be fed further sources from all subperiods and subregions established by extralinguistic research. As the database does not yet contain material on the necessary scale, a more limited and evidently simpler goal would be to computerize responsa of particular periods as part of the retrieval system.

The next step should thus be to bolster the dialectological data on rabbinic Hebrew, even going beyond responsa and selecting works according to place and period—given that linguistic phenomena clearly belonging to some subsystem will not be a matter of a specific literary genre, while the first phenomena to be examined may be those already used for the initial dialect classification. Examples of literary genres are biographies, historiography, regulations, and communal records.

To organize the data into quasi-dialectal language maps, with the optimum isoglosses, we will need to delineate very sharply the dates and places of the authors being used. A particular generation of authors may turn out to be a convenient basis for distinguishing different dialects of written Hebrew.[17]

Semantic Fields

Establishing the syntactic and lexical facts is more than just a matter of recording particular data in isolation. One may seek to organize them into semantic fields, with a view to revealing the pattern of relations between one element in the field and another. Once set up for the various sublanguages, such fields lend themselves to comparison and contrast. Changes in a language can also be detected; we are thus, in fact, fashioning a sensitive tool for diachronic Hebrew research whose day will come (see below).

The semantic field we shall take to illustrate this method of investigation is the field of adverbs known as intensifiers, such as *me'od* מאד and its like. Being already in possession of this field for biblical and mishnaic Hebrew,[18] we can begin analysis for responsa Hebrew with the question of whether, say, the responsa of Early Ashkenaz were closest to biblical, mishnaic, or Babylonian Talmud usage. Were they perhaps altogether very different?

The writings selected to test this field were the responsa of Rabbi Me'ir ("Maharam") of Rothenburg.[19] We first called up from the responsa database for *Rishonim* of Ashkenaz—in line with the preliminary classification derived from historians' research—all intensifiers qualifying past tense verbs.[20] At that stage, we found the following intensifiers, in descending order of frequency: *me'od* מאד (10),[21] *beyoter* ביותר (4), *kol kakh* כל כך (3), *yoter mi-dai* יותר מדאי (3), *yafeh* יפה (3), *harbeh* הרבה (2), *yafeh yafeh* יפה יפה (1), *me'od me'od* מאד מאד (1), and in quasi-citations *hetev* היטב (3), *mah* מה (2), *kamah* כמה (1).

No occurrences were found of the biblical intensifier *yoter* יותר, mishnaic *le-ahat* לאחת, or the Babylonian talmudic forms *ad le-ahat* עד לאחת (Hebrew) and *tuva* טובא (Aramaic). Note too that we have not yet explored the intensifiers in Eretz-Israel talmudic Hebrew (i.e., in the Jerusalem Talmud and contemporary Midrashim).

Summarizing the details: *me'od* מאד intensifies verbs denoting mental processes and qualities (*ka'as, harah le, hikpid, yakhol lematek* יכול למתק, הקפיד, חרה ל-, כעס), deadjectival verbs (*yisge* ישגא quoted from Job 8:7), predicative adjectives (*katan, tzarikh le, kasheh* קשה, צריך ל-, קטן), a predicative quantifier (*harbeh* הרבה); the word order is NUCLEUS followed by *me'od* מאד, but see *me'od me'od* מאד מאד.

Beyoter ביותר as an intensifier[22] comes with a predicative adjective (*geru'ah mi-perutzah beyoter* גרועה מפרוצה ביותר "much worse than a whore," *tovah mi-perutzah beyoter* טובה מפרוצה ביותר "much better than a whore," *milta de-lo shekhihah beyoter* מלתא דלא שכיחה ביותר "a thing that is not very common") or an attributive adjective (*ela le-divrei kerovav beyoter . . .* אלא לדברי קרוביו ביותר "only to his very close relatives") and not with a verb.

Kol kakh כל כך as an intensifier comes with a verb denoting a mental process or action or a predicative adjective (always negative: *lo iyannu kol kakh* לא עיינו כל כך "we have not considered it so much," *eynam tzerikhim kol kakh* אינם צריכים כל כך "they do not need it so much," *eyn lah tzorekh gadol kol kakh* אין לה צורך גדול כל כך "she does not have so great a need"). The normal word order is NUCLEUS + INTENSIFIER, but the reverse can be found. An entirely different, and frequent, use of *kol kakh* כל כך is as a pronoun: *eyn lo kol kakh* אין לו כל כך "He does not have so much" [i.e., so great an amount].

Yoter mi-dai יותר מדאי intensifies a verb with mental-spiritual connections (*lehaḥmir aleyhem yoter mi-dai* להחמיר עליהם יותר מדאי "to be too stringent with them"), a predicative adjective (*im yesh lo shnei sarbalim eḥad yafeh yoter mi-dai* אם יש לו ב׳ סרבלים אחד יפה יותר מדאי "if he has two mantles, one of them too beautiful"), and a noun implying a qualitative adjective (*ani noten lekha sekhirut yoter mi-dai*> *sekhirut yafah, tovah, merubah* אני נותן לך שכירות יותר מדאי <שכירות יפה, טובה , מרובה "I am going to pay you a very good rent").

Yafeh יפה as an intensifier comes with mental verbs (replacing biblical *hetev* היטב)—the phrases found are: *lo dikdaktem yafeh* לא דקדקתם יפה "you did not scrutinize it thoroughly," *timtza mevo'ar yafeh* תמצא מבואר יפה "you will find it well explained"—and verbs of physical activity: *she-lo teda lekaneaḥ yafe* שלא תדע לקנח יפה "because she would not be able to wipe it off thoroughly."

Harbeh הרבה intensifies following a mental verb: *ve-dikdakti sham harbeh* ודקדקתי שם הרבה "and I have thoroughly scrutinized it," *ve-tamahti harbeh al ha-davar* ותמהתי הרבה על הדבר "and I have been greatly puzzling over the matter."

Yafeh yafeh יפה יפה intensifies a verb of physical activity: *tekaneaḥ yafeh yafeh* תקנח יפה יפה "she would wipe it off very thoroughly."

Me'od me'od מאד מאד apparently appears only in a question rather than a responsum, and only as a biblical imitation[23] (with word order inverted): *ḥasid me'od me'od na'alah* חסיד מאד מאד נעלה "the highly, highly venerated pious man."

The intensifiers *hetev, mah, kamah* כמה , מה ,היטב were only found in citations or quasi-citations.

It emerges that the Hebrew of Maharam of Rothenburg features intensifiers from the Bible (*me'od, me'od me'od, harbeh, hetev, mah* מאד מאד מאד, הרבה, מה, היטב); from mishnaic Hebrew (*beyoter, yoter mi-dai, yafeh* ביותר, יותר מדאי, יפה); and also from Babylonian Talmudic Hebrew (*kol kakh (yafeh, yoter mi-dai), yafeh yafeh* יפה יפה),[24] יפה, יותר מדאי, (כל כך). The numbers for each group, respectively, are 18, 11, and 4. The small number makes it hard to talk of preferences or linguistic similarities. The major novelty is the co-occurrence of intensifiers from different sources—though the similarity to biblical Hebrew by way of imitation is growing.

Another study revealed that it was not just the combination of various sources that was new but also the types of words being intensified. With *me'od* מאד, for instance, Maharam of Rothenburg preferred just some of the options provided in the Bible: mental verbs (cf. *vayiḥar lekayin me'od* ויחר לקין מאד "and Cain was very angry," Gen. 4:5, *vayir'u ha-anashim me'od* וייראו האנשים מאד "and the men were very afraid," Gen. 20:8), adjectives, and quantifiers. Such selectivity is also at work with the intensifiers *kol kakh, yoter mi-dai, yafeh* יפה, יותר מדאי, כל כך. The upshot is that the verbs with which Maharam of Rothenburg uses an intensifier denote primarily processes and activities of the mind.[25]

For another angle, we can look at the relative weight of the intensifiers: close to half of Maharam's intensifier use involves biblical *me'od* מאד (31%) and talmudic[26] *beyoter* ביותר (12%), which makes him quite different from his sources.[27]

Out of this comes a diachronic hypothesis about a Hebrew semantic field. The biblical field of intensifiers, a homogeneous one dominated by just two intensifiers (one accounting for 84% of occurrences), gradually gains heterogeneity: mishnaic Hebrew has three main intensifiers, the most dominant accounting for 46%, whereas in Babylonian talmudic Hebrew the most dominant reaches just 30%. More heterogeneous still are the intensifiers of Maharam of Rothenburg: the most dominant (not the same one as in the Talmud) reaches 31%, but the combined weight of all the intensifiers of any real frequency is still a mere 43%.

The Diachronic Angle

Diachronic description rests largely on comparison: comparison of synchronic descriptions will show up changes over time. Even comparing contemporaneous states of language can tell us about change—along geographical or sociocultural axes.

The language of the responsa invites such comparisons, and a combination of both geographical and sociocultural data can be incorporated into analyses of later synchronic states of language. Change can be explained—along either (perhaps both) of two lines: (a) internal evolution of preexisting forces, (b) external linguistic influences. Internal evolution is liable to provide acceptable explanations; for example, Maharam of Rothenburg can be seen as reshaping his field of intensifiers out of a combination of intensifiers inherited from the biblical, mishnaic, and talmudic Hebrew of his literary sources—but highlighting certain latent features in these sources through his preoccupation with a certain aspect of life (mental processes and activities).

Influence from other languages is often highly conjectural. Sometimes, to be sure, the facts speak for themselves: the auxiliary *hayah* היה combined with a further past tense verb may crop up in responsa influenced by Arabic,[28] as will such expressions as *min ha-nimna, lavash tzurah* לבש צורה, מן הנמנע, while *sitra aḥara, bidḥilu u-rḥimu* בדחילו ורחימו, סיטרא אחרא will appear in texts of Spanish or ex-Spanish scholars privy to the Zohar and the beginnings of Kabbalah.[29] But one cannot always be sure which language was involved. What can we say for sure about the source of the syntactic pattern NOUN PHRASE + *hu* הוא + ADJECTIVE (such as *ha-rimonim hem adumim* הרמונים הם אדומים)? What is plain is that this pattern is not inherited from the Bible or Mishnah. It may be Romance, or Germanic, or Slavic in origin, and we shall have to leave it at that; but stimulating comparative research remains to be done.

Notes

1. See Urbach 1980: 521–70.
2. See Goldenberg 1971; 1636f.; 1974: 650.
3. Selecting these phrases allows us to display the results of the detailed description due to appear in full in Kaddari (1991).
4. The full material appears in Kaddari (1991).
5. See Albeck 1987.
6. See Edelberg 1969, Gilon 1984, Halperin 1947, Nobel 1959.
7. See Glinert 1990 on the grammatical usage of Ibn Ezra.

8. Such as Rabin 1945 on the language of Rabbi Avraham bar Hiyya and Kogut 1973 on *Sefer Hasidim.*

9. Choueka (personal communication).

10. In assembling the forms of the verb system, for instance, the most efficient method may be to select the frequent verbs (plus inflexions) in responsa Hebrew rather than to call up all verbs beginning with the affix ת.

11. In these phrases -ש is bracketed because of the present technical impossibility of calling up one-letter strings.

12. Unavoidably, current descriptive work on responsa Hebrew is based on the common printed editions that have been fed into the computer. Concordances as well as broader contextual reading of the texts rest upon such printed editions. (Full biobibliographical data on the works and their authors are available from the computer. Verification and control checks were carried out on copies of the works in the Responsa Project Library.) As linguists lack a suitable collection of manuscript (and particularly autograph) data of responsa texts—though a start has been made among historians—bibliographical research will have to be encouraged in this virgin territory. The very presence of a manuscript text alongside a printed version can stimulate comparison with reference to questions arising in linguistic analysis. The same obtains, for instance, in the field of Midrash: the text of the Theodor-Albeck edition of Bereshit Rabba rubs shoulders in the database with the Vilna printed text. Naturally, such a dual database will encourage the creation or use of software for the computer to do the comparing itself.

These computer-based differences will be important to the linguistic description provided due regard is paid to the minutiae of morphology and syntax (such as distinctions between prepositions within the preposition phrase, word order variation within a construction, or sentence order within a discourse). The work involves special methodological difficulties. A tentative inference from this research, still in full swing, is the need for full synchronic studies of each author in the database. We must for the moment leave comparisons and historical conclusions for the next stage in the work: we must first lay the basis for as complete a description as possible of the language of major authors from each period of importance to this genre. The full description will embrace morphology and syntax, followed by the lexicology of that author. To get from such a question to a synchronic description of responsa texts of various periods is no easy task. Urgently required is a model, a kind of working plan, to guide linguists in their choice of descriptive base (random sample or corpus), in focusing their mind on the various domains of linguistic description, and in presenting the key phenomena—all this to ensure that we derive as instructive and cohesive a picture as possible from the work that is done.

13. Bezer (1990) has addressed this theme, encompassing the verbal and pronominal systems.

14. See Kaddari (1991).

15. See, for example, Soloveitchik 1987.

16. Before even performing this reexamination, one can detect an answer to one difficulty: why does the language of Nachmanides provide such a striking deviation from the practice of Spanish scholars in its use of *mi-kol makom* מכל מקום?

17. This explains the proposal to establish a descriptive corpus of selected linguistic phenomena from responsa of Haskalah times (see note 13). There is similar justification for exploring a particular feature of responsa of the *Rishonim* period (tenth to thirteenth century). See below.

18. The Bible has the following intensifiers (not in order of frequency): *me'od, me'od me'od, mah, hetev, yoter, harbeh, kamah* כמה, הרבה, יותר, היטב, מה, מאד מאד, מאד. Mishnaic Hebrew has: *yoter mi-dai, me'od me'od, mah, beyoter, le-aḥat* מדי יותר מאד מאד, מה, ביותר,

לאחת. Babylonian talmudic Hebrew has: *yafeh yafeh, beyoter, kol kakh, yoter mi-dai, yafeh, hetev, me'od, le-aḥat* לאחת, מאד, היטב, יפה, יותר מדאי, כל כך, ביותר, יפה יפה.

19. The database was fed Moshe Arye Bloch's edition, part 4 (Budapest 1895), based on the Prague printed edition.

20. Since we were dealing with a short time span, filtering was able to wait until the computer had supplied the data.

21. This figure includes two examples with the verg *saga* שגא based on Job 8:7.

22. "As an intensifier" implies that the expression acting as intensifier appeared in other senses too.

23. This is not a real citation, as the biblical word being intensified is a verb (*me'od na'alah* מאד נעלה, Ps. 47:10), whereas in the responsum we have an attributive adjective (*ḥasid me'od me'od na'aleh* חסיד מאד מאד נעלה).

24. *Yafeh* יפה and *yoter mi-dai* יותר מדאי are found in both mishnaic and talmudic sources.

25. Only *yafeh* יפה and *yafeh yafeh* יפה יפה come with a "physical" verb (*tekaneaḥ* תקנח); the stative verb *shagah* שגה comes twice with *me'od* מאד (following Job 8:7).

26. This is a relatively widespread intensifier in the Babylonian Talmud (25% of intensifiers), but much less so in mishnaic Hebrew (7%).

27. However, a handful of intensifiers does not almost sweep the board, unlike biblical Hebrew (*me'od* מאד 84%, *mah* מה 11%: total 95%) or mishnaic Hebrew (*kamah* כמה 46%, *yafeh* יפה 20%, *yoter mi-dai* יותר מדאי 10%: total 76%). Individual intensifiers in the Babylonian Talmud are not preponderant to any such degree (*yoter mi-dai* יותר מדאי 27%, *beyoter* ביותר 25%, *yafeh yafeh* יפה יפה 30%).

28. See Kaddari 1980.

29. See Kaddari 1985.

References

ALBECK, ORLI. "Shibutz u-Makor: Hatza'ah le-Nisuaḥ Formali" (Inclusion and Source: A Proposal for Formal Formulation). *Hebrew Computational Linguistics* 25 (1987): 7–18.

BEZER, ZVI. "Morphology of the Verb and Pronoun in 18th Century Responsa Hebrew." Ph.D. diss. Bar-Ilan, 1990 (Hebrew with English summary).

EDELBERG, S. "Lashon ve-Haba'ah be-Sifrut ha-She'elot u-Teshuvot" (Language and Expression in the Responsa Literature). *Leshonenu La'am* 20 (1969): 120–27.

ELDAR, ILAN. *Masoret ha-Keri'ah ha-Kedam-Ashkenazit: Mahuta ve-ha-Yesodot ha-Meshutafim La u-le-Masoret Sefarad (The Hebrew Language Tradition in Medieval Ashkenaz, ca. 950–1350 C.E.).* 2 vols Jerusalem: Hebrew University Language Traditions Project, 1979.

GILON, M. "'Ro'eh ha-Ḥeshbon': Ha-Mevaker be-Ma'arkhot ha-Shilton ha-Yehudi ha-Penimi, Gilgulav shel Munaḥ Ivri" ('Ro'eh ha-Heshbon': The Revisor in Jewish Self-Government, the History of a Hebrew Term). *Iyyunim be-Vikoret ha-Medinah* 38 (1984): 1–28.

GLINERT, LEWIS H. "Did Pre-Revival Hebrew Literature Have Its Own *Langue?* Quotation and Improvization in Mendele Mokher Sefarim." *Bulletin of the School of Oriental and African Studies* 51 (1988): 413–27.

———. "The Unknown Grammar of Abraham Ibn Ezra: Syntactic Features of *Yesod Diqduq*," in F. Diaz Esteban, ed. *Proceedings of the International Symposium on*

Abraham ibn Ezra and his Age. Madrid: Asociación Española de Orientalistas, 1990, pp. 129–36.
GOLDENBERG, ESTHER. "Medieval Hebrew." *Encyclopedia Judaica* 16 (1971): 1636–42.
———. "Ivrit Rabbanit" (Rabbinic Hebrew). In the entry "Ivrit, Lashon." *Entziklopedyah Ivrit (Hebrew Encyclopedia)* 26 (1974): 648–51.
GROSSMAN, AVRAHAM. *Ḥakhmei Ashkenaz ha-Rishonim (The Early Sages of Ashkenaz).* Jerusalem: Magnes, 1981.
HALPERIN, Y. "Leket Milim mi-Teḥum ha-Tarbut shel Yahadut Ashkenaz" (Collected Words from the Domain of Ashkenaz Jewish Culture). *Leshonenu* 15 (1947): 190–97.
KADDARI, M. Z. "Homonimyah u-Polisemyah be-Tzurot Nitpa'al bi-Leshon Sifrut ha-Shut" (Homonymy and Polysemy in the *nitpa'al* in Responsa Hebrew). *Bar-Ilan Annual* 18–19 (1980): 233–47.
———. "Leshon ha-Kabbalah ve-ha-Meḥkar ve-Hashpa'ata al ha-Ivrit ha-Modernit" (The Language of Kabbala and Research and its Influence on Modern Hebrew). In Menahem Zohari et al., eds. *Ummah ve-Lashon* (Nation and Language: Studies in Memory of Prof. Aryeh Tartakower). Jerusalem: Brit Ivrit Olamit, 1985, pp. 371–76.
———. *Iyyunim ba-Taḥbir u-va-Semantikah shel ha-Ivrit she-Le'aḥar ha-Mikra (Studies in Postbiblical Hebrew Syntax and Semantics).* Bar-Ilan: University of Bar-Ilan Press, 1991.
KAHANA, Y. Z. "La-Leksikografyah be-Sifrut ha-Teshuvot" (On Lexicography in the Responsa Literature). *Leshonenu* 13 (1947–48): 46–50.
KOGUT, S. "Ha-Mishpat ha-Murkav be-'Sefer Ḥasidim'" (The Complex Clause in Sefer Hasidim). Ph.D. diss. Hebrew University of Jerusalem, 1976.
———. "Shimushim Miloniyim ba-Ivrit shel Sefer Ḥasidim" (Lexical Usage in the Hebrew of Sefer Hasidim). *Proceedings of the Sixth World Congress of Jewish Studies,* Section 4 (1973): 183–96.
———. "Matzav ha-Meḥkar shel ha-Ivrit shel Yemei ha-Beynayim" (The State of Medieval Hebrew Research). *Bikoret u-Farshanut* 16 (1981): 9–31.
KUTSCHER, Y. *A History of the Hebrew Language.* Jerusalem: Magnes, 1982.
LUZZATO, S. D. *Toledot Leshon Ever (The History of Hebrew)* (Hebrew translation from the Italian by Y. H. Castiglioni): Krakow, 1985.
NOBEL, S. "Targumei She'ilah mi-Yidish ba-Ivrit ha-Rabanit" (Loan Translations from Yiddish in Rabbinic Hebrew). *Leshonenu* 23 (1959): 172–84.
RABIN, C. "Rabbi Avraham bar Ḥiyya u-Teḥiyat Leshonenu ha-Ivrit ba-Me'ah ha-Aḥat-Esreh" (R. Avraham bar Hiyya and our Hebrew Revival in the Eleventh Century). *Metzuda* 3–4 (1945): 158–70.
———. "Hebrew." In T. A. Sebeok, ed. *Current Trends in Linguistics* 6. The Hague: Mouton, 1970, pp. 304–30.
———. *Ikarei Toledot ha-Lashon ha-Ivrit (A Short History of Hebrew).* Jerusalem, 1972.
RAZHABI, YEHUDAH. "Leshonot be-Sifrut She'elot u-Teshuvot" (Terms in Responsa Literature). *Leshonenu* 33 (1982): 99–113.
SHAPIRA, NOAH. "Ha-Lashon ha-Tekhnit ba-Sifrut ha-Rabanit" (Technical Language in Rabbinic Literature). *Leshonenu* 26 (1962): 209–16.
SOLOVEITCHIK, HAYYIM. "Religious Law and Change: The Medieval Jewish Example." *AJS Review* 12 (1987): 205–21.
TA-SHEMA, YISRA'EL. "She'elot u-Teshuvot" (Responsa). *Entziklopedyah Ivrit (Hebrew Encyclopedia),* 31 (1979): 369–71.
URBACH, EFRAYIM. *Ba'alei Ha-Tosafot (The Tosaphists).* 4th expanded edition. Jerusalem, 1980.

6

On the Role of *Melitzah* in the Literature of Hebrew Enlightenment

MOSHE PELLI

In the study of the writers of the Haskalah ("Enlightenment") and their language, few issues are as problematic as their use of Haskalah-type "melitzah" ("high-flown figures of speech," "euphuism").[1] Scholarly treatment of the underlying nature of such melitzah leaves much to be desired. The very definition of melitzah is uncertain; nor do we have a clear picture of how it was employed in Haskalah literature. The topic has, of course, attracted its fair share of Hebrew scholars—one might single out Boaz Shabevitch, in particular, for his studies on the language of Naftali Herz Wessely[2]—but a comprehensive picture based on a systematic, scholarly analysis of the melitzah of the Haskalah is still wanting.

In a survey of the various definitions of melitzah in dictionaries and scholarly works, Shahevitch has found that the general use of the term is a derogatory one. And sure enough, the definition for melitzah provided in the Gur dictionary is: "empty words couched in an imprecise style (in ridicule).[3] Even-Shoshan defines melitzah as "bombastic phraseology, scriptural verses and snatches of verses inserted into sentences, high-sounding diction;[4] so too *Otzar Ha-Lashon Ha-Ivrit*: "a bombastic style tending to use snatches of scriptural verses."[5]

Shahevitch observes that scholars such as Lachover and Klausner used the term melitzah interchangeably in its variegated meanings, usually to derogatory effect. He notes that the word originally denoted "rhetoric"—an aesthetic and artistic use of language—but later it "fell into disrepute and acquired a pejorative meaning." Shahevitch then proceeds to enumerate all the accusations levelled at melitzah: that it is overextended and verbose, that it is imprecise, a patchwork of verses and snatches of verse, that it is ornate, it makes excessive use of puns, it cherishes biblical hapaxlegomena, it is cliché, it is empty and bombastic. Shahevitch argues that this long litany of argumentations fails to provide a unique characterization of *melitzah;* and they are equally applicable to other styles of writing.[6]

In effect, concludes Shahevitch, these criticisms of melitzah relate in the main to the "extreme" "verbosity as a quantitative extreme, *shibutz* [an "inlay" of segments of biblical verses] as an extreme of associations, the ornamental as a qualitative extreme, the use of rare words as an extreme of the unique and the unusual." The Maskilim ("enlightened") employed Hebrew as a language "acquired from the

Scriptures," and were not sensitive enough to distinguish "the levels of words and expressions" (Shahevitch 1970: 667). Thus even Shahevitch comes to subscribe to the negative conception of melitzah.

A better understanding of the negative attitudes to melitzah may be found in the writings of one of the giants of twentieth-century Hebrew literature, Hayyim Nahman Bialik, who certainly had a hand in determining this attitude to the melitzah of the Haskalah. It is now over fifty years since Bialik came out strongly against the *shibutz* ("inlay" or "mosaic") style of the *piyyut* poetry that had endured up until the period of the Haskalah. He defines this usage as "language which emits the flash of the occasional block-busting word or stirring expression, sometimes with half-verses culled from Holy Scripture."[7] The Hebrew poets had imitated Arab poets in the use of words—"They saw the importance of the word not in its being a small piece of an artistic work but as a precious stone with an independent value all of its own" (ibid.: 12).

To Bialik's mind, the Hebrew poets "employed rhymes and *shibutz* prose rather than perpetuating the Biblical forms, in which there is no external ornament and in which the beauty of the word derives from the place it occupies and not from itself...." Herein lay the "grating" strangeness in reading their prose. "There is no inner beauty in it, nothing in which form and content are equally matched." For Bialik, it was precisely this that flawed the writings of the Haskalah too; and on this basis he claimed that M. H. Luzzatto (RaMHaL, 1707–47), who "threw down the gauntlet to the *shibutz* style of Hebrew prose," was the first modern Hebrew poet (ibid.: 14–15).

Elsewhere, Bialik argued that until Mendele Mokher Sefarim (Shalom Yaakov Abramovitch, 1835–1917) Hebrew literature had amounted to an artistic "zero." "They had forever been scratching around on the surface of the shell, but their pen never seemed to get inside . . . for portraying nature, it was again a case of two or three well-worn coinages lifted from the Bible. . . ."[8] "Until Mendele what we had were linguistic tricks and games, linguistic capers, linguistic shreds and patches; Mendele handed us one language that was a whole. . . . He was virtually the first in our modern literature to stop imitating the Book—he imitated nature and life" (ibid.: 327).

Bialik thus gives voice to that negative response to Haskalah style, an attitude that has taken a hold on our literary life, even penetrating into literary criticism and historiography of literature, realms which are supposed to be balanced and objective.

Of course, when we turn to more recent scholarly studies of medieval Hebrew poetry, we find a somewhat different picture of the use of the biblical *shibutz*, and a different attitude to melitzah. Ezra Fleischer, dealing with sacred poetry, explains, "the stylistic bond between the preclassical *piyyut* and biblical melitzah":

> The biblical *shibutz,* i.e. the insertion of fragments of Tanakhic verses and phrases into the stylistic fabric of a literary work, is one of Hebrew literature's old and established ornamental devices. Each and every period in Hebrew literature "inlaid" biblical quotations into its style, some more, some less. The inlay adds prestige to the literary text, enriching it with the harmonics that the inlaid word brings from its original "environment," lending it the charm of the unexpected. And the hearer is

aroused to an appreciation of the writer's talent, of his excellent command of the Scriptures and his skill in taking words from another time and place—from another topic even—and welding them so smoothly together with a text being composed in the here and now.[9]

Dan Pagis, in his study of secular Hebrew poetry, has explained the phenomenon of the *shibutz* style as a "consequence both of the biblical revival and of contemporary poetics."

It is a truism that the Hebrew poetry of medieval Spain utilized not only a biblical vocabulary but also whole verses and parts of verses, integrating them into the poem in a new context. . . . An intertwining of the biblical is already a feature in the earliest of these Spanish poets, and in some poems the very linguistic fabric is a weave of verses from here and there in Scripture. Now the Bible was an inseparable part of the education of every Maskil: a snatch of a verse was an allusion to the text in its entirety. Readers could derive a special, sometimes a surprising, flavor from the new knit of old familiar verses and from the new context set up by the poem. An inlay of verses at their best . . . is no mere collection of high-flown, euphuistic quotations but a new and dynamic creation.[10]

Dan Miron is one of the few modern literary critics to have addressed the subject of inlaid melitzah in Haskalah literature from a literary angle, in his discussion of the style of Avraham Mapu (1808–67). Miron explains that the sweeping dismissals of the melitzah of the Haskalah were necessary and understandable in their time, within the context of a literary reevaluation. However,

the entrenchment of such views in criticism and in routine exposition of the history of literature up to our own day betokens a laziness of thought and a lack of sensitivity and understanding for our literary heritage. The inlay style, like any of the other devices of *"melitzah"* literature, is not intrinsically worthless; only the bad instances . . . are worthless . . . the literary taste evident in the inlay style is not inferior but merely different from our own conventional taste. The aesthetic-poetic notions upon which it rests do not conform to the notions on which . . . our own literary judgment is based.[11]

Examining the positions that have been held since Bialik, Miron has attempted, in the article just cited, to arrive at a definition of the *shibutz* style (as compared to the "free" poetic style presented by Bialik) as

a system of linguistic connective practices, which seeks to convey a certain expressive meaning by combining linguistic units—perceived as pre-constructed and as possessing a linguistic-aesthetic value of their own—without there being a link between these units and the one-off meaning which they effect. Thus the controlling power of meaning in the linguistic organization of the utterance is rather limited, sometimes being reduced to the selection of units that appear to be roughly appropriate and to stringing these units syntactically together. In no case may the meaning blur the independence of these units or melt them down to the point of destroying the autonomous wholeness which they had already acquired, as it were, before the creation of the contextual and syntactic bond between the unit and the whole. This wholeness has its source mainly in those familiar literary sources from which the units derive.

And Miron continues: "Most characteristic of the Hebrew inlay style is the use of phrases from sacred texts, particularly the Tanakh, as fixed, finished elements which the author may only string together in different orders but may not radically alter" (ibid.: 28–29).

Miron has proposed utilizing the analysis of Mapu's writings "as point of departure for a reexamination" of "the essential quality and artistic value of the *melitzah*." In a brilliant presentation, he dwells upon the sophisticated art of the melitzah in Mapu and its tie-in with the system of structures running throughout Mapu's work. He argues that "in order to comprehend the art of the *melitzah,* one must train the ear to listen to the stereophony of the language." Sometimes, indeed, "the polyphony of the *shibutz* style expands . . . from stereophonic to triphonic or even polyphonic effect" (ibid.: 33).

The Hebrew writer of the Haskalah, at the start of that period, was forced to grapple with a newly emerging Hebrew tongue and with the new demands of modern composition. He sought to express a new path and a new approach, and in his sensitivity to the language problem he was rebelling, first of all, against the rabbinic style, which he saw as expressing an old world. The Hebrew Maskil sought new and modern means of expression to convey the new world-picture he wished to draw. The wish to address oneself to a new style may in itself appear commendable, but achieving this style was no simple matter; certainly, not all the Maskilim found their way to this goal. The early Maskilim drew upon that very same old cultural world against which they rebelled; thus, despite their efforts to escape rabbinic idiom, we find several of them using the old-style expressions that they so condemned.[12]

As I have pointed out in my book,

> there was a natural tendency by *Maskilim* to use the Tanakhic idiom, which they saw as representing pure Hebrew at its best. And indeed, they contrived to apply Tanakhic Hebrew to the epic poem and the poetic drama, which revolved in part around biblical themes, and thus succeeded in achieving a harmony between style and content. However, this was not the case with their philosophical writings or in their essays on themes of language, let alone on topical themes—in matters pertaining to education, science, and society. Trained as they were in the philosophical and theological Jewish writings of the Middle Ages, . . . the *Maskilim* tended to opt for a medieval Hebrew for writing in the non-belletristic sphere (ibid.: 23).

The assumption that biblical style predominates throughout the literature of the Haskalah is a false one.[13] "The utilization of the familiar, conventional idiom, derived from the rich array of sources in the Hebraic cultural heritage, led . . . to the creation of the Haskalah-type melitzah, in its modern use" (ibid.: 24).

It should be emphasized that a Haskalah text in a melitzah style—such as the one to be analyzed in the present study—depends for its reading and comprehension upon the reader too. One of the problems in reading a Haskalah text today resides not in the text itself but in today's Hebrew reader, who connects differently to the textual sources than did the Haskalah readership. Educators are duty-bound to be aware of this problem when teaching the literature of the Haskalah and to draw the student's attention to the sources underlying the text. Needless to say, the task is as important as it is difficult—and one that confronts anyone making a serious study of Hebrew literature through the ages, modern literature included.

Melitzic *shibutz*-inlays are not all of a kind. Pagis (ibid.) distinguishes various types of medieval *shibutz,* and his distinctions can be called upon in examining the *shibutz* of the Haskalah. He lists three types:

(a) "A neutral *shibutz,* primarily linguistic in function"—using words, phrases and bits of verses without allusion to the Tanakhic context (ibid.: 17).

(b) "A *shibutz* that acts primarily via a knowledge of the source-text, though it can in fact be self-contained" (ibid.: 72). As an example: the inlay that undergoes meaning-shift—not only divorcing the source-verse from its original context but changing the meaning of the words, satirically or sarcastically on occasions (73).

(c) "An inlay or system of inlays acting on the whole, or the major portion of, the poem as a conceptual or descriptive center, or as part of its inner structure" (75).

With the use of the biblical melitzah, the biblical text being alluded to may sometimes become a subtext underlying the modern story. Where compatible with the event or description, it contributes to these and enriches them with the original substance and colors, and where incompatible with the modern story it creates an ironic contrast, potentially enriching it in terms of irony. Of course, incompatible melitzah can cause incongruity between the surface text and the (biblical) text being alluded to, thus creating a tension which the author had not intended (assuming that we can monitor such intent, or that it is the critic's affair) and which does not enrich the text. This would be an unsuccessful use of melitzah.

I will explore the functions of melitzah in the writings of a number of Hebrew Maskilim, with particular reference to Shmuel Romanelli's *Masa Ba'rav* (1792), a book that belongs to the genre of travelogues. Romanelli describes his real-life journey to North Africa and his four year sojourn there. The analysis presented here forms part of a broader treatment I have undertaken of the travelogue genre in the Hebrew Haskalah.[14]

At the start of his book Romanelli describes a break for lunch during a journey. He begins with the time: *vayehi hashemesh el mahatzit hayom* ("and the sun was at midday"). Further on, he gives the event: *vaneshev le'ekhol lehem* ("and we sat to eat bread"). Forthwith, a description of the location: *bine'ot deshe tahat tse'elei atzei hasadeh el mikhal mayim hanigarim balat uvenahamat hesed* ("in a green pasture under the boughs of the trees of the field by a stream of water flowing discretely with a kindly murmur"). Having depicted the location, the narrator describes the setting of the table: *hamelitz riped smikhah al hehatzir* ("the interpreter spread a blanket on the grass"), and finally the meal: *vayikhreh lanu kerah makolet mibeyto dei hashiv et nafshenu* ("and he served us a feast of food from his home, sufficient to restore our souls").[15]

Romanelli employs conventional Tanakhic imagery and conventional scriptural expressions to convey his experiences and impressions. When he gives the time, he means to say, in the elevated literary style current today: *amdah ḥamah be'emtza harakia* ("the sun stood in the middle of the sky"), but using the melitzah style he says: *vayehi hashemesh el maḥatzit hayom*. Romanelli employs the Tanakhic expression *vayehi hashemesh* ("and the sun was"), taken from the verse *vayehi hashemesh lavo vetardemah naflah al avram* ("And when the sun was going down, a deep sleep fell upon Abram"), Gen. 15:12.[16] And he transfers it to the situation described in his story, combining it at the same time with the expression *maḥatzit hayom* ("mid-day"), drawn from Neh. 8:3: *min ha'or ad maḥatzit hayom* ("from the morning until midday"). The two inlaid expressions are tied together by the preposition *el*. Romanelli has changed the sense of the first sentence and omitted the verb *bo,* which in collocation with "the sun" denotes "setting," and has thus broken down the original biblical meaning, fashioning it into a different and original sense. Nonetheless, he has left us to infer an omitted verb *ba'ah*—though with a change in its meaning—from the tie-in with the original verse, as if saying: *vayehi hashemesh ba'ah el maḥatzit hayom* ("and the sun *was coming* to midday"). The usage *vayehi . . . el* is generally found in the Bible as a linguistic convention indicating an opening to a prophecy, such as *vayehi devar hashem el . . .* ("and the word of the LORD came to . . ."), and the basic figure of Verb + Noun + Preposition has to an extent been preserved here too.

The continuation of the sentence, *vaneshev le'ekhol lehem* ("and we sat to eat bread"), appears to be founded on the verse *hu yeshev bo le'ekhol leḥem* ("he shall sit in it to eat bread"), Ez. 44:3—with a change in person and with the "conversive *vav*" common in similar cases: *vayeshev hamelekh al haleḥem le'ekhol* ("and the king sat him down to the meal to eat", I Sam. 20:24)—or *le'ekhol leḥem im ḥoten moshe* ("to eat bread with Moses' father-in-law"), Ex. 18:12. Romanelli's language would appear economical and to the point, and functions well in supplying information about the meal.

The sentence, *bin'ot deshe taḥat tze'elei atzei hasadeh* ("in green pastures under the boughs of the trees of the field"), describing the location, stitches together pieces of verse that are well-suited to the description: *bin'ot deshe* is based on the verse *bin'ot deshe yarbitzeni* ("he maketh me to lie down in green pastures"), Ps. 23:2, minus the verb. Note that for readers conversant with the Bible, its style and its phraseology, both during the Haskalah and in our own day, the idyllic Tanakhic image conjured up by the underlying original *bin'ot deshe yarbitzeni* and the sequel (not mentioned here) *al mei menuḥot yenahaleni* ("he leadeth me beside the still waters") infuses a calm even into Romanelli's modern tableau. By using a scriptural verse that also features in the prayers,[17] he reinforces the contextual-Tanakhic allusion of the *shibutz*.

The description of the location continues: *taḥat tze'elei* ("under the boughs of"), based on the original *taḥat tze'elim yishkav* (AV: "he lieth under the shady trees," NEB: "under the thorny lotus he lies"), Job 40:21, minus the verb as the author is depicting a place, and with the noun *tze'elim* switched into the construct form.[18] The rare use of the name of a shrub or tree, thus called originally because its boughs cast shade *(tzel),* in the sense of "bough," serves to hark back to the scriptural source of this tree name and its meaning, "caster of shade." Furthermore, the use of *tze'elei* adds a homophonous quality and a musical sound that connote the desired image of "shade."

Tze'elim has been made construct to *atzei hasadeh* ("the trees of the field"), derived from Is. 55:12: *vekhol atzei hasadeh yimḥa'u khaf* ("and all the trees of the field shall clap their hands"), et passim,[19] transposed here minus the word *kol* and the verb.

In the phrase, *el mikhal mayim hanigarim balat uvenahamat ḥesed* ("by a brook of water flowing gently with a kindly murmur"), the preposition *el* is used here meaning "by" (e.g., *vayehi hem yoshvim el hashulḥan* "as they sat at the table", 1 Kings 13:20). *Mikhal mayim* ("brook of water") is taken from 2 Sam. 17:20: *avru mikhal hamayim* ("they be gone over the brook of water"), stitched together with *mayim nigarim* ("flowing water") based on *ki mot namut vekhamayim hanigarim artza* ("for we must needs die, and are as water spilt on the ground"), 2 Sam. 14:14. The two turns of phrase are thus interwoven by use of the shared word *mayim,* to form an "original" inlaid melitzah. The adverb *balat* is not used biblically of water, and figures in Judges 4:21: *vatavo elav balat* ("and went discretely unto him"); it has been revamped to mean "slowly, gently."

The expression *nahamat ḥesed* ("a kindly murmur") is apparently an innovation of Romanelli's, based perhaps on *kenahamat yam* ("like the roaring of the sea"), Is. 5:30, or *minahamat libi* ("by reason of the disquietness of my heart"), Ps. 38:9, the construction . . . *ḥesed* being patterned on *veahavat ḥesed* ("and to love kindness"), Mi. 6:8. Innovation is achieved by replacing *ahavat* with *nahamat,* identical in vocalization and rhythm, while preserving the internal rhyme *a-a-at.*

The sentence, *hamelitz riped smikhah al heḥatzir* ("the interpreter spread a blanket on the grass"), appears altogether modern, with none of the direct Tanakhic turns of phrase or scriptural references. Particularly noticeable is the absence of the "conversive *vav.*" Nonetheless, the Tanakhic connection is there, fairly witty and sophisticated. The author is relying on the reader to trace the alluded biblical reference of the expression by making the association between the verb *riped* ("spread") and the noun *smikhah* ("blanket") by reference to the verse *samkhuni ba'ashishot rapduni batapuḥim* ("stay me with flagons, comfort me with apples"), Song of Songs 2:5. In the source-text the verbs *simekh* and *riped* are in complementary parallelism. The author is counting on this parallel and on the reader's ability to spot the wit and novelty in the inlaid melitzah. The term *hamelitz* is biblical (Gen. 42:23) and it is used here in its biblical meaning, "the interpreter."

Al heḥatzir ("on the grass") is borrowed from the biblical word that frequently denotes wild grass (but not specifically dry), e.g., *matzmiaḥ ḥatzir labehemah ve'esev la'avodat ha'adam* ("He causeth the grass to grow for the cattle, and herb for the service of man"), Ps. 104:14. It may be supposed that the author had some difficulty getting Scripture to yield a description of picnic preparations, and therefore went for a description of the repast itself: *vayikhreh lanu kerah makolet mibeyto dey hashiv et nafshenu* ("and he set out a feast for us of food from his home, sufficient to restore our souls"). *Vayikhreh lanu kerah,* based on *vayikhreh lahem kerah gedolah* ("and he prepared great provision for them"), 2 Kings 6:23 changes the suffix in *lahem* to suit the tale and drops the inappropriate adjective *gedolah.*

Makolet mibeyto follows the pattern of *makolet leveyto* ("food to his household"), 1 Kings 5:25, with a change of preposition. *Dey hashiv* is given on the basis of the verse *ve'im lo matz'ah yado dey hashiv lo* ("but if he be not able to restore it to him"), Lev. 25:28, while the expression *hashiv et nafshenu* rests upon *lehashiv nafsho* ("to being back his soul"), Job 33:30, in line with the story and with added *et,* the two expressions being stitched together to form a blend.

Romanelli's innovation lies in blending two biblical expressions sharing the same link-word, to form a turn of phrase with an altogether biblical ring about it.

Insight is gained into Romanelli's way with Biblical *shibutz* by making comparisons with similar descriptions of luncheons in the language of the early *Haskalah* and in the Hebrew and non-Hebrew travelogue.

In the fable-like idyll *Gideon Haro'eh* ("Gideon the Shepherd"), published in the periodical *Ha-Me'asef,* Hayyim Keslin uses an economical Scripture-based style to depict lunch as follows: *vayehi be'et hatzohorayim ve'ehav yashvu le'ekhol velishtot* ("And it came to pass at noon time that his brothers sat down to eat and drink").[20] Notice that the time is specified here with none of the graphic quality found in Romanelli, who described midday with an image of the sun. The meal too is conveyed in generalities, using the verbs *yashav* ("sat") and *akhal* ("ate"), plus the verb *shatah* ("drank") not found in Romanelli.

A similar method of conveying time is to be found in *Mashal Hasheleg, Ha'adamah Vehanahar,* printed in the same issue of *Ha-Me'asef: vayehi le'et hatzohorayim vehashemesh yatza al ha'aretz* ("And it came to pass at noon time that the sun came out upon the Earth"). Rather than specifying the hour, the author uses a conventional figure of time.[21] It appears that the tendency is to refer to time in generalities, using conventional terms rather than exact reference to time.

An interesting comparison can be made with a similar picnic tableau by the Haskalah author and editor of *Ha-Me'asef,* Isaac Euchel. His letters, too, belong to the literary genre of the travelogue, and were also written at a point of time close to the composition of Romanelli's book. We thus have a special interest in Euchel's description, though the ambience is a more cultured one from a European point of view than Romanelli's:

> *malon ahat al em haderekh, po nish'anu tahat ha'etz lish'of tzel kehom hayom, ve'akhalnu lehem tzohorayim me'et asher nitztayadnu, veyashavnu sham ad asher kilu ha'avadim le'esor et hamerkavah* ("an inn at a crossroads, where we reclined beneath a tree to breathe in some shade in the heat of the day, and we ate a noontime repast from what we had packed, and sat there until the servants were done with saddling the carriage").[22]

Euchel makes short shrift of describing the location, merely talking of an inn at a crossroads, which suits his well-planned travel more than Romanelli's and is also more suited to the company of ladies journeying with him. The tree appears here again but without any of the detail or linguistic ornament of Romanelli. Euchel explains the stop as a pause for rest and as a chance to ready the carriage (to change horses?), so the verb *nish'anu* ("we reclined") serves its purpose. There is no adverbial of time here, but there is an adverbial of circumstance relating to the noontime—*kehom hayom* ("in the heat of the day")—which is a Tanakhic inlay (Gen. 18:1 et passim). Close to it is the phrase *lish'of tzel* ("to breathe in some shade"), itself a Tanakhic inlay based on Job 7:2: *ke'eved yish'af tzel* ("like . . . a slave longing for the shade"). The combination of the two phrases yields an image of a hot day.

The expression *lish'of tzel* sounds bizarre to the modern ear, but in terms of Tanakhic inlay Euchel has plucked the verb *yish'af* from its scriptural context, where it parallels the verb *yekaveh* (*ukhesakhir yekaveh fo'olo* "and as an hireling looketh for the reward of his work")—originally an abstraction from the act of inhalation (*sha'af = kivah*)—and has restored it to its original sense. However, using the verb in a non-abstract sense has left it somewhat estranged from its object—for one cannot inhale shade as one inhales the breeze. Yet the metonymous image is an attractive one, both witty and original, of shade being inhaled as if it were a breeze. . . . The information about the luncheon is limited, with added details of the carriage not found in Romanelli's description.

A travel description like Euchel's is found in the writings of the traveller Lempriere, who visited Morocco just when Romanelli was staying there: "At noon I fixed upon the most shady spot I could find, and, agreeably to the Moorish fashion, sat down cross-legged on the grass and dined."[23]

Lempriere conveys time with the sparing adverbial "at noon," without mention of where the sun stood in the sky. The search for shade is stressed, and a little local color added with the detail of the Oriental way of sitting (found elsewhere in Romanelli: 13/40, 29/61). Where he sat, on the grass, is given the maximum brevity, as is the information on the meal. The comparison of Romanelli's style with the others illustrated here reveals a linguistic richness and poetic craft that are a standing credit to Romanelli's name.

To our mind, the Tanakhic linguistic routine, though it may be full of generalities, ill-designed for self-expression and unsuited to relaying personal experiences, enjoys the great advantage of rousing the reader to an involvement in the events described. Moreover, the compositional technique of the inlaid melitzah works to create a bond between author and reader through the game of spotting sources and uncovering the way they have been reworked and recast.

With generality, however, come—more often than not—loss of detail, superficial description, and lack of a concrete sense of happenings and places. And thus, routinely: luncheon is *be'emtza hayom* ("in the middle of the day"), a repast is *vaneshev le'ekhol lehem* ("and we sat to eat bread"), a picnic is held on the grass in the shade of a tree. Even the picture of a flowing brook has a conventional look about it, as in the contemporary romance or idyllic tableau, although the linguistic mode of expression of Romanelli is particularly lofty in the use of biblical hapaxlegomena (e.g., *mikhal hamayim*—"the brook of water," *balat*—"gently," *kerah*—"food," *makolet*—"provisions") and there is something special about the new phrases being coined (*hanigarim balat*—"flowing gently," *uvenahamat hesed*—"and with a kindly murmur," and the like).

The description of the blanket appears matter-of-factly at the picnic, with none of the Tanakhic linguistic routine—perhaps owing to its "modern" character—

aside from Romanelli's aforementioned innovation of the expression *riped smikhah* ("spread a blanket").

On the other hand, the repast vouchsafes us nothing concerning what they ate, and how much or how they ate. The generality or abstraction, *karah kerah* ("prepared food"), "covers" for all possibilities and fills the gap. As we noted, however, even Euchel's travelogue does not go into the details of a meal.

It should be borne in mind that the idyllic portrait of the surroundings occupies a respectable portion of the passage concerned: two out of six sentences, thirteen out of thirty-four words, are devoted to depiction of landscape. Note that scenery and landscape serve as indirect characterization for the figures in the narrative while the idyllic picture reflects their mood. The emphasis on nature and its tranquility marks the Haskalah's Rousseauesque trend of "back to nature," far from the tumult of civilization.

Romanelli espoused linguistic and literary conventions that invoked the phraseological routines of Tanakh. This phraseology led, by its very nature, to a generalization of experience rather than to a precise and distinctive description reflecting unique personal experience. The use of the linguistic conventions will not validate an experience or event through description per se. Conversely, generality can point toward universally shared elements, thereby involving the reader in the experience itself.

We cannot accept the term "shreds of verses"—conventionally employed, it will be recalled, in criticism of the melitzah style—as being true of Romanelli. What one has here, as we have seen, is no abritrary or random shredding of verses but an artistic use of verse "off-cuts" to enhance the description or serve the narrative. Klausner was thus correct when he spoke of the melitzah in Romanelli's *Masa Ba'rav;* Shahevitch's claim that "his [Romanelli's] language is virtually melitzah-free"[24] does not hold up.

As we have argued elsewhere,[25] while the luxuriant style of melitzah was artificial, clumsy, and at times hazy and inappropriate to everyday language, it had qualities that served the Hebrew authors well, enabling them to embrace the whole multi-layered history of the language. Literary Hebrew thus evolved subtly with all its array of allusions and fine distinctions; this evolution, in fact, was itself a reflection of all that is problematic in the duality of Jewish existence in the modern, secular world. Hebrew in this manner was being expanded from a sacred into a secular, mundane tongue.

Notes

1. An additional article of mine on melitzah has been published in the journal *Lashon ve-Ivrit* and another will be published in the journal *Bikoret U-Farshanut*.
2. One chapter in Shahevitch 1963; idem, 1967; 1968a; 1968b; 1970b.
3. Grazovsky-Gur 1935: 538.
4. Even-Shoshan 1966: 1366.
5. Canaani 1968: 2959. And see, e.g., Rivlin 1934: 96: "There were "authors" for whom melitzah was the main thing and who put no thought into it. However, even those who had something to say . . . could not find the *mot juste* for their thought, and melitzah so

clouded their thinking that one could not tell what they wished to say." Melitzah is also referred to in derogatory terms in Sokolow 1933-34: 40.

6. Shahevitch 1970b; and compare Shahevitch 1965 and Sadan 1965.
7. Bialik 1935a.
8. Idem 1935b. Compare Bialik's use of the word *melitzah* in the translation of *Don Quixote, the Man of La Mancha* (1961: 43): *"uleshon hasfarim af hi amukah ukhvedah veniftalah mehavin, lo hadar la velo ta'am, kulah melitzah al melitzah, ishah tfelah mere'utah"* ("and the language of the books too is profound and heavy and contorted beyond comprehension, without beauty or taste, entirely *melitzah* upon *melitzah*, each one more insipid than the last").
9. Fleischer 1975: 103-104.
10. Pagis 1976: 70.
11. Miron 1979: 32-33.
12. And see the discussion in Pelli 1988a: 23-24.
13. As already observed in Halkin 1984: 100-101.
14. Pelli 1988b.
15. Romanelli 1792: 2 and p. 26 in 1969 edition.
16. Similarly, Gen. 15:17: *vayehi hashemesh ba'ah va-alatah hayah* ("And it came to pass that when the sun went down and it was dark").
17. In *kabalat shabat* ("Introduction of the Sabbath") of the Sefard rite and after Washing of the Hands in Hasidic custom.
18. In the next verse, Job 40:22, one reads *yesukuhu tze'elim tzilelo, yesubuhu arvei-nahal* ("The shady trees cover him with their shadow; the willows of the brook compass him about").
19. Ez. 17:24: *veyad'u kol atzei hasadeh* ("and all the trees of the field shall know") et passim.
20. H . . . K. = Hayyim Keslin 1785: 21.
21. R-K. 1785: 85.
22. Euchel 1785: 137.
23. Lempriere 1813: 69.
24. Shahevitch 1967: 236 n.
25. Pelli 1988a: 24.

References

BIALIK, HAYYIM NAHMAN. "Le-Toldot ha-Shirah ha-Ivrit ha-Hadashah" (On the History of Modern Hebrew Poetry). *Devarim she-be-al-Pe* 2. Tel Aviv (1935): 9-18.

———. "Mendele u-Shloshet ha-Krakhim" (Mendele and the Three Volumes). *Collected Works* 2. Tel Aviv (1935): 320-26.

———, translator. *Don Kishote Ish La-Mansha (Don Quixote the Man of La Mancha)*. Tel Aviv (1961).

CANAANI, YAAKOV. *Otzar ha-Lashon ha-Ivrit (Treasury of the Hebrew Language)*. Vol. 9. Tel Aviv (1968).

EUCHEL, ISAAC. "Igrot Yitzhak Euchel" (Letters of Isaac Euchel). *Ha-Me'assef* 2 (1785): 116-121, 137-142.

EVEN-SHOSHAN, AVRAHAM. *Milon Hadash (New Dictionary)*. Vol. 3. Jerusalem: Kiryath Sepher (1966).

FLEISCHER, EZRA. *Shirat ha-Kodesh ha-Ivrit bi-Ymei ha-Beinayim (Sacred Hebrew Poetry in the Middle Ages)*. Jerusalem: Israel Academy of Sciences and Humanities (1975).

GRAZOVSKY, YEHUDA. *Milon ha-Safah ha-Ivrit (Dictionary of the Hebrew Language)*. Tel Aviv: (1935).

HALKIN, SHIMON. *Zeramim ve-Tzurot ba-Sifrut ha-Ivrit ha-Hadashah (Trends and Forms in Modern Hebrew Literature)*. Jerusalem: (1984).

KESLIN, HAYYIM. "Gideon ha-Ro'eh" (Gideon the Shepherd). *Ha-Me'assef* 2 (1785): 21.

LEMPRIERE, WILLIAM. *A Tour through the Dominion of the Emperor of Morocco*. 3rd ed. Newport: (1813).

MIRON, DAN. *Beyn Hazon le-Emet (Between Vision and Truth)*. Jerusalem: Bialik Institute (1979).

PAGIS, DAN. *Hidush u-Masoret be-Shirat ha-Hol ha-Ivrit: Sefarad ve-Italyah (Innovation and Tradition in Secular Hebrew Poetry: Spain and Italy)*. Jerusalem: Keter (1976).

PELLI, MOSHE. *Be-Ma'avkei Temurah (Struggles for Change)*. Tel Aviv: (1988).

———. "Sifrut ha-Masa'ot ke-Sugah Sifrutit ba-Haskalah ha-Ivrit: 'Masa Ba-'rav' li-Shmu'el Romanelli (The Travelogue as a Literary Genre in the Hebrew Enlightenment: Shmuel Romanelli's 'Masa Ba-'rav')." In Stanley Nash, ed. *Migvan: Mehkarim ba-Sifrut ha-Ivrit u-ve-Giluyeha ha-Amerikaniyim (Spectrum: Studies in Hebrew Literature and its American Manifestations)*. Lod: Habermann Institute (1988), pp. 299–321.

———. "Tefisat ha-Melitzah be-Reshit Sifrut ha-Haskalah ha-Ivrit." *Lashon ve-Ivrit* 8 (1991): 31–48.

RIVLIN, Y. "Beyt Midrasha shel Yerushalayim" (The Jerusalem Study-House). *Moznayim* 1 (1934): 96–98.

R-K. "Meshal ha-Sheleg, ha-Adamah, ve-ha-Nahar" (The Fable of the Snow, the Earth, and the River). *Ha-Me'assef* 2 (1785): 85.

ROMANELLI, SHMUEL. *Masa Ba-'rav (Travail in an Arab Land)*. Berlin (1792) and Jerusalem: Dorot (1969).

SADAN, DOV. "Hidush she-Sofo Shigrah—Keytzad?" (How Can an Innovation Become a Routine?). *Abstracts of the Third World Congress of Jewish Studies*. Jerusalem: (1965): p. 152.

SHAHEVITCH, BOAZ. "Be'ayot be-Signon ha-Prozah ha-Masa'it shel Reshit ha-Sifrut ha-Ivrit ha-Hadashah al-pi ha-Prozah shel R. N. H. Weisel" (Problems in the Essay Prose Style of Early Modern Hebrew Literature, with Reference to the Prose of N. Wessely). Ph.D. diss., Hebrew University of Jerusalem, 1963.

———. "Ha-'Melitzah' mahi?" (What is melitzah?). *Abstracts of the Third World Congress of Jewish Studies*. Jerusalem (1965), pp. 146–47.

———. "Arba Leshonot: Iyunim shel Sifrut bi-Leshon ha-Maskilim al-pi 'Ha-Me'asef'" (Four Tongues: Literary Studies in the Language of the Maskilim with Reference to 'Ha-Me'asef'). *Molad* (new series) 1, 2 (1967): 236–42.

———. "Mi'ut-Panim ve-Ribuy-Panim ba-Dimuy" (The Few-Faceted and the Multi-Faceted in the Figure). *Tarbiz* 37, 4 (1968): 374–96.

———. "Rovdey Otzar ha-Milim be-'Divrei Shalom ve-Emet'" (Layers of Vocabulary in 'Divrei Shalom ve-Emet'). *Leshonenu* 32 (1968): 304–307.

———. "Shi'uro ve-Givun Shi'uro shel ha-Mishpat bi-Khtivat ha-Iyun she-be-Ivrit" (The Measuring and Measuring Variation of the Sentence in Essay Writing in Hebrew). *Leshonenu* 34 (1970): 210–24.

———. "Beyn Amur la-Amirah: le-Mahutah shel ha-'Melitzah'" (Between Saying and Said: On the Nature of Melitzah). *Ha-Sifrut* 2, 3 (1970): 664–66.

SOKOLOW, NAHUM. "Magefat ha-Melitzah ha-Nokhriyah" (The Plague of the Alien Melitzah). *Moznayim* 1, 6 (1933–34): 38–56.

7

A Duty Too Heavy to Bear: Hebrew in the Berlin Haskalah, 1783–1819: Between Classic, Modern, and Romantic

YAACOV SHAVIT

> The Enlightenment gave the Jews who hitherto lacked a language not one language but two: German and Hebrew
>
> I. M. Jost

> The Hebrew readership of the day . . . , unlike the generation of the Haskalah, is not looking for Hebrew to serve as a "primer" from which to proceed toward another world. They are reading Hebrew because they *are* Hebrew and feel in their soul an inner bond with the national tongue and its literature.
>
> Ahad Ha'am

1

The period of the Haskalah ("Jewish Enlightenment") in Germany is regarded as the start of the "revival of Hebrew" as a literary, i.e., written, tongue. In Germany proper, this revival ended by petering out as early as the end of the eighteenth century, "bequeathing" the "revival of Hebrew" to an Eastern European "Enlightenment." At the same time, the German Haskalah is regarded as opening the way to the integration of Jews into German culture.

The Berlin Haskalah did not intend to "revive" Hebrew as a sole and exclusive language, as *the* national written and spoken medium. Its practical intention from the outset was to create and propagate a "new Hebrew language" to function alongside other languages. This language was cast in a defined role within the Jewish polyglossic system in Germany (and Eastern Europe). As much as they gave their full weight to the ideology and praxis of the "revival of Hebrew," so too did the Maskilim (proponents of Haskalah) insist with equal faith and fervor upon the need for study and knowledge of "the language and literature of the people among whom we dwell,"[1] for it was evident to them that without the foreign language there could be no emancipation and no "reform" of Jewish life. Thus, from the outset, they subjected the Jew who lacked mastery of Hebrew and the "vernacular" (notably German) to a dual burden, with the aim of creating a new situation of diglossia,[2] with the new foreign tongue in the main role. Alongside it, the equally new Hebrew language was allotted new, clearly-defined goals.

If this were not enough, the new Hebrew language was assigned several social and cultural functions: the "modern" Jew, and not just the Maskil, was thus asked at the dawn of the new age to acquire, urgently and simultaneously, a mastery of two new languages with differing functions. Moreover, in this polyglossic system Hebrew was accorded a variety of simultaneous value concepts: "classicizing," "Romantic," and "modern." And so Maskilim drew up a string of far-reaching demands that were incapable of fulfilment; with the multiple demands of their linguistic-cultural *tendenz* went an exceedingly high level of expectations, designed for the most part to lend legitimation and encouragement to their demands—in the cultural context in which they were uttered. When these expectations failed to find fulfilment, the resulting disillusionment and desolation was due in no small measure to the high expectations fostered by Haskalah rhetoric.

Notwithstanding, the Berlin Haskalah was a significant, even a critical, turning point in the history of Hebrew and Hebrew culture. This turning point was somewhat paradoxical, for it involved a variety of options, which may be defined as follows: the Berlin Haskalah created the new ideology of Hebrew as a modern language of culture and communication, and gave an impressive display of Hebrew's range of possibilities and capabilities in almost every domain of the written word. To be sure, before this time Hebrew had served the day-to-day life of the community, but in an "integrated" function, whereas now it was being accorded a role and status associated with an ideological mission and was being used to convey things that were radically new. At the same time, the declining mass and status of Hebrew in Germany even before the end of the eighteenth century created a situation in which, despite the retention of Hebrew study in various frameworks and its continuing fragmented use as a "modern" written medium, it had here to fall back on the role of being little more than a sacred tongue, a functionally restricted language of prayer (and as such, sometimes merely in conjunction with German).

This decline in the status of Hebrew, following its "revival" and its attendant expectations, prompted considerable wonderment as to the "true" intent of the Berlin Maskilim.[3] In later generations, particularly from the vista of the Hebrew national movement, the circle of Maskilim was depicted as the last generation of Hebrew aficionados in Germany;[4] *après eux,* the masses who betrayed and forsook the Hebrew tongue, going so far as to disgrace it in public. Such people were portrayed by the journal *Hamaggid* in the mid-1850s as having violated the language and then buried her, declaring that "the Hebrew tongue is as alien to us as Latin, Greek or Arabic," in flagrant disregard of the fact that Hebrew was not only the historic-national language but also the common unifying medium of the entire Diaspora, a living language, not an "archaeological tongue" like Egyptian or Akkadian.[5] So the Berlin Haskalah was adjudged not only to have launched a first, revolutionary stage in the history of modern Hebrew but also to have done so with insincere motives, and even to have promoted an emancipatory ideology whose encouragement of acculturation and whose conception of the foreign language as sole "vehicle of culture," nay as the national language of the Jew, led inexorably from "day one" to the abandonment of Hebrew as just one more ex-language. A further criticism was later appended (in the years that saw the moulding of the Hebrew nationalist ethos), to the effect that a majority of Maskilim had been antinationalist, or else unwitting agents of a deadly ambivalence in the Jewish mind and psyche—through seeking to impregnate it with a bilingualism whose result was a dualism, "a national catastrophe striking both at the faculty of thought and at the creative force."[6] The blame for the abandonment of Hebrew was laid not only upon *Wissenschaft des Judentums* (The science of Judaism) and the Reform Movement but also upon "virtually every rabbi and preacher in Germany," even among whom, as Peretz Smolenskin wrote with some exaggeration, "there cannot be ten percent who can comprehend Hebrew...."[7]

As early as the late eighteenth century, Yitzhak Euchel, a prime mover of the Berlin Haskalah, was able to utter a lament over the "death" of Hebrew in Germany, over the vanished Hebrew students and the desertion of the Maskilim who "have despised the tongue of their fathers and cast it behind them"; and indeed, he continued in philosophical and pessimistic vein, "times change, and people and opinions with them";[8] and in this vein he was not alone. The hopes and future of Hebrew thus lay in Eastern Europe. There are Jews there, wrote I. M. Jost in 1839, who read and write Hebrew, while "in Germany the knowledge of Hebrew is almost a thing of the past."[9] This was the dominant mood, although periodicals, anthologies, and textbooks in Hebrew continued to appear through the second decade of the nineteenth century and later still.

This gloomy picture of a rise and an immediate decline was an exaggeration, insofar as any assessment of the knowledge of Hebrew must measure the number of readers, writers, and speakers at a given time in relationship to some earlier date, while also asking what level of Hebrew and which Hebrew. Haskalah activity created the impression of a sudden leap in the number of Hebrew readers, an exaggerated impression due to the very nature of the revolutionary phenomenon. For the present discussion, I shall limit myself to an attempt to elucidate the declared ideological goals of the "Hebrew revival" in the context of the period—the last quarter of the eighteenth century and the first decade of the nineteenth—as well as the reasons for the inability of this ideology to achieve fulfilment.

I intend to locate the "inner cause" in the fundamental multifunctionality assigned to Hebrew in Haskalah ideology (and to which I have already alluded), whereas the "objective cause" is to be found in the nature of the circle of Maskilim as well as in its addressees and in the broad historical milieu in which they operated. To my mind, the significance of the ideology and the practical "Hebrew revivalist" activity within the Berlin Haskalah is not only that it was a historical turning point but also that it embodied Hebrew's three roles, which in fact would only come together some one hundred fifty years after the appearance of the periodical *Ha-Me'assef (Der Sammler)*, the Hebrew journal of the German Haskalah (1784–97, 1809–11), i.e., within a national "Hebraic" society in Eretz-Israel.[10]

2

Hebrew, of course, was not a "dead language" in the framework of traditional society but rather continued to exist in a range of day-to-day textual activities, and was "integrated" as a living tongue in the various layers of linguistic activity in Jewish society, as both a written and a spoken medium. There are various testimonies to the low level of Hebrew knowledge among rabbis and cantors. These are primarily by way of impression, historiographical material intended not so much to paint a full and faithful picture of the status of Hebrew and the knowledge of it in traditional society as to point to the fact that rabbis, as well as Maskilim, were aware of its straitened circumstances and were calling for it to be cultivated. But the fundamental difference between traditionalist circles and Maskilim was that the latter accorded Hebrew entirely different functions and significance than the former.[11] The fact that the periodical *Ha-Me'assef* could not reach more than some three hundred subscribers (and of course one must also take account of "objective" and ideological causes) and that it gradually expired between 1790 and 1797 indicates that Hebrew as a modern language was being read by the tiniest circle of readers,[12] but says nothing about the potential number of readers for Hebrew as a whole. This number may be contrasted, for example, with the seven hundred fifty purchasing the first edition of the *Bi'ur* (the German translation by Mendelssohn and others of the Five Books of Moses, with the attendant Hebrew commentary, the *Bi'ur*), those reading *Shulamit* (which appeared in 1806) in German, and the number of those requesting the Friedlander-Euchel German prayer-book, published in 1786 and being sold even before coming out in a print-run of about one thousand.[13] While there are no major divergences here between Hebrew and German readers, they led Katz to conclude that German had made rapid strides in Jewish public life in Germany in the short period of less than a single generation,[14] in complete contrast to the progress of Hebrew.[15]

This growth itself would appear to testify not so much to the achievements of Haskalah ideology as to a deepening process of acculturation and assimilation among German Jewry. Sociocultural processes were considerably stronger than ideology. What began in fact as early as the close of the eighteenth century in the small circle of the high bourgeoisie (thus *Ha-Me'assef* of 1786 writes of "Jewish girls who all know how to speak perfectly in Gentile languages and cannot speak Yiddish") spread among wider circles. Katz even holds that the choice of Hebrew as the language of the German Haskalah was more pragmatic than ideological: the Maskilim did not, for the most part, know German, but they did know Hebrew. This knowledge of Hebrew was in all likelihood the fruit of traditional study and self-instruction. Euchel tells of his first encounter with a group of Maskilim in Koenigsberg, just after his arrival from Lithuania: "They knew Hebrew beautifully." At the same time, he represents the members of the circle from which he himself came as benighted individuals: "The Hebrew language which You chose for your Torah is in rather poor shape."[16] The fact that their intended readership did not yet read German, while Yiddish was regarded by the Maskilim as a despicable patchwork language,[17] was another factor compelling them to use Hebrew. But once they had mastered German, they no longer had a need for Hebrew within their own close circles, and it was merely fashioned as a medium of communication with Maskilim further East, one component of a shared consciousness.

Pragmatic reasons naturally carried great weight. It should, however, not be forgotten that *Ha-Me'assef* began appearing in 1783, before the French Revolution, when the prospects for emancipation were still nonexistent. The processes of acculturation and apostasization were not motivated by a conscious ideology, while the Maskilim were developing just such a collective consciousness and ideology. Hebrew for them was more than just the medium of communication among themselves and with their readership during that brief interlude—a single generation—in which German became an acquired language; Hebrew was the language that created a common consciousness and anchored it in a linguistic conception that was more than a "technical" means of communication, at the same time expressing the sense of mission that the Maskilim harbored toward traditional society. Since they aimed at two levels of change in Jewish society—change from within and change in relations with the surrounding society (and vice versa)—they were obliged to support the creation of a bilingual (Hebrew-German) rather than monolingual Jewish public. As for the "simple folk," the young Jews meant to undergo a process of "productivization," it was enough, according to Wessely, that they learn the local vernacular necessary for the acquisition of skills and for restricted social contact, and there was no need to study Hebrew as a "language of culture." The function of Hebrew had thus been diminished. Paradoxically, it was the Orthodox that adopted it as a secondary "everyday language."

In Wessely's words, "just as Hebrew has its domain, so German has its domain, the former for sacred matters, faith and Torah, the latter for wordly matters in business and human affairs" and for what was considered "neutral knowledge" (science, philosophy etc.). The linguistic situation was designed to reflect the ideal cultural situation as seen by a "conservative" religiously observant Maskil: an absolute division between the Jewish "inner life" and the Gentile "outer life," between the Torah and the "external disciplines," embracing various fields of knowledge. Indeed, one might say that the belief that such a division was possible was reflected in the assumption that each social and cultural sphere within the Jewish society is able to set its own separate language,[18] in other words to draw a linguistic distinction between "sacred" and "profane." The Berlin Haskalah, as is well-known, did not follow Wessely's line, and used Hebrew for "external disciplines" too, an accurate reflection of its cultural-intellectual world which found expression in the belief that one could imbibe "alien" ideas and arrive at an integration of "external disciplines," science and metaphysics included, with the Torah and the Jewish belief system. It was thus the vanguard of "secularization," for Hebrew, hitherto the sacred tongue, served as a vehicle for familiarization with literature and for literary exegesis, undermining the system of beliefs and the traditional historical outlook. At the same time, it should not be forgotten that the German Haskalah was not "secular" and that within it Hebrew was widely used as a medium for literature with an out-and-out religious message.

The Maskilim themselves were forever making high-flown declarations about the character of the "linguistic revival." Their position on the language and its nature reveals a parallel between conceptions of language in medieval Jewish philosophy and eighteenth-century philosophy of language.[19] Upon the foundations of their great social weakness, the Maskilim thus constructed a series of broad arguments: Hebrew is the most ancient of tongues and must be "raised from the dungheaps of disgrace."[20] It is the language in which the Scriptures and prayers were composed, and so only by understanding it can one reach an understanding of the Bible; Hebrew is a language of many facets, host to a sublime literature and capable of expressing the whole range of human feelings, but also philosophy and science, etc.[21] These declarations in praise of Hebrew have already been set out and analyzed in the literature and we need not rehearse them here.[22] Without doubt, another reason that Maskilim opted for Hebrew was its dual function in their struggle within traditional Jewish society: on the one hand, it expressed and embodied the "radical" core of the Haskalah, for the stress on Hebrew in the Jewish Enlightenment, as in the Renaissance and Reformation in the Christian World, signified a return to the ancient source and an unshackling from the authority of the official (rabbinic) canonical exegesis.[23] The return to Hebrew and to the Bible also created in practice and in appearance a shared cultural platform for Maskilim and Protestant society. Since Hebrew enjoyed no small prestige in Protestant eyes, its "revival" by the Maskilim was liable to give them prestige among the surrounding intelligentsia. The return to the biblical tongue, and with it the highlighting of its literary dimension, thus became one of the major signs of the intellectual reorientation of the Berlin Haskalah. Linguistically, this ideology placed an added burden upon Hebrew by insisting on restricting it to a single historical phase of the written language. Putting it another way, not only poetry was to be couched in biblical language but science too—which would prove to be impossible from the outset.

The eighteenth century assigned a central value to human language, and to national languages in particular; a process was underway that may be termed "the discovery of language"—meaning the various languages outside the European language family—and a speculative debate raged over the principle of where language originates and the way in which language mirrors cultural and literary circumstances; a classification was also made of the characteristics of the various languages and language families. This great interest in language led the Maskilim too to focus on language and is what gave it the standing it henceforth possessed in the new Jewish historical consciousness, as they turned it into a sign of belonging and continuity and an expression of a cultural essence—and in fact into the source of its cultural manifestations and spiritual content.

Only in the second half of the eighteenth century, be it noted, did the emergence of High German as a "cultural vehicle" reach its decisive phase. This process aimed at the formation of the literary norm of the German national language and the creation of an authentic general German language *(Gemeindeutsch)* and linguistic unity.[24] German was now asked to replace both Latin and French and expected to be capable of "conveying new ideas": "to try to make the German language say things in a different way, in a new way, even sometimes to make it say new things."[25]

In revamping the language, the aim was to replace Latin as the vehicle of "high" scholarly culture, and sure enough German was transformed into the language of the Enlightenment, with all its sociomoral values, and the language of science. The

Napoleonic Wars strengthened the desire for liberation from the influence of the French language, quickening German's transformation into the vehicle of national culture—the basis for turning the Germans into a *Kulturnation,* a nation with a shared national-cultural political consciousness which enhanced the status of its language. Such is the concise, action-packed time span in which the Berlin Haskalah operated.

All this was also being done in a culture in which philosophical debates were held between "rationalists" and "mystics" concerning the origin of natural language and its nature, a debate in which the history and character of Hebrew occupied a place of honor. The Hebrew language was considered a *lingua humana,*[26] and for mystics such as J. G. Hamann (1730–88) it was the most sublime and profound of all ("Das Heil kommt von den Juden");[27] while for others Greek held the absolute advantage. But Hamann did not consider a language's clarity to be the absolute criterion for style, whereas the Maskilim aspired, as we said, to just such a stylistic and linguistic clarity. They did not intend for Hebrew to convey a metaphysical conception but rather a response to Nature, a thrilling to the wholeness and complexity and harmony thereof; above all it had to be a language of wit: a language of the parable, the moralistic-didactic message, of knowledge and science.

The contemporary interest in the qualities and characteristics of Greek vis-à-vis biblical Hebrew found expression in such seminal compositions as those of Robert Lowth (1787)[28] and Thomas Blackwell (1736),[29] and it is to such sources that one may apparently trace the pronounced tendency by the Maskilim to roll off the list of Hebrew's qualities and characteristics, particularly *qua* language of literature and poetry: a language that can express humanity's position vis-à-vis the world and the religious and aesthetic impression the world invokes in it,[30] equal, if not superior, to Greek—a classical tongue like Greek, a "classic" source-language of civilization.

What the poetry of Homer was to European culture, the Bible was to the Jewish Maskilim, in particular the poetic layers which under pre-Romantic and then Romantic influence were perceived first as an expression of the classical and later as an expression of the sublime.[31] The state of the language, to them as to the medieval philosophers, now represented a mirror of the state of the nation, and as far as the Maskilim were concerned, that meant the cultural and social situation in the Diaspora as a closed, petrified society (they could not, of course, espouse Maimonides' view that life in the land of Israel is the sole condition for a "pure" language),[32] which must be "reformed" as part of the European society. Language, wrote Thomas Blackwell, "is the conveyance of our Thoughts" and the Greek language at the time of Homer "was brought to express all the best and bravest of the human Feelings and retained a sufficient Quantity of its *original, amazing, metaphoric* Tincture."[33] Of especial influence, of course, were Herder's ideas that language is a mirror of understanding ("ein Spiegel des Verstandes"), of the individual group, and the mirror of the state of a civilization. In his words, "the genius of language is thus the genius of the literature of a nation. . . ."[34] The return to the classical was therefore a "corrective" return, a return to the pure, ideal state of things. There was thus a direct and fundamental nexus between the ideology of a consummate Jewish society and that of the revival of the "pure" classical Hebrew, for language was seen as influencing thought and, by extension, civic behavior.[35] An "eclectic" language, such as Yiddish, is therefore like a mirror of an imperfect ossified society, incapable either of perfection from within or of integration into the civic society around it.

Thus to a very great extent German and Hebrew were designed to replace Yiddish, just as in the East the local vernacular together with Hebrew was fully to usurp it. Even if we cannot establish a direct inspiration, we have here a parallel to the outlook prevalent in the selfsame place and around the same time: Behind the move to "purify" Hebrew lay not only a rejection of Yiddish (*Ivri-Taytsh,* the Yiddish translation of Scripture) and the world it represented but also, simultaneously, that same national-cultural trend that was fuelling the activity of language expansion by Germans. They too, like the Maskilim, had to demonstrate that the national tongue was in a position to express "the new activities and results and disciplines that were springing up every day."[36] The criticism of Talmudic language, it should be remembered, did not reflect the attitude of Maskilim to the Talmud as a whole, for they turned to the Talmud for legitimation to study "foreign disciplines," in particular for a go-ahead to learn the local vernacular.[37] The legitimation for this might be found in the Talmud. But the Maskilim rejected the Talmud's practice of adopting words and concepts from a foreign tongue. In their articles and books, the Maskilim expended huge efforts on "Hebraizing" the concepts and terms and names, but for the most part they set the foreign source word alongside its Hebrew translation.

To this end it was necessary to translate the ideology of a "pure language"—reflecting an "ideal," primal as far as possible, state of affairs—into outright rationalistic practice, i.e., into an organized establishment of "artificial" norms. By a linguistic norm we mean the definition of a rational principle introduced into the language by means of conscious efforts on the part of the educated and by artificial conscious standardization.

The majority of Maskilim, admittedly, were not particularly intent on demonstrating the metaphorical richness of Hebrew, but they could not accept its portrayal as a language bereft of poetic qualities and qualifications and as a language of simple structures (as Robert Lowth put it, "its form is simple above every other ... nor capable of much variety").[38] They meant to prove that it could express the whole spectrum of human feelings and could portray "Nature."

Indeed, within a short space of time, intensively and simultaneously, Hebrew had to demonstrate capability in prose and science ("a language of reason") and in poetry ("a language of passions"). As a medium for a new "secular" literature, Hebrew was burdened with two herculean tasks, as a classical tongue engendering a classicist poetics and, at the same time, as a modern language creating a scientific literature in Hebrew.

3

There were thus two aspects to the "classical" dimension in the linguistic-literary activity of the Maskilim: (a) an attitude to Hebrew as a "classical" tongue, the language of classical civilization reflecting the golden age of "national culture," a knowledge of which was deemed equivalent to a knowledge of Greek (or Latin) among the European intelligentsia; (b) an attempt to create a "classical" Hebrew by "purging" it of postbiblical accretions. However, the Maskilim, as already observed, saw Hebrew literacy as more than just a means of understanding a classical Hebrew civilization from a distant past and the deeper and correct meaning of the Bible, and as more than just a classical layer upon which to mount a modern German-language culture. Hebrew literacy also had an active value in the creation of something new. For these purposes, biblical Hebrew was on a par with the medieval German now being revamped for modern times. Here, then, we find the second motif in the linguistic philosophy of the Berlin Haskalah and of the Jewish Enlightenment as a whole. Hebrew was regarded as a tool of *modernization* (and even acculturation). Putting it another way, the "modern" Jew's acquaintance with world culture, and with modern culture in particular, was to be effected in part by means of Hebrew.

"Modernization via Hebrew"—and certainly not through Yiddish which symbolized the despicable, the eclectic, the nonauthentic and a traditional conservative society to boot—meant "modernization via translation," for this was not a case of "original" scientific creation but of an intensive, ongoing attempt at transfer and adaptation, to enable the new Hebrew reader to find the knowledge he or she needed about the "world around them" and its culture, through Hebrew. To this end the Haskalah had to maintain a constant watch for what was happening around it and had to have classificational and selectional criteria (what was worth translating and adapting?) as well as ways of ingesting the selected material into the new Jewish cultural ambience. Equally, it had to espouse new literary genres or to alter the content (occasionally even the form) of traditional genres (an outstanding example would be the parable), and the lexicon had to be expanded, so that it might be possible to import the words and concepts of modern culture. It was not just Hebrew's *poetic* capability that had to be put on show—it was widely held to be inherently limited— but also its capacity to talk the *"language of science"* and the abstract language of philosophy. And in the background, let us not forget, was a ubiquitous dogma which went from strength to strength as the nineteenth century wore on, even being adopted by various Jewish spokesmen,[39] namely that Hebrew lacks the wherewithal to express abstract philosophical concepts. As literary Hebrew was not intended to be a classical language alone, the Maskilim from the first *Ha-Me'assef* onwards invested considerable energy toward "modernizing" it.

The Maskilim, it goes without saying, did not fancy that enlightened Jews, i.e., they themselves, would be able to make do with whatever was translated or adapted for them. They therefore defined themselves as "enlightened men" with a knowledge of both Hebrew and other languages, and attached great importance to learning German.[40] On the other hand, or so their attitude seemed to be, they believed that the general Jewish public at large, particularly in the East, would be satisfied with a "modernization via Hebrew." And this indeed is what happened in the second half of the nineteenth century, when many among the broad band of Jews open to the influence of modern culture received this culture via Hebrew.[41] As Ahad Ha'am showed in his article *"Riv Ha-Leshonot"* (The Language Conflict), in Haskalah times Hebrew was "the beginning of knowledge."[42] In any event, it is scarcely surprising that as German extended its domination among "modern" Jews in Germany, Hebrew was unable to meet their quest for knowledge and cultural integration, and when the gates of German culture were thrown open to them linguistically, all hope was lost that Hebrew might function as the language of modern culture; it was no longer necessary or useful, to Reformers and Orthodox alike.

Nor was there the motivation in Germany to fight the transformation of the Jewish vernacular into a literary medium or to mount a linguistic and cultural Hebrew opposition, as was indeed the case in later years with the Nationalist Maskilim in Eastern Europe—for Yiddish was pushed aside by German. The key factor in the waning of Hebrew in Germany as the nineteenth century began was the shrinking readership. However, one must not forget that many continued studying Hebrew as a second or secondary language and set themselves the goal of reading Hebrew at some level or other,[43] nor that texts of sundry kinds went on appearing in Hebrew until the 1830s.[44] Thus it was not a total ignorance of Hebrew that drove it to the margins of German Jewish culture, nor even the fact that it had from the start been allotted a minor place in the diglossic system, but above all the attempt to transform it into the language of modern culture within a society undergoing mounting acculturation from the turn of the century. This society now lived amidst a culture which ascribed prestigious weight to its own language and literature and which, by its successes and pulling power, had come to symbolize modern culture at its very best. To ignore its influence was an impossibility, and there was scant desire to do so. *Wissenschaft des Judentums* and the Reform Movement were not alone in regarding German as the language of culture and the national tongue; so too did Orthodoxy. S. R. Hirsch wrote of the German language:

> Die Sprache unseres Denkens and Dichtens, die Sprache unserer Liebe and Anhänglichkeit, die Sprache, mit der wir mit jedem Nerv unseres Seins verwachsen sind, bleibt für uns deutsche Juden unsere Muttersprache, unsere schöne deutsche Sprache.[45]

German also served to transmit outright "Jewish" values. And what had been in the cards from the start of the Berlin Haskalah, namely the move to modernization and acculturation via German, and even the move to translate Hebrew religious literature into German, drew further strength from a chain of sociocultural circumstances which carried all ideological resistance before them.

4

The Haskalah also signalled a third avenue, the conception of Hebrew as a national language, i.e., a language that not only unifies all sections of the nation but also expresses the "inner form" of the individual Jewish spirit, the essence of their *Volksgeist,* and their manner of interpreting the world, translating it and giving it order, form, and content. In this way, the Haskalah paved the way to the conception of Hebrew held by the National Movement in the last quarter of the nineteenth century. It is of course conceivable that even without the precedent or breakthrough of the Haskalah such a process could have happened, as a result of internal features of Eastern European Jewish society and the influence of nineteenth-century

Romantic nationalism. But the Berlin Haskalah not only engendered ideological assumptions but even showed that Hebrew has the potential of a language that is classical, modern, and national at one and the same time.

It was the "national" rhetoric of the Haskalah, responsible for a multitude of expectations and subsequently for their much criticized nonfulfilment, that created the new platform for projecting language as a central element of individual national consciousness. The German *Aufklärung* (Enlightenment) had already preempted the Romantic movement with this idea of language as expressing the special unique individuality of the national group, inter alia as a rejection of the universalistic rationalism of the "Western" Enlightenment. Language is the expression and embodiment of the *Volksgeist,* and the national tongue, the mother tongue, was seen as the absolute and authentic substantiation of the individualism of the group: "Man thinks only through his mother language. Every man has a mother; a mother tongue is enough for him," wrote Friedrich Ludwig Jahn, the prophet of German nationalism, in his popular book *Das deutsche Volkstum* (1810).[46] Those among the Berlin Haskalah who are also termed "nationalists" were of course not nationalists in the conventional sense. They did not subscribe to a return of the Jewish people to its land or to territorial nationalism, nor to the possibility of a full and exclusive Hebrew national culture in the Diaspora. Nationalism such as this was more than just beyond their horizons—it contradicted their goals. Thus the national dimension of the language, in their view, lay in being the key both to understanding the ancient national literature, now considered the authentic "national" *chef d'oeuvre,* and to connecting with this literary expression of the "national spirit" and culture by the direct medium of its language—as well as adding to it. In Haskalah doctrine, language now attained new status as a central element in a Jew's identity and in his consciousness of historical continuity.

This explains the "mystic," indeed "organistic," relationship of Maskilim to Hebrew as bearer of an inner national-cultural value. Is is not surprising that they were giving expression to this outlook on the nature of language as early as the 1780s; as already indicated, ideas in this vein had been voiced within the *Aufklärung* even before the Romantic hegemony. Johann David Michaelis, for example, in his prize-winning treatise of 1759, had observed that "languages are an accumulation of the wisdom and genius of nations."[47] Other Germans turned to the German literature of the Middle Ages to discover the "natural," "pure" German. For the Maskil, of course, there was no medieval literature or "popular, organic Hebrew"; for him, the Bible was the alternative literature.

Summing up, the Berlin Haskalah operated against a backdrop of a German cultural environment: from it, they learned to admire the classical languages and learned to see language as mirroring the circumstances of a culture, as being the platform for cultural unity and for the creation of an original national culture; from German, they learned about the concerted effort to create a new normative language while evicting dialects (and casting Yiddish as a colloquial) and about equipping such a language to function on all levels of modern culture. This was no "vision of national revival," as has often been claimed,[48] but rather a rhetoric shielding the recognition that the modern Jew would be diglossic and that one must therefore transform Hebrew into his second language and assign it other roles. But the second-language roles that were assigned in the West were too much for it to bear. The real circumstances, sociocultural and political processes of erosion, led to Hebrew being allotted from the outset a secondary, restricted position on the multilingual German-Jewish scene—restricted but multifunctional.

The achievement of the Berlin Haskalah was not only to prove that Hebrew could act as a modern cultural medium. With this proof went a carefully argued ideology that saw Hebrew as a secular national tongue, "secular" not in the sense of an essentially scriptural medium that also happens to be integrated into national life, but of a medium by which Jews could develop the full spectrum of national secular culture, as an ultimate alternative to the traditional culture. The Berlin Maskilim were conscious of the cultural revolution which they sought to bring on and in which Hebrew figured so prominently. Their historical role is to be found not just in what they did to Hebrew but also in the sense of value and mission they gave it.

The Berlin Haskalah also created the first "modern" Hebrew readership, and their activity transformed the language into a school subject. The study and knowledge of Hebrew were propagated through anthologies and children's literature. In other words, the three impossible functions that they assigned to Hebrew in Germany continued to operate in various parts of the Jewish world, although the following generations in Germany found that the three could not operate as an integrated whole—and so too in Eastern Europe, as the nineteenth century wore on. It took further historical developments in Jewish society in the "East" for it to become a possibility there.

In the generations to come, Hebrew would again be called upon to play two roles. The first role: "modernizer" of the Jew and vehicle of his interaction with European culture and ingestion of its values. The second role: a national language, the language of new, original literary works. These two roles, far from being complementary, contradicted each other or went their own separate ways, but as the end of the nineteenth century approached they were fulfilling this dual role for a growing swathe of society. What made this possible was that, unlike Germany or its spheres of influence, general Eastern European society was bilingual or even multilingual. This dual role was emphasized in ideology and rhetoric: Hebrew (rather than a foreign language) was viewed as the main bridge from "piety and ignorance" to modern European civilization and—at one and the same time—as the cherished national tongue, "the remnant of our treasures of Antiquity," i.e., as a cultural tongue in the "classical" and "modern" sense. In Eastern Europe, too, Hebrew was called upon to play the dual role of national-classical language and living artery of modern civilization. Objectively speaking, the Maskilim in the East were in an easier position than those in Germany: for the former, German could not be the natural "language of culture," and Polish and Russian did not strike them as being on a par. So Yiddish was left to provide the main and only opposition. And indeed, the position of Hebrew vis-à-vis Yiddish on the one hand and Russian on the other was to be a bone of contention from the 1860s on between the "radical Maskilim" working for russification and the "national Maskilim," and a source of inner doubts and cultural duality.[49] In any event, Hebrew in the West could not be the medium of Enlightenment nor a national secular tongue; in the East, it was both of these, and at the same time the language of religious life.

Notes

We begin in 1783 as the year in which the *Hevrat Dorshei Leshon Ever* (Society of Friends of Hebrew) joined forces with Moses Mendelssohn. The year 1819 saw the foundation of the group *Verein für Cultur and Wissenschaft der Juden* and the start of the *Wissenschaft des Judentums* school. The "generation of the Me'assefim" extends (with intermissions) across the years 1797–1811. In 1811 the last of *Ha-Me'assef He-Hadash* ceased to appear.

1. Wessely 1782: I,7. Diglossia for him had to involve Hebrew and German. In this, Wessely followed the philosophy of Mendelssohn; see Eliav 1960:25–51. Another reason for Wessely's opposition to the use of Hebrew as an "everyday language" was his fear that a wider Jewish public might thereby come under the influence of the "alien wisdoms"; German, by contrast, could only be the possession of a minority of Jews.

2. See Even-Zohar 1970, 1971, 1986; and Wexler 1971.

3. See Raisin 1913, who writes that the editors of *Ha-Ma'assef* held as their guiding idea that "Hebrew was to be utilized as a means of introducing Western civilization. Afterwards it was to be relegated once more to the Holy Ark." See too the detailed discussion by Tsamriyon 1988: 72–106. The controversy surrounding the "true" intentions of the Maskilim does not always distinguish the various functions knowingly assigned to the two languages. There is also an underlying assumption that the rebirth of Hebrew as a national tongue and acculturation are intrinsically opposites. In the words of Pelli 1979:82, ". . . the Maskilim did not see any dichotomy in their attitude toward the two languages. To them, the two went hand in hand." However, "nationhood" in the world view of the Maskilim was of a "restricted" kind, seeking primarily to create new layers of awareness not as a shield against acculturation but rather as an accessory and aid to it.

4. See Dinur 1972: 250–52; and also Barzilay 1956 and 1959.

5. "Divrei Shalom ve-Emet," *Ha-Maggid* (7 April and 15 April 1858).

6. In the celebrated words of H. N. Bialik 1930. Bilingual writers such as Bialik, equally at home in two languages, at least as regards reading and speaking, were not averse to preaching this opinion.

7. Smolenskin 1925. Smolenskin regarded Mendelssohn and his circle as having deliberately given legitimation to German as an exclusive cultural medium, thereby paving the way to assimilation.

8. See Cohen 1866. Euchel made this statement around the turn of the century, see Letteris 1784 = 1862: 46. See also Pelli 1979: 90. n. 3 and also Ben-Ze'ev 1808 in his introduction, pp. 17–18.

9. I. M. Jost in a letter to Ehrenberg roughly a year before the appearance of the Hebrew periodical *Zion* under his editorship in 1840 (see Michael 1983: 139). In the foreword to the first issue of *Zion* Jost wrote to "a friend living in Poland" that the periodical was intended for the knowledge-thirsty Jewish reader not versed in German or any other European language. See Eliav 1960: 162–76.

10. See in this regard the two comprehensive articles by Harshav 1990 and Morag 1990; as well as Rabin 1980.

11. See the controversy between Yehudah Friedlander 1987 and Me'ir Gilon 1987. Gilon is right to stress that rabbis and Haskalah writers did not share the same aim when writing of the need to study Hebrew. Mendelssohn's *Bi'ur* evoked sympathetic responses by rabbis—along with trenchant and unbridled criticism—because they regarded it as a fitting and reliable substitute for the Latin translation rather than as a rival to the Hebrew. Mendelssohn himself, incidentally, did not intend the *Bi'ur* to be a Jew's "teach-yourself German"; see Greenberg 1983: 113–20. On the rabbinic opposition to the *Bi'ur* see Eliav 1960: 30–36. The Maskilim, be it noted, saw Hebrew not only as a means of understanding the prayer book or as a layer in everyday life but as a classic vehicle of "modernization."

12. In its first year *Ha-Me'assef* had just eight subscribers in Poland and Lithuania, a number that would increase as the years passed. *Ha-Me'assef he-Hadash* already boasted many more subscribers outside Germany, three hundred apparently. See Tsamriyon 1988: 47. However, this says less about Hebrew literacy than about the size of the readership that considered Hebrew the vehicle of Haskalah ideas and the channel of communication of the new social set. On *Ha-Me'assef,* see also Röll (1985).

13. Meyer 1988: 24–25.

14. Katz 1973: 65. Katz highlights the fact that those behind *Ha-Me'assef* changed their name in 1785 from *Dorshei Sefat Ever* (Friends of Hebrew) to *Die Gesellschaft zur Beförderung des Guten und Edlen,* signifying the rapid and radical ideological shift in their world view.

15. Strictly speaking, the nexus between these two facts is far from automatic. Modern Jewish education at that time was also producing new Hebrew users, alongside those who were there at the birth of *Ha-Me'assef* thanks to their traditional schooling. It is patently impossible, however, that the knowledge of the two languages could evolve in parallel fashion.

16. Euchel 1832. On Euchel, see Feiner 1987 and Pelli 1979: 190–230.

17. On the attitude of the Maskilim to Yiddish, see Tsamriyon 1988: 87–88, and Shemueli 1986.

18. It will be recalled that Wessely in *Nahal Absor* (i.e., *Nahal Ha-Besor*), ed. Letteris: p. 8, designated German for "worldly affairs of business" and for "general learning" unrelated to Torah. Thus linguistic stratification was also to reflect social stratification, expressing, to my mind, a "conservative" social standpoint that distinguished elite from masses in the new sociocultural context.

19. The compliments paid to Hebrew allude—and even refer directly—to Aggadic Midrashim extolling Hebrew as well as to statements to this effect by Maimonides, Yehudah Halevi, Rashi, and others. See Tsamriyon 1988: 72–106 and n. 67. On Maimonides' viewpoint on the special nature of Hebrew and his attitude to the "confusion of tongues" resulting from the Exile, see Twersky 1989 and Levinger 1989: 94–98. Maimonides held that the purity of Hebrew had been sullied by life in exile and could only be restored by resettling the Holy Land (and thus no Maskil could be "national" by this philosophy!). He was, however, not party to the fundamental criticism of mishnaic Hebrew. A mordantly negative stand against Hebrew polyglossia was taken by Joseph Kimhi, of a classically purist persuasion. A different view was voiced by Jonah Ibn Janah and others who espoused the cause of comparative philology—see Talmage 1989. For views on the origin of language—conventional or natural—see Wolfson 1950: 609–22. The Maskilim concurred that language possesses a "pure (classical) state" which must be regained, in line with the view of contemporary German literati who sought to return German to its *"rein Deutsch"* or *"rechte deutsche Sprache"* state.

20. "Our entire purpose is to raise the horn of Judea that languishes in the ashes of oblivion and in the dungheaps of disgrace." *Ha-Me'assef* (1774): 192 *et passim.* Here too there is

an overlap with the widely-held belief that the state of a language is an embodiment of the general cultural state of a nation. See also Gilon 1979.

21. Altman 1973: 88 states that "Mendelssohn wished to show that biblical Hebrew was capable of expressing all moods of human life—sorrow, joy, anger etc. In other words, classical Hebrew could serve as an organ of expression even in modern times."

22. For full details of such declarations, see Yitzhaki 1970, Pelli 1979, and Tsamriyon 1988.

23. See Pelli 1988: 18–22.

24. On the "discovery of tongues," see Pederson 1962 and Guxman 1977.

25. Blackall 1959: 1.

26. See Katz 1982: 43–87. For brief discussion of Hebraism in Germany, see the section "Hebräisch und Bibelstudien," in Harlfinger 1989: 306–35.

27. On Georg Hamann (1730–88), see Blackall 1959: 430–37. Hamann was of course a fierce critic of Mendelssohn and regarded language as a manifestation of revelation, cf. the dispute there between the rationalist and mystical approach to the character of biblical language. The Rationalists denied its "clarity" (which they considered the prime quality of language), whereas Hamann rejected the use of clarity as an absolute criterion of style.

28. Lowth 1969. See the introduction by Vincent Freimarck, v–xxxvi. For Lowth's influence on Shelomo Levisohn, see Tova Cohen 1988: 32–33.

29. Blackwell 1976. On the book's powerful influence upon the German Aufklärung, see Reil 1975: 203–204.

30. See Gilon 1979: 55–74. *Kohelet Mussar* (1755–56), like the contemporaneous German journals and literary periodicals (*moralische Wochenschriften,* "moral weeklies"), aimed to foster and propagate a correct style. See Van Dülmen 1986 and Blackall 1959: 49–101.

31. Cohen 1988: 49–55, is at pains to emphasize the influence of the English pre-Romantic poetics of the sublime, and of course Levisohn's direct acquaintance with the *Peri Hypsoys* of Longinus in its Latin translation. On the other hand, she allows no room for the contemporaneous poetics and philosophy of language of the German Enlightenment.

32. Twersky 1989.

33. Blackwell 1976: 36, 46–47.

34. Irmacher 1985: 137–73. Herder held that "every language has its own genius," and this is a source of inspiration for views like Bialik's (cf. note 6) and the nationalist-Romantic concept of the Hebrew language in modern times.

35. On the influence of this outlook on the tie between language, culture, and society in the U.S.A., see Bynack 1984: "To establish a national standard." Social and national cultural reform were seen as bound up with correctness and purity of language.

36. Tsamriyon 1988: 78–84.

37. I discuss this matter in my book (in press), *Judaism in the Greek Mirror.*

38. Lowth (p. 39) stated that compared to the Hebrew, Greek "beyond every other language (and Latin next to it) is a copious flowing, and harmonious, possessed of a great variety of measures, of which the impression definite, the affects so striking. . . ."

39. See, for example, Shavit 1987.

40. German was more highly esteemed than other European languages as a language of culture by the Maskilim and Jewish intellegentsia in particular throughout the nineteenth century and beyond. French, by contrast, represented a "decadent culture."

41. Mendele Mokher Sefarim in his story *Ha-Avot ve-ha-Banim* (reprinted 1963): 14–15, writes that Hebrew was the beginning of the Haskalah: "for among them too, the desire for knowledge and intellect only begins to stir through the Hebrew language. It opens their eyes and gives them the basics."

42. Ahad Ha'am 1930.

43. On the place of Hebrew in the Jewish school curriculum in Germany, see the detailed description by Eliav 1960. In the school in Wolfenbüttel (p. 108), for instance, in 1818 the first two classes had 5 hours of Hebrew, 5 of German, 4 of French, 4 of Latin, and 2 of Greek. In 1843 they were taking 9 hours of German and 4 of Hebrew; the other languages had gone.

44. The first Hebrew textbooks in the natural sciences appeared in the mid-eighteenth century. On the Hebrew literature for younger readers, see Zohar Shavit 1987.

45. Breuer 1986: 83. Geiger 1861 wrote in similar vein of language being a creation of the spirit and emotions and thus the fact that Hebrew was no longer a living tongue or even a language of enlightenment or religious expression created alienation. Hence the desirability that prayer too (even in private) should be in German.

46. Jahn 1810.

47. Michaelis 1769: 12. Note that this is a matter of the national language of the *Kulturnation*, not of a politically united nation.

48. See Tsamriyon 1988 and others.

49. See Breiman 1954.

References

AHAD HA'AM. "Riv ha-Leshonot" (The Language Quarrel). In *Al Parashat Derakhim*. Vol. 4, 2nd ed., Berlin 1930, pp. 116–123.

ALTMANN, ALEXANDER. *Moses Mendelssohn: A Biographical Study*. London: 1973.

BARZILAY, ISAAC E. "The Ideology of the Berlin Haskalah." *Proceedings of the American Academy for Jewish Research* 25 (1956): 1–37.

———. "National and Anti-National Trends in the Berlin Haskalah." *Jewish Social Studies* 22 (July 1959): 165–92.

BEN-ZE'EV, YEHUDAH. *Otzar Ha-Shorashim*. Vienna: 1808.

BIALIK, HAYYIM NAHMAN. "Hevlei Lashon" (Language Travail). *Collected Works*. Vol. 2. Tel Aviv: 1930, pp. 211–23.

BLACKALL, ERIC. A. *The Emergence of German as a Literary Language 1700–1755*. Cambridge: 1959.

BLACKWELL, THOMAS. *An Enquiry into the Life and Writings of Homer*. Hildesheim and New York: Olms Verlag (1736) 1976.

BREIMAN, S. "U. Kovner and Hebrew Criticism." In Simon Rawidowicz, ed. *Metsudah: (Fortress) Essays and Studies*. London, 1954, pp. 416–57 In Hebrew.

BREUER, MORDECHAI. *Jüdische Orthodoxie im deutschen Reich 1871–1918: Die Sozialgeschichte einer religiösen Minderheit*. Frankfurt-am-Main: Jüdischer Verlag bei Atheneum, 1986.

BYNACK, V. P. "Noah Webster's Linguistic Thought and the Idea of American National Culture." *Journal of the History of Ideas* 45, 1 (January–March 1984): 99–113.

COHEN, SHALOM. *Ketav Yosher, Safah Berurah*. Epistle 2. Lemberg, 1866.

COHEN, TOVA. *Melitzat Yeshurun by Shelomo Levisohn: The Work and its Author*. Ramat Gan: Bar-Ilan University Press, 1988 In Hebrew.

DINUR, BENZION. *Historical Writings*. Vol. 1. Jerusalem: 1972 In Hebrew.

ELIAV, MORDECHAI. *Jewish Education in Germany in the Period of Enlightenment and Emancipation*. Jerusalem: 1960 In Hebrew.

EUCHEL, ISAAC ABRAHAM. *Sefat Emet. (Language of Truth)* Koenigsberg: 1832.

EVEN-ZOHAR, ITAMAR. "The Nature and Functionalization of the Language of Literature under Diglossia." *Ha-Sifrut* 2,2 (January 1970): 286–302 In Hebrew.

———. "Literature Written in Language with a Defective Polysystem." *Ha-Sifrut* 3,2 (November 1971): 339–40 In Hebrew.

———. "Language Conflict and National Identity: A Semiotic Approach." In Joseph Alpher, ed. *Nationalism and Modernity: A Mediterranean Perspective.* New York: Praeger 1986, pp. 126–35.

FEINER, SHEMUEL. "Yitzhak Euchel, ha-'Yazam' shel Tenu'at ha-Haskalah be-Germanyah" [Isaac Euchel, "Entrepreneur" of the Haskalah Movement in Germany.] *Zion* 52,4 (1987): 427–69.

FRIEDLANDER, YEHUDA. "Hebrew Satire in Germany in the Late Eighteenth Century: Dissection of a Critique." *Zion* 70,4 (1987): 510–23 In Hebrew.

GEIGER, ABRAHAM. *Notwendigkeit and Mass einer Reform des jüdischen Gottesdiensts.* Breslau: 1861.

GILON, MEIR. *Mendelssohn's Kohelet Mussar in its Historical Context.* Jerusalem: 1979 In Hebrew.

———. "Hebrew Satire in the Age of Haskalah in Germany: A Rejoinder." *Zion* 70,4 (1987): 524–30 In Hebrew.

GREENBERG, MOSHE, ed. *Jewish Bible Exegesis: An Introduction.* Jerusalem: 1983 In Hebrew.

GUXMAN, M. M. "Formation of the Literary Norm in the German National Language." In Philip A. Luelsdorff, ed. *Soviet Contribution to the Sociology of Language.* The Hague: Mouton, 1977, pp. 7–30.

HARLFINGER, DIETER, ed. *Graecogermania: Griechstudien deutscher Humanisten (1469–1523). Ausstellung und Katalog.* Wolfenbüttel: Herzog August Bibliothek, no. 59, 1989.

HARSHAV, BINYAMIN. "Masah al Tehiyat ha-Lashon ha-Ivrit." *Alpayim* 2 (1990): 9–54.

IRMACHER, HANS DIETRICH. *Introduction to Johann Gottfried Herder's "Abhandlung über den Ursprung der Sprache" (1770).* Stuttgart: Reclam, (1966) 1985.

JAHN, FRIEDRICH LUDWIG. *Das Deutsche Volkstum.* Lübeck, 1810. Reprinted in Louis L. Snyder, *The Dynamics of Nationalism.* Princeton, NJ: Princeton University Press, 1964, pp. 149–53.

KATZ, DAVID S. *Philo-Semitism and the Readmission of the Jews to England 1603–1666.* Oxford: Oxford University Press, 1982.

KATZ, JACOB. *Out of the Ghetto: The Social Background of the Jewish Emancipation, 1770–1870.* Cambridge, MA, 1973.

LETTERIS, MEIR. "Toldot he-Hakham R. Yizhak Euchel." *Ha-Me'assef,* 1784 = Vienna, 1862.

LEVINGER, JACOB S. *Maimonides as Philosopher and Codifier.* Jerusalem: 1989 In Hebrew.

LOWTH, ROBERT. *Lectures on the Sacred Poetry of the Hebrews.* Hildesheim: Olms Verlag, (1753, in Latin, 1787) 1969.

MENDELE MOKHER SEFARIM. *Collected Works.* Tel Aviv: Dvir, 1963 In Hebrew.

MEYER, MICHAEL. *Response to Modernity: A History of Reform Movement in Judaism.* New York and Oxford: Oxford University Press, 1988.

MICHAEL, REUVEN. *I. M. Jost, Founder of Modern Jewish Historiography.* Jerusalem: 1983 In Hebrew.

MICHAELIS, JOHANN DAVID. *A Dissertation on the Influence of Opinions on Language and of Language on Opinions.* (1760 in German), London: 1769.

MORAG, SHELOMO. "Modern Hebrew–Some Sociolinguistic Aspects." *Cathedra for the History of Eretz Israel and its Yishuv* 56 (June 1990): 70–92 In Hebrew.

PEDERSON, HOLGAR. *The Discovery of Language: Linguistic Science in the Nineteenth Century.* Bloomington, IN: Indiana University Press, 1962.

PELLI, MOSHE. *The Age of Haskalah: Studies in Hebrew Literature of the Enlightenment in Germany.* Leiden: 1979. Chapter 4: "The Revival of Hebrew and the Revival of the People: The Attitude of the First Maskilim towards the Hebrew Language."

———. *Struggle for Change: Studies in the Hebrew Enlightenment in Germany at the End of the Eighteenth Century.* Tel Aviv: 1988 In Hebrew.

RABIN, CHAIM. "What Was the Revival of Hebrew?" In Avraham Even-Shoshan, ed. *Sefer Shalom Sivan.* Jerusalem, 1980, pp. 125–40.

RAISIN, JACOB *The Haskalah Movement in Russia.* Philadelphia: 1913.

REIL, PETER HANS. *The German Enlightenment and the Rise of Historicism.* Berkeley: University of California Press, 1975.

RÖLL, WALTER. "The Kassel 'Ha-Me'assef' of 1799: An Unknown Contribution to the Haskalah." In Jehudah Reinharz and Walter Schatzberg, eds. *The Jewish Response to German Culture: From the Enlightenment to the Second World War.* Hanover: University Press of New England, 1985, pp. 32–50.

SHAVIT, ZOHAR. "From Friedlander's *Lesebuch* to the Jewish Camp—The Beginnings of Hebrew Children's Literature in Germany." *Leo Baeck Institute Year Book* 32 (London 1987): 385–416.

SHAVIT, YAACOV. "Semites and 'Aryans' in Modern Hebrew Polemics." In Shmuel Almog et al., eds. *Israel Among the Nations: Essays Presented in Honor of Shemuel Ettinger.* Jerusalem, 1987, pp. 215–41 In Hebrew.

SHEMUELI, EPHRAIM. "Hevlei Tarbut—Hevlei Lashon: Moshe Mendelson u-Va'ayat Ribuy ha-Leshonot be-Sifrut Yisra'el." *Kivunnim* 33 (1986): 136–44.

SMOLENSKIN, PERETZ. "Et Lata'at." *Essays.* Vol. 2. Jerusalem: 1925, pp. 235–37.

TALMAGE, FRANK. "Rabbi Joseph Kimhi: From the Depression of Jerusalem in Sepharad to the Canaanites in Zarephath." In H. Ben-Sasson, R. Bonfil, and J. R. Hacker, eds. *Culture and Society in Medieval Jewry.* Jerusalem: 1989, pp. 315–28 In Hebrew.

TSAMRIYON, TSEMAH. *Ha-Me'assef: The First Modern Periodical in Hebrew.* Tel Aviv: 1988 In Hebrew.

TWERSKY, ISADORE. "Maimonides and Erets Israel: Halakhic, Philosophical, and Historical Aspects." In H. Ben-Sasson, R. Bonfil, and J. R. Hacker, eds. *Culture and Society in Medieval Jewry.* Jerusalem: 1989, pp. 271–368 In Hebrew.

VAN DÜLMEN, RICHARD. *Die Gesellschaft der Aufklärer: Zur bürgerlichen Emanzipation und aufklärerischen Kultur in Deutschland.* Frankfurt-am-Main: 1986.

WESSELY, NAFTALI HERZ. *Divrei Shalom Ve-Emet.* 1782.

WEXLER, PAUL. "Diglossia, Language Standardization, and Purism: Towards a Typology of Literary Languages." *Ha-Sifrut* 3,2 (November 1971): 326–38 In Hebrew.

WOLFSON, HARRY A. "The Veracity of Scripture in Philo, Halevi, Maimonides, and Spinoza." In Saul Lieberman, ed. *Alexander Marx Jubilee Volume.* New York: The Jewish Theological Seminary of America, 1950. English Section, 603–30.

YITZHAKI, YOSEF. "The Views of the Writers of the Haskalah on the Hebrew Language and their Methods of Extending and Renovating it." *Leshonenu* 34 (1970): 287–305, 35: 39–59 and 140–155.

8

What Did "Knowing Hebrew" Mean in Eastern Europe?

SHAUL STAMPFER

Knowledge of Hebrew, its role in Jewish society, and its function in any given period is best understood by looking at it in its social context. When we do so for Hebrew in its nineteenth century East European setting we find that knowledge of Hebrew and changes in the place of Hebrew were closely related to basic issues and developments in that society. Knowledge of Hebrew can mean various things. It can refer to a technical ability to read a Hebrew text, to an ability to write in Hebrew letters as well as to an ability to read a text in Hebrew and to understand it. We will first examine the data available on different types of knowledge of Hebrew in traditional East European Jewish society, the role of Hebrew in that culture and finally what changes took place in the nineteenth century and why.

Virtually every male in traditional East European Jewish society studied Hebrew and texts written in Hebrew (and Aramaic) for about ten years, and this should have guaranteed some level of literacy for all. However, the results were not identical for all and determining what they were, even for some of them, is not that easy. There is no good source for quantitative data on literacy in Hebrew. Even defining Hebrew literacy is not simple. The term "literacy" refers in normal English usage to the ability to read and write. In most Western schools, reading and writing are taught together. Both skills are very practical, necessary in modern society, and they reinforce each other. During the Middle Ages there was an added virtue to studying the two together. Books were in short supply and students copied the texts they would study.

The coming of the printing press changed all of this. In most European societies, the increased availability of books was paralleled by a rise in literacy among the population. However, East European Jewish education took advantage of the new technology and the drop in the price of books by dropping penmanship from the standard curriculum of the *ḥeder* or Jewish elementary school.[1] Reading the holy writ was one thing and writing a shopping list was another, and it was unbefitting for a *ḥeder* devoted to the teaching of the word and will of God in the form of Torah and Gemara to devote time and effort to such mundane, though practical, skills.[2] Thus, when dealing with early modern Eastern Europe, we have to distinguish between the two skills, and reading ability cannot simply be measured by what is known about the ability to write.

In any case, there is precious little evidence for the percentage of the population who could write. The ability to sign is often used for these purposes, even though it is well known that not all who can sign their name know how to write. Unfortunately, there were few situations where Jews had to sign documents. One of the few cases of this type was in Poland. A study of marriage registration forms found that in 1845/6 about a quarter of the Jewish males could not sign, neither in Polish nor in Hebrew, and fifteen years later there was no significant difference.[3] According to this data, about half the signatories in 1845 could write in Polish and fifteen years later, two thirds. The problem with this evidence is that there are few reasons to assume that what happened in Warsaw was typical for any place other than Warsaw, and even in Warsaw there might have been discrimination against signing in Hebrew. Signed membership lists of organizations could serve as another possible source but most of these lists are made up of upper and middle class individuals who were most likely to know how to write. In this respect, membership lists of craft guilds can be useful. The few that have been carefully studied reveal an interesting pattern of mistakes. An error such as writing the name Mordechai with a *het* or Nathan with a *samekh* is an error made by someone who knows how letters sound and not someone who learned at one stage how to sign a name without knowing how to read and simply forgot which letters to use. However, many found any writing difficult. When the members of a water carriers guild in Minsk signed their charter in 1829, eight out of thirteen used a proxy to sign for them and eight out of twenty-five tailors used a proxy in Sokolov in 1835. In records from a tailors guild in Bialystok, only one or two out of the thirty to forty members could not sign themselves.[4] In an agreement signed by guild representatives who presumably were from the worker elite, in Wlodawa (Eastern Poland, near Brest Litowski) in 1743, one out of eight was unable to sign.[5]

More promising from a quantitative point of view, and probably more significant as well, is to try to find data on the ability to read Hebrew. Here as well the data available on ability to read Hebrew in traditional Jewish society is limited.

The census of the Czarist empire made in 1897 does not give reliable data on Hebrew literacy so it can be ignored. In a careful survey taken in 1901 of Jewish workers in Minsk, about 10 percent of the male masters and about a quarter of the journeymen and apprentices were reported as unable to read Hebrew or Yiddish.[6] A 1913 study of Vilna, Warsaw, Berdichev and Busin found negligible percentages of individuals totally unable to read Hebrew.[7] A careful study of immigrants to the United States found that about 15 percent were illiterate in Hebrew and any other language.[8] All of these groups were nonrepresentative in that they came from the working classes which were proverbially ignoramuses. This data seems to support the traditional stereotypical view that almost every male in East European Jewish society could read.

Here as well, the question remains as to what an ability to read means. In other words, how well did Hebrew readers understand what they were reading? As we shall see, most males probably could read but they had a very limited ability to understand an unfamiliar text in Hebrew.

The reason for the limited mastery of Hebrew among most males in Eastern Europe lies in the framework for elementary education.[9] Almost all boys began their study in the *ḥeder*. These were private one-room schools. Most of the teachers in these schools were very poor and entered teaching after failing at other attempts to earn a living. Many were neither very learned nor good teachers and they often made up for their lack of pedagogical skills by administering violent physical punishment to their pupils. Since parents picked the teachers and paid them directly, a situation arose naturally in which the better off and highly motivated paid more than the going rates to secure the few good *ḥeder* teachers for their children, and these parents often paid a premium so that the *ḥeder* teacher would take only a limited number of pupils. The result was that most children studied with poor teachers and in large classes together with other children of low-motivated parents. These were certainly not ideal conditions for study.

Study began at the age of four and continued more or less until the age of thirteen. At that point pupils who were able to study the Talmud independently could go on to advanced study. The others, and they were the vast majority, went out to work and/or to learn a trade. The end of formal education at the age of thirteen or fourteen served as a cutoff point. A student who did not reach a satisfactory level by that point would have no chance to reenter the framework of education and to go on to advanced study. At certain periods, such as the eighteenth and early nineteenth century, it was common for outstanding Talmud students to marry very early—around the age of thirteen. They would then live in their father-in-law's house and study full time in the local *bet midrash* (community study hall) with all of their material needs taken care of by the father-in-law. This of course was a way to demonstrate to the entire community, who prayed regularly in the local study hall, the wealth and the devotion to Torah of the father-in-law.[10]

When drafting for service in the Czarist army began on the initiative of Nicholas I, young Talmud scholars were generally safe from the danger of the draft. Moreover, scholars in *batei midrash* were supported by pious families who provided them with meals—modest but regular—and many of their other needs. Study in a *bet midrash* was tuition-free and even provided status in the traditional society. The only condition for studying in a *bet midrash* was an ability, acquired in *ḥeder,* to study the Talmud independently. In short, a young scholar had every possible reason to devote himself to study in a *bet midrash.* To be sure, the onset of the draft led to an increase in the number of *bet midrash* and *yeshiva* students, but these institutions were not flooded with students.[11] Given the terror with which the draft was regarded, the limited number of students who went to communal study halls is strong evidence that in 1828 most boys were not able to prepare a page of Talmud independently—even if their lives depended upon it.

It therefore seems clear that even though most men could read Hebrew, they were at the same time unable to study Talmud on their own. Doing the latter requires a knowledge not only of Hebrew but also of Aramaic and requires much more than technical reading skills. Determining what was the level of most men between these two extremes is not easy, and most of our evidence is circumstantial in nature. It is directly based on an understanding of the role of Hebrew in East European Jewish society.

It has been pointed out by many that the Jewish community in Eastern Europe was characterized by diglossia. That is to say, there was a literary language and a spoken vernacular. In this respect, Hebrew filled a role very much like that of Latin. It was the language of texts written in a revered past and it was studied and used by individuals in various lands who spoke a variety of vernaculars. Hebrew had the additional quality of being regarded as a holy language since it was believed by Jews (and Christians) that God had given the Torah in Hebrew and had even commanded the creation of the world by speaking in Hebrew.

Not surprisingly, an analysis of how Latin functioned in Christian society sheds light on the place of Hebrew in Jewish society. The similarities between the role of Hebrew and that of Latin are many. The higher educational program of most European societies took a knowledge of Latin for granted. This was not a simple matter, for learning Latin was a long process which could take over eight years.[12] However, it was necessary for the individual who wanted to go on to advanced study. The curriculum of the medieval university was based on texts written in Latin and much scholarly work, depending of course on the time and place, was done in Latin. Therefore, "Before the student could profitably attend university lectures, he must have learned to read, write, and understand such Latin as was used in the schools,"[13] and this knowledge was the basic academic precondition for admission to the medieval university. University freshmen were "as a rule ... between thirteen and sixteen"[14] and most of their pre-university study was devoted to learning Latin.

Much, if not all, of this advanced education could have been in the spoken language. Indeed, the rapid spread of use of the vernacular in post-Renaissance periods shows how little education is dependent on knowledge of Latin. There is little doubt that the classical literature is well worth studying. However, for the level of understanding that most people reach, a translation is almost as good as the original. What the concentration on Latin did achieve was to weed out the number of students who reached advanced study. Tuition itself cost money. Moreover, it required a long-term commitment, for the study of Latin was worthwhile only if the long course of study necessary to reach even an elementary proficiency in Latin was completed. This meant that only children of a certain level of society could in practice prepare themselves for admission to university and higher study. Access was restricted, by using language as a hurdle on the way to valuable knowledge. This in a sense is what kept up the value of the knowledge since it was not readily available to most people. To get information most people had to go to one of the individuals who had learned Latin and had access to the knowledge written in it. The change to the use of the vernacular as the language for scholarly and religious writing meant that one major barrier to the direct acquisition of information was eliminated.

Jewish education in Eastern Europe concentrated on the Babylonian Talmud, virtually ignoring the Bible, the Jerusalem Talmud, Midrash and other potential texts for study. Medieval education was equally centered on an agreed-upon list of classical authors. However, this use of language and an agreed-upon body of classical literature was not unique to Jewish or medieval Christian society. In Chinese culture as well, there was a concentration on the writings of Confucius; and examples from other cultures are not difficult to find.

One characteristic all of these societies had in common was a commitment to very similar views as to what characterized the ideal leader. In a comparative study of Victorian England and classical China, Wilkinson found the following characteristics of what he termed "the gentleman ideal," and they are as applicable to East European Jewish society as they were to England and China:[15]

> ... there are two secondary characteristics of the gentleman concept that are particularly important. ... The first is classical learning and the second is the possession of leisure. Both were concerned with an aesthetic ideal of elegant ease—or at least a posture of ease. ...
>
> To the gentleman, and those who respected him, classical culture was supposed to confer moral advantage by providing select access to past wisdoms. Confucian doctrine stated quite explicitly that great virtue could only come through learning. In England, the moral claims ... were fainter, but in tacit form they existed.
>
> Both societies, however, made familiarity with a classical body of knowledge a matter of aesthetic, as well as moral, advantage. "Puns, euphemisms, allusions to classical quotations, and a refined and purely literary intellectuality were considered the conversational ideal of the genteel man" [in China and] ... the power of the apt and witty classical allusion carried advantage in England. ...
>
> Classical culture ... contributed to the differentiated style that gave the gentleman elite its magical aura. ... For by definition, a classic only becomes a classic when it gains a measure of antiquity; when it appears to conform to a well-ordered structure and when it follows absolute and unquestionable rules.

In traditional East European Jewish society, leading citizens spent much of their time in study in the communal study hall—which demonstrates that they did not have to work at that time. This unconscious demonstration is very close to what Wilkinson called "a posture of ease." In this society the rabbinic literature and especially the Talmud was regarded as the repository of all virtue and certainly the best source of guidance for correct behavior in accordance with God's will. Status and membership in the intellectual elite, which was to no small degree correlated with membership of the socio-economic elite, was demonstrated through "talking in Torah," i.e., demonstrating through conversation an easy familiarity with the concepts and terminology of rabbinic literature as well as scope of knowledge as shown through quotations.

One of the virtues of Hebrew appears to have been the fact that a good knowledge of the language and of the literature[16] was limited. The relative failure of the *ḥeder* to produce graduates with a good knowledge of Hebrew was in this respect a very desirable goal from the point of view of the elite. It should be emphasized that both the elite and the masses were totally unaware of this function of education.[17]

However, even the restricted knowledge of Hebrew that most males received did of course have its purpose. It enabled them to use a prayer book and to read a limited number of texts, namely the Torah with Rashi's commentary—which was a central element in the *ḥeder* curriculum—with some understanding, even though reading an unfamiliar text would have posed severe difficulties. Hebrew knowledge, however limited, had an additional function. It set apart men from women or—if one wants to put it bluntly—it gave them (and women) a sense that men were superior. Some, perhaps many, women could read a vocalized Hebrew text. However, few women understood any Hebrew, and when they took a book in hand, it was in Yiddish and not in Hebrew.[18]

How much reading was necessary in Eastern Europe after all? One of the interesting characteristics of Hebrew publishing in Eastern Europe in the eighteenth and early nineteenth century is the relatively small number of books published in Hebrew and directed to the nonlearned reader. Most books published in Hebrew were directed to a learned audience or were prayerbooks, Bibles, and similar books designed for ritual use. There was a widespread genre of ethical tracts designed for a more general audience,[19] but even these texts, in their Hebrew versions, took a fair amount of education for granted. It was the Yiddish versions of these books which were directed not only to women but to the large numbers of uneducated men.[20]

Jewish society in Eastern Europe was in many respects a profoundly oral society. Despite the widespread ability to read among men, information which determined both belief and behavior was generally obtained orally. One important reason for this is that knowledge that was deemed valuable was written in Hebrew while the same information in a Yiddish translation was regarded as nonauthoritative.[21] Since understanding Hebrew was a problem for most male readers, they could not rely on their own reading for information.[22] This can be seen in a number of areas.

In Eastern Europe, it was assumed by most Jews, up until the modern period, that the correct observance of Jewish law was a precondition for a good fate in the world to come. This involved a very complicated system of commandments and prohibitions. At the same time, most people learned what to do through imitation of parents and through asking a rabbi or learned acquaintance. Relatively little information was acquired through direct reading of guides. The most likely candidate for such a book was the *Shulḥan Arukh,* published in 1565. Indeed, when it first came out, it was criticized precisely on the grounds that unlearned readers might use it to decide questions of Jewish law without turning for guidance (accepting the authority and power) from the rabbis.[23] The book was neutralized in this respect by the fact that, from the seventeenth century on, it was never published without a commentary. The minute a handbook or guide appears with a commentary or commentaries, presenting differing views on the contents, it is no longer useful as a guide for the untutored reader. He may be able to read the contents and understand them, but how is he to decide which of the commentaries he should accept?

Practical knowledge for commerce and crafts was also not learned from books. There was little technical development in the crafts of Eastern Europe and what there was could be picked up through imitation. Jewish trade was based to a large extent on contacts and very often it skirted the law.[24] There was little to write about and little to learn from books that would not be learned more efficiently from an apprenticeship—formal or informal.

Even the study of religious texts was very oral in character in Eastern Europe. Most males studied in the framework of *ḥevrot,* in communal study halls as mentioned above, and not in solitude.[25] There were *ḥevrot* devoted to various texts which would gather in the same study hall for study. There was a hierarchical structure to these *ḥevrot* based on the difficulty/status of the text. Highest in status was the *ḥevra* devoted to the study of the Talmud *(ḥevrat shas).* Lower were *ḥevrot* devoted to the study of Mishnah or to Ein Yaakov (a compilation of the aggadic portions of the Talmud) and the lowest were the *ḥevrot* devoted to the saying of chapters of Psalms in unison.[26] In the *ḥevrot* devoted to study, participants did not study as a group nor did they take turns giving the lesson. Rather, they had a teacher who read the text and explained it. To be able to follow the lesson and to ask a good question required a background in study, but participants were not expected to be at the level where they could study the material on their own.

Within the traditional East European Jewish community, perhaps the most important source of information on religion and especially belief were not books but the lectures or sermons given on Saturdays. These *drashot* were usually not given by official communal rabbis. It would have been beneath their dignity to speak in a popular style to the masses every Sabbath. Rather, these talks were given by *darshanim* or preachers—some of whom were official communal preachers and some of whom wandered from community to community preaching for a living.

The gap between oral and literary culture can be seen while leafing through almost any book of rabbinic sermons. They are all in Hebrew, with full citations of textual sources and full of learned asides. It is easy to forget that these sermons were given only in Yiddish because only in Yiddish were they understandable to a wide audience. At the same time, no *darshan* would ever dream of writing down or printing his sermon in the language in which it was originally given. Translation meant editing as well, so that in their printed form these sermons were directed to a learned audience and not an audience identical to the listeners of the sermons.

The Hasidic movement was the product of oral more than written propaganda. While great attention has been paid to the Hasidic story in general and to the first collection of stories about the Baal Shem Tov, *Shivḥei HaBesht,* it is worth noting the complicated history of the book. It was first published in Hebrew in 1815, and some five editions came out in the next three years. However, from 1818 to 1828 no editions were printed and in the next thirty years, only two. Three or four Yiddish translations appeared between 1815 and 1817, but they too were not reprinted for decades. There was clearly a market for the book. In the early days of Hasidism, the printing presses in the areas in which Hasidism arose were busy printing esoteric kabbalistic works alongside halakhic and rabbinic works but not popular texts aimed at the common reader.[27] This may have contributed to the atmosphere of interest in Kabbalah among the initiated readers but, once again, these books were not aimed at the masses. The rarity of popular Hasidic printed texts may have been due to formal and informal censorship. Whatever the reason or reasons for the limited use Hasidism had for the press, it is clear that Hasidism spread quite nicely among the masses without great recourse to the printed word.[28]

Few efforts were made to ease the entry of a student or interested adult into literate culture. Despite the great emphasis on the study of the Talmud, no commentary or introduction to the Talmud was published in Yiddish—despite the fact that this would have helped many off to a start in Talmud.[29] There were no Aramaic-Yiddish or Hebrew-Yiddish dictionaries which also would have helped a reader with limited Hebrew to deal with a text on his own. As a result, Hebrew played a peripheral role in the activity of most Jews, even though almost all could read.

The nineteenth century saw a number of significant changes in the use of Hebrew and its readership. The attempts of the Maskilim to revive Hebrew have been carefully studied. The Maskilim themselves came from the educated elite (many—or at least so they claim—were child prodigies when it came to Talmud study) and their efforts shed little light on the scope of knowledge of Hebrew among the Jewish population.

Expansion in the use of Hebrew was not limited to the modernizing elements of the community. An early and interesting effort to reach the average reader through Hebrew was the publication of the first practical guide to Jewish law or halakhah in the modern period. This was *Hayyei Adam,* written by Abraham Danzig and published in Hebrew in Vilna in 1810.[30] The author stated that his goal was to provide a useful guide for advanced students, but in reality it was most popular among the less learned. Over eighty editions of the book have appeared so far. The way this book was received reflects once again the oral nature of study and even book use. Soon after it came out, *hevrot* were set up all over the Pale, to study *Hayyei Adam.* In other words, even though the author intended the book for the advanced student, it was used as a textbook for communal study. Thus its popularity and printing history do not really indicate how many people actually *read* it.

Newspapers were one of the most important areas of creativity in Hebrew, but it is not easy to draw conclusions from their spread. There was generally a fair amount of interest in news, but the high cost of the newspapers (ten rubles was a standard subscription rate) did not make it easy for individuals to subscribe. There is very little information on the numbers of subscribers to Hebrew newspapers, but it appears that in 1885 HaMelitz had 2500 subscribers.[31] If we are generous and assume a readership of 15 for each copy of the newspaper, then the newspaper reached an audience of about 60,000. This was certainly a respectable figure, but considering a Jewish population of close to five million in the Czarist empire alone, it is not so large. The readership of the Yiddish press was far larger.

Nonetheless, the end of the nineteenth century was noted for a rise in the readership of Haskalah literature and Hebrew literature in general.[32] This was the period when modern Hebrew literature began to develop rapidly, and it was at this time that efforts began to be made for the revival of Hebrew as a spoken language.[33]

Hebrew was an elite language up to the end of the nineteenth century, and the aura and status of the language contributed to its survival. In many respects, traditional Jewish society in Eastern Europe fitted the pattern of a closed semiliterate society.[34] It restricted access to authoritative texts, which strengthened the authority of the traditional leadership. This situation emphasized the importance of rabbis and gave power to communal leaders and in this respect it had a very conservative impact. At the same time, the fact that access to authoritative texts was limited made it possible for traditional society to adapt itself to new situations and for halakhah to be flexible, with a minimal sense of the novelty in these adaptations.[35]

The Hebrew used in traditional writing was medieval rabbinic Hebrew. This usage was opposed by the Enlighteners who called for a return to biblical Hebrew, just as they called for a rejection of rabbinic values and a return to more original sources.[36] Had this call been heeded, the fate of Hebrew might have been no different from that of Latin. The medieval Latin was rejected in favor of Ciceronian Latin on the grounds that the latter was more "correct." Since the latter, like biblical Hebrew, is far more difficult to study, the ultimate result was that fewer could learn the language and, ultimately, that the language stopped being used.

However, with acculturation, Hebrew could no longer keep its status as the sole elite language, and it quickly lost ground to Polish or Russian. This was true even in circles where one might have anticipated a strong identity with Hebrew. In 1911 the Russian-language Zionist newspaper *Rassvet* had a circulation of about 8000 while its Hebrew language sister newspaper *HaOlam* had just 3000 subscribers. By 1916, *Rassvet* was up to 17,000.[37] One reason is that for an acculturated individual, the authoritative texts were no longer Hebrew ones. Moreover, there were changes in patterns of study. Children of the elite and even the not-so-elite began increasingly to study in gymnasia rather than in traditional educational institutions. By 1886, the number of Jewish students in gymnasia had reached over 9000.[38] A generation earlier these would have been the bearers of Hebrew. Now, their sights were set on Russian.[39] At this point in history, the ineffectiveness of Hebrew education in traditional society and the absence of practical uses for Hebrew knowledge were no longer advantages but clear disadvantages. The elite had less and less use for Hebrew; and for much of the traditionalist nonelite, there were not enough means or incentives to work toward a mastery of Hebrew. The new role of Hebrew as a means of national identification required both a convincing ideology and a resetting of personal career goals to justify the effort necessary for language study. This was not to be done easily.

In the twentieth century, literary creativity in Hebrew and publication in Hebrew continually lagged behind that of Yiddish in Poland. Of about a thousand Jewish books published in Poland in 1928, about a quarter were in Hebrew.[40] Two years later, the share of Hebrew books was under 20 percent.[41] This does not necessarily mean that there was a decline in the readership of Hebrew. The drop might well be the product of increased imports from Eretz-Israel. What it does mean is that patterns of Jewish publishing were becoming more and more like those of other nations in that vernaculars took the lead. The role of Hebrew had changed radically.[42] In the past, Hebrew was widely used and little understood; now, in pre-Holocaust Poland, the purchasers of Hebrew books were the members of a subgroup in the Jewish community with a specific nationalistic outlook. What they bought they could read. Their language indicated their location in society—not as a scholarly or socioeconomic elite but as a self-conscious national group.[43] It was not a group which all or even most Jews aspired to enter. Hebrew remained a language of a minority, an elite if you wish. However, now its minority status was clear to all, while a hundred years earlier the image of Hebrew had been a very different one.

Notes

1. Note that almost no descriptions of the Ḥeder up to the latter part of the nineteenth century mention learning how to write and that schoolboy pranks in ḥeder do not involve quills or ink bottles.
2. I discussed this point in Stampfer 1988.
3. Kowalska-Glikman 1981: 2, Table 3, p. 42.
4. The data on craft guilds is found in Halpern 1968: 171, 188.
5. Weinryb 1950: 226 in the Hebrew section. In 1774 the same name appears again along with another nonsignatory among ten signatories of another legal document. See p. 228. I am very grateful to Dr. Murray Rosman for the reference.
6. "To the Question of the Situation of Jewish Workers," *Voskhod* 20, 39 (21.6.1901). In Russian.
7. Margolin 1915.
8. *Jewish Immigrants,* Senate Document 611, 63rd Congress, 2d Session (Washington DC 1914).
9. The analysis here is based on my analysis in Stampfer 1988.
10. See Stampfer 1987.
11. See Shohat 1986.
12. See the comments and references in, for example, Lawrence 1970: 62.
13. Rashdall 1936, 3:341–42.
14. Ibid, p. 353
15. See Wilkinson 1970: 128.
16. I am well aware that the Talmud is written in Aramaic but at the time there was no distinction between the knowledge of the two languages—he who knew one knew the other.
17. For an exploration of this theme from a very original but somewhat different approach, see Funkenstein and Steinsaltz 1987.
18. See Stampfer (forthcoming). The exclusion of most women from access to Hebrew explains why this article deals only with males.
19. Dan, 1975.
20. See Chava Weissler (forthcoming).
21. I discuss this issue in greater detail in Stampfer (forthcoming).
22. One of the unintended consequences of this situation is that women, whose education was usually looked down on, probably acquired more of their Jewish knowledge from books (which they read in Yiddish) than did most men!
23. See Twersky 1976: 330; and, in Hebrew, Katz 1984.
24. There are some Hebrew travel guides and lists of fair dates but they were not a standard element of the merchant's library. Commercial calendars became popular toward the end of the nineteenth century.
25. On ḥevrot see for example Goldman 1975: chaps. 11, 12, 13. A more recent study of the dynamics of contemporary ḥevrot is Heilman 1983.
26. Interestingly enough, there were no ḥevrot devoted to study of Torah—perhaps on the assumption that this was best studied in a ḥeder.
27. See Lieberman 1950.
28. Of course, books written by important personalities in the movement, such as *Toldot Yaakov Yosef,* may have had a great impact on their readers. However, these were books aimed at a learned and, by definition, elite audience.
29. It is perhaps worth noting today's mixed reaction to Rabbi Adin Steinsaltz's translation and commentary on the Talmud. Much of the opposition to it from traditional circles seems to be related to the fact that it demystifies the Talmud and enables anyone to study it.

30. See Goldrat 1973.

31. See Ungerfeld 1954: 148.

32. See the thought-provoking Miron 1987, part I.

33. Since most of the efforts in this direction and all of the success was in Eretz-Israel, I leave this topic out of the discussion here.

34. Here I am following the terminology used by Abraham Stahl 1973: esp. p. 13 and 22. See also Jack Goody's introduction to Goody 1968: 11–17.

35. Elijah Gaon's attempts to bring current practice into line with the requirements of the written sources run counter to the general tendency of this and other traditional societies to determine behavior on the basis of past precedents.

36. On the different types of Hebrew see Kutscher 1982: chaps. 7 and 8.

37. See the data and sources in Slutsky 1978: 252.

38. See the data cited by Slutsky 1970: 17.

39. For a rare view of the impact of Russian on readership see Solomon Goldenberg's (1907) report on the Jewish library in Poltava. According to his data, 80% of the reading material that circulated was in Russian. Of the readers, 65% could read only Russian. An article by A. Kirzhnits ("Towards a Characterization of the Contemporary Jewish Reader," *Vestnik Obshchestva Prosveshchenia Evreev* 1-2 [1910]: 29–46) also provides data. From 1907 to 1909, about 40% of the books checked out in the Kiev library of the Society for the Spreading of Enlightenment Among Jews were in Hebrew. However, during those years there was a drop in the percentage of Hebrew books checked out and a rise in Yiddish books read. At the same time, in Bobruisk in the same years, 70% of the books checked out were in Russian and only about 15% in Hebrew. Clearly, different libraries had varying readerships and policies so that decisive conclusions cannot be drawn from this kind of data. However, it is clear that the role of Russian was growing. I thank Prof. Steven Zipperstein for the references.

40. Levinson 1935: 211. According to the data there, of the 2.1 million copies of Jewish books printed that year, 15% were in Hebrew.

41. Ibid p. 212. Of the 5.5 million copies that appeared that year, only 5% were in Hebrew.

42. Unfortunately, we have no data for convenient comparison of the number of publications of Jewish interest in Polish with publications in Jewish languages. Such a comparison, over time, could be quite interesting.

43. In this respect, the use of Hebrew was no different from that of Yiddish.

References

DAN, JOSEPH. *Sifrut ha-Musar.* Jerusalem: Keter, 1975.

FUNKENSTEIN, AMOS and ADIN STEINSALTZ. *Sociology of Ignorance.* Tel Aviv: University of the Air, 1987.

GOLDENBERG, SOLOMON. "Are There Hebrew Readers." *HaShiloah* 17 (1907): 417–22 In Hebrew.

GOLDMAN, ISRAEL. *Life Long Learning Among Jews.* New York: Ktav, 1975.

GOLDRAT, A. "On the Book 'Hayyei Adam' and Its Author." In *Sefer Margaliot.* Jerusalem: Mossad Harav Kook, 1973, pp. 255–78.

GOODY, JACK, ed. *Literacy in Traditional Societies.* Cambridge: Cambridge University Press, 1968.

HALPERN, ISRAEL. *Yahadut Mizrah Eiropa.* (East European Jewry) Jerusalem: Magnes Press, 1968.

HEILMAN, SAMUEL. *The People of the Book: Drama, Fellowship, and Religion.* Chicago: Chicago University Press, 1983.

KATZ, JACOB. *Ha-Halakhah ve-ha-Kabbalah.* Jerusalem: Magnes, 1984.

KOWALSKA-GLIKMAN, STEFANIA. "Ludnosc Zydowska Warszawy w Polowie XIX W. W Swietle Akt Stanu Cywilnego." *Biuletyn Zydowskiego Instytutu Historycznego* 2 (1981): 118.

KUTSCHER, EDUARD. *A History of the Hebrew Language.* Jerusalem: Magnes, 1982.

LAWRENCE, ELIZABETH. *The Origins and Growth of Modern Education.* Harmondsworth: Penguin, 1970.

LEVINSON, ABRAHAM. *Ha-Tenu'ah ha-Ivrit ba-Golah* (The Hebrew Movement in the Diaspora). Warsaw: Brit Ivrit Olamit, 1935.

LIEBERMAN, CHAIM. "Legends and Truth About Hassidic Printing." *YIVO Bletter* 34 (1950): 182–208. In Yiddish.

MARGOLIN, S. *Sources and Research on Jewish Industrial Craftsmen.* Vol. 2. St. Petersburg: ORT, 1915. In Russian.

MIRON, DAN. *Bodedim be-Mo'adam* (When Loners Come Together). Tel Aviv: Am Oved, 1987.

RASHDALL, HASTINGS. *The Universities of Europe in the Middle Ages.* F. M. Powicke and A. B. Emden, eds. New edition. Oxford: Oxford University Press, 1936.

SHOHAT, AZRIEL. "The Cantonists and the 'Yeshivot' of Russian Jewry during the Reign of Nicholas I." *Jewish History* 1 (1986): 33-8, Hebrew Section.

SLUTSKY, YEHUDA. *The Russian-Jewish Press in the Nineteenth Century.* Jerusalem: Mossad Bialik, 1970.

———. *The Russian-Jewish Press in the Twentieth Century.* Jerusalem: Mossad Bialik, 1978.

STAHL, ABRAHAM. "Historical Changes in the Culture of [the People of] Israel and their Consequences for Dealing with Deprived Children." In Abraham Stahl, ed. *Literacy and Cultural Change.* Jerusalem: Magnes, 1973.

STAMPFER, SHAUL. "Ha-Mashma'ut ha-Hevratit shel Nisu'ei Boser be-Mizrah Eiropah ba-Me'ah ha-Tesha-Esreh." (The Significance of Premature Marriages in Nineteenth-Century Eastern Europe). In Ezra Mendelsohn and Chone Shmeruk, eds. *Studies on Polish Jewry: Paul Glikson Memorial Volume.* Jerusalem: Institute for Contemporary Jewry, 1987, pp. 65–77.

———. "Ḥeder Study, Knowledge of Torah and the Maintenance of Social Stratification in Traditional East European Jewish Society." In Janet Aviad, ed. *Studies in Jewish Education.* 3 (1988): 271–89.

———. "Gender Differentiation and the Education of the Jewish Woman in Nineteenth Century Eastern Europe." *Polin.* Forthcoming.

TWERSKY, ISADORE. "The Shulhan Aruk: Enduring Code of Jewish Law." In Judah Goldin, ed. *The Jewish Expression.* New Haven: Yale University Press, 1976.

UNGERFELD, M. "Igrot Alexander Zederbaum." *HeAvar* 2 (1954): 145–6.

WEINRYB, BERNARD. *Texts and Studies in the Communal History of Polish Jewry.* New York: Proceedings of the American Adademy for Jewish Research, 1950.

WEISSLER, CHAVA. "For Women and for Men Who Are Like Women." *Journal of Feminist Studies in Religion.* Forthcoming.

WILKINSON, RUPERT. "The Gentleman Ideal and the Maintenance of a Political Elite." In P. W. Musgrave, ed. *Sociology, History and Education.* London: Methuen, 1970.

9

From Traditional Bilingualism to National Monolingualism

ISRAEL BARTAL

National movements springing up in nineteenth-century Europe associated what they termed the "National Revival" with a crucial set of features, without which such a revival could not take place. Outstanding among these, along with territory and historical heritage, was the "national tongue." Generally, this "national" tongue was a particular dialect that became the state language and ousted alternative dialects—or else the language of an ethnic group that had been ousted by the "state language" and whose revival or renewal entailed a struggle for "national rights." These two types of "national tongue" arose in tandem with the historical disparity between national-movement types in modern times. The national "state language" arose decades or centuries before the age of modern nationalism as part of the processes that brought about the emergence of the new centralized state, attaining cultivation and final form at the hands of the authorities under the enlightened absolutist regimes of the late eighteenth century; nineteenth century Romanticism and historico-national dogmas had already added a "national" layer to an existing state of affairs. The languages of the ethnic groups who in the nineteenth and twentieth centuries waged a struggle for their uniqueness or even for mere recognition of their legitimate right to a separate existence had, by early modern times, gone through a stage of declining prestige and now lagged behind, relatively speaking, in their development. Supporters of the development of these languages generally appealed to the historical legacy of an earlier age, in which these languages seemed to be main languages, recognized and endowed with cultural value and prestige.

The history of cultural nationalism in Central and Eastern Europe is replete with outstanding examples of the confrontation between these two types of "national tongue," which were even known to intermingle—as time and political development would have it. The Ukrainian language, for instance, was officially ousted by Russian. Just as the Ukrainians were dubbed "Little Russians," so too their language was adjudged in the nineteenth century to be a colloquial unworthy of cultivation; indeed, restrictions were imposed by the Russian authorities on promoting it and publishing in it. The renewed efflorescence of Ukrainian as a national cultural tongue drew upon the image of bygone prestige—but also upon its claim to be a historical alternative to the state language, identified with the suppression of the Ukrainian nation by the Russian regime. It was only from the mid-nineteenth century that Polish ceased to function as a state language of administration in broad areas of Eastern Europe, despite Russian control. In Lithuania, Polish was a language of administration and of the higher echelons of society, at least until the Polish Revolt of 1831—following which its status diminished sharply in the western provinces of Russia. An attempt was later made, after the failed Polish Uprising of 1863, to replace Polish by Russian in the autochtonous areas of Poland too, but the stage intermediate between "state language" and "national tongue" barely existed in this case.

The great interest shown by the national movements in the place of language in national life, and the propensity to view the past through a national prism, made their mark of course upon national historiography. "Revivals" of nations and cultural and literary "rebirths" occupied center stage in the historical consciousness. Anything preceding the "revival" stage was portrayed as leading toward modern nationalism or conversely as incompatible with it. Social radicalism, allied to Romantic world-views in the various national movements, equated the language of the "nation" with the tongue of the "people" and linked national and social suppression with the decline of national tongues. To an observer unencumbered by the national-radical image of the past, it sometimes seems bizarre that the potent influence of national ideas could so befog the mind, erasing anything that was out of line with the national direction. Yosef Klausner (1930) was able to write a massive study on the rebirth of Hebrew literature, dismissing as culturally irrelevant the fact that the prime architects of the modern national culture used another *Jewish* language besides—or more than—Hebrew in their writing; in describing the poetic creation of Naphtali Herz Wessely, Klausner paid no attention to the fact that Wessely's *Shirei Tiferet* also needed expounding against the backdrop of the Yiddish biblical poetry widespread in Ashkenaz in the generations that preceded the Haskalah.[1] Eliezer Ben-Yehuda (1949: 12), in the Great Introduction to his thesaurus, all but ignores the fact that in the absence of a living Hebrew another language is being spoken by his compatriots. Only when he enumerates the sources of his thesaurus does the existence of a "popular tongue" suddenly surface, termed (like other such vernaculars) "corrupt languages spoken among our people, Sephardim, Ashkenazim, Yemenites, etc." But even in the field of Jewish history many more years would pass before attention was turned to the complex nexus of history and language—a complexity to which the diverse national images cannot do justice. There is no comprehending the place of language in the Jewish national revival unless one addresses the social changes that have come upon Jewry in its encounter with modernity, changes in which language, or better, languages, have played so significant a role.

The "opening situation" of the Jewish people in Europe and the Mediterranean rim on the eve of modern times is of a corporation with uniquely defined and agreed features, in the Jewish mind as in the mind of the Gentile environment. One distinctive marker, unchallenged as a principle or a value, is the linguistic: just as Jews dress distinctively, dwell apart and eat just of their own, they have a language all of their own. Notwithstanding, the corporation's linguistic reality is quite unlike what one finds in some national historiographies: it is a *bilingual* reality. In this "diglossia" two languages function side by side: the "vernacular," the everyday spoken language and the language of writing in certain spheres, and the "holy tongue" *(leshon ha-kodesh),* the language of liturgy and religious composition. The vernacular varies according to place and period, changing form like any living language; it has set functions and a known social status; there are things that may be said only in the vernacular, while other things are never written in it. The vernacular has considerable space for Hebrew and Aramaic influence but draws its main influence from the languages of the environment and maintains itself even after a change of environment due to migration, expulsion, change of surrounding population (or its language), or change of regime. The vernacular contains layers of earlier colloquials, such as Judeo-Greek in the Judeo-Spanish of Anatolia and the Balkans, or memories of Slavic tongues in the ancient stratum of Yiddish. *Leshon ha-kodesh* is the language that embraces Hebrew with its various historical components, from the biblical and up to the rabbinic of late medieval times—and Aramaic of various kinds.

The modern period heralds a dramatic switch in this diglossia of the Jewish corporation. New ideas, finding material expression in the policy of European governments toward the medieval corporations as a whole and the Jewish community in particular, seek to snap the bond between vernacular and *leshon ha-kodesh*. The European Enlightenment heralds a challenge to the legitimacy of dialects and argots; rules of the "enlightened despot" type aid and abet the imposition of the "state language" as an obligatory language of administration and cultural medium. The demands of the men of Enlightenment, Jewish and Gentile, over the language issue sit well with the goals of enlightened absolutism: replacement of the vernacular by the "state language"—or in the concrete terms of the day, a demand that the Jews of the Austrian Empire replace the use of Yiddish by German in documents, bills of sale, and communal records and adopt German as their spoken tongue. Maskilim and state officials alike deemed Yiddish unseemly, both linguistically and socially. Insofar as the Maskilim saw the vernacular as the expression par excellence of human reason, the spoken language of Ashkenazi Jewry bore witness to their base spiritual circumstances:

> And this language which we speak in this land [Russia], borrowed from the Germans and called German-Jewish, is utterly corrupt, being mingled with corrupt words lifted from Hebrew, Russian, French, Polish and the like, and even the German words are worn and shapeless, and thoroughly disfigured; nor is this language of ours of any use save for simple chatter, and as if this were not all, when we wish to name some sublime concept, our language deserts us. . . . And of those who lack knowledge of those languages [of Europe] we may say what the prophet Isaiah (28:11) said: "for with stammering lips and another tongue will he speak to this people," and thereby they earn the contempt of the nations among whom we dwell . . . for the man who lacks a pure and lucid language and script is a man despised.

Thus Isaac Baer Levinsohn in his book *Te'udah be-Yisra'el* (pp. 34–35) composed in the 1820s. Yiddish, the vital component in the traditional diglossia, is not a rational language, nor an aesthetic one, and cannot supply the needs of self-expression and communication. The Jewish Enlightened in Russia require knowledge of a language of "elegance" and "breadth"—one of the European languages. And which European language is best substituted? For the Maskilim of Berlin and Koenigsberg, the matter was a relatively simple one, for Yiddish in those parts was perceived as just another dialect, or argot, of German. What was demanded of the Jews was not essentially different than what their other compatriots were supposed to do: to adopt the "state language" as evolved in Berlin in the eighteenth century.

However, in the multilingual empires of Eastern Europe the situation was a different and infinitely more complex one. The replacement of the vernacular component in the traditional diglossia involved deciding which was the alternative: Russian, Polish, or even German? And the distance between East European Yiddish and Slavic languages did not afford so simple a transition as from Western Yiddish to German, the transition recommended by the Maskilim of Prussia. And sure enough, the Maskilim of Eastern Europe did not come down squarely for the one or the other but opined, like the absolutist rulers themselves, that the Jews were free to opt for one of the European tongues as a substitute for Yiddish. Levinsohn (p. 39) could thus advise his readers in Russia to change from Yiddish either to Russian *or* to German:

> And so too we can say in this country [Russia]: Why Judeo-German [Yiddish]? Either elegant German—or Russian, this being the language of the land and, in particular, an exceedingly broad and elegant language, lacking nought in tone and beauty and in all the sublime qualities that are counted towards linguistic perfection (as I have explained in the book "Yesodei Leshon Rusya" [Foundations of the Russian Language] that I have written for the benefit of Jewish youth . . .).

However, the second element in the diglossia, *leshon ha-kodesh,* the language of religious creativity and of prayer, and the traditional channel of communication among the elite of Jewish society in premodern times, was also intended to undergo a change in make-up, standing and functions. The views of the early Maskilim in Germany concerning a return from *leshon ha-kodesh* to the language of the Bible also found acceptance among the Maskilim of Eastern Europe, coming to fruition in their literary creations and grammatical activities. Their desire to distance themselves from the language of the Mishnah and Gemara, from the language identified with the Talmud and rabbinic writing, led to a real change in the role of the Hebrew language. To remove the postbiblical strata was to throw down the gauntlet to the spiritual world of traditional Jewish society. This was, moreover, yet another clear manifestation of a submission to the ascendant rationale of Christian society and an accession to influential literary trends in contemporary European culture. In Galicia, Volhynia, and Lithuania, as in Germany, the Hebrew language began to fulfill functions unknown—or uncommon—in traditional Jewish culture up until the nineteenth century. "Linguistic expansion," as this change in Hebrew functions was defined, included poetic and prose composition, a new and almost unknown brand of communication (newspapers, periodicals), translations from European belles lettres, and translated adaptations from the scientific, philosophical, and historiographical works that enjoyed a wide European currency.[2]

Thus the vision of the Eastern European Haskalah was aimed not at *ending* the diglossia but at *replacing* the two component languages: the state language or a European language (most commonly, German) for Yiddish, and biblical Hebrew for *leshon ha-kodesh*. The new Haskalah-style bilingualism may have reflected, more than all else, the dual character of the Haskalah: the premodern corporative features were indeed to give way to an identification with the centralized state, while the language of worship and spiritual composition was to be cleansed and flushed free of purportedly corrupt substrata. In fact, the more radical the views of a particular group of Maskilim, the more space was made for the state language and the less space for Hebrew, leading to its virtual elimination; in this way, the Maskilim edged ever closer to their vision of integration into the society of subjects of the centralized state. On the other hand, the moderates of the Eastern European Haskalah extended the functions of Hebrew far beyond the "religious" segment of spiritual and cultural life. This contributed in no small measure to its conversion into a secular tongue in which one might write on scientific or general historical subjects or pen stories and poems as in the literatures of European languages. The "secularization" of Hebrew was a central plank in the cultural change brought upon traditional Eastern European society by the Haskalah. Hebrew continued, among other things, as a distinctive feature of Jewish separateness in the new political reality. For many Maskilim in Galicia, Poland, and Lithuania, biblical Hebrew in its Maskilic incarnation became a key element in Jewish identity. While preaching sociopolitical integration in their states of abode and challenging the very existence of the Jewish corporation in all its manifestations, they used Hebrew as a focus of identification with the Jewish past and as a legitimate channel of communication with their coreligionists already cut off from their traditional environment—as well as with Jews from other lands. The Lithuanian Jewish author, Abraham Mapu, gave fine expression to this new relationship to Hebrew:

> Pay heed to this, you who fear for the holy things of Israel, who aspire to the earth of the Holy Land and desire its stones; do we not cherish a clod of earth, do we not adore fragments of stone from the Holy Land, recalling that maybe on this earth and on these stones our forefathers' feet once strode—so how can we not cherish their holy tongue, the thoughts of their heart and the utterance of their lips, within which is all the life of their spirit? Are these not the Holy Scriptures, neglected by the generation who preceded us and who have denied the delight of Israel to the Children of Israel, unknown in our days too save to a couple here and a handful there ... and how I rejoiced to see my books tugging at the hearts and minds of our best people, the healers of Israel, after they had all but forgotten the Hebrew tongue in their student days.[3]

In the alternative *bilingual* vision of the Eastern European Haskalah, the traditional spoken language, Yiddish, was to vanish and *leshon ha-kodesh* was to change. Although the Haskalah movement's views on the language question exerted a powerful influence on the diverse streams that appeared within Eastern European Jewry in the second half of the nineteenth century, it differed in one thing from modern Jewish nationalism: the Haskalah movement did not strive for monolingualism as a normal feature of a distinctive Jewish identity. It was precisely in this sense that the Haskalah so well perpetuated the traditional linguistic lifestyle, which had never known monolingualism until the nineteenth century.

On the other hand, the Haskalah had a highly problematic attitude toward the linguistic reality arising out of the modernization of Jewish society: the Maskilim took up a negative, almost unequivocal, stand on the role of the vernacular. Yet they used it, willy-nilly, as a channel of communication with the traditional masses whom they sought to improve and to change. The first Maskilim in Germany wrote in Yiddish, penning mordant comedies, for example, in which they made sophisticated use of the multilingual reality of the changing Jewish society. In Eastern Europe the authors of the Haskalah went on composing in this language, thus unwittingly abetting a continued cultural activity in Yiddish and lending legitimacy to its use. Modern Yiddish literature and journalism actually came about as an unavoidable if undesirable bridge to the end goals of the Haskalah. Within a few decades, they became a serious competitor for the place of the Hebrew component in the Haskalah-promoted diglossia.

The Haskalah's attitude to the "state language," by contrast, faithfully represented a sociopolitical trend characteristic of Eastern European Jewish society. The Jews tended to adopt the imperial languages: German in the portions of Poland that passed into Austrian and Prussian control, and Russian in the domain of the Czars. But the acculturation in practice to either one of these state cultures was, in the social circles concerned, more rapid and more vigorous than the Maskilim had expected. And so the chances were not great for Hebrew to survive as a component in diglossia as envisioned by the Maskilim. Moreover, in an age of stirring nationalism in multinational empires, to adopt the language of the imperial center was a highly political act, calculated to sharpen the tension between Jews and surroundings in which a revival of the local "national" tongue was being touted.

Thus the beginnings of the modern Jewish national movement partook, on the one hand, of a Maskilic linguistic vision in which a state of diglossia would be preserved but with a change of components. On the other hand, the fin-de-siècle reality found itself facing an exceedingly complex *triglossia,* containing the elements of a traditional linguistic way of life alongside the products of a partial acculturation to the cultures of the state. In the Jewish national movement several new elements were added that were not dominant in the Haskalah's attitude to the language question and which were inherently contradictory: legitimation was given to the "popular language" and to the culture of the popular strata, affording a new conception of Yiddish; and it was henceforth possible to identify the "state language" with the "national language," insofar as the vision of a national political rebirth in a Hebrew-speaking state might be realized. This last new element was nicely formulated by Eliezer Ben-Yehuda (Perelman) in a letter to the editor printed in Peretz Smolenskin's periodical *Ha-Shaḥar* in 1880 (p. 244):

> But we shall be quite unable to revive the Hebrew language save in a land whose Hebrew inhabitants outnumber its Gentiles. So let us increase the number of Jews in our barren land and restore the remnant of our people to the soil of its fathers; let us revive the nation, and the language will come to life!

Modern Jewish nationalism was heralding, for the first time, an idea that was alien to the members of the traditional Jewish corporation: the nation possesses *one* language, fulfilling all functions. In other words, an *end* to diglossia:

Just as Jews can only be a truly living people when they return to the land of their fathers, so too they can only be a living people when they return to the language of their fathers and use it not only in books, not only in matters sacred or philosophical, as argued by Peretz Ben Moshe [Smolenskin], the editor of *Hashaḥar,* but in actual talk by great and small, women and children, boys and girls, on all things of life and at all hours of day and night, like any other nation with its very own tongue.[4]

Thus the ending of a bilingual state of affairs and the presentation of monolingualism as normal was a complete innovation on the part of modern nationalism; and although not universally accepted in its sharpest form, it did constitute the greatest break with traditional bilingual culture. Which would be the "national language" in the new monolingual situation—the cast-off popular Yiddish idiom rediscovered in the spirit of Romanticism, populism, and social radicalism that had captured the minds of Eastern Europe, or the "historical" tongue heralding in its revival a liberation from exile and a return to a distant, many-splendored past? And what was the political situation that might permit an identity of "state language" and "national language"? A wide variety of answers was forthcoming in turn-of-the-century Eastern Europe. But not by chance, the claims of the proponents of the various languages were sometimes more alike than dissimilar, the new nationalist idea leaving its imprint all around and blurring a simple fact that none but the Orthodox continued to acknowledge at this time of transition from Haskalah to national radicalism: the fact that diglossia was Jewish society's *normal* state of affairs—and one whose elimination was truly revolutionary.

It is no coincidence that this study of the incarnations of the linguistic system of East and Central European Jewry has ended with the focus on the Orthodox. Having proposed alternative limits for the traditional corporation now deprived of its defenses and robbed of its ramparts, the Orthodox also set up linguistic defenses; in parallel to the early Haskalah, which preached replacement of Yiddish by the state language, Orthodoxy began preaching the *maintenance* of Yiddish. In Orthodox thought, the vernacular acquired an ideological significance, akin to the maintenance of distinctive Jewish dress:

It is Jewish law to be different at all times from the nations of the world. . . . Let Israel be distinguished from them and known in its dress and other actions just as it is distinguished from them in its knowledge and its traits. . . .[5]

Two precepts are incumbent upon a father: to talk to his son in the Holy Language and to teach him Torah, and our rabbis have said . . . that our Jewish language [Yiddish] is to be counted as a Holy Language of . . . sorts but on the day that the child begins talking they speak a foreign tongue or Hungarian to him, or change his Hebrew name, they uproot his soul and he is bound to end up going off the straight and narrow.[6]

These writings of Rabbi Akiva Yosef Schlesinger in his book *Lev Ha-Ivri* against the Jewish circles that had undergone acculturation to Hungarian language and culture in the mid-nineteenth century are essentially similar to the strictures of Rabbi Shalom Ber against the Zionists in the 1910s. This leader of the Lubavitch Hasidim vented his wrath upon the portrayal of the Hebrew language as the national language and demanded that his followers vigorously maintain the traditional diglossia that assigned a sacred function to *leshon ha-kodesh* and a colloquial role to the vernacular. In a letter to several rabbis, Rabbi Shalom Ber stated inter alia that except for the First Temple period—when "all God's people were holy"—the Jewish people had never been monolingual:

> And in Eretz-Israel and Babylonia the Holy Tongue was spoken only by the scholars engaged constantly in Torah, i.e., the Tannaim and Amoraim—including after the destruction of the Temple—whose total occupation was Torah, whereas the masses engaged in worldly matters did not speak the Holy Tongue . . . and in Eretz-Israel as in Babylonia the masses spoke another language.[7]

Indeed, Schlesinger, in a period prior to the rise of the modern national movement, was assuming a situation in which the Jewish people would return to its land and revive the holy language. However, he saw this as a sacred state of affairs, with diglossia coming to an end as part and parcel of the redemption and the Jewish people being cut free entirely from the baneful influence of European modernity. As long as the people is at risk from integration into the cultures of surrounding peoples, the traditional state of diglossia is one of the most commendable means of self-defense against the Enlightenment, religious reform, and the loss of a distinctive Jewish way of life.

By contrast, Rabbi Shalom Ber of Lubavitch represents the extreme Orthodox position against secular nationalism, which had challenged the state of diglossia in the name of the idea of national monolingualism. He distinguishes (pp. 21–22) the *leshon ha-kodesh* of Torah-true Jews from the *ivrit* of the Zionists, prohibiting the latter's use entirely:

> But the fathers of the Zionist idea, who have adopted an entirely different approach and replaced the whole Torah by the nationalist idea, saying "this is your people, Israel, a people like any other people or tongue" . . . and they have therefore made a mighty effort to take hold of the Holy Land, not for its sanctity and purity sake but for the sake of a nationalism which is bound up with land, for there is no nationalism without a country . . . and they have therefore also taken hold of the language, for there is no self-respecting nation without a language . . . and they pay no heed to the value of its sanctity, rendering it a spoken tongue for an entire people and for saying all things, a function that the language cannot really bear, as we have explained, and the whole study of the language is now for language sake alone. . . .

These words are in fact an absolute criticism of the ideas of Eliezer Ben-Yehuda, who, as stated earlier, saw the language and land as the bases of the new nationalism and aimed to turn *leshon ha-kodesh* into an only language for the entire people at all times.

The defensive maintenance of bilingualism, in response to Enlightenment and then to Zionism, gave new significance to the place of Yiddish but also added new weight to the use of *leshon ha-kodesh.* The secularization of the Hebrew language, which had already begun in the Haskalah period and had contrived to cut it loose from the talmudic-rabbinical language, was loaded with hostile signification for the values of the traditional corporation. Faced with a modern nationalism that assigned an absolute value to *one* of the two languages in the traditional diglossic system (Hebrew or Yiddish), Orthodoxy sprang to the defense of diglossia, but the very act gave an entirely new meaning to the maintenance of the diglossic situation. At times Orthodoxy accepted the possibility of replacing Yiddish by the state language (German, and later English)—but vehemently opposed the secularization of the *leshon ha-kodesh* component in the system. And thus, out of opposition to the assignment of a hostile ideological value to a language (Hebrew or Yiddish) and absolute revulsion at language secularization, Orthodoxy created an alternative ideological value for the traditional diglossic system.

In the final analysis, the Haskalah movement, which preached a switch in the diglossic components of traditional Ashkenazi society in its desire to adapt to the changing times, and the Orthodox reaction to the challenges of modernity yielded quite similar attitudes to diglossia. The new nationalist movements, whether preaching Yiddishism or Hebraism, strove for monolingualism. In the historical reality of Eastern Europe and in the successive incarnations of Ashkenazi Jewry in the upheavals of the twentieth century, these trends have left us with the monolingualism of a modern Jewish, Hebrew-speaking state and the bilingualism of a modern Orthodoxy in which *leshon ha-kodesh* and Yiddish (or English) are new heirs to an old diglossia.

Notes

1. See Klausner 1930: 118–28. In this respect, Klausner was perpetuating Wessely's (1782: chap. 7) own disregard for Yiddish biblical poetry: "And why have several successive generations not produced a single celebrated poet in German or Polish parts? . . . And some of the great Gentile poets of our generation have affirmed that the splendor and beauty of Scripture have no equal among the most celebrated poems, even going back to Antiquity . . . and wherefore have *we* abandonned them and not followed in their path? But all this has befallen us because we have been raised since childhood under the hand of blithering teachers, who taught us to speak in crass and common figures [i.e., Yiddish]." On Yiddish biblical poetry and knowledge of it, see Shmeruk 1978: 117–36.

2. The term *harḥavat lashon* (language extension) already appears in *Kohelet Musar* edited by Moses Mendelssohn in 1750, p. 161: "Let us learn from other nations who have their language in their land. They did not rest until they had extended the frontiers of their language. . . . And the Hebrews will observe that our language is ready for any eventuality. To weep aloud. To sing songs to the joyful or to condemn the wicked in the gate."

3. Mapu 1939: 457.
4. Ben-Yehuda 1949, *Great Introduction*, p. 2.
5. Schlesinger 1872: 28b.
6. *Idem*, p. 85a.
7. Schneersohn 1980: 18.

References

BEN-YEHUDA, ELIEZER. *Milon ha-Lashon ha-Ivrit ha-Yeshanah ve-ha-Hadashah* (Dictionary of Ancient and Modern Hebrew). Jerusalem and Tel Aviv, 1949.

KLAUSNER, YOSEF. *Historyah shel ha-Sifrut ha-Ivrit ha-Hadashah* (History of Modern Hebrew Literature). Vol. 1. Jerusalem: Achiasaf, 1930.

MAPU, AVRAHAM. *Hozei Hezyonot* (Visionaries). In *Collected Works of Avraham Mapu,* Tel Aviv, 1939.

MENDELSSOHN, MOSES. *Kohelet Musar* (Digest of Reproach). M. Gilon, ed. Jerusalem, 1976.

SCHLESINGER, AKIVA YOSEF. *Lev ha-Ivri* (The Heart of the Hebrew). Lvov, 1872.

SCHNEERSOHN, SHALOM BER. *Leshon ha-Kodesh ve-ha-Dibur Ba* (The Holy Tongue and Speaking in It). In Y. Mondschein, ed. *Sefer Migdal Oz.* Kefar Habad, 1980.

SHMERUK, HONE. *Sifrut Yidish: Perakim le-Toldoteha* (Studies in the History of Yiddish Literature). Tel Aviv, 1978.

WESSELY, NAFTALI HERZ. *Divrei Shalom ve-Emet* (Words of Peace and Truth). Berlin, 1782.

10

Cartoons about Language: Hebrew, Yiddish, and the Visual Representation of Sociolinguistic Attitudes

JOSHUA A. FISHMAN

Language attitudes abound in all societies, even in those in which it is not customary, or even not permitted, to study them. This is all the more so in multilingual societies. The multiplicity of languages, and, therefore, usually the multiplicity of ethnolinguistic groups, heightens language consciousness, at the very least, and may also heighten language conflict, i.e., the competition between languages for more prestigious functions or the efforts of one ethnolinguistic group and its internally recognized language "authorities" to be free from the influence or regulation of other groups and their "authorities." Under such circumstances, it is particularly likely that language attitudes will be consciously held, more clearly (although perhaps not always openly) formulated, and become the objects of language-planning efforts on the part of various spokesmen, on an *inter*group as well as on an *intra*group basis.

A substantial literature has come into being dealing with language attitudes, particularly during the past two decades.[1] However, a review of this literature reveals that it is only the *verbal* manifestations of language attitudes that has been studied thus far. This is unfortunate. Verbally expressed and expressible language attitudes represent only part of the total attitudinal constellation. Language attitudes may also possess visual dimensions,[2] i.e., they may pertain to sociolinguistic phenomena that are expressible graphically rather than (or rather than only) verbally. Indeed, the visual expression of language attitudes may become just as culturally established, just as symbolically recognized and accepted, just as ideologically tinted, as are verbal attitudinal expressions vis-à-vis language. Language is, of course, the major symbol system of our species. Accordingly, it is quite predictable

---

Joshua Fishman, "Cartoons about Language," reprinted from *Trends in Linguistics, Studies and Monographs 54: Languages in Contact and Contrast*, edited by V. Ivir and D. Kalogkera, published by Mouton de Gruyter, 1992. Reprinted by permission of Mouton de Gruyter, a division of Walter de Gruyter & Co., Publishers.

that most attitudes *toward* language will be expressed *via* language. However, visual symbols may be used as well, and not only in *concert* with linguistic symbols but, also, as a metaphor for the linguistic designations. Visual symbols pertaining to language are, therefore, metasymbols, i.e., just like language per se, visual symbols become symbols about symbols.

Where do visual representations of language originate? Who initiates them? To what extent do they become consensual on a society-wide or speech community-wide basis, rather than remain the individual innovations of one or another visual communicator? Under what societal circumstances are societal consensual representations more common and less common? Why do some visual representations of language become entrenched, even to the point of intergenerational acceptability, while others are more ephemeral? These are some of the questions that I hope to place on the agenda of sociolinguistic research via the following case study.

The Case of Yiddish and Hebrew

Jewish cultures in the Diaspora have commonly been diglossic, both for intragroup as well as for intergroup purposes.[3] For intragroup purposes a local Jewish language and Hebrew are typically involved in complementary functional distribution. The local Jewish language is commonly allocated to vernacular, intimacy, and popular literacy functions, as well as to the sanctity-proximate functions of the oral discussion and oral as well as written translation of hallowed texts. Hebrew, on the other hand, is commonly the language of sanctity per se, whether in prayer, textual study, or oral ritual, as well as the language of all phenomenologically "important" communal or personal records, of scholarship and of status-stressing communication more generally. Among Central and Eastern European Jews (Ashkenazim) this diglossic pattern, involving Yiddish and Hebrew, had generally existed peacefully enough from roughly the year 1000 CE through to the end of the eighteenth century. With modernization, secularization, increased contact with coterritorial vernacular cultures and the attainment of citizenship, this traditional diglossic pattern began increasingly to come apart. It was already under some strain by the latter part of the eighteenth century, particularly in Polish and Austro-Hungarian Galicia, and by the end of the nineteenth century it was no longer tenable in most parts of Eastern Europe, except in those Orthodox circles least influenced by modernization and secularization. Both languages, which had existed side by side for centuries in complementary functional distribution, came to be developed by "bearers of enlightenment" (Maskilim) for one and the same set of nontraditional purposes (e.g., secular literature for adults, modernized education for the young, theater, community self-regulation, etc.). Both languages underwent independent modernization, cultivation, and standardization at approximately the same time by differently oriented elites, each of which came to aspire to control the *entire* intragroup sociolinguistic repertoire, rather than to share it, as had been the case in premodern arrangements. A modern press arose in each language at approximately the same time, and it is in this press that we begin to find the first signs of visual representation of these languages via the work of cartoonists.

Cartoons about Language 153

Classical Visual Imagery

The earliest visual representations of Yiddish and Hebrew that I have encountered stem from the first decade of this century.[4] They depict two female figures that obviously differ in status. Hebrew is depicted as an older, wealthier, more cultured woman and Yiddish is depicted as her younger, poorer, less refined maid-servant. Figure 10.1, portraying Nokhem Sokolov (1859–1936), basically a Hebrew writer but one of the many who initially also wrote quite frequently in Yiddish, portrays him as a "literary bigamist." He has two "girlfriends" and proudly displays them both. The age and status differences between them is clear. Note that Yiddish, the figure on Sokolov's left, wears an apron, as befits a servant girl, even though she is a very robust and self-satisfied servant girl, to be sure. The imagery utilized is far

Fig. 10.1. "Nokem Sokolov: Literary Bigamist." Yiddish is the female figure on the right (Sokolov's left). The text below the cartoon informs the reader that Sokolov also has other girlfriends (i.e., that he also writes in other languages, in addition to the two depicted in the cartoon).

from accidental; nor is it an innovation of the artist. It is the visual representation of a well-established verbal metaphor which had already been used by several writers for at least a century by the time this cartoon appeared.[5] In the frequent (and increasingly acrimonious) debates that raged among Maskilim in the nineteenth century as to the permissible or desirable roles of Yiddish, it had become a commonplace among the detractors of Yiddish to refer to Hebrew as the *bas shemayim*[6] (daughter of heaven) and to Yiddish as the *shifkhe* (maid servant). This verbal metaphor, derived from the traditional relationship between the two languages in the domain of textual sanctity (where Yiddish was never used independently but, rather, as a mere assistant, or "servant," in the service of translating or clarifying Hebrew), was easily appropriated by cartoonists, since it provided them with readymade consensually recognizable figures to represent the two languages. Languages do not have to be visually represented as human figures, but if the cultures to which particular languages pertain already have a tradition of such personification, then

Fig. 10.2. Heading: "No, this is not an illicit love affair." Hebrew, walking arm-in-arm with Bialik, asks: "What's this Khayim Nakhmen, an illicit love affair?" Child (Bialik's writings in Yiddish) shouts "Daddy!" Servant girl (Yiddish) addressing Hebrew: "Don't be so surprised, madam; Khayim Nakhmen knows me since childhood!"

this traditional usage provides one obvious point of departure for visual representation.

If Sokolov was initially pleased to go about arm-in-arm with two "girlfriends" (the early supporters of the revival/revernacularization[7] of Hebrew initially had to make the difficult choice between remaining completely true to their convictions and, therefore, reaching only a very small readership, composed primarily of better educated males, or compromising with their ideals and writing *also* in Yiddish— often on behalf of Hebrew—in order to reach a much larger and more diversified readership), such was decreasingly the case as time went by, both for Sokolov and for other initially bilingual authors. In figure 10.2, we see Khayim Nakhmen Bialik (1873–1934) abandoning the maid-servant, Yiddish, with whom he has already "had a child" (many of his poems and essays had appeared initially in Yiddish or had subsequently been translated into Yiddish by Bialik himself) and walking off with Hebrew alone. In figure 10.3, we note the precisely opposite choice by Yits-

Fig. 10.3. Heading: "Perets's Folksy Romance." While old and wealthy Hebrew protests that she is being abandoned in favor of an unworthy rival, Perets showers endearing phrases upon young and lovely Yiddish. The designation "folksy" in the heading of the cartoon is borrowed from one of Perets's volumes of short stories, "Folksy Tales."

khok Leybush Perets (1852–1915). In the latter instance, Yiddish is not only younger; she is no longer wearing an apron, i.e., she is no longer a servant girl but, rather, a modern, liberated young woman. The basic metaphor is still recognizable, but the artist's own sentiments are recognizable too; and the metaphor is adapted, as metaphors usually are, in order to fit the attitudes and interpretations of the one who invokes it.

Adaptation of the Traditional Imagery

In the course of continuing modernization the traditional imagery continues to be used, but it also continues to be additionally altered and adapted in order to fit the message of the artist. In figure 10.4, we again find the two female figures we have grown to expect, but now their circumstances are considerably changed and reversed. Hebrew (attempting to gain support for a weekly of its own in the USA,[8]

Fig. 10.4. Heading: "Charity saves one from death." Hebrew, selling the *Hadoar:* "Don't be so stingy, mademoiselle! Donate a little publicity!"

where the Jewish press was, and still is, overwhelmingly dominated by Yiddish) is depicted as old and infirm, dependent upon young, stylish and affluent Yiddish for charitable support in order to attract readers and contributors. A further example of the adaptability of the traditional metaphor is shown in figure 10.5. Here we find the writer Osip Dimov (1878–1959) being torn apart by the three languages in which he wrote: Hebrew, Yiddish, and Russian. The fact that Russian too is depicted as a female figure is of particular interest here. The traditional imagery, referring to languages as female figures, is now extended to apply to a language outside of the Jewish fold. This extension may rest both on the visual habit that we have discussed thus far and on grammatical habits, since in both Yiddish and Hebrew the most common words for "language" are feminine.

The traditional imagery is obviously both robust and flexible. Within its metaphorical bounds, Yiddish and Hebrew can still be depicted as females, no matter how altered their relative circumstances may become, and other languages too can easily be rendered consensually recognizable. The latter languages can tap the already available visual metaphor, a metaphor that associates languages with female figures, a metaphor that is shared by artists and readers alike. Thus, the tradition can be both flexible and stable, rather than merely being "the dead hand of the past."

Fig. 10.5. Heading: "Three in One Osip Dimov." His friends [referring to panel on the right] claim that two literatures [Russian and Yiddish] are eager to possess him. His enemies [referring to center panel] claim that he has actually been torn in half by the struggle. The truth is that he is the hero of one of his own dramas [The Eternal Wanderer] in his constant alternation between one language and the other. Dimov's backpack is overflowing with mss in both languages.

The Tradition Breaks Down

However, as social change continues and accelerates, all traditions (including visual ones) may come to the end of their adaptive, reinterpretive capacity. New generations may arrive on the scene for whom the old metaphors no longer have the connotations and associations that render them doubly meaningful, i.e., meaningful as visual symbols in their own right and meaningful as the visual counterparts of earlier, once well recognized, verbal symbols. In the case that we are discussing, however, the tradition did not break completely in favor of some totally new set of visual conventions. Instead, as we approach the most recent decades, male figures come to be increasingly used to represent the languages in question. This may, perhaps, be interpreted as due to the growing role of technology and undisguised power, phenomena that are widely identified in modern societies as primarily masculine characteristics. In figure 10.6, we find Yiddish still depicted as a female figure, but one that is much abused by Hebrew (in Palestine, where its adherents resorted to brute force to combat Yiddish[9]). This is the first time that Hebrew, the oppressor, is depicted as a male figure. In figure 10.7, Yiddish too is depicted as a male figure; however, in this instance a biblical metaphor is being exploited. The story of Abraham's readiness to sacrifice Isaac, in order to prove his own obedience to God, is

Fig. 10.6. Last line under cartoon: "Strong complaints based upon a morally weak point of view." Hebrew writers in Palestine (male figure): "We protest against the Soviet Union for persecuting Hebrew."

Fig. 10.7. Heading: "The Sacrifice of Yiddish." Angel, to the Independent Order of Brith Abraham, brandishing a resolution against Yiddish: "Abraham! Abraham! Do not sacrifice your own child [Yiddish]. Sacrifice the ram [Anglo-Jewish press] instead." On the curious resolution of the IOBA Convention calling upon members to read the Anglo-Jewish press rather than the Yiddish press.

transformed into a parable on American Jewry's willingness to sacrifice Yiddish in its pursuit of unbridled anglification.

The latter cartoon may be an instance of one traditional visual symbol being replaced by an even earlier, more basic, more deeply ingrained visual representation of a verbal metaphor. By the third decade of the twentieth century the depiction of Jewish languages as females had, perhaps, become less acceptable or recognizable. However, their depiction as human figures had not. Given that the prior visual tradition had become unserviceable, human figures drawn from biblical texts were the most consensually recognizable ones to which the artist could appeal.

The Absence of Consensual Visual Metaphors

Visual traditions may crumble, but the visual representation of languages goes on. Modern artists, living in decreasingly traditional societies, i.e., in societies more marked by *Gesellschaft* than by *Gemeinschaft,* still seek to communicate about language. If they lack a consensual metaphor for doing so, they may need to fall back on their ingenuity and imagination. Their metaphors may become highly individualistic, but they may still communicate, edify, amuse. Even when their substantive theme remains constant, widely different visual metaphors may be resorted to by different artists, precisely because the previously unifying visual traditions have retreated or disappeared. Modern, technological societies may suffer from a relative lack of integrative visual metaphors, even as they are less integrated in many other respects relative to their more traditional predecessors. Artists use more individualistic and, therefore, a wider variety of visual metaphors to discuss their concerns, even when they share the same point of view on a particular issue.

Let us consider, e.g., the degree to which many Jews in Palestine/Israel implemented the mainstream Zionist stance that Diaspora languages (whether Jewish or coterritorial) should be barred from intragroup communication and that only revernacularized and modernized Hebrew should be utilized for this purpose. How should the long-continued use of *loazit* (foreign, non-Jewish languages) and the under-utilization (even nonacquisition) of Hebrew be depicted in visual terms? What visual metaphors should be employed in referring to Hebrew in this connection—a matter of widespread intellectual concern? As figures 10.8 to 10.12 reveal, in an ultra-modern society in which no traditional visual consensus is widely operative, an amazing variety of representations are encountered, even when both topic and attitude are fully shared. In figure 10.8, the physician tries to find out what has happened to Hebrew inside the patient's throat, since, obviously, no Hebrew is coming out of there. In figure 10.9, the waiter regretfully informs a patron that he cannot provide him with a newspaper, because all of the cafe's newspapers are at that moment being read by other customers. Obviously, there are still several newspapers hanging on the wall, but they are all in Hebrew and no one wants to read them. In figure 10.10, the reader of a presumably bilingual newspaper (Hebrew and Hungarian) is really interested only in the non-Hebrew part of the paper and is totally blind to the Hebrew section. In figure 10.11, the amazing and disconcerting diversity of languages publicly displayed prompts an observer to ask, "Have we returned to Babel?" Note that no traditional imagery pertaining to the biblical Tower of Babel is utilized, but, rather, the artist's own representation of an Israeli street scene. In figure 10.12, the most recent acquisition to my collection, the modern Israeli penchant for learning English is satirized. Instead of remaining exclusively loyal to Hebrew, English is increasingly and unnecessarily utilized, to the utter confusion of one and all. The English "who" sounds just like the Hebrew *hu* (which means "he"). The English "he" sounds just like the Hebrew *hi* (which means "she"). The English "me" sounds just like the Hebrew *mi* (which means "who"). And so it goes, confusion compounding confusion, when a foreign tongue is utilized.

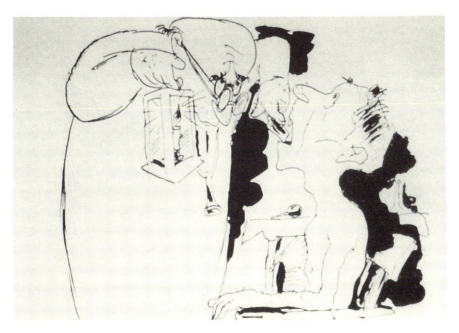

Fig. 10.8. (Dentist to patient) "I can't find any Hebrew in your throat." A commentary on the fact that many older immigrants speak little if any Hebrew.

Fig. 10.9. Waiter to cafe customer: "Sorry sir, all of our newspapers are being read by other customers." Obviously, several newspapers, all of them in Hebrew, are not being read, but no one wants to read them.

Fig. 10.10. Bilingual newspapers are not a halfway house en route to Hebrew. Their readers merely shut their eyes to the Hebrew sections and read only the sections written in their Diaspora mother tongues.

Summary and Discussion

The visual representation of languages and of sociolinguistic attitudes is a dynamic mode of symbolic communication. Where it is possible to do so, it makes use of previously established verbal metaphors and provides a visual counterpart to them. However, even under traditional societal circumstances it adapts, alters, and expands upon these metaphors. By doing so, visual metaphors tend to become, at least in part, consensually recognizable and interpretable symbols *in their own right,* i.e., they present in graphic terms various overtones of cognitive and affective communication relative to language matters that are unmentioned or unstressed in any of the original verbal metaphors that preceded them. Age, beauty, wealth, power, and other attributes of one language or another may only be implicitly mentioned in verbal discourse or in verbal imagery, but they may become explicit (although not necessarily highlighted) aspects of visual representation.

Under circumstances of rapid sociocultural change, consensual visual metaphors may be difficult to preserve, particularly so when the available set of underlying verbal metaphors on which the visual representations are so frequently based have themselves been lost. On the other hand, visual metaphors may continue in very stable fashion, even when rapid social change is underway (note, e.g., the continued tradition of depicting Uncle Sam and La Belle France as rather stereotyped

Fig. 10.11. The streets in Israel are cluttered with signs in a large variety of languages other than Hebrew. This leads new arrivals to ask "What? Have we returned to Babel?" and then to proceed to do likewise, i.e., to utilize their Diaspora mother tongues rather than Hebrew.

figures for roughly two centuries), as long as that change is within controllable bounds and its underlying verbal imagery has been retained.

Finally, there is no reason to suppose that older, once abandoned visual conventions cannot be returned to. Both on historical as well as on grammatical grounds, I would predict that if a consensual representation of Hebrew or Yiddish were to once more come into being, each of these languages would again be depicted as females. However, a strong component of cultural stability is needed for visual symbols to consolidate on an intergenerational basis. Since such stability is increasingly difficult to come by, the stabilization of visual metaphors, and even more so, the revival of those that existed in the past, strike me as increasingly unlikely occurrences. On the other hand, the innovation of visual metaphors pertaining to languages and to sociolinguistic attitudes should continue unabated. Just as language

Fig. 10.12. Not only is English not Hebrew, but, to make matters worse, it is confusing too.

change is more rapid in modern than in premodern times, so visual representations of language (and of visual metaphors more generally) can be expected to change more frequently in modern societies. The exact correlation between change in the verbal and in the visual realms remains to be established however. This is but another reason why the entire area of visual representations of language should be given far greater research attention by sociolinguists in the future than has been the case thus far.

Notes

This paper is dedicated to Prof. Rudolph Filipovic, Zagreb, in honor of his seventieth birthday, with warmest good wishes and sincerest admiration. May he "live to a hundred and twenty years" and continue his admirable example of stimulating research on the languages of Yugoslavia, both at home and abroad.

 1. For extensive bibliographies on language-attitude research, theory and methodology, see Roger W. Shuy and Ralph W. Fasold, eds., *Language Attitudes: Current Trends and Prospects* (Washington, DC, Georgetown University Press, 1973); and the two issues of *The International Journal of the Sociology of Language* devoted to this topic, both of them assembled

by Robert L. Cooper: 3 (1974) and 6 (1975). The field of language-attitude research has become so voluminous that it is now possible to follow it carefully only via international abstracting and bibliographic tools such as *Linguistics and Language Behavior Abstracts (USA)* and *Linguistics Abstracts (England)*.

2. Another nonverbal aspect of language attitudes that remains to be examined is the auditory one. We often hear individuals say that certain languages sound strange, ugly, harsh, musical, guttural, etc. These designations have yet to be either experimentally or situationally investigated, although they are probably closely related to more pervasive attitudes toward the languages in question.

3. The diglossic nature of the sociolinguistic repertoires of traditional Diaspora Jewish communities is discussed in my, "The Sociology of Jewish Languages from a General Sociolinguistic Point of View," in Joshua A. Fishman, ed., *Readings in the Sociology of Jewish Languages* (Leiden: Brill, 1985), pp. 3–21. In the same volume, this pattern is documented for Hebrew, Greek, and Aramaic (Judeo-Aramaic) in first-century CE Palestine by Bernard Spolsky, for Judezmo (Judeo-Spanish) and Spanish by Haim Vidal Sephiha, for Mugrabi (North African Judeo-Arabic) and Arabic by David Cohen, and for Judezmo and Mugrabi in Morocco by Joseph Chetrit. The basic conceptualization of diglossia situations involving Yiddish in Central and Eastern Europe was initially formulated by Max Weinreich in a 1959 publication (in Yiddish) and more fully developed by him in his *History of the Yiddish Language,* trans. Shlomo Noble and Joshua A. Fishman (Chicago, University of Chicago Press, 1980) from the three-volume Yiddish original, *Geshikhte fun der yidisher shprakh* (New York: Yivo Institute for Jewish Research, 1973). For more specific efforts to relate Yiddish-Hebrew diglossia to modern sociolinguistic theory see my *Never Say Die! A Thousand Years of Yiddish in Jewish Life and Letters* (The Hague: Mouton, 1981).

4. Figures 10.1–10.7 are from the American Yiddish press during the first three decades of this century. Figures 10.8–10.12 are from the Israeli press since the end of the Second World War. The cartoons discussed in this paper are a representative sample selected from a collection of nearly one hundred dealing with Hebrew and Yiddish. The author would greatly appreciate receiving copies of additional cartoons, whether dealing with these or with other languages.

5. The earliest reference that I have come across to Yiddish as a "servant girl," in relation to Hebrew, is in Tuvye Feder's *Kol meḥatsetsim* (written and distributed in MS in 1813, but not published until 1853), a vitriolic mock-trial of Mendl Lefin, who had prepared a folksy and free-standing Yiddish translation of the biblical Book of Proverbs (1815).

6. In this paper, transliterations of Ashkenazi Hebrew *(Loshn Koydesh)* will follow the Ashkenazi pronunciation of Eastern European Jews. Transliterations of modern Israeli Hebrew will follow the Israeli-Sefardi pronunciation. Items derived from Yiddish publications will generally be presented in the former transliteration, whereas items derived from Israeli publications will generally be presented in the latter transliteration. Exceptions to the above-stated principle are made in connection with certain proper nouns that have attained well-established transliterations of their own based on other conventions.

7. For a discussion of the revival/revernacularization of Hebrew, clearly indicating that the latter rather than the former was the major challenge facing Hebrew advocates in the latter part of the nineteenth and the early part of the twentieth century, see Jack Fellman, *The Revival of a Classical Tongue* (The Hague: Mouton, 1973). Also see his "A Sociolinguistic Perspective on the History of Hebrew," in J. A. Fishman, ed., *Readings in the Sociology of Jewish Languages* (Leiden: E. J. Brill, 1985), pp. 27–34.

8. *Hadoar* ("The Post") was founded as a daily in 1921, was briefly discontinued in 1922, and then resumed publication as a weekly. Except for a brief period in 1925, when it was once again discontinued, it has remained in operation continuously since that date.

9. For a detailed discussion of the strong-arm tactics used by extremist champions of Hebrew in Mandate Palestine in order to undercut Yiddish see chapters 1 through 5 of Arye Leyb Pilovski, *Tsvishn yo un neyn* (Tel Aviv: Veltrat far yidish un yidisher kultur, 1986). Other instructive articles by Pilovski on this same topic are his "La querella hebreo-yiddish en eretz-israel, 1907–1921, y sus proyecciones nacionales, politicas y culturales," *International Journal of the Sociology of Language* 24 (1980): 75–108; and his "Yiddish Alongside the Revival of Hebrew: Public Polemics on the Status of Yiddish in Erets Israel, 1907–1929," in J. A. Fishman, ed., *Readings in the Sociology of Jewish Languages* (Leiden: E. J. Brill, 1985), pp. 104–24.

11

Hebrew and the Habad Communication Ethos

NAFTALI LOEWENTHAL

The spiritual perspective on the Hebrew language is a feature of some of the earliest known kabbalistic texts and continued to be expressed in many works written in the Middle Ages. At the dawn of the modern period, the Hasidic movement began. This essay considers the teachings on the mystical dimension of Hebrew in the Habad school of Hasidism and suggests that they were and continue to be an important medium for the transmission of spiritual values and perspectives to the members of the Habad fraternity. In addition, the Habad teachings on Hebrew in relation to non-Hebrew languages have a significant role in the self-perception of this branch of Hasidism in relation to other sectors of society. This is relevant to the general question of the position of traditional Judaism in the post-ghetto contemporary world.

The Sacred Tongue

The Hasidic movement arose in the second half of the eighteenth century among the Jews of Eastern Europe. In this society the language of daily life was Yiddish, while Hebrew was in the main reserved for Torah study and prayer. It need hardly be stated that Hebrew was viewed as "the sacred tongue," particularly as a written language. Thus, as is well known, although Yiddish was generally employed in oral teaching of Torah, the language in which the lecture or inspired sermon would eventually be redacted was Hebrew. This applied to talmudic discourses, ethical exhortations, and also to the new Hasidic teachings.

Among the scholars there seems to have been no tension in this interaction between the two languages, although there was occasional recognition of deficiencies in the translation process.[1] At the same time it was understood that Yiddish had a role to play in promoting ethical teachings among the masses and the women in the community, who by and large could not understand Hebrew even if they could pronounce the words of the Prayer Book or Psalms. Again, it was obvious to all that Hebrew had the primary role as purveyor of the sacred; the use of Yiddish was a deliberate popularization. The function of Hebrew as the language of the scholarly elite was heightened by the fact that without vowel points, it could not be read by the ignorant. When a kabbalistic prayer book[2] was published in Zolkiew in 1781, the head of the Beth Din of Lemberg, Rabbi Mordechai Zev, gave his approbation to the publication of this highly esoteric work because the mystical text was being printed without vowel points "so that not everyone will be able to use it."

During the third and fourth generations of the Hasidic movement, now in the early nineteenth century, we find two contrasting developments concerning language. Both of these relate to the central ethos of Hasidism: the communication of the spirituality of the esoteric heritage through the broad reach of Jewish society. Instead of a heightened sense of contact with the Divine being reserved for the tiny elite of kabbalists, many of them greatly revered—at a distance—by the surrounding populace, Hasidism sought to make the spirituality of Judaism available to the wider community of scholars and ultimately to the many[3]. One effect of this, which has long been noted, was a new emphasis on the use of Yiddish. The popular language could reach far wider echelons of society, particularly including women, and also intrinsically had more power than the literary Hebrew to reach the "gut" level of the scholar. Thus we find Hasidic works being printed in Yiddish, and also Yiddish interpolations in Hebrew texts. A collection of stories about the Baal Shem Tov was published in Yiddish as well as Hebrew,[4] and Rabbi Nachman of Braslav (1772-1810) was concerned that his kabbalistic stories should be printed with a Yiddish translation.[5] The second leader of Habad, Rabbi Dov Ber of Lubavitch (1773-1827), wrote a Yiddish tract[6] which, within the Habad fraternity, became an important guide to the inner life of the Hasid. In his Hebrew writings Yiddish interpolations abound.[7]

A second development concerning language manifesting the communication ethos was the transmission by certain Hasidic leaders of spiritual or mystical teachings about Hebrew, the sacred tongue. Let us consider this in its context.

The ideal of broad communication of the esoteric presented a challenge: how could a sense of spirituality be imparted to the person who is not naturally inspired? A number of the most salient features of Hasidism, such as the role of the *Zaddik,* the Hasidic leader, can be better understood in terms of this general aim. The *Zaddik,* making himself accessible to his followers, succeeded in personally communicating to them some of his own enthusiasm; his teachings, drawn from the Kabbalah, but with a distinctive Hasidic flavor, revealed an inspired approach to standard Torah texts, prayer, and the observance of the Commandments. Much of this has been explored in the now considerable scholarly literature concerning the Hasidic movement. An area which has not yet been examined in its own right concerns the concept of Hebrew. Language, by its very nature, is a medium of communication. In Hasidism teachings *about* language, in particular about Hebrew, became an important instrument in striving to communicate the intense spirituality and sense of "radiance" which was perceived by the Hasidic masters and which they sought to transmit to others. Through these teachings, the sacred tongue became a vehicle to impart overt intimations of "holiness" to those for whom encounter with Hebrew texts was a natural part of everyday life. This process begins with the founder of Hasidism, Rabbi Yisrael Baal Shem Tov (1698-1760).

A Teaching about Hebrew Letters

In a famous letter by the Baal Shem Tov, addressed to his brother-in-law in the Holy Land, we find an interesting teaching about the spirituality of Hebrew.[8] This is the letter which describes a mystical "ascent of the soul,"[9] the climax of which was an encounter with the Messiah. The Baal Shem Tov asked "when will you come?" The answer was a demand for the communication of spiritual power to others: "when your teachings are publicized and revealed in the world, and your fountains will be spread to the outside . . . and they too will be able to make 'unifications'[10] and ascents like you."[11]

This letter, which has been called "the manifesto of Hasidism,"[12] expresses clearly the communication ethos which became the central feature of the new movement. There is a demand that the Baal Shem Tov should transmit to others something of his own spiritual attainment. The letter continues with information about the way he responded to this demand. At first he was dismayed, because he thought this would be very difficult and take a long time. Then he was appeased somewhat, because during this same spiritual journey he was given a mystical teaching which would be "easy to study and to explain." He thought that by means of this teaching, his spiritual power could be transmitted to at least some of his contemporaries, possibly a close circle of intimate disciples.[13] However, he then states that he was forbidden to do this. Two contrary forces seem to be at work: the traditional restriction of mystical power to a small elite, and, by contrast, the new goal of communication. The Baal Shem Tov writes that he sought permission to reveal this "easy" teaching to just one individual, the intended recipient of the letter, R. Gershon of Kuty, himself a kabbalist of note.[14] This too was denied. How then could the Baal Shem Tov fulfill the spiritual task which had been given to him? At this point we come to the crux of the letter, the transmission by the Baal Shem Tov of a teaching which *was* permitted. This concerned the spirituality of the Hebrew letters and words:

> However, of this I will inform you. . . . During your prayer and study, in every single word, have the intention to achieve "unification" there. For in every single letter there are worlds, and souls, and G-dliness, which rise and join and unify with each other. Then the letters join and unify together and become a word. They achieve a true unity with G-d. You should include your own soul with them at every step. . . .[15]

Thus while the Baal Shem Tov was forbidden to transmit a direct and overt teaching, even one which was "easy," the teaching about the spirituality of Hebrew was permitted. Through drawing attention to the holiness of the letters, and revealing that within them there are "worlds, and souls and G-dliness," the Baal Shem Tov found a permissible path to transmit to others the sense of the spiritual and the holy as a living experience. The context of this awareness is, naturally enough, prayer and Torah study, activities which are centred on texts in Hebrew. But the Baal Shem Tov's teaching transmits a further dimension, relating to the kabbalistic heritage of divine names, letter combinations and other verbal "keys" of the Merkavah tradition, by means of which the soul of the mystic would ascend to ever higher supernal realms.[16] If the person praying or studying is made aware of this further dimension and is able to "include" his own soul in the spiritual pathways which are opened up, then he too will share in the otherworldly power which the Baal Shem Tov understood it was his task to transmit.

Teachings about the spirituality of the Hebrew letters are found repeatedly in the records extant of the sayings of the Baal Shem Tov. In those of his disciple, Rabbi Dov Ber, the Maggid of Mezeritch (d. 1772), they appear in a more overtly kabbalistic form.[17] These teachings are in the main addressed to people of considerable spiritual stature for whom the demand to be aware of and respond to the otherworldly dimension of the letters was within reach—people like R. Gershon, and the members of the intimate circles of the Baal Shem Tov and the Maggid, many of whom were seen as important Hasidic leaders in their own right. But to what extent were these teachings relevant to the normative scholar, to the intellectual brought up on a diet of talmudic analysis and halakhic (legal) codes?

It is here that we come to the Habad school, a branch of Hasidism which was particularly concerned with the communication ethos of Hasidism. In Habad a systematic philosophy of the nature of Hebrew was expounded, both as the divine language which generates all existence and also as an important element in the mystical psychology of the individual. This philosophy of language is central to the Habad system of contemplation, a system intended for the normative intellectual, not just for a small elite of the inspired. In addition, these teachings concern not only the sacred tongue, Hebrew, but also by extension other languages, which in certain circumstances are deemed spiritualized, "elevated." As a number of writers have shown, the sanctification and elevation of the mundane is a central theme in Hasidism.[18] The Habad teachings on Hebrew were thus an important vehicle for transmitting Hasidic ideals to the members of the fraternity.

Language and Contemplation

In 1796 Rabbi Shneur Zalman of Liadi (1745–1812), the founder of the Habad school, published a volume of Hasidic teachings which eventually became known by the general title *Tanya* ("We have learnt..."). The first edition[19] comprised two sections: a tract on the nature of the soul and on divine service, and a second, briefer work on the nature of existence. The chief purpose of this second section, entitled *Sha'ar ha-Yihud ve-ha-Emunah* ("Gate of Unity and Faith"), was to provide material for contemplation before or during prayer. In this text for contemplation, a central theme is the role of the Hebrew language as the divine dimension of all existence.

The starting point for this idea is the account of creation in Genesis. Ten divine "utterances" brought the universe into being: "let there be light," "let there be a firmament," and so on.[20] Rabbi Shneur Zalman states in the name of the Baal Shem Tov that this was not simply an event in the past: the utterance "let there be a firmament," in the form of a flow of "words and letters" from the divine, continues to give existence to the firmament, i.e., the heavens. "If the letters were to disappear for a moment ... and return to their source, all the heavens would be absolutely naught as if they had never existed."

He adds that this is also the case for "all created things in all worlds, upper and lower, even this physical world and the inanimate things: if the letters of the Ten Utterances with which the world was created ... were to disappear for a moment, Heaven forbid, [all] would return to naught as before the six days of creation."

On this level, the "words and letters" which give existence to the world seem to be purely divine, remote from human language. But R. Shneur Zalman presents the idea, citing the great sixteenth-century kabbalist, Rabbi Isaac Luria, that everything "including stones and dust" has a spiritual aspect, which gives it existence. The spiritual dimension of any object is "the name which it is called in the Sacred Tongue." The letters of this name, i.e., the Hebrew noun, are described as being derived from the brief text of the Ten Utterances. The ancient *Book of Creation,* an early treatise of letter mysticism, is cited as the source of the method of deriving one letter from another, by a kind of mystical system of interchange which in effect provides the facility to substitute any letter for any other.[21] Apart from letter interchange and substitution, R. Shneur Zalman also speaks of the *gematria* method of transformation, whereby a Hebrew word is considered spiritually related to another because of their respective numerical values.[22] (See Dan in this volume.)

R. Shneur Zalman makes no attempt to impart any of the esoteric teachings concerning the actual method of letter interchange. Without doubt he considered such instructions as unsuitable for the intended reader of his book. He simply makes clear that there is such a system implicit in the inner structure of the universe. The knowledge that he does want to transmit to his reader is the idea that given the existence of these divine methods of interchange, the brief text of the Ten Utterances—some ten verses in Scripture—can be seen as the basic source from which all nouns in the Hebrew language are generated. The Ten Utterances are part of the Torah, and "the Torah and the Holy One, Blessed be He, are One."[23] Hence the divine creative power which is in the Ten Utterances extends also to *all* nouns in Hebrew. However, since these nouns are only derived indirectly from the Ten Utterances, by means of letter interchange and *gematria,* the creative power in ordinary nouns is milder than in the Ten Utterances themselves. It has been "stepped down" by the process of interchange and substitution. This is an important aspect of the system, because it links the linguistic model for existence with the kabbalistic one of downchaining worlds of ever decreasing spiritual force:

> ... the individual things created are not able to receive their life-force directly from the Ten Utterances in the Torah, for the life-force which flows from them is too great for the capacity of the individual created things. They are able to receive this life-force only when it descends and is progressively diminished, degree by degree, by means of exchange and interchange of letters and *gematriot,* the numerical value of the letters, until it is able to contract and be enclothed in and give life to an individual created thing. And this is its name in the Holy Tongue....[24]

The teaching which R. Shneur Zalman is imparting is about existence in relation to the Divine, but it is expressed in terms of the spirituality of Hebrew. Highly esoteric teachings are referred to, not in order to teach "Practical Kabbalah"[25] but in order to impart a more general awareness of the spiritual nature of existence. The focus of this awareness concerns the spiritual function of Hebrew, both as the divine speech in the ethereal beginning of creation and also as the sacred language which enters and gives life to the physical details of the daily world.[26]

The next chapter of this tract explores further the idea that existence is continuously dependent on the Divine. With echoes of Maimonides' *Guide for the Perplexed*[27] it enters the arena of philosophic argument about divine providence and the miracles described in the Torah. This synthesis of philosophy and mysticism is an important aspect of Habad thought.[28] However, the chapter soon returns to the theme of Hebrew, this time describing another feature of R. Shneur Zalman's mystical cosmology. The stream of letters from the Divine which give existence to the universe have another, parallel function: they enter the mind of the Prophets, and "are enclothed in their minds and understanding, in their prophetic visions, and also in their thought and speech."[29] In this form they are not reduced in power, but flow directly from an exalted spiritual level.

This additional concept helps us to appreciate the continuum of spirituality of which R. Shneur Zalman sought to make his followers aware. The sacred letters of Hebrew flow from the Divine, giving existence to everything; at the same time other, even brighter letters are there in the prophetic teachings written in the Torah and the sacred texts which comprise the Prayer Book. This is reminiscent of the instruction in the letter of the Baal Shem Tov, to be aware of the "worlds, and souls, and G-dliness" in the Hebrew letters of Torah and prayer. Yet in R. Shneur Zalman's teaching it is the letters themselves which bear the spirituality: be aware, he is saying, of the continuum of Hebrew letters. R. Gershon of Kuty, the intended recipient of the letter of the Baal Shem Tov, himself a kabbalist, would surely have been able to conceive of the "worlds, and souls and G-dliness" within the letters. But the normative scholar who was the expected reader of *Tanya* might well not be able to cope with this demand. He was not a mystic, but a talmudist. The awareness demanded from him was of the letters themselves, as the key to the spiritual in Torah, prayer, and life. With this demand he could cope, and thus a spiritual perspective on existence, drawn from profoundly mystical sources, was made a part of his life.

Inner Communication

Early Habad teachings also expound a theory of language as an aspect of the inner life of the individual. Employing the ancient theme of the parallel between microcosm and macrocosm, these ideas also apply to the process of the divine creation of and interaction with the universe. However, while one aspect of the Habad teachings on language concerns the discovery of the spiritual within the mundane, a second approach to the same material generates a heightened awareness of the communication process which takes place within a person during both contemplation and the activities of daily life.

R. Dov Ber (1773–1827), the son and successor of R. Shneur Zalman, in his

Tract on Contemplation, taught of "letters" *(otiot)* as the medium of translation from one level of consciousness to another. "Through the letters, that which is hidden becomes revealed."[30] R. Dov Ber describes levels which are beyond any kind of definition, and which are beyond communication or transmission. However, by taking form as "letters," which means undergoing a process of concretization, the spiritual force of that ethereal realm can be translated into a form relevant to a lower level of being or of consciousness. Thus the abstract plane of "pure will and delight," the innermost domain of consciousness to which the person has access, becomes transformed into the "letters of the will," a tangible expression of specific desire. The same process of concretization through "letters" takes place when tangible will becomes translated into specific intellectual categories, the "wisdom" and "understanding" required to implement the will. The "letters" of the intellect define the desire further, and make it more precise.

The next step described by R. Dov Ber is from intellect to emotion. This means the arousal of a positive enthusiasm leading towards real achievement and implementation of what began as a purely abstract, wordless idea. In this step too, "letters" are involved: emotion is conceived of as needing something tangible on which to feed. In the following stage of thought the "letters" come to the fore in the more obviously linguistic sense. One begins to think clearly about the idea and the next step forward. After this comes speech itself, described as the stage which follows thought and communicates it to others, and finally action. In this too there are "letters." Action is considered the implementation of speech, expressing its "letters" in practical form. It is the final concretization of the ladder of speech, thought, emotion, wisdom, and ultimately will, the source of all.

At every step in this process, "letters" are involved. Inner communication, in the form of a kind of internal language, leads from wordless intimations to tangible reality. Where does this language originate? What is the source of the "letters"? How do they have such power to transform the ethereal into the practical?

The answer to this is perhaps the most intriguing aspect of R. Dov Ber's system. "The root of the letters is in the very essence of the soul." His father, Rabbi Shneur Zalman, too speaks of the idea that "the soul (i.e., the essence) is full of letters."[31] In the very essence of being there is the basic parameter of language, in terms of which all other dimensions of consciousness and expression can take form. At every stage of the process of transformation and translation from idea to action, there is, necessarily, reference (albeit largely unconscious) to this inner language, the "letters" of the soul.

The letters are, as we might expect, Hebrew letters. A teaching by Rabbi Shneur Zalman, published in 1814 by his son R. Dov Ber, states that all speech, in whatever language, is based on the Hebrew letters.[32] Through the medium of the Hebrew letters within the soul, a human being functions as such, and his or her consciousness can proceed from intimations of spirituality to thought and speech in any language. In the pages of *Tract on Contemplation,* as elsewhere in Habad teaching, this structure is depicted in terms relevant both to the microcosm and the macrocosm. The contemplative can ponder on the chain from the Infinite to the teacup on the table, or be sensitive to the nature of the stages of transformation from level to level within his own inner world. Contemplatation and life can thus be seen as a form of protolinguistic communication. Indeed, R. Dov Ber describes the "veils" which, in the Lurianic Kabbalah, conceal the Divine, as letters, "but the letters are disorganized" and convey no meaning. This too is the nature of all *Zimzum,* the source of the finite (and also problematic) quality of existence.[33] However, when the jumbled letters are rearranged in an organized way the meaning of all life—the ultimate reality, the boundless oneness of the Divine—shines through. This revelation of the meaning in the letters is the mystical, all-transcending step of "breaking through the veil."[34]

Gematria and Other Teachings

Apart from general conceptual structures involving language, such as those described above, in early Habad teachings there is constant reference to the spiritual significance of Hebrew. *Gematria,* the numerical value of the words, is often employed as a means to demonstrate a point. Thus the fact that one of the divine names has the same numerical value as the word for nature *(ha-teva)* illustrates teachings on the way the Divine gives life to and is concealed in nature.[35] The word ואהבת *ve-ahavta,* "and you shall love," has twice the numerical value of אור *or,* "light," for there are two kinds of spiritual radiance involved in true love of the Divine: first the radiance of Torah study and observance of the Commandments, then the radiance of pure love, which comes as a gift from heaven.[36]

Sometimes the grammatical features of a word are also used in the exposition of a mystical teaching. Thus the Tetragrammaton is explained as a form of the verb "to be," for the Divine gives existence to the universe; it is in the imperfect tense, which is interpreted as meaning continuous action (as in Job 1:6: ככה יעשה איוב *kakhah ya'aseh Iyov*), because this imparting of life and being is a continuous process.[37]

As in the Talmud, etymology is another medium of communication. מִצְרַיִם *Mitzrayim,* "Egypt," is interpreted as מְצָרִים *metzarim,* "limitations," "straits": for the exile in Egypt, on a personal level, is the inner spiritual limitation from which a person has to break free.[38] Further, the word מצוה *mitzvah,* "commandment," is explained as relating to the Aramaic צוותא *tzavta,* "connections," for the observance of a commandment creates a bond with the Divine.[39]

This aspect of the power of a mitzvah is also emphasized by pointing out that when the first two letters of this word (Mem and Tzaddik) are transmuted through the *AT BaSh* system, in which Alef is replaced by Tav, Beit by Shin, Gimmel by Resh and so on, they are transformed into Yud and Heh, which together with the last two letters of the word (Vav and Heh) make the Tetragrammaton.[40]

The spiritual dimension of Hebrew, expounded in a variety of ways, continued to be a feature of Habad thought, through the nineteenth century and into the present. The third leader of this branch of Hasidism, Rabbi Menachem Mendel, known as the *Zemah Zedek* (1789–1866), left extensive teachings which have recently been anthologized in the form of extracts arranged in order of subject, constituting in effect a large encyclopedia of his ideas.[41] The entry on the Hebrew "Letters" is almost two hundred pages long. One might say this also tells us something about the interests of the present day Hasidic compilers of the encyclopedia. At the beginning of the entry is a list of topics covered. This includes:

> Drawing down the letters [from above] through fire, water, and wind; that they are fixed in the essence of the soul; are termed "stones" . . . their form and matter; the difference between letters of speech, thought, and those in the essence of the soul . . . three types of letters [in the text of Scripture]—large, normal, and small; the final letters; the five kinds of consonant; letters of prayer and Torah study, the letters of the Torah corresponding to the number of Jewish souls; sacred and profane letters; elevating letters through incense; the crowns on the letters; letter interchange; letters which are written and those which are engraved.[42]

Concern for the spiritual dimension of the Hebrew language is also expressed in another literary project of modern Habad. This too is an encyclopedia, written at the behest of Rabbi Menachem Mendel Schneerson (b. 1902), the Lubavitcher Rebbe. Its author is one of the leading scholars in the Habad-Lubavitch community in Brooklyn, R. Yoel Kahn.[43] In this work, only part of which has as yet been published, two large volumes concern "Letters," that is, the significance of the Hebrew letters and language, as expounded in earlier Habad teachings. On the letter Alef, for example, there are some ninety pages. The following is a representative passage, discussing the fact that the Alef is written as a Yud above, a Yud below, and a line, seen as a Vav, between the upper and lower Yud:

> The two letters Yud of the Alef represent the realm of *Azilut* [the highest of the four kabbalistic worlds] and the lower worlds, respectively. The fact that these two letters Yud are together in one letter [the Alef] indicates that *Azilut* and the lower worlds are joined together. [We might think they are completely separate] . . . Although the separation between *Azilut* and the lower worlds is immense—for the Veil between them completely interrupts and conceals—nonetheless, since from the point of view of the Divine there is no concealment at all, ultimately (that is, from the divine viewpoint) the lower worlds are joined with the higher.

> Further, through the service of study of Torah and obervance of the mitzvot one can bring about that this unity of the lower and upper realms be revealed also to humanity [rather than just to G-d]. This is one of the reasons why the Giving of the Torah was with an Alef (the Alef of the word *Anokhi,* "I am"). For at the Giving of the Torah there was transmitted the power to achieve this unity for the "lower waters" which are below the firmament (which means the lower realms, and even more, physical existence), that they too should be joined to the Divine.[44] (So much so, that after they are elevated they rise higher than the "upper waters." This is shown by the fact that the lower Yud joins the central line at a higher point than does the upper Yud)[45] (See fig. 11.1.).

These encyclopedias provide evidence of interest in modern Habad in the earlier teachings concerning Hebrew. At the same time, it is noteworthy that there is a strong focus on the Hebrew language and the significance of the forms of the Hebrew letters in a twentieth-century text, called *Bati le-Gani,* which is known to be a central document of the contemporary Habad-Lubavitch movement.

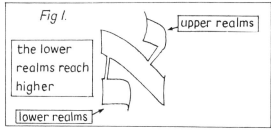

Fig. 11.1. Joining the upper and lower realms by means of the Alef of the Giving of the Torah

Letter Mysticism in the Twentieth Century

Bati le-Gani is a long discourse of Hasidic teaching written by the previous Lubavitcher Rebbe, Rabbi Yosef Yitzhak Schneersohn (1880–1950). It has twenty chapters, and its name comes from the opening words, "I have come into my garden" (Cant. 5: 6). Shortly before R. Yosef Yitzhak passed away he had this discourse printed and issued instructions that it should be studied by the Hasidic followers on the tenth day of Shevat, the anniversary of his grandmother's death. However, on that day R. Yosef Yitzhak himself passed away, and *Bati le-Gani* became a final statement of guidance and instruction.

In 1951 the present Rebbe, after a year of reluctance, formally accepted the leadership of the Lubavitch movement. His acceptance took the form of reciting a discourse, at a Hasidic gathering, on 10th Shevat, the first anniversary of the demise of the previous Rebbe. This discourse was itself based on *Bati le-Gani.* While it encompassed the basic outline of the original, it also included a detailed discussion of the first of its twenty chapters. Since then, the Lubavitcher Rebbe annually recites a discourse based on the original *Bati le-Gani,* each year particularly focusing on the exposition of another chapter, in order. After twenty years, the 10th Shevat discourse returned again to the first chapter.[46]

The *Bati le-Gani* discourse has an important role in the life of the Habad community. It is extensively studied, by women as well as men, and has been translated into English.[47] It is noteworthy that there is a strong focus, both in the original discourse and in its later expositions, on aspects of letter mysticism and the spiritual significance of the Hebrew language.

The first few chapters concern the task of humanity: to create a dwelling for the *Shekhinah,* the divine "presence." The *Shekhinah* was in the Garden of Eden, but receded from it after the sin of Adam and Eve, and receded yet further due to subsequent evil actions, such as Cain killing Abel. Then came Abraham, a Zaddik who drew the *Shekhinah* a little way back toward the world; his successors Isaac, Jacob, and so on continued this task, until the seventh such *Zaddik.* This was Moses, who built the Sanctuary, in which there dwelt the *Shekhinah,* in the Holy of Holies. The task of life is to construct an inner "sanctuary,"[48] and the discourse continues by expounding various aspects of this sanctuary in terms of the life of the individual. R. Yosef Yitzhak depicts qualities of self-restraint, self-transformation, and the reach for a transcendent dimension of action (which he calls "sacred folly"[49]) as being represented in various features of the sanctuary.

Then in chapter 6 there is a discussion of the "planks" used to construct the Sanctuary, as described in Exodus 26: 15–30. The term used for a plank is *keresh*. The discourse describes the way a person seeks to transform "falsehood", שקר *sheker*, the negative aspects of being, into קרש *keresh*, a sacred plank in the Sanctuary. The theme of transformation is central to Hasidic thought; here it is expressed through the fact that the two words, Hebrew *sheker* and *keresh*, have the same letters. The discourse then discusses the nature of these letters more deeply, starting with quotation of the passage in the Zohar which tells of the Hebrew letters rising before the Creator, each pleading that the world should be created through it.[50] Shin, Kuf, and Resh are the letters under discussion. According to the Zohar, Kuf and Resh are letters which have a negative aspect, so in order to exist they take the letter Shin with them, "a letter of truth." Hence *sheker*, falsehood, starts with the letter of truth, Shin, and then has the negative letters Kuf and Resh. "From here [we learn] that anyone who wants to tell a lie should first take a basis of something true, and then his lie will stand firm"[51] (fig. 11.2a).

Despite the negativity of Kuf and Resh, however, the ultimate purpose is to transform them into something holy, the *keresh* (plank) of the Sanctuary (fig. 11.2b). To explain this process, R. Yosef Yitzhak continues with an exposition of the nature and form of these letters. He states that Kuf and Resh are negative because they are negative expressions of the sacred letters Heh and Daled. In both cases the forms of the letters are similar: Kuf is like a Heh, but with an extended left "foot"; Resh is similar to a Daled and even has the same meaning: both *resh* and *dal* mean "poor." However, while "poor" as an expression of Daled means the humility of the sacred, the poverty of Resh is the poverty of evil, due to its lack of connection with the Divine.[52]

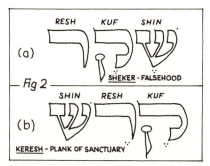

Transforming falsehood and evil (a) into the holiness of the Sanctuary (b)

Fig. 11.2. Transforming falsehood and evil (a) into the holiness of the Sanctuary (b). In section (a): *Sheker*, Falsehood. In section (b): *Keresh*, a Plank of the Sanctuary

The spiritual difference between Resh and Daled is very great: the first verse of the Shema has the word *eḥad* ("one"), the oneness of the Divine, written Alef, Ḥet, Daled, with a large Daled in the Hebrew text of Scripture (Deut. 6:4).[53] This emphasizes that the word means "one," contrasting with Exodus 34:14, in which the word *aḥer* ("other"), Alef, Ḥet, Resh, is written with a large Resh. This word refers to idols: "do not bow down to any *other* god." The Daled therefore signifies the holiness of the Divine, the Resh the unholiness of idolatry[54] (fig. 11.3).

The key to the distinction between the forms of Resh and Daled is based on analysis of the forms of these letters. R. Yosef Yitzhak explains that the difference between these two letters is that the Daled is like a Resh but has a Yud added to its back. This totally transforms it, for "the letter Yud signifies *bitul*," a term meaning self-abnegation and humility. This quality is missing from the Resh, which therefore signifies pride (fig. 11.4). In Hasidic thought in general, but particularly in Habad, humility denotes the realm of the holy, while pride is the expression of evil. At this point there is an exposition of these qualities, based on the forms of the letters.

The discourse then explores the relationship of the Kuf and the Heh.[55] The Heh is actually a Daled, expressing sanctity, with the further addition of a Yud as its left "foot." The right "foot" and "roof" of the Heh represent sacred thought and speech, and the left "foot" (which is not joined to the "roof") signifies sacred action. The separation of the left "foot" from the "roof" is because of the way that action is separate from the inner person, while thought and speech are more direct expressions of one's inner qualities. However, the right kind of action can of course be an expression of holiness, and this is depicted in the letter Heh (fig. 11.5). R. Yosef Yitzhak describes how this is manifest in the life of a person, giving the example of the official in charge of distributing charity, who may have to stand firm on certain issues but yet must be gentle and sensitive in his relations with others, "avoiding pride to the furthest extreme,"[56] thus expressing the humility which characterises the domain of holiness.

Just as the Heh is a product of the Daled, and is its fulfilment in practical terms,

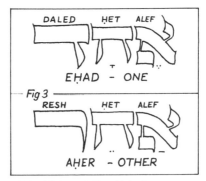

The Holy and the Unholy

Fig. 11.3. Holy and Unholy. The large Daled and large Resh in the words *Eḥad* ("One") and *Aḥer* ("Other")

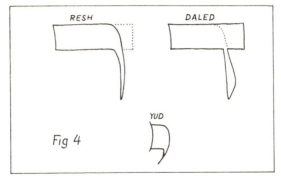

Fig. 11.4. The difference between Resh and Daled is a Yud, symbol of humility

so too the Kuf is a product of the Resh. Here however we are dealing with the unholy rather than the holy. The Resh lacks the humility of the Yud appended to the back of the Daled; as thought and speech, the Resh therefore signifies bad thoughts and negative speech. These then are complemented by the left "foot" of the Kuf, again representing action. But this time, instead of being level with the rest of the letter, as in the case of the Heh, the left "foot" descends below the line, to the unholy depths, "her feet going down to death" (Prov. 5: 5) (fig. 11.6). Thus through bad action the Kuf is made, representing the realm of the unholy *kelipot* which are described in kabbalistic sources as "an 'ape' *(kof)* compared with a man."[57] The ideal of course is to return to being a "man," אדם *adam,* of which the Alef represents thought, i.e., thoughts of holiness (for Alef denotes the divine), and the Daled and Mem sacred "speech" (דבור *dibbur*) and "action" (מעשה *ma'aseh*) respectively.

The service in one's inner sanctuary is the process whereby the long "foot" of the Kuf is cut back, so that it is more like a Heh; through Torah study and contemplative prayer, the Kuf will be filled with divine radiance and will be transformed. Thus the negative word *sheker,* falsehood, the falsehood of the profane world, will

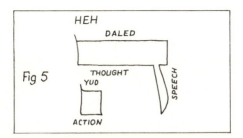

Fig. 11.5. The Heh represents sacred Thought, Speech, and Action

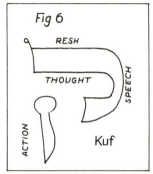

Fig. 11.6. Kuf is a negative form of Heh. Unholy action (the left foot) descends to the depths

thereby become the positive *keresh,* "plank" of the sanctuary. Through this, spiritual darkness is changed to light, which is the purpose of existence.[58]

Bati le-Gani is a product of modern Habad. It utilizes teachings from the Zohar and Lurianic Kabbalah in order to transmit the ethos of Hasidism to followers in the United States, modern Israel, and other countries. As in the early generations of the movement, it is the spirituality and inner meaning of Hebrew, the sacred tongue, which is an important medium for the communication of the basic themes of Hasidism.

Beyond Hebrew

One more aspect of the Habad teachings on Hebrew needs examination: the relationship of Hebrew to other languages. The emphasis on the holiness of the sacred tongue could well lead to a "ghetto" structure, in which the lone preserve of holiness is surrounded by a hostile sea of the profane.[59] It is characteristic of Habad and the communication ethos that this does not take place. Rather, Habad teachings emphasize that it is in the power of the sacred to transmit its essential quality to the nonsacred. The teachings on non-Hebrew languages in Habad texts, like those on the forms of the Hebrew letters explored above, are an important medium for the expression of the relationship of the Divine and the earthly in terms relevant both to the life of the individual and to society as a whole.

Thus in a teaching delivered in the early spring of 1808 Rabbi Shneur Zalman presented a conceptual structure linking Hebrew, the sacred tongue, with the languages encountered by the Jews in exile.[60] The teaching starts with the idea that letters can be compared to "stones," as those used for building. This image derives from the ancient kabbalistic text *Book of Creation,* which was mentioned above. This text refers to the different combinations possible with a group of letters (two from two letters, six combinations from three, twenty-four from four, and so on) as the number of "houses" which can be built with the "stones" of the Hebrew letters. The audience of Hasidic followers listening to R. Shneur Zalman's discourse was quite familiar with this idea. His teaching presented them with a development of this image: there are two kinds of stones for building, those which are literally stones, fashioned by G-d, and those which are actually bricks, made from clay by human beings.

The divinely fashioned stones represent the letters and words of Hebrew, the sacred tongue, revealed by G-d in the Torah. The man-made bricks signify the letters of other languages:

> There are letters which do not come from above [as does Hebrew] ... but they are formed below by man, similar to bricks, which are made by man so as to resemble stones. ... These are the combinations of letters of the seventy languages of the seventy nations of the world, and similarly other letters of worthless talk, [anything] other than letters of the Sacred Tongue which are in the Torah, for each nation speaks its own language.[61]

R. Shneur Zalman explains that these non-Hebrew languages are elevated to holiness by the religious devotion of the Jews. Scattered in exile, they speak the languages of the nations of the world and use those languages for their daily affairs. When the Jew prays "with self-sacrifice" and also uses the Gentile language for discussion of Torah[62], he elevates it to a higher level. Then

> one raises all the combinations of letters used in one's speech to the level of Upper Purity beyond the downchaining of the worlds. ... This is called "the ordinary which is prepared with the purity of holiness."[63] This means that even though the combinations of letters of the seventy languages are completely non-holy, they are nonetheless brought to the purity of the upper holiness. For they are raised above, so that they too should be "Letters," like the letters of the Sacred Tongue in the Written Torah and similar.[64]

R. Shneur Zalman goes on to emphasise that this process can only take place through the intensity of divine service of the Jew. Just as clay has to be heated in a furnace in order to become bricks, so the ordinary language of everyday life has to go through the "furnace" of enthusiastic prayer in order to be elevated to holiness.

This teaching, expressed in terms of sacred and profane language, is one of the central teachings of Hasidism: that ordinary life can become sacred. The discourse emphasizes this theme by reference to another biblical image. Exodus 24:1–11 describes Moses and the elders of the Israelites ascending Mount Sinai and seeing a vision of the Divine. The climax of this included seeing that "under His feet was a paving of sapphire bricks, pure as the essence of Heaven" (Ex. 24:10). R. Shneur Zalman explains that "under His feet" means the way that divine radiance extends below, to the very lowest realm of existence. On that very lowest level, through the process of making "bricks" from the letters of the profane languages, one is able to make the radiant bricks of sapphire described in the verse, "for the beginning is joined in the end,"[65] in other words, on the lowest level one discovers the highest level: the profane letters become sapphire.

R. Shneur Zalman now asks how this is possible. How can the letters of the profane languages be elevated to such a high level? His answer is that the essence of all language is in fact Hebrew, the sacred tongue. All language is expressed by a variety of consonants. (This is an allusion to a passage in the *Book of Creation,* 2:1, which refers to gutturals, velars, dentals, sibilants, and labials.) Since these consonants are in Hebrew, one can say that Hebrew is the source of all language. All language can therefore be elevated to its source, the sacred tongue:

> The voice divides into the five kinds of consonant, as is known, and we can see that the letter Alef, which is a guttural, is identical in other languages. The same Alef expressed in the Holy Tongue is also the Alef expressed in other languages of the seventy languages, such as Yiddish.[66] For the five types of consonant are simply the source of the division of the letters, into gutturals and so on. Hence the five types of consonant are the source of the division [of the letters] in all languages equally. Therefore the seventy languages have a spiritual source above, in the spiritual source of speech, which is the Divine Attribute of Kingship. . . .[67] For this reason the combinations of letters [of profane languages] can be transformed into the Sacred Tongue.[68]

This teaching on the nature of language is a remarkable expression of the communication ethos of Habad. Ultimately everything can be embraced by holiness, for the source of everything is holiness. Further, it is precisely by reaching the lower level, the profane level, that the "paving of sapphire" can be made. As it stands, this teaching concerns the inner spiritual life of the Hasid. Any inference it may have carried for R. Shneur Zalman's followers regarding the non-Jewish world around them remains a matter of conjecture. In fact relations with that world were then at a very low ebb.

At this time the Jewish community was faced with the tragic consequences of the harsh Statute Concerning the Jews of 1804, which began to be put into effect in January 1808. Thousands of Jews were expelled from the villages and taken forcibly to the towns.[69] R. Shneur Zalman himself was very active in trying to care for these unfortunates on a practical level. The guidance he gave through the medium of his Hasidic teachings was to maintain a defiant stance of dedication to Judaism despite the current atmosphere of oppression.[70] There is a possibility that the teaching we have been discussing could be understood as meaning that through the mystical movement of elevating the profane and everyday aspect of life, the nations of the world, including the oppressor, would also be elevated and changed from evil to good. A somewhat similar teaching by R. Shneur Zalman is known, dating from 1805.[71] It is noteworthy that here, in the discourse of 1808, this idea is expressed in terms of a linguistic transformation.

Early Non-Hebrew Works

It is reasonable to suggest that this aspect of Habad thought would tend to promote publication of works in Yiddish and eventually in other languages. In a work on halakhah published in 1794, R. Shneur Zalman states that the sages in talmudic times would give talks about practical Jewish law every Sabbath "in a language that could be understood by the women and the ignorant."[72] While as far as is known R. Shneur Zalman himself did not publish any work in Yiddish, his son and successor, R. Dov Ber, did so. Around 1817 his Yiddish tract entitled *Pokeaḥ Ivrim,* "Opening the Eyes," was printed. This was intended to spread the teachings of Hasidism beyond the confines of the ranks of the scholars.

According to Habad tradition *Pokeaḥ Ivrim* was originally written by R. Dov Ber in order to provide guidance for a specific individual, who had left the Jewish community and had married a Gentile. An encounter with a scholarly Habad follower eventually led to his return to Jewish life. The Yiddish tract provided guidance for him as a penitent, a *baal teshuvah*.[73] Presumably there was felt to be a wider need for this kind of book, for it was then printed.[74]

The tract is noteworthy as a manual of spiritual guidance for the unlearned man who cannot understand Hebrew, but it probably also had a considerable effect in shaping the style of service of the scholars. In addition, there is some internal evidence that this book by R. Dov Ber was intended also for women.[75] In 1821 another work, this time a tract on halakhah by R. Shneur Zalman, was published in a bilingual edition with both Hebrew and Yiddish. This was a guide to the halakhically complex subject of which blessings to say on various occasions.[76] It is likely that this publication too was aimed at strengthening both the spirituality and practical observance of the unlearned men and the women in the community.[77]

Of course, publication of works in Yiddish was not a new phenomenon. A number of ethical works and the halakhic tract *Lev Tov* had been printed many times before the nineteenth century. However, the fact that a movement such as Habad should be involved in Yiddish publishing is interesting. The other works by R. Dov Ber are profound mystical treatises on contemplation and ecstasy in prayer and on subtle pathways of divine service on the highest level. We might think he could legitimately leave the work of Yiddish publishing to others. But this view does not take into account the central feature of Habad: the communication ethos, the goal to transmit the teachings at the heart of Judaism to society at large. These Yiddish works are manifestations of that ethos. The presence of a developed theory of the Hebrew language and of the potential spiritual significance of other languages complemented the practical fact of publication on a theoretical level.[78]

A further example of an early Habad tract in a language other than the sacred tongue is a rather remarkable work by R. Dov Ber which he wrote in Hebrew but, it seems, then had translated into Russian. Only the Hebrew text has survived. The occasion for writing this was R. Dov Ber's arrest in the autumn of 1826, due to false charges by the Mitnagdim (opponents of Hasidism): he was accused of plotting rebellion, that his study hall had the same dimensions as the Temple, and that he was sending money to the Sultan (a charge based on records of the charity funds he was sending to the Habad community in the land of Israel).

The tract was addressed to the governor general of Vitebsk, named Chovansky, who was in charge of his case. Letters by R. Dov Ber are extant in which he asks a certain R. Leib to work in some way on a text he had written in connection with the trial. It is likely that this work was the translation into Russian of the tract. The recipient was told he might depart slightly from the original text by expanding or abbreviating "but should not omit completely even a small part" of its contents.[79]

The tract as we see it in Hebrew is an exposition of Habad Hasidic teaching on the nature of leadership. It includes a diagram of the divine attributes *(Sefirot)*, and expounds the importance of following the middle path of balance, going neither too far to the side of kindness (the right), which would permit people to steal, nor to the side of severity (the left). Only the central path, from Crown *(Keter)* to Kingship *(Malkhut)*, is the true path, expressing the quality of *Tiferet*, splendor. Further, this tripartite division exists at every level of being: in one's mind, in the emotions, and in action. It is the responsibility of leadership to follow the central path and express it in wise judgment.[80]

On one level this is a subtle plea by a prisoner; on another, it is a fascinating kabbalistic tract addressed to a non-Jew. The belief that such a work could be written at all, translated into Russian, and given to a powerful Gentile to read may well stem from the belief in the spiritual power of translation, and in the ability of the sanctity and spirituality of Hebrew to extend into a Gentile tongue.

Translation in the Twentieth Century

As we might expect, the teaching about the potential spirituality of languages other than Hebrew is emphasized in modern Habad. In the early spring of 1962 Rabbi Menachem Mendel Schneerson (b.1902), known as the Lubavitcher Rebbe, gave a talk *(siḥah)* on the subject of the first word of the Ten Commandments: *anokhi* ("I"). A Midrash states "*anokhi* is in Egyptian."[81] The talk discusses this statement, emphasizing the kabbalistic idea that the word *anokhi* expresses the divine essence, and includes within it all the Mitzvot of the Torah.[82] How can it be that this all-important word should be in the Egyptian language? The answer given is:

> In the very first word which G-d said at the Giving of the Torah, He hinted at the intention of the Giving of the Torah: why was *anokhi* (that is, not just the radiance of the Divine, as previously, but the very Essence of G-d) revealed—for the sake of the Egyptian language. The purpose of Torah is to transmit holiness not only to aspects of the Sacred Tongue . . . [but to] descend into the seventy languages, indeed into the Egyptian language . . . and to transmit holiness also on that level. And this is so also from below to above: when and how can one reach the *anokhi* [i.e., the Essence of the Divine]? Through the Egyptian language. . . .[83]

This process is explained in this talk not in terms of literary translation, but as the quest for a non-enclave mode of living, which applies both in social terms and in relation to the psychology of the individual:

> One cannot be satisfied just with one's own aspects of holiness, one has also to be active in the world. [Divine] service has to be in two ways: a) not to lock oneself away in one's own four cubits, but also to make the world into a vessel for G-dliness; b) also concerning one's [Divine] service with oneself, it is not enough just to be involved with study of Torah, prayer, and keeping mitzvot. There also has to be the [concept of] "know Him in all your ways" (Prov.3: 6). . . . In your ways, ordinary worldly aspects . . . there should also be the "know Him," the knowledge of and . . . bonding to G-d.[84]

In this teaching the concept of extending sanctity to non-Hebrew is used to communicate two ideas: the demand to have an involvement with "the world" beyond the confines of the Ultraorthodox community; and also the imperative to implement the classical Hasidic theme of *devekut,* cleaving to G-d in worldly aspects of life, beyond the domain of the narrow interpretation of the "holy."[85]

Later in 1962 the first volume of the English translation of Rabbi Shneur Zalman's *Likkutei Amarim—Tanya* was published. In a preface to this work, written in English, the Lubavitcher Rebbe discusses the concept of translation. He presents this as the employment of a basic "resource," "the vehicle of human language and communication." This can be used to elevate both the individual and the world around him. Further, through this process the non-Hebrew language is itself transformed:

> ... any of the "seventy tongues," when used as an instrument to disseminate the Torah and Mitzvoth, is itself "elevated" thereby from its earthly domain into the sphere of holiness, while at the same time serving as a vehicle to draw the Torah and Mitzvoth, from above downward, to those who read and understand this language."[86]

In a talk a year later on the festival of Shavuot, celebrating the Giving of the Torah, this theme was reiterated. Citing the Midrash that the divine voice at the theophany "divided into the seventy languages,"[87] the point is made that this means that a translation of Torah has holiness in its own right:

> One might think that the Torah which one studies in the seventy languages does not have the holiness of Torah as it was at the Giving of the Torah—so one is told that the great Voice of the Giving of the Torah divided into the seventy tongues. It has descended and clothed itself in lowly garments, but the inwardness of the Voice is the same as the great Voice saying "I am G-d, your G-d" (and in fact, it has a yet deeper source, for "anything which is higher descends lower").[88]

Thus the translation into the non-Hebrew language is affirmed, not only as something positive, but as holy in its own right. There is even a suggestion that in some way it draws from "a deeper source" than the Hebrew original, perhaps because through the translation what was called earlier "the purpose of the Torah" is being fulfilled.

While the importance of the task of translation is affirmed, there is also recognition of the dangers inherent in the translation process. There might be distortion or misrepresentation of the original. A later talk by the Lubavitcher Rebbe discusses the rabbinic statement that the day the Torah was translated into Greek "was as grievous as the day the [Golden] Calf was made, for the Torah could not be translated properly."[89] The reason for this critique, states the Rebbe, was the possibility of error and misinterpretation. Nonetheless, the need for modern translations of Torah thought, including Hasidic teachings, is endorsed.[90]

Such translations are of course intended for the benefit of the Jewish community, or for those who are Jews but are outside the normal communal structure. But another aspect of the 1963 talk discussed above concerns the theme of the seven Noahide laws. As described by Maimonides, who goes into the subject in considerable detail, these are teachings which are relevant to all humanity. They originate from divine instructions to Adam and Noah, and were ratified in the revelation to Moses at Sinai; further, the Jew has the responsibility to communicate these teachings to society at large.[91] In the hostile atmosphere of the medieval world the Jew was clearly not able directly to express this aspect of Judaism, the duty to be "a light to the nations." Modern Habad however, in the post-ghetto age, lays considerable emphasis on this area of Jewish teaching.[92] The communication ethos in its contemporary form therefore reaches beyond the confines of the Jewish community.

In the talk we have been discussing, given in 1963, this ideal is expressed in linguistic terms. The fact that, according to the Midrash, the "great Voice" at the giving of the Torah divided into the seventy tongues is explained with reference to the Noahide laws. The Jew has a duty to encourage the observance of these laws. However:

> In order that one should not think that their Seven Laws are something secondary, unrelated to the Giving of the Torah, the Torah states: "a great Voice. . . ." The Voice of the Giving of the Torah "divided into the seventy tongues," so that also the laws for the seventy tongues, the nations of the world, come from the great Voice of the Giving of the Torah.[93]

We thus see that in a teaching on the relationship between Hebrew, the sacred tongue, and the other languages, the spiritual responsibility of the Jew for the world community is emphasized. In other discussions of this topic, the halakhic parameters of this aspect of the role of the Jew are explored and defined.[94] He or she is encouraged to implement the potential moral and spiritual effect of the Jew on the world.

The basis of this perception of the nature of the Jew is the idea that the divine revelation at Sinai, on account of which the Jew was "chosen" by G-d "from among all peoples,"[95] includes also a universal dimension. From this perspective, chosenness, a concept inherent in the ancient theme of the sacred tongue, does not mean withdrawal into an enclave of sanctity, but rather imparts the responsibility and the power to affect and transform the seventy tongues, the nations of the world.

Language and Limits

This survey has attempted to show the way that Habad teachings about Hebrew express the communication ethos, the most important single characteristic of the early Hasidic movement. Habad is distinguished for the espousal and implementation of that ethos, both at the beginning of the movement, when it underwent harsh criticism on this account,[96] and also in modern times. The large body of teachings about Hebrew, the divine language, helped in the task of relaying spiritual awareness to the members of the Habad fraternity. They are also complemented by teachings on the relationship between Hebrew and other languages.

Central to all these teachings are the Hasidic ideals of "elevation" and "transformation": to elevate one's perception of existence, and of one's own being, seeing not just matter, or even psyche, but the spirituality within; and to elevate (rather than hide from) the negative dimensions of life and to transform them from falsehood and negativity to the holiness of the Sanctuary. On the social level, there is the demand on contemporary Jewish scholars and Hasidim to go beyond their immediate "four cubits" of Torah study and prayer, to reach out to elevate and transform the wider Jewish community, translating hitherto closely guarded Torah teachings into other languages to facilitate this task. The furthest reach demanded of them, as Jews, is that they should see Judaism as the attempt to fulfil a responsibility to all humanity.

This teaching too is expressed in terms of language, the basic human mode of communication. Hebrew, the sacred tongue, has the power to interact with the many languages of the nations of the world. The communication ethos of Hasidism is so powerful that it does not stop at the border of the Jewish community. Here, perhaps, we see its real significance.

The fall of the ghetto raised important questions about the transmission of the traditional, spiritual modes of Jewish life and thought from the medieval world to the modern age. Could traditional Judaism survive without the protection of the ghetto wall? Did it have to draw in on itself, forming new, deliberate enclaves within modern Jewish society, let alone the wider, non-Jewish world? Or, would it rather have to undergo a process of secularization, retaining some aspects from its rich past but necessarily relinquishing others? The modern history of Hebrew itself shows clearly both these avenues. On the one hand, the creation of a new, secular language; on the other, the attempt to create a linguistic enclave of the sacred tongue (rather than *Ivrit*), with Yiddish for daily usage—which is the impression conveyed by some sectors of the Ultraorthodox community.[97]

The Habad teachings on Hebrew and language in general show another path. Indeed, Hebrew is sacred and, in modern Habad-Lubavitch thought, in certain ways so too is Yiddish.[98] Indeed these languages should be known and used in daily life as, ideally, the languages of Torah study and the home. But they do not need walls around them in order to survive. The essence of the Divine is beyond limitations and can and even must reach the *anokhi* of the most foreign of tongues.

These teachings on the validity of translation of sacred texts into non-Hebrew languages for the sake of Jews who cannot understand Hebrew, on the potential transformation of those languages by this process, and on the responsibility of the Jew to the non-Jewish world, suggest a post-ghetto form of traditional Judaism in which the spiritual heritage is preserved intact. As we have seen, this spirituality itself is expressed in terms of teachings about Hebrew, the language of Creation, the language of the Essence which reaches everywhere.

Notes

The illustrations of Hebrew letters are by the scribe Aryeh Freeman.

1. R. Shneur Zalman comments that sometimes the oral Yiddish of the Baal Shem Tov was not correctly translated into Hebrew in printed collections of his teachings, a fact which could give rise to misunderstanding (*Tanya* Pt.IV, sec. 25, fol. 141a).

2. It is entitled *Seder ha-Tefilah;* this was at the beginning of the spate of kabbalistic and Hasidic publications which was a feature of the last two decades of the century.

3. On the communication ethos of early Hasidism, see Scholem 1961: p. 342. It is discussed at length in Loewenthal 1990a.

4. Dov Ber ben Shmuel, *Shivhei ha-Besht* published in Hebrew in Kopyst, 1815, and in Yiddish in the same year in Ostraho and in Koretz (Korcek) in 1816. Trans. D. Ben-Amos and J.R. Mintz 1970.

5. *Sippurei Ma'asiyot* (Berdichev, 1815). There are several English translations. Rabbi Nachman's concern that these stories should be accessible to women is mentioned by his disciple R. Natan Sternhartz, *Hayei Muharan* (Jerusalem, 1962), "Sihot ha-shayakhim la-torot," p. 16, sec. 25. See also Rabbi Nachman's *Likkutei Muharan* I no. 60, sec. 6.

6. R. Dov Ber of Lubavitch, *Pokeah 'Ivrim* (1817; Kfar Habad: Kehot Publication Society, 1973).

7. The same is true of the writings of his contemporary, Rabbi Nathan Sternhartz, the leader (but not rebbe) of Braslav after the death of Rabbi Nachman.

8. The text of this letter was first published by R. Yakov Yosef of Polonoye, a leading disciple of the Baal Shem Tov, at the end of his *Ben Porat Yosef* (Koretz, 1781). Other versions of the letter have been published by D. Fraenkel (1923) and Y. Mondschein 1980: 119–26.

9. This mystical experience is the central theme of the ancient "Merkavah" (Chariot) school of mysticism. Moshe Idel 1988: 88–95 claims that the practice of spiritual ascent enjoyed continuity among kabbalists until the nineteenth century.

10. A kabbalistic practice involving connecting ("unifying") spiritual forces such as souls.

11. *Ben Porat Yosef* 128a. The text published by Mondschein is similar, but the Fraenkel text reads only "when your teachings are spread throughout the world."

12. Dubnow 1975: 60.

13. See A. Rubinstein 1970:135, and Mondschein 1980: 124 n. 10.

14. See Heschel 1985: 46.

15. *Ben Porat Yosef* 128a. Thus too the Mondschein version, but not that of Fraenkel.

16. There is a wide literature on this. See Idel 1985: 92, 97ff.

17. In the teachings of the Maggid there are numerous references to the "World of Speech," signifying the divine attribute of Kingship *(Malkhut)*. See Rivkah Schatz-Uffenheimer 1968: chap. 9. There are also teachings on how, through elevating language to its divine source, the Zaddik has the power of blessing or even of miracles. See *Maggid Devarav le-Yakov*, ed. Schatz-Uffenheimer (Jerusalem: The Magnes Press), 1976, pp. 94–96.

18. See Tishby and Dan 1977: cols. 808–809, and Scholem 1971: 206.

19. Printed in Slavuta, 1796. The second edition (Zolkiew, 1799) included a third section *Iggeret ha-Teshuvah*. The teachings of early Habad are discussed in Jacobs (1963), Mindel (1974), Elior (1982), Etkes (1986), Hallamish (1987), Loewenthal (1990a).

20. Thus the Mishnah: "With ten utterances the world was created" (Aboth 5:1). The word *be-reshit* ("In the beginning") is considered one of the ten—otherwise there are only nine. See B. T. *Rosh ha-Shanah* 32a.

21. The 22 letters of the Hebrew alphabet produce 231 possible pairs, termed "gates." By means of these "gates" any letter can be transformed into any other letter. This is presented here as a divine process, without any suggestion that it might be accessible to humans.

22. See Scholem 1974: 337–42.

23. See *Zohar* I 24a, *Tikkunei Zohar* (Jerusalem, 1965) sec. 6, fol. 36b.

24. *Tanya* Pt. II (Vilna, 1900), chap. 1, 77a.

25. Kabbalah can be divided into "speculative" Kabbalah, which is primarily a system of theosophic study and contemplation, and "practical" Kabbalah, which is ecstatic and theurgic in quality, granting direct entry to metaphysical realms.

26. For more extensive treatment of R. Shneur Zalman's teachings on Creation see Y. Jacobson 1976.

27. Compare *Tanya* fol. 77a with Maimonides, *Guide* Pt. I, end of chap. 69.

28. See Loewenthal (1990b).

29. *Tanya* Pt. II chap. 2, 77b.

30. R. Dov Ber of Lubavitch, *Sha'ar ha-Yihud (Tract on Contemplation)* in *Ner Mizvah ve-Torah Or* (Brooklyn: Kehot Publication Society, 1974: chap. 38, fol. 28b).

31. See *Maamarei Admur ha-Zaken*, 5567 (Brooklyn, 1979: 392, 236). See also *Tanya* Pt. IV, chap. 5.

32. *Tanya, Iggeret ha-Kodesh,* chap. 19 fol. 129a.

33. In the Lurianic Kabbalah, there is a process of divine concealment (apparent withdrawal, or veiling) called *Zimzum* which is a necessary concomitant to the act of creation. If the Divine were totally revealed, there would be no "room" for a finite world; hence concealment is necessary. The purpose of life is to reveal the Divine despite this concealment, to "break through the veil" and draw the Infinite into the finite.

34. *Sha'ar ha-Yihud,* chap. 51, fol. 37b.

35. *Tanya,* Part II chap. 6, 80a.

36. *Tanya,* Part I, chap. 43, 62b.

37. *Tanya,* Pt. II, chap. 4, 79a.

38. *Torah Or,* 49d.

39. *Likkutei Torah, Behukotai,* 45c.

40. Ibid., *Vayikra,* 2a.

41. *Sefer ha-Likkutim,* 27 vols. (Brooklyn: Kehot Publication Society, 1977–82).

42. *Sefer ha-Likkutim,* entry *Otiot,* p. 716.

43. *Sefer ha-Arakhim,* 6 vols. (Brooklyn: Kehot Publication Society, 1971–80).

44. Creation was a process of dividing the "waters" by means of the "firmament" (Gen. 1: 6–8). The upper waters represent the spiritual realm, the lower waters the physical. The symbolism of the Alef is applied here too: the upper and lower Yud symbolise the upper and lower waters, respectively, and the Vav is the firmament (*Sefer ha-Arakhim, Otiot,* entry "Alef", col. 219).

45. Ibid., cols. 221–22. The text is fully annotated showing the sources in rabbinic, kabbalistic, and Hasidic teachings. Concerning the idea that through the Mitzvot, the lower, physical realm achieves a higher level than does the upper realm of spirituality, see Loewenthal (1987).

46. The original, and first twenty subsequent discourses are collected in *Sefer ha-Maamarim Bati le-Gani* (Brooklyn: Kehot Publication Society, 1977). The original discourse is also in *Sefer ha-Maamarim 5710* (Brooklyn: Kehot Publication Society, 1970), pp. 111–55.

47. *Bati Le-Gani 5710* (Brooklyn: Kehot Publication Society, 1980).

48. *Sefer ha-Maamarim Bati le-Gani* (henceforth *BLG*), p. 1.

49. Ibid., pp. 7–8.

50. *Zohar,* I 2b–3b.

51. *BLG,* p. 9.

52. Ibid., p. 10.

53. Throughout the Hebrew Scriptures, certain letters are written "large" or "small" in contrast to the rest of the text. See Maimonides, *Yad, Hil. Sefer Torah,* 7:8.

54. *BLG,* p. 9.

55. Ibid., pp. 11–13.

56. Ibid., p. 13.

57. Ibid.

58. Ibid., pp. 13–15.

59. See Glinert and Shilhav (1991) for discussion of this possibility.

60. There are two versions of this, which differ slightly. One is in *Torah Or,* fol. 77c–88a. This version is probably based on a transcript by R. Yehudah Leib, brother of R. Shneur Zalman, which was edited by R. Menahem Mendel, the *Ẓemaḥ Ẓedek,* his grandson. The other, probably a transcript by R. Dov Ber, the oldest son of R. Shneur Zalman, is in *Maamarei Admur ha-Zaken 5608,* pp. 66–69. For information on the editing and publishing of R. Shneur Zalman's writings see Loewenthal 1986: 69 n. 31, and 1990a: 67–68.

61. *MAHZ 5608,* p. 67. The image of making "bricks" is derived homiletically from Gen. 11:3, a verse which aptly concerns the making of the bricks for the Tower of Babel. The idea that there are seventy original nations, speaking seventy languages (the source of all later languages), corresponding to the seventy members of Jacob's family, is found in Rabbinic interpretations of Deut. 32:8. See *Sifrei* and Rashi ad. loc.

62. This point is in the version in *Torah Or,* fol. 77d: the text points out that Aramaic, a profane language, is used in the Talmud.

63. In Rabbinic literature this refers to food which, although ordinary food to be consumed at home, is prepared with the same level of purity as if it were part of the Temple service.

64. *MAHZ 5608,* p. 67.

65. A quotation from *Book of Creation,* 1:5.

66. *La'az* in the text, which at this period refers to Yiddish.

67. The relationship of the attribute of Kingship with speech is found in the second introduction to *Tikkunei Zohar:* "Kingship is the mouth. . . ." (fol. 30a of the Jerusalem, 1965 ed.). To explain this relationship the verse "For the word of the king is power" (Eccl. 8:4) is sometimes quoted.

68. *MAHZ 5608,* p. 68.

69. See Dubnow 1916: 1:351.

70. This is discussed in Loewenthal 1986.

71. See ibid., p. 71, and *MAHZ 5565,* pp. 402–403.

72. *Hilkhot Talmud Torah* (Brooklyn: Kehot Publication Society, 1968: end of chap. 1, p. 22).

73. See *Pokeaḥ Ivrim* (Kfar Habad: Kehot Publication Society, 1973), including additional material, pp. 33–34, and Rachel Elior 1976: 372.

74. See *Pokeaḥ Ivrim,* p. 5, which quotes a Habad tradition that this was the first of R. Dov Ber's own works to be printed. See also Haberman 1948–52: no. 20.

75. See the discussion of this work in Loewenthal 1990a: 194–205.

76. *Luaḥ Birkhot ha-Nehenin,* Berditchev, 1820. Y. Mondschein (1984: 212) points out that the true place of publication was Sdylakov. The Hebrew version of this tract by R. Shneur Zalman was first published in his *Siddur,* 1803, entitled *Seder Birkhot ha-Nehenin.* (An earlier work, somewhat different, entitled *Luaḥ Birkhot ha-Nehenin* was published in Shklov in 1800 and again in Zolkiew, 1801.

77. The saying of blessings on food and other occasions is not only a practical halakhic matter but also directly concerns the spiritual dimension of life. It enhances the sense of the presence of the Divine, and the awareness of the Divine as the source of all sustenance. The reciting of daily blessings with mystical *devekut* ("cleaving to the Divine"), or at least deep feeling and enthusiasm, was an early feature of the Hasidic movement. See Loewenthal, (1991).

78. It is noteworthy that the teachings of R. Nahman of Braslav also include an exposition of the spiritual nature of Hebrew and its relationship with other languages. Although this teaching expresses the mystical tension and sense of confrontation typical of Braslav thought, it also embodies the idea that the Ẓaddik can elevate Aramaic, the intermediary between the

holy tongue and other languages. See *Likkutei Muharan* I, sec. 19. Braslav too is noted for Yiddish publishing: in 1815 R. Nahman's kabbalistic stories were published in bilingual form, with parallel Hebrew and Yiddish versions on each page.

79. *Yagdil Torah* Year 4, no. 2 (33), p. 126.

80. See *Bad Kodesh* (Brooklyn: Kehot Publication Society, 1963), pp. 11-18. See also Loewenthal 1990a: 206-208. According to Habad tradition, on the day the tract was given to Chovansky, R. Dov Ber was released. See H.M. Hielman, *Beit Rebbe,* pp. 200-201.

81. *Yalkut Shimoni* Yitro, remez 286, referring to the Egyptian absolute pronoun for the first person singular, *ynk* or Coptic *anok.*

82. See *Likkutei Sihot,* 3: 892, also p. 891; *Likkutei Torah,* by R. Shneur Zalman, sec. *Pinhas,* 80b: "*anokhi* . . . is above the Tetragrammaton . . ."; and *Zohar,* 2: 85b: "at the moment when *anokhi* was said all commands of the Torah . . . were included in this word."

83. *Likkutei Sihot,* 3: 893-94.

84. Ibid., p. 894.

85. See Scholem 1971: 203-27.

86. This is on p. 760 of the Soncino bilingual edition of the *Tanya* (London: Soncino, 1973). Rabbi Schneerson cites as a source for this concept the discourse of 1808 which was discussed above.

87. *Shemot Rabbah,* end of chap. 28.

88. *Likkutei Sihot,* 4: 1095.

89. *Soferim,* 1: 7.

90. *Likkutei Sihot,* 24: 1-11.

91. *Yad, Hil. Melakhim,* 8:10-10:12.

92. See *Likkutei Sihot,* 26: 135-37, 143-44. This encouragement by the Lubavitcher Rebbe has led to a number of publications, such as an interactive video on moral issues for non-Jewish middle-school children, called *The Outsider,* produced by the Chabad Film Unit in London. There are also Lubavitch campaigns for a moment of silence in the American public schools, and for an annual Education Day or Day of Reflection: see *Congressional Record* for March 30, 1982: H.J.R. 447.

93. *Likkutei Sihot,* 4: 1094.

94. See *Likkutei Sihot,* 26: 132-44.

95. Thus the text of the "Blessing on the Torah" recited daily.

96. See Braver 1924, and Loewenthal 1990a: 50-54, 77-86.

97. See Glinert and Shilhav (1991).

98. It is noteworthy that many volumes of *Likkutei Sihot,* by the Lubavitcher Rebbe, are in Yiddish. This might have been, originally, in order that women should be able to read them. On the redaction of *Likkutei Sihot,* see P. Salinger (1991). Concerning the significance and near sanctity of Yiddish in modern Habad thought, see the talk by Rabbi Schneerson transcribed in Y. Weinberg's *Shiurim be-Sefer ha-Tanya,* vol. I (Brooklyn: Kehot Publication Society, 1983), pp. 9-14. At the same time this talk is a strong affirmation of the ideal of translation and communication. The volume to which it forms the introduction comprises the text of a twenty-year series of Yiddish radio broadcasts teaching *Tanya.*

References

BEN-AMOS, D. and MINTZ, J.R. *In Praise of the Baal Shem Tov.* Bloomington In: Indiana University Press, 1970.

BRAVER, A.J. "Al ha-Mahloket she-beyn ha-Rashaz ve-R. Avraham mi-Kalisk," *Kiryat Sefer* 1 (1924): pp. 142-150, 226-238.

DUBNOW, S. *History of the Jews in Russia and Poland.* Philadelphia: Jewish Publication Society of America, 1916.

———. *Toledot ha-Ḥasidut.* 4th ed. Tel Aviv: Dvir, 1975.

ELIOR, R. "The Theory of Divinity... in the Second Generation of Hasidut Habad." Ph.D. diss., The Hebrew University, Jerusalem, 1976. In Hebrew.

———. *The Theory of Divinity of Hasidut Habad: Second Generation.* Jerusalem: The Magnes Press, 1982. In Hebrew.

ETKES, I. "R. Shneur Zalman as a Hasidic Leader." *Zion* 50 (1986):321–54. In Hebrew.

FRAENKEL, D. *Mikhtavim me-ha-Besht.* Lvov: 1923.

GLINERT, L. and SHILHAV, Y. "Holy Land, Holy Language: A Study of an Ultra-Orthodox Jewish Ideology," *Language in Society* 20 (1991): 59–86.

HABERMAN, A.M. "Shaarei Ḥabad." *Alei Ayin: The Salman Schocken Jubilee Volume* (Hebrew). Jerusalem: 1948–52.

HALLAMISH, M. *Netiv la-Tanya.* Tel Aviv: Papyrus, 1987.

HESCHEL, A.J. *The Circle of the Baal Shem Tov.* Chicago: University of Chicago Press, 1985.

IDEL, M. *Kabbalah: New Perspectives.* New Haven: Yale University Press, 1988.

R. JACOBS, Dobh Baer of Lubavitch. *Tract on Ecstasy.* Ed. and Trans. Jacobs, L. London: Vallentine, Mitchell, 1963.

JACOBSON, Y. "Torat ha-Beriah shel R. Shneur Zalman mi-Liadi." *Eshel B'er Sheva 1* (1976): pp. 307–368.

LOEWENTHAL, N. "Early Hasidic Teachings—Esoteric Mysticism, or a Medium of Communal Leadership?," *Journal of Jewish Studies* 37 (1986): 58–75.

———. "The Apotheosis of Action in Early Habad," *Daat* 18 (1987): V-XIX.

———. *Communicating the Infinite: The Emergence of the Habad School.* University of Chicago Press, 1990a.

———. "'Reason' and 'Beyond Reason' in Habad Hasidism," Moshe Hallamish, ed. *Alei Shefer: Studies in the Literature of Jewish Thought Presented to Rabbi Dr. Alexander Safran.* Bar-Ilan University Press, 1990b: 109–126.

———. "Early Ḥabad Publications in Their Setting," D. Rowland Smith and P.S. Salinger, eds. *Hebrew Studies (British Library Occasional Papers 13).* London: The British Library, 1991: 94–104.

MINDEL, N. *The Philosophy of Chabad.* Brooklyn, Kehot Publication Society, 1974.

MONDSCHEIN, Y. *Migdal Oz.* Kfar Habad: Makhon Lubavitch, 1980.

———. *Sifrei Halakhah shel Admur ha-Zaken, Torat Ḥabad,* Kfar Habad: Kehot Publication Society, 1984.

RUBINSTEIN, A. "Iggeret ha-Besht le-R. Gershon mi-Kutov," *Sinai* 67 (1970): pp.120–139.

SALINGER, P.S. "Publishing Developments of Ḥabad Teachings, 1794–1989." In Smith D. Rowland and Salinger P.S. eds. *Hebrew Studies (British Library Occasional Papers 13).* London: The British Library, 1991, 105–110.

SCHATZ-UFFENHEIMER, R. *Ha-Ḥasidut ke-Mistikah.* Jerusalem: The Magnes Press, 1968.

SCHOLEM, G. *Major Trends in Jewish Mysticism.* 3d ed. New York: Schocken Books, 1961.

———. *The Messianic Idea in Judaism, and Other Essays on Jewish Spirituality.* London: George Allen and Unwin, 1971.

———. *Kabbalah.* Jerusalem: Keter, 1974.

TISHBY, I. and DAN, Y. "Ḥasidut" In *The Hebrew Encyclopedia,* vol. 17. Collected in Rubinstein, A., ed., *Perakim be-Torat ha-Ḥasidut u-ve-Toledoteha.* Jerusalem: Merkaz Zalman Shazar, 1977.

12

Why Did Ben-Yehuda Suggest the Revival of Spoken Hebrew?

GEORGE MANDEL

Eliezer Ben-Yehuda first became well known to readers of the Hebrew press for his energetic advocacy of two radical ideas. One was *yishuv Eretz Yisra'el,* the large-scale resettlement of the Land of Israel by Jews. The other was *teḥiyyat ha-dibbur ha-Ivri,* the revival of spoken Hebrew, i.e., turning Hebrew from a language used mainly for literary and liturgical purposes into the everyday spoken language of the Jews in Palestine. In this article I want to consider what made Ben-Yehuda adopt these ideas. It is generally of interest to historians to know why people change their allegiances. The case of Ben-Yehuda is of particular interest to historians of Zionism because, as we shall see, he came to his Jewish-nationalist views four years before the Russian pogroms of 1881—that is, at a time when very few Jews had espoused such beliefs—and because anti-Semitism seems to have played no part in the process by which he reached them.

The form that Ben-Yehuda's version of Jewish nationalism took from its inception (unlike, say, that of Smolenskin before 1881) gives us some justification for referring to his views by the name "Zionism," even though the word was not coined until nearly twenty years later. Jacob Katz, discussing the so-called "forerunners" of Zionism, has written that they were characterized by the belief "that the future existence of the Jewish nation is conditioned by [read: conditional upon?] its return to the historical homeland" (Katz 1971: col. 1034), which is precisely what Ben-Yehuda argued in various articles that appeared in the Hebrew press from 1879 onwards. Had Ben-Yehuda died early in 1881, before the pogroms, he would probably have been classified as such a forerunner. As it is, he lived on well into the era of Zionism proper and became an enthusiastic supporter of Herzl's political Zionism as soon as Herzl appeared on the scene. Ben-Yehuda rightly saw his support for Herzl not as a break with his earlier views but as a natural continuation of them. To all intents and purposes, therefore, it seems permissible to describe him as a Zionist *tout court,* as long as one bears in mind that this is, strictly speaking, an anachronism.

The chief source of information about Ben-Yehuda's early life is his autobiography, *Ha-Ḥalom ve-Shivro* (The Dream and its Realization),[1] which was written in 1917–18. A useful supplement to it is an entry on him in a biographical dictionary of Hebrew writers, *Sefer Zikkaron le-Sofrei Yisra'el (Sefer Zikkaron* 1889: 188-92), which is important because it is by far the earliest biography of Ben-Yehuda to have appeared (it was published only seven or eight years after Ben-Yehuda settled in Jerusalem) and the source of the information in it was almost certainly Ben-Yehuda himself. We have no memoirs by anyone who knew Ben-Yehuda during the relevant period, i.e., before he emigrated to Palestine in the autumn of 1881, so we must assume that the works mentioned are our most reliable sources of information. Biographical statements about Ben-Yehuda in the following that appear without specific sources are based on these two works. (The biographies by Ben-Yehuda's widow, Hemdah, and by Joseph Klausner are demonstrably inaccurate for this period of his life. (See Mandel 1988: 6-8.)

Ben-Yehuda was born in Lithuania, within the domains of the Russian Empire, in 1858. During his childhood he received the traditional education of an Orthodox Jew in Russia in those days: that is, one devoted entirely to Jewish religious and legal texts. When he was thirteen or fourteen years old the head of his yeshiva, who was a secret Maskil, introduced him to the Haskalah; more particularly, to Hanau's textbook of Hebrew grammar, *Tzohar ha-Tevah,* and to *Kur Oni,* Rumsch's Hebrew version of *The Adventures of Robinson Crusoe.* These works, and the enthusiasm of his teacher, made a powerful impression on Ben-Yehuda, and he became a fervent devotee of the Hebrew language and of the literature of the Haskalah. More than forty years later he wrote in his memoirs:

> From then onwards, the fire of love for the Hebrew language burned within my soul, a fire that a flood of events later in my life could not extinguish. It was this love for Hebrew that saved me from the danger that lay in wait for me.
>
> (Sivan 1978: 60.)

The danger in question was of being drawn into the Russian revolutionary movement and entirely away from Jewish interests. Three years or so after first seeing the "light" of the Haskalah, Ben-Yehuda—having, through private study, acquired a sufficient knowledge of Russian and other necessary subjects—was admitted to the government high school in Dünaburg.[2] There, like most of the other students—especially the Jewish ones—he fell under the influence of the revolutionary movement and became a nihilist, believing that his life should be devoted to the service of "the people," and losing interest in nearly everything to do with Jews and Judaism: "Nothing in Jewish life interested me any more, and I felt myself—or at any rate I believed that I felt myself—entirely Russian" (Sivan 1978: 62). Nonetheless, one thread did still connect Ben-Yehuda to Jewish interests: his love for the Hebrew language and its new literature, a passion from which he could not free himself even though Jewish concerns in general now seemed trivial to him, and despite the fact that his readings in Russian literature soon made him realize the inferiority of the Hebrew literature produced by the Haskalah movement.

However, Ben-Yehuda's residual attachment to Hebrew was itself a danger, and from a surprising source—the Hebrew writers themselves:

> That was the time when the Russian Maskilim in general despaired of the Hebrew language. Moses Leib Lilienblum himself pronounced sentence of death on it,

declaring, in Rodkinson's newspaper *Ha-Kol,* that the Hebrew language's time had passed, that it had no more role to play in Jewish life, and that if he and others were still writing articles in Hebrew it was only because there were still some Jews who did not know Russian ... the attitude of the Hebrew writers toward the language was slipshod and lazy, and they used to slip Aramaic and Russian phrases into their writing; for Hebrew was of no importance to them since it was in any case due to be abandoned very soon.

These being the words of the Hebrew writers themselves, how could I, who had already nearly passed the point of no return, be expected to find anything to attract me in that language or that literature? And no doubt I would in the end have abandoned the literature, together with the language in which it was written, had it not been for Smolenskin's journal *Ha-Shahar,* in which I detected rather more signs of life....

Thanks to *Ha-Shahar,* the embers of love for the Hebrew language, which had nearly been smothered by the ashes of nihilism, did not go out ... and only a breath of wind was needed to make them blaze up again.

And the wind came suddenly, from the Balkans. The Bulgarians had rebelled against the Turks and throughout Russia the cry went up that it was a sacred duty for the Russians to hasten to the assistance of "their little brothers," to free them from the yoke of foreigners, and restore the Bulgarian nation to its ancient borders. All the Russian newspapers gave voice to this call.

Thirstily, I drank in these words from the newspapers, without at first sensing what they had to do with me. I saw only one thing: I was more interested in the news from the battlefield than any of my fellow-pupils, rejoiced more than they did in every Russian and Bulgarian victory, and derived deeper satisfaction from newspaper articles about the freedom of the Bulgarian people and their country.

Then, late one night, after several hours of reading newspapers and thinking about the Bulgarians and their approaching freedom, I suddenly felt as though a flash of lightning had passed before my eyes. My thoughts flew from the Shipka Pass in the Balkans to the banks of the Jordan in the Land of Israel, and I heard a strange voice within me calling:

The Revival of Israel and its Language on the Ancestral Soil!

... Changing and contradictory feelings fought one another in my soul. On the one hand, the great Russian people and the exalted notions about laboring for its freedom; on the other hand, a vision that filled my soul with boundless joy, the vision of Israel revived in its sacred land. ... Thus, two nations struggled within me: the Russian in me and the Jew in me fought one another angrily....

And the Jew won. My fate was decided. My life and my strength were henceforth to be dedicated to working for the revival of Israel and its language on the soil of its ancestors.

(Sivan 1978: 63–65.)

It is obvious that, for Ben-Yehuda, becoming a Zionist performed an important psychological function: that of resolving the tension in him between his new, Russianized, way of life and the "advanced" ideas that went with it, on the one hand, and his continuing attachment to Hebrew literature and, by implication, his Jewish origins, on the other. In the new Palestine as he conceived it in his imagination, it would be possible to be both a Jew and a modern man without feeling any conflict between the two. It has been said of the Russian Maskilim who became Zionists that for some of them:

> Zionism came as a bold and dazzling solution to a problem that had become heart-breakingly baffling: how to adapt to the modern world without ceasing to be a Jew. The *maskilim* who chose Zionism were reintegrating their personalities.... (O'Brien 1986: 48).

Ben-Yehuda was almost certainly the first Russian Jew for whom Zionism was to have that significance.

The war between Russia and Turkey broke out in April 1877 and ended in January 1878. The available evidence suggests strongly that Ben-Yehuda's conversion to Zionism took place very soon after the outbreak of the war, before the end of the school year in the summer of 1877 (Mandel 1985: 144–145.).

Having left school that summer, Ben-Yehuda went to Paris with the intention of qualifying in medicine before emigrating to Palestine. It was in Paris that he made his first attempt to formulate his ideas in writing in an article that was published under the title *She'elah Nikhbadah,* "A Weighty Question."[3] This famous essay was written early in 1879 (Mandel 1981: 34–35), nearly two years after the night of its author's conversion during the Russo-Turkish war. One of its main arguments is that, under modern conditions, the Jewish people is in danger of disappearing through assimilation among the Gentiles. This can only be prevented by bringing about a concentration of Jews in a single country, the Land of Israel: "If we wish, then, to prevent Israel's name from being blotted out completely, we must do something ... and that is—settlement of the Land of Israel" (Ben-Yehuda 1879a: 364–65).

If the existence of the Jewish people is in danger then so, obviously, is the continued survival of Hebrew as a language in active use, since the latter will not exist without the former:

> In vain [will be] all the effort of our writers to revive the language if the entire people remains scattered in different lands among nations speaking different tongues. All our work will be in vain, for it will not succeed. In vain will we boast that there is no means of making us disappear from the face of the earth, in vain!
>
> (Ben-Yehuda 1879a: 364.)[4]

If, however, the Land of Israel is resettled by Jews, then "the language, too, will flourish, and literature will spawn writers in plenty.... Only then will our literature renew its vigor..." (Ben-Yehuda 1879a: 366).

It is evident from *She'elah Nikhbadah* that Ben-Yehuda saw the settlement of Jews in Palestine as necessary for the survival of Hebrew literature which, he thought, could not survive in the Diaspora. What was his attitude at the time he wrote the article towards the *speaking* of Hebrew? As we have seen, Ben-Yehuda said in his memoirs that he was converted to the idea of "The Revival of Israel *and its Language*" while he was still at school in Dünaburg. In *She'elah Nikhbadah,* too, in one of the passages just quoted, we find a reference to efforts "to revive the language." However, some caution is required when reading these words. It should not be assumed that by "revival of the language" Ben-Yehuda necessarily meant the revival of *spoken* Hebrew. In later years the two phrases *teḥiyyat ha-lashon* (revival of the language) and *teḥiyyat ha-dibbur* (revival of spoken Hebrew) were often used almost interchangeably, but it should not be taken for granted that the former necessarily implies the latter in Ben-Yehuda's writings. The well-known fact that Ben-Yehuda subsequently devoted himself with such zeal to *tehiyyat ha-dibbur* makes it natural to assume that that is what he had in mind when he suddenly conceived the idea, late one night during the Russo-Turkish war, of "The Revival of Israel and its Language." However, the need to be on our guard against such an assumption is apparent from the words Ben-Yehuda uses in *She'elah Nikhbadah*. As we have seen, Ben-Yehuda refers there to "the effort of our writers to revive the language." The word "writers" suggests that Ben-Yehuda was not thinking of any attempt to revive *spoken* Hebrew, but was referring to the *literary* revival that had taken place as part of the Haskalah movement. No less than eighteen months after the publication of *She'elah Nikhbadah* Ben-Yehuda referred in another article to "Our Maskilim, who labored to revive the Hebrew language . . ." (Ben-Yehuda 1880c: 297). The Maskilim, of course, had as their ideal the creation of a flourishing Hebrew literature, not the restoration of the spoken register to Hebrew.

Evidently the words "revival of Hebrew" as used by Ben-Yehuda at that time, and as recalled by him in his autobiography, did not necessarily refer to spoken Hebrew. We have seen that during Ben-Yehuda's "nihilist" period in Dünaburg the Maskilim in general had come to despair of any future for Hebrew literature, that Lilienblum himself was actually calling (in Hebrew!) for the death of that literature, and that all this had impressed itself powerfully on Ben-Yehuda's consciousness. In the light of these facts, the words "The Revival of Israel and its Language" in Ben-Yehuda's autobiography should not be taken as evidence that Ben-Yehuda conceived the ideas of *yishuv Eretz Yisrael* and *tehiyyat ha-dibbur* simultaneously on the night of his conversion. Rather, they mean that Ben-Yehuda had perceived that Hebrew literature would stand a better chance of being saved from its apparently imminent extinction if there were to be one country where the Jews formed a majority and had control over their internal affairs. At that stage in Ben-Yehuda's thinking, and until after he had started writing *She'elah Nikhbadah,* "revival" meant, first and foremost, "survival," and referred only to *written* Hebrew.

Any doubt about this conclusion is dispelled by another account Ben-Yehuda gave of the events of 1877–79 (Ben-Yehuda 1948: 1–2, Arabic pagination)[5]. In *Ha-Mavo ha-Gadol,* the introductory volume of his great dictionary, Ben-Yehuda writes that the words that flashed through his mind during the Russo-Turkish war were "The Revival of Israel on the ancestral soil!" (Ben-Yehuda 1948: 1, Arabic pagination.) That is, there is no mention (unlike in his autobiography) of reviving the Hebrew language. Ben-Yehuda then describes how he wrote the article with which he made his literary debut, and says in unequivocal terms that the idea of *tehiyyat ha-dibbur* came to him only after this (Ben-Yehuda 1948: 1–2, Arabic pagination).[6] This confirms that the words "revive the language" in *She'elah Nikhbadah* are not to be taken as referring to *spoken* Hebrew.

The commonly held view that Ben-Yehuda actually intended to suggest the revival of spoken Hebrew in *She'elah Nikhbadah* is mistaken. What he envisaged at the time he began writing the article was that the Jews would continue in Palestine to speak the languages they had spoken in the Diaspora, so that several languages would be spoken in the country. This is evident from a careful and unprejudiced reading of the article itself, and is supported by other writings by Ben-Yehuda in which he refers to the composition of *She'elah Nikhbadah.* (Mandel 1981.) (It is also, more or less, what Theodor Herzl was to suggest seventeen years later in *Der Judenstaat.* See Herzl 1967, 70). In *She'elah Nikhbadah* Ben-Yehuda even referred to Switzerland, Belgium, and other countries as providing precedents for such an arrangement, (Ben-Yehuda 1879a: 362.) The distinctive feature of the Jewish settlement, which had no parallel in Switzerland or Belgium, was to be the use of one and the same language—Hebrew—for literary purposes by all the inhabitants, no matter what language they normally used in speech. The well-known words in *She'elah Nikhbadah* that are often taken as a proposal for *teḥiyyat ha-dibbur*— "we have a language even now in which we can write anything we care to, and it is also in our power to speak it if only we wish"—actually mean that Hebrew can be spoken when circumstances make that necessary or convenient, i.e., between two Jews with no other language in common (Mandel 1981: 31–32.) This is not the same as turning Hebrew into the everyday spoken tongue of the Jews in Palestine. (It is important to be aware that in many reprints of *She'elah Nikhbadah* emphasis has been added to these words that is not present in the original version in *Ha-Shaḥar.* The punctuation of the sentence, too, has been changed in such a way as to give these words greater weight.[7])

Why, then, did Ben-Yehuda change his mind after writing *She'elah Nikhbadah,* and decide that Hebrew should become an everyday spoken language?

Perhaps it was inevitable that he should do so once he had started on the line of thought revealed in that essay. If the Jews were to become a nation like every other nation, as he was proposing, then it was natural to suggest that Hebrew become a language like every other language—which, in modern times, for a European, meant one that possessed both the spoken and the written registers. Be that as it may, Ben-Yehuda did not at the time present the case in that way. His published writings during the year and a half following the publication of *She'elah Nikhbadah* give us some insight into the process by which he reached his new conclusion.

Between November 1879 and May 1880 three articles by Ben-Yehuda dealing with the question of Jewish education and "enlightenment" appeared in the Jerusalem weekly *Ḥavatzelet* (Ben-Yehuda 1879b, 1880a and 1880b.).[8] Ben-Yehuda criticized the modern schools recently established in Jerusalem by European Jewish philanthropic organizations such as the Alliance Israélite Universelle. He claimed that these schools would act as agents of assimilation. Instruction in them was in French, German, or English (according to which organization had set up any particular school) and the children who attended them would, in Ben-Yehuda's view, be bound to grow up to speak these languages and to despise or even forget the languages of their parents. Something similar had already happened in Russia, where the attempt to educate Jewish children in the modern spirit had led to a state of enmity between the generations, due to the huge difference in outlook between parents and their children, not least in linguistic matters:

> The fathers speak Yiddish, since they don't know Russian, and the children talk Russian because they would be ashamed to talk Yiddish. . . . Is it any wonder that the

old generation looks askance at this Haskalah, which steals their offspring from them and from their people?

(Ben-Yehuda 1879b: 50.)

Ben-Yehuda had observed the process of Russification among enlightened Jewish youth in Russia: "Day by day the number of those who know our language [Hebrew], and of those who want to know it, grows smaller" (Ben-Yehuda 1880b: 204). He was afraid that a comparable process would take place in Palestine as a result of attempts to bring a modern education to Jewish children in that country. He had abandoned the optimistic belief, expressed in *She'elah Nikhbadah,* that a concentration of Jews in Palestine would of itself guarantee the survival of Hebrew literature there. Even if the Jews were in a majority in the country, the process of modernization was likely to lead to the replacement of (spoken) Yiddish and (written) Hebrew by European languages, if the latter were the vehicles of that modernization. It made no difference that the modern schools included Hebrew in their curriculum. If all subjects were taught in French, the pupils would acquire a complete mastery of that language. Not only would their knowledge of French far exceed their knowledge of Hebrew, but—and this was the more important point—it would render knowledge of Hebrew superfluous, since French was far more useful than Hebrew for practical matters, as well as opening the door to a rich and attractive culture. Hebrew would then be like Latin and Greek, which people studied dutifully while they were at school and promptly forgot thereafter.

The solution Ben-Yehuda proposed was for Hebrew itself to become the language of instruction in the schools in Palestine. Hebrew was not, he asserted, a dead language: "... we can say anything we care to in it, we can use it for all of life's purposes, within the household and in large gatherings...." (Ben-Yehuda 1879b: 51). If Hebrew were to become the language of teaching in the schools it would be possible to have a system of education that was at one and the same time modern and, in a Jewish sense, national.

One of Ben-Yehuda's fears concerning the existing modern schools was that they would bring about a permanent linguistic change in their pupils. The latter would continue to speak French or German after they had left school, as far as circumstances allowed, and would usually regard these as their main languages. Evidently Ben-Yehuda hoped that the reform he was advocating would do the same, but in favor of Hebrew rather than of some prestigious European language. We have seen that he referred to the possibility of Hebrew being spoken within the home and in public. A little later we find him arguing that the children in Palestine should get used to speaking Hebrew "always, even for personal and intimate matters" (Ben-Yehuda 1880a: 91), and calling on the wealthy Jewish philanthropists and the Maskilim to "give us our land ... return our language to us ... found schools there to teach our offspring in Hebrew, and let us lead a Hebrew life!" (Ben-Yehuda 1880b: 211–12.)

Although what Ben-Yehuda was advocating clearly meant that Hebrew would become a spoken language once again, he did not, at that stage, use the word "revival" in connection with the speaking of Hebrew. Nevertheless, he was proposing something that he had not proposed in *She'elah Nikhbadah,* and his reason for doing so was a growing recognition on his part that if the Jews of Palestine did not *speak* Hebrew, they would soon not read or write it either. Diglossia had almost died out among the Christian nations of Europe, and Ben-Yehuda's instincts had evidently told him (though he never expressed it in such terms) that social forces akin to those that had killed diglossia among the non-Jews were now at work among the Jews, too, and would be the more effective the more Jewish life was modernized. Soon Jews, like other people, would be using one and the same language in speech and writing. Ben-Yehuda wanted modernization but, recognizing that it would spell the doom of diglossia, he saw that if Hebrew was to survive at all it would have to become the everyday language, spoken as well as written, of the new society in Palestine. That was his reason for coming to believe in the necessity for *teḥiyyat ha-dibbur*.

Ben-Yehuda set out his revised program for the Jewish future in a series of articles that appeared in *Ha-Maggid* in September 1880 under the title *Degel ha-Le'umiyyut* (The Banner of Nationality) (Ben-Yehuda 1880c.)[9] Although the articles in *Ha-Maggid* contain much that is of an ephemeral nature, they are also the place where Ben-Yehuda brought together the main elements of his new outlook for the first time. This, and the fact that these articles have largely been neglected so far in the literature on Ben-Yehuda, make it worth quoting some of their more interesting passages.

In *Degel ha-Le'umiyyut* Ben-Yehuda made his most determined effort to persuade his readers of the inevitability of assimilation in Europe:

> The days when we Jews could choose which path to take—those happy days have gone. . . . Since the day we began to pull down the wall dividing us from our Christian brothers we have ceased to walk along a separate path. Whether we like it or not, we follow the ways of the peoples among whom we are scattered, and are powerless to deviate from them. We are enlightened, whether we like it or not, because the nations among whom we dwell are enlightened.[10] . . . We will speak their language, like it or not . . . It is a law of nature, for they are the many and we are the few; they are the ocean and we are the drop. . . .
>
> Our national-minded authors cry "Teach your children Hebrew": excellent advice, but we are powerless to follow it, because children do not do everything that their parents want them to. The young will not obey our command to learn Hebrew, just as we disobeyed our parents' instructions not to follow the prophets of the Haskalah. Time and place influence a man strongly and determine his direction in life. In our days, and in the lands where we dwell, no amount of effort to teach our children Hebrew will succeed. It's a dead language for the new generation, no better than Greek or Latin, and just as pupils abandon these languages when they leave school, so Jewish children will abandon Hebrew. . . .
>
> Let those who have tried to teach their children Hebrew stand up and say whether I'm not right! Which of our Maskilim and learned men have children who know Hebrew and care about it? Let the learned S.S. testify whether he did not labor in vain to teach his two sons our language and to plant the love of our nation in their hearts! . . . Our language and all our heritage are alien to them. Yet who loves his people, its language, and its wisdom, as much as Mr. S.? Let Professor Joseph Halévy testify whether the pupils of the Ecole Orientale in Paris didn't tell him that they had

no need of the Hebrew language, "for a man can be Israelite without it." Yet . . . the Director [of the Ecole Orientale] reminds his pupils every day that they are Jews, that they have a duty to love their people, to love our language and our learning, that that is the only reason for the Alliance's benevolence towards them—and what is the result?

(Ben-Yehuda 1880c: 298.)

Ben-Yehuda's remarks about the Ecole Normale Israélite Orientale, a school set up in Paris by the Alliance Israélite Universelle to train teachers for the network of Alliance schools in the Orient, were based on his own observation when he had briefly been a pupil there and attended a class taught by Halévy. The incident he is referring to is described in his autobiography (Sivan 1978: 77–78.) The initials S.S. (*shin, zayin* in the original Hebrew) probably refer to the well-known Hebrew scholar Senior Sachs, who had been living in Paris since 1856.[11]

The conclusion Ben-Yehuda drew from these gloomy considerations was clear:

Will our language and our literature last much longer if we don't put it into the mouths of our descendants, if we don't *revive* it, if we don't make it a *spoken* language? And how can we succeed in making it a spoken language other than by making it the language of instruction in the schools? Not in Europe, nor in any of the lands of our exile! In all these lands we are an insignificant minority, and no amount of effort to teach our language to our children is going to succeed. But in our land, the Land of Israel, in the schools that we shall found there, we must make it the language of instruction and study.

(Ben-Yehuda 1880c: 316.)

This is the first place in Ben-Yehuda's writings where he uses the word "revive" specifically in the sense of *teḥiyyat ha-dibbur*.

Ben-Yehuda made a great effort to persuade his readers of the inevitability of assimilation because he had grasped something that the older generation of Maskilim, including Smolenskin, had not grasped. They had succeeded in giving themselves a modern education and in learning European languages while retaining a knowledge of, and attachment to, Hebrew, and they could not see why succeeding generations of Jews should not do the same. When they saw that their children were nonetheless abandoning Hebrew their only remedy was to reprove them and exhort them ever more fervently to mend their ways. Ben-Yehuda, however, understood that the older Maskilim had been able to combine modernization with Jewish learning only because, in their childhoods, *before* coming under the influence of modern ideas, they had been through the traditional, closed, purely Jewish, education system of the *ḥeder* and the *yeshivah*— institutions to which they had no wish to send their own children because they regarded them as reactionary, in both the content and the method of education. Strange as it may seem to us today, the Maskilim of the 1870s had not yet understood the power of assimilatory influences. Smolenskin, for instance, could not understand why Jews in European countries where they had been granted legal equality should not be brought up to use Hebrew side by side with their European language, albeit using the former only in its written form. He believed that an adequate minimum standard—the ability to read biblical Hebrew fluently—could be imparted to all Jewish children within the general (non-

Jewish) school system. (Smolenskin, 1925: 170–78.) Ben-Yehuda understood that this was not possible, and his awareness of the power of the non-Jewish environment to influence the Jews was close to the core of his national ideology: "In the nineteenth century . . . a nation cannot survive for long in a foreign country" (Ben-Yehuda 1880b: 211).

Smolenskin's writings abound in attacks on Moses Mendelssohn and his followers, whom he blames for having led the Jews astray. Ben-Yehuda, too, criticized them in *She'elah Nikhbadah*. By the time he came to write *Degel ha-Le'umiyyut*, however, he had changed his mind. In that article he absolves Mendelssohn from responsibility on the grounds that "enlightenment" and assimilation would have overtaken the Jews no matter what the Maskilim of Berlin did or said, and even if their movement had never existed:

> The Jews were foolish to wage this war [against Haskalah], for how can a dwarf fight a giant? How can a small drop stand up against a mighty wave coming to engulf it? The first Maskilim didn't give birth to the phenomenon; they weren't the fathers of the Enlightenment. European history conceived it and modern times gave birth to it. When the waves of the Englightenment arose and its breakers were above them, they were simply the first [among the Jews] to submit, for it is better to be one of the drops of the wave than a drop against the wave. The Jews of Russia and Poland thought otherwise, and tried to resist—but in vain!
>
> (Ben-Yehuda 1880c: 316–17.)

To summarize our main conclusions so far: Ben-Yehuda advocated settlement of the Land of Israel because he did not think the Jews could survive as a nation if they stayed in the Diaspora, where they were a minority everywhere; later, he also advocated that Hebrew become the spoken language of the Jews in Palestine because he thought that otherwise it would die out even as a literary language.

It may be worth mentioning that after writing *She'elah Nikhbadah* Ben-Yehuda changed his mind not only about how Hebrew was to be used in the Land of Israel, but also about at least two other things. One is the question whether all Jews should be considered Jewish by nationality. In *She'elah Nikhbadah* he had sought to prove that the Jews were a nation, by considering the meaning of nationality—in particular, John Stuart Mill's definition of it—and trying to show that it applied to the Jews. (Ben-Yehuda 1879a: 362–63.) Less than a year later he wrote that nationality was a matter of feeling, not of logic. Those who felt themselves to be "Hebrews" required no proofs of their Jewish nationality; equally, those who declared themselves to be French or German by nationality, and Jews only by religion, had every right to do so. He explicitly disavowed what he had said on the subject in *She'elah Nikhbadah*. (Ben-Yehuda 1880a: 89–90, esp. n. 3.)

Ben-Yehuda also changed his mind about the nature of the danger that was facing the Jewish people and threatening to lead to its disappearance. In *She'elah Nikhbadah* he had agreed with Smolenskin and another writer, E. Schulman, that it was the teachings ascribed to Moses Mendelssohn and his followers that were causing the damage. (Ben-Yehuda 1879a: 361–62.) As we have seen, by the time he wrote *Degel ha-Le'umiyyut* he had rejected this view. It is not surprising that

Ben-Yehuda twice referred to *She'elah Nikhbadah* as an immature work. (Sivan 1978: 74; and Ben-Yehuda 1948: 2, Arabic pagination.)

The questions that have been discussed above—what made Ben-Yehuda become a Zionist, and what made him propose the revival of Hebrew speech—were considered a few years ago by Shlomo Avineri in his book *The Making of Modern Zionism* (Avineri 1981: chap. 8).[12] Since Avineri's answers are different from those given above, it may be worthwhile to look at them and the evidence for them in some detail.

According to Avineri, Ben-Yehuda's starting-point was his awareness of the low artistic level achieved by the Hebrew writers of his day in the literature of the Haskalah. Ben-Yehuda's explanation for this, we are told, is that Hebrew is not a spoken language:

> ... true literature can emerge only in a social environment speaking the language in which that literature is being written. *Haskala* literature in Russia is artificial, alienated from the sources of true artistic creativity—life itself. . . . A Hebrew literature, Ben-Yehuda argues, can develop only in a society which speaks Hebrew. . . .
> (Avineri 1981: 85.)

However such a society cannot be created in countries where the Jews are a minority. At this point Avineri quotes Ben-Yehuda directly:

> We will be able to revive the Hebrew tongue only in a country in which the number of Hebrew inhabitants exceeds the number of gentiles. There[fore], let us increase the number of Jews in our desolate land; let the remnants of our people return to the land of their fathers; *let us revive the nation and its tongue will be revived too!*
> (Avineri 1981: 85.)[13]

Thus, according to Avineri, Ben-Yehuda's chief aim was the creation of a superior Hebrew literature. Revival of spoken Hebrew was a necessary means to this end, and the settlement of the Land of Israel by Jews was a means to the means.

It is evident that this view conflicts with the conclusions reached earlier in this article. In order to decide between the two views it will be necessary to examine the evidence adduced by Avineri in support of his conclusions, but there are two points worth making first.

One of the clear-cut differences between Avineri's view and that argued in this paper lies in the matter of chronology. We saw that Ben-Yehuda came to believe in the need for settlement of the Land of Israel during the Russo-Turkish war, while he was still at school in Dünaburg, whereas he adopted the idea that Hebrew had to become a spoken language again only after he had left school and gone to study in Paris. The evidence for this sequence of events is very strong. Avineri's view requires these events to have occurred in the reverse order, that is, for *teḥiyyat ha-dibbur* to have preceded *yishuv Eretz Yisa'el* in Ben-Yehuda's ideological development. This alone constitutes powerful, perhaps decisive, evidence against Avineri's thesis.

The second point concerns the war between Russia and Turkey. Ben-Yehuda attached great importance to it as the immediate cause of his change of outlook.

This is clear not only from the section of his autobiography that was quoted earlier but also from the introduction to his dictionary (Ben-Yehuda 1948: 1, Arabic pagination) and from the biographical article of 1889 (*Sefer Zikkaron* 1889: 189). Yet Avineri, in a chapter purporting to explain why Ben-Yehuda became a Zionist, does not mention the war. The impression given by this chapter of his book is that Avineri was not aware, when he wrote it, of the contents of Ben-Yehuda's autobiography, or of the other sources just mentioned. It is perhaps significant, even if the point itself is a minor one, that Avineri states that Ben-Yehuda published most of his early articles in *Ha-Shaḥar* (Avineri 1981: 83). In fact, Ben-Yehuda published more articles during the same period in *Ha-Maggid* and many more in *Ḥavatzelet*. Even if one excludes the articles in these two newspapers that do not deal directly with Jewish nationalism, those that are left still outnumber Ben-Yehuda's articles in *Ha-Shaḥar*.

What evidence, then, does Avineri bring in support of his view? It turns out that it is all taken from one piece of writing by Ben-Yehuda, an open letter to Smolenskin, the editor of *Ha-Shaḥar*, from which Avineri quotes three times. The impression given is that in this letter Ben-Yehuda discusses the low artistic level of the Hebrew literature of his day:

> An open letter by Ben-Yehuda . . . sets forth his ideas in their most concise form. . . . Ben-Yehuda ask[s] . . . why is it that the Hebrew literary attempts of the Haskala were not successful in producing truly masterful aesthetic and artistic achievements? . . . In his letter to Smolenskin, Ben-Yehuda's answer is fairly simple: true literature can emerge only in a social environment speaking the language in which that literature is being written.
>
> (Avineri 1981: 84–85.)

In fact, though, Ben-Yehuda's open letter (Ben-Yehuda 1881) does not discuss this question and is hardly about Hebrew literature at all.[14] It is hardly surprising, therefore, that none of the direct quotations from the letter in Avineri's book, one of which has been reproduced above, has anything to do with the question of the artistic level of Hebrew literature. The open letter was written in December 1880, about three months after *Degel ha-Le'ummiyut* was published in *Ha-Maggid*. Its argument is essentially a more concise version of the one that appears in the extracts from *Degel ha-Le'ummiyut* that have been cited in this article: the Jewish people and the Hebrew language are in danger of dying out, the danger is caused not by the Haskalah of Berlin but by the conditions of modern life, and the only solution is to bring about a Jewish majority in the Land of Israel and make Hebrew a spoken language there.

It is true that Ben-Yehuda was aware of the poor quality of the Hebrew literature of his day. He says so in his autobiography (Sivan 1978: 63), but there is no indication there that he ascribed the inferiority to the fact that Hebrew was not a spoken language. As it happens, there is one place where Ben-Yehuda does, by implication at least, offer an explanation of the phenomenon, and that is at the end of *She'elah Nikhbadah*. If Jews settle the Land of Israel as he has been suggesting then, writes Ben-Yehuda,

> [Hebrew] literature will spawn writers in plenty, because there literature will be able to reward its servants, and it will become an art in their hands, as is the case with

other literatures. Only then will our literature renew its vigor, because writers will serve it not for love alone, but also for reward; and they will not be forced to write at unearthly hours as they do now—for our writers have to make a living [by nonliterary means], since at present they receive no reward for their [literary] labors.

(Ben-Yehuda 1879a: 366.)

In other words, the reason for the poor quality of Hebrew literature is that writers cannot make it their full-time occupation. We have seen that Ben-Yehuda changed his mind about several things that he had written in *She' elah Nikhbadah* and it is possible that a year or two later he would have given a different explanation for the low artistic level of the Hebrew literature of his day. What is relevant here, though, is that he gave the explanation cited above at precisely the time he first publicly advocated settlement of the Land of Israel, and before he began arguing for the revival of spoken Hebrew.

For Ben-Yehuda, the fight against assimilation and the fight to preserve Hebrew as a language in active use were one and the same. Neither could succeed in a non-Jewish environment under modern conditions. Insofar as the need for *tehiyyat ha-dibbur* was connected in Ben-Yehuda's mind with the specific question of Hebrew literature, his purpose in wanting to turn Hebrew into a spoken language was to rescue that literature not from mediocrity, but from extinction.

In the epilogue to his book Avineri seeks "to identify . . . precisely the specific successes of Zionism" (Avineri 1981: 217). In spite of what he wrote about Ben-Yehuda in an earlier chapter, he does not discuss here whether an improvement in the artistic level of Hebrew literature is one of these successes. It might not be easy to answer such a question. One the one hand, there is no doubt that the literature produced by Hebrew-speaking Jews in Israel has risen to heights far greater than those attained by the writers of the Haskalah movement whose works Ben-Yehuda read in his youth. On the other, it is generally agreed that the improvement began with writers who were born and brought up in Eastern Europe, and who grew up speaking Yiddish. Most of them were Zionists, but even these did not, except perhaps at the ends of their lives, live in a Hebrew-speaking environment.

Given what Ben-Yehuda's actual reasons for advocating his Zionist views were, however, it is clear that a different question ought to be asked: is the *survival* of Hebrew literature one of the "specific successes of Zionism"? It is much easier to give a clear-cut answer to this question. The fact is that Ben-Yehuda's views have been proved right. Hebrew literature has died out as an active force in the Diaspora, and flourishes today only in the one country where there is a Jewish majority and where Hebrew is a spoken language, officially recognized and fostered by a Jewish government. Ben-Yehuda gave an accurate diagnosis of the disease that threatened the life of Hebrew literature more than a century ago and was the first person to explain clearly the nature and cause of that disease. Moreover, he prescribed a cure that has proved successful, and he labored strenuously to put the cure into effect. Although Ben-Yehuda was far from being either a great writer or a great literary critic, he surely deserves a place not only in the political history of the Jewish people and in the history of the Hebrew language, but also in the history of Hebrew literature.

Notes

1. First published in installments in *Ha-Toren,* New York, 1917–1918. Reprinted in Ben-Yehuda 1941: 1–69 (Hebrew pagination) and in Sivan 1978: 55–132. An English translation by T. Muraoka is in preparation.
2. In Latvia. The town was later called Dvinsk and is known today as Daugavpils.
3. The article was first published in *Ha-Shahar* (Ben-Yehuda 1879a). It has been reprinted several times but the reprints are not all accurate; see note 7, below, and the relevant text. Quotations from *She'elah Nikhbadah* in the present article are based on the translation by D. Patterson (Ben-Yehuda 1981).
4. In the reprint of *She'elah Nikhbadah* in Sivan 1978, a line has accidentally been omitted from the passage quoted here. (Sivan 1978: 45.) On the meaning of the phrase "revive the language" in this passage, see below.
5. Reprinted in Sivan 1978: 136–38.
6. For an English translation of part of this passage, see Mandel 1981: 28.
7. The sole exception appears to be the reprint of *She'elah Nikhbadah* in Brainin 1918: 75–83, where this passage has been reproduced accurately. However, there is a misleading footnote there on p. 75 implying that *She'elah Nikhbadah* appeared in about 1877, whereas the correct year is 1879. The translation by Patterson (Ben-Yehuda 1981) reflects the original text of 1879 faithfully.
8. All three articles have been reprinted in Ben-Yehuda 1941: 43–47, 51–56 and 59–64, Arabic pagination.
9. Reprinted in Ben-Yehuda 1941: 73–85, Arabic pagination.
10. Ben-Yehuda is using the word "enlightened" *(Maskilim)* here in the sense of "familiar with modern secular culture."
11. I am indebted to Professor R. Loewe of University College London for suggesting this identification.
12. A Hebrew version of the same work, *Ha-Rayon ha-Tziyyoni li-Gevanav,* was published in Tel Aviv in 1980. The chapter on Ben-Yehuda there is chapter 9.
13. The alteration of Avineri's "there" to "therefore" is in accordance with Hertzberg's translation (Hertzberg 1959: 164), which is the source cited by Avineri. It is also in accordance with the Hebrew original. (Ben-Yehuda 1881: 244.)
14. An English translation is available in Hertzberg 1959: 160–165. The Hebrew version has been reprinted in Ben-Yehuda 1941: 27–33, Arabic pagination, and in Sivan 1978: 49–54. Neither reprint follows the original precisely.

References

AVINERI, SHLOMO. *The Making of Modern Zionism: The Intellectual Origins of the Jewish State.* London, 1981.

BEN-YEHUDA, ELIEZER. "She'elah Nikhbadah," *Ha-Shahar* 9 (Vienna, 1878–79): 359–66. (1879a)

———. "She'elat ha-Hinnukh." *Havatzelet* 10 (21 November 1879): 49–52 (1879b).

———. "Al Devar ha-Hinnukh." *Havatzelet* 10 (2 and 9 January 1880): 89–91, 97–99 (1880a)

———. "Self Maskileinu." *Havatzelet* 10 (29 April and 6 May, 1880): 203–205, 211–13 (1880b)

———. "Degel ha-Le'umiyyut." *Ha-Maggid* 24 (1, 9 and 16 September 1880): 297–99, 306–307, 316–17 (1880c)

———. "Mikhtav le-Ven Yehuda." *Ha-Shaḥar* 10 (1880–82): 241–45. (1881)
———. *Kol Kitvei Eliezer Ben-Yehudah.* Vol. I. Jerusalem-Talpioth, 1941.
———. *Millon ha-Lashon ha-Ivrit . . . Ha-Mavo ha-Gadol.* Jerusalem-Talpioth, 1948.
———. "A Weighty Question," Transl. David Patterson. In Silberschlag 1981: 1–12.
BRAININ, REUVEN, ed. *Sefer Zikkaron le-Eliezer Ben Yehudah.* New York: 1918.
HERTZBERG, ARTHUR. *The Zionist Idea.* New York, 1959.
HERZL, THEODOR. *The Jewish State: An Attempt at a Modern Solution of the Jewish Question.* Transl. Sylvie d'Avigdor. London, 1967.
KATZ, JACOB. "Forerunners [of Zionism]." *Encyclopaedia Judaica.* Jerusalem, 1971. 16: 1033–37.
MANDEL, GEORGE. "*She'elah Nikhbadah* and the Revival of Hebrew." In Silberschlag 1981: 25–39. Reprinted in S. Morag, ed. *Studies on Contemporary Hebrew.* Jerusalem, 1987.
———. "Ben-Yehuda be-Paris." *Ha-Kenes ha-Ivri ha-Madda'i ha-Ḥamishi be-Eiropah* [*Kenes Paris, 1982*]. Jerusalem: Brit Ivrit Olamit, 1985, pp. 136–46.
———. *Eliezer Ben-Yehudah u-Profesor Yosef Halevy.* Jerusalem: Brit Ivrit Olamit, n.d. [1988].
O'BRIEN, CONOR CRUISE. *The Siege: The Saga of Israel and Zionism,* London, 1986.
The editorial board of *Ha-Asif. Sefer Zikkaron le-Sofrei Yisra'el ha-Ḥayyim itanu ka-Yom.* Warsaw, 1889. Photographic reprint with introduction by G. Kressel. Jerusalem, 1980.
SILBERSCHLAG, EISIG, ed. *Eliezer Ben-Yehuda: A Symposium in Oxford.* Oxford, 1981.
SIVAN, REUVEN, ed., Eliezer Ben-Yehudah. *Ha-Ḥalom ve-Shivro: Mivḥar Ketavim be-Inyenei Lashon.* Jerusalem, 1978.
SMOLENSKIN, PERETZ. *Ma'amarim.* Vol. I. Jerusalem, 1925.

13

The Emergence of Modern Hebrew: Some Sociolinguistic Perspectives

SHELOMO MORAG

In recounting the history of Modern Hebrew one can talk of three main phases: (1) from the beginnings of rural settlement starting with the first *moshavot* in 1882 up to the end of Ottoman rule in 1917; (2) from the establishment of the Mandate until the creation of the State of Israel; and (3) on till the present. It is quite natural that these phases should correspond to the three major chapters in a century of Jewish life in Eretz Israel. And it hardly needs stating that the history of the Yishuv and the State during this period runs parallel to the history of the language. The foundation work, the step-by-step consolidation, the preparation for confrontation, the all-consuming struggles, leading ultimately within these one hundred years to a one hundred and twenty-fold explosion of a Jewish population that in 1882 had numbered just 30,000 (out of a total of 350,000),[1] now living in an independent state and maintaining a culture of its own—these stages have their parallels in the history of the Hebrew language over the past one hundred years. One might also say that any historian who regards as historically unique the phenomenon of a people's return to its land after dispersal among the nations will regard as linguistically unique the phenomenon of the revival of Hebrew.

The term "revival" of Hebrew is not strictly accurate. Down the long centuries in which the Jewish communities both in the Diaspora and in Eretz-Israel used Jewish languages as their vernacular (Yiddish, Judeo-Español, Judeo-Arabic of various kinds, and other such languages), Hebrew was far from dead. Its use as a written medium for a multifaceted literature and even for workaday letters is well-known. But throughout those times it also existed as an oral medium.

All Jewish communities maintained the heritage of oral Hebrew in two corpora: the Classical Hebrew Corpus and the Integrated Hebrew Corpus. The first corpus was constructed from a number of components: the communal tradition for reciting Scripture, in particular the Torah, Haftarot, the five Megillot, and the Psalms, and its relationship with the *nikkud* system accepted by the community; the communal tradition for reciting the Hebrew parts of postbiblical literature, especially the Mishnah—whether by itself or as part of the Babylonian Talmud; the phonetic and morphological tradition for reading the prayers; and the linguistic and literary knowledge, i.e., the degree of grammatical and lexical understanding of, and the familiarity with, the written texts. The components of the Classical Hebrew Corpus differed in breadth and depth from community to community and from country to country—all according to the solidity and prestige of its cultural tradition, and of course the members of a community were not all guardians of the Classical Hebrew Corpus to the same extent. Be this as it may, there was no traditional community that lacked this Hebrew dimension. Sociolinguistically, moreover, there emerged among the various sections of world Jewry a special two-language system: a spoken vernacular alongside a traditional language of culture, Hebrew.

This is a relatively rare situation of "diglossia"; this term usually denotes the existence in a language of two varieties, or standards, a higher (for more formal occasions and in writing) and a lower (for everyday conversation). Examples of diglossia would be colloquial vis-à-vis literary Arabic or Swiss German dialects vis-à-vis Literary German.

This was not the case as regards the status of Hebrew in relation to the vernaculars of the Jewish communities: in the Jewish traditional society Hebrew served as the transmission medium for the cultural legacy; it was not a language spoken in ordinary social circumstances. To know Hebrew, and with it Aramaic, meant chiefly to be potentially able to recite the Scriptures and postbiblical literature in line with local tradition, and—for more learned members of the community and scholars—to comprehend these texts. This potential ability was an important measure of a Jew's prestige in his community. So the relationship between the Classical Hebrew Corpus and the communal vernacular ought not to be regarded as a run-of-the-mill case of diglossia but as one existing between a store of linguistic knowledge employed (e.g., in Torah recital) in servicing the society's cultural heritage and a language of everyday speech. Let us call this relationship "socioglossia."

Alongside the Classical Corpus the Jewish communities maintained another Hebrew corpus of their own, which we shall call the Integrated Hebrew Corpus: in the Jewish languages numerous Hebrew and Aramaic words had been preserved, expressions and phrases, biblical quotations and allusions, words from the Mishnah and Talmud, as well as many words that came into being during the long years of exile.

We are wont to assume that these Hebrew words that took firm hold in the vernacular as stock items of vocabulary came from the sphere of religion and heritage—take שבת (*shabat,* "Sabbath"), חתן (*hatan,* "bridegroom"), כלה (*kalah,* "bride"), חתונה (*hatunah,* "wedding"), גט (*get,* "divorce document"), שמיטה (*shemitah,* "sabbatical year"). But this is simply not so. The Hebrew elements are part of each and every sphere of the lexicon, serving to express both abstract and concrete in every field of meaning. We are calling these components "integrated" because, as used by any speaker in his respective community, they do not exist as independent linguistic units but rather as a part of the overall spoken system. Thus, for example, in the spoken Arabic of Yemenite Jews one finds Hebrew words such as דמיון (*dimyön,* (originally: "similarity,") denoting "etrog, citron"),[2] כהן (*kohen,* denoting "ruler"), מלך (*malakh,* (derived from מלאכה *melakhah,* "work,") as "(he) performed work"),[3] צערוריה (*ṣa'aruriyyah,* as "pain, grief"). In the ordinary speech of Baghdad Jews, Baghdadi Jewish Arabic, צרעת *ṣara'at,* (originally: "leprosy,") denotes "all manner of disease" and also "an evil person", קבורה *qaburah,* (originally "burial,") is "to hell," "I will never be so lucky", מצוה *miṣwah* is "funeral bier."[4] In the spoken Aramaic of the Jews of Zakho in Iraqi Kurdistan, *ḥammas* (חומש) denotes any kind of book, שמעתי, *shama'ti* (originally: "I heard") is an epithet for "a yes-woman, a bride who always obeys her mother-in-law," *mi'uggenes* (מעוגנת) besides its original sense of "stranded wife" also means "anything that languishes unused for a long period" and "neither forbidden nor permitted."[5] In Judeo-Español, *arninu* (from הרנינו, *harninu*, "rejoice"), used for denoting "Thursday," which used to be pay day, alludes both to the joy of being paid and to the Psalm for Thursday, which opens הרנינו לאלהים עוזנו (*harninu lelohim 'uzenu*, "rejoice to God our might.")[6]

Yiddish, of course, is awash with Hebraisms and Aramaisms. Some examples from its Integrated Hebrew Corpus: בעלן (*baylen*, "interested"), חסידים (*khasidim*, "Hasidim"), מנין (*minyen*, "prayer quorum"), עבירה (*aveyre*, "sin"), מעשה (*mayse*, "tale"), רשע (*roshe*, "evil man"), רשעות (*rishes*, "evil"), אן א שיעור (*un a*) *shier*, "(without) limit," and from Aramaic: מהיכא תיתי (*mekhteyse*, "with great pleasure").

Thus in both corpora, the Classical and the Integrated, grammatical and lexical information about Hebrew was transmitted down the generations. The two corpora are of course quite different, but they do have their points of contact and parallels. Also, both possessed a powerful potential which helped trigger the change in the status of Hebrew during the First Aliyah (1882–1903) and the Second Aliyah (1903–14)—a period largely tantamount to the first phase in the history of Modern Hebrew.

This change ensued from the cultural revival created by the Return to Zion. The return to Eretz-Israel, the foundation of the first settlements *(moshavot),* and the nascent consolidation of the Jewish presence in Palestine, brought with them the return to Hebrew, the Full Return to the national tongue. By the expression "Full Return to Hebrew" we mean the aspiration to bring Hebrew to normalcy, to establish it as an all-purpose vernacular, and the realization of this aim. Denoting this process as "Full Return" strikes us as more apt than naming it "Revival," for we have seen that Hebrew was in no way a dead language during the lengthy exile. It was not a mother tongue, the language in which mothers spoke to children among Jews in this period, but neither was it dead.[7]

The basic notion that Hebrew possessed the potential to make the Full Return a possibility, and the linkage between the Return and the Return to Zion, were tellingly expressed by Eliezer Ben-Yehuda in his article *She'elah Lohatah"* ("A Burning Question")[8] published in *Ha-Shaḥar* in 1879. Before quoting some sentences from this article, we would observe that the article primarily addresses not the topic of language but the issue of achieving the ends of nationalism; language is a means towards these ends:

> For we have a language in which we can now write whatsoever we desire, *and we can speak it too if we so wish.* . . . In vain all our toil if we do not create a center for nationalism . . . in vain all the toil of our writers to revive the language, if the whole people remains dispersed among peoples of diverse tongue.[9]

The Full Return to Hebrew was both a means to achieving the cultural revival and at one and the same time a major objective of this same revival. This combined function of the Full Return was of unique import for the process of cultural consolidation.

As in any process of cultural revival or renaissance, this was from the outset a selective, eclectic continuation of a heritage.[10] A selective continuation involves a mix of perpetuation on the one hand and of rejection on the other. Any renaissance maintains certain aspects of a heritage, rejects others, and creates yet others in their place. Views regarding the nature and scale of the rejected components and the new ones naturally differ among the leading figures in a renaissance. Differences of attitude have here too engendered debate, often heated and sometimes bearing the seed of future ideologies. The Full Return to Hebrew too was at root a process of selective continuation; this is also disclosed by the differing attitudes to the question of which pronunciation, the Ashkenazi or the Sephardi, should be adopted. To this question we shall return later.

The vanguard of the newly-emerging culture had to confront problems that went way beyond the bounds of language. These were questions at the heart of the nascent native-born culture—problems of mutual relations of language and society, of language and literature, problems of how to change, to develop, and to fashion—problems that were semiotic in nature. From a semiotic point of view "culture" is the set of possible signs available to society as a whole and to its individuals, enabling communication in any of the attendant circumstances. Central to the challenge was how to find substitutes for the semiotic cultural heritage of the first and second waves of Aliyah.[11] The need for these semiotic, i.e., linguistic and behavioral, substitutes stemmed from the very nature of the Return to Zion. The perception of the semiotic substitutes as a whole by those involved was not intrinsically of the same kind; whether they differed or agreed, their actions were fired with enthusiasm for the renascent language.

Among those active in the process of the Full Return, the following should be mentioned:[12] Eliezer Ben-Yehuda, steersman and man of action, wedded to his objective and unceasingly preoccupied with reconditioning a vocabulary to meet the needs of the moment; the teachers of the generation, men like David Yellin, David Yudelevitch, Simḥa Wilkomitz, Yehuda Grazovski (later: Gur) and many others,[13] who bore the burden of restoring their pupils to Hebrew; public figures, thinkers and researchers, like A. M. Luncz and Y. M. Pines; and, from the Second Aliyah on, the immigrants-turned-workers *(ha-po'alim)* and the offspring of the founders of the settlements in Judea and the Galilee.

How strong the emotional charge of those involved was can be seen from a letter of 1889 by the author Neḥamah Pukhachevsky.[14] She tells of a group that came up from Rishon Le-Zion to Jerusalem during the Intermediate Days of the festival of Sukkot:

> A great caravan of some thirty people came during the Intermediate Days of Sukkot to Jerusalem—one would have to have witnessed the caravan to have appreciated how cherished is the thought of Jerusalem to the Jew. On the eve of the first day of the festival at ten o'clock I went up to the main street of the settlement. There, at the top of the street, stood three wagons full of men, women, and children. Many of the travellers were still walking to and fro outside, with the Holy Tongue on their lips, and their expressions and words spoke for the love of Zion and Jerusalem that burned within them . . . This caravan made a strong impression in Jerusalem. All of the trav-

elers walked about together at all times, speaking Hebrew in the streets, paying visits to Jerusalem's wise and great, and all welcomed them with joy. But the folk of Jerusalem could not believe their eyes: "Godless people[15] talking the Holy Tongue! Indeed, this is something as yet unheard of . . ." Our youngsters also saw a play on the stage in Jerusalem. The school pupils directed by the teachers put on "Zerubavel"[16] translated by Mr. Yellin the son-in-law of Mr. Pines. All the pupils spoke good Hebrew and only in a Sephardi accent, and they made a powerful impression on the audience. One of the youngsters who told me about the play wept bitterly as he spoke, so strong an effect did the play have on him. Here too [in Rishon Le-Zion] the schoolteachers wish to stage it, but we will not succeed for it is too hard for us; we are talking just a little in the Holy Tongue, but to mount a complete play is beyond us.

Like the Jewish population, the traditional Hebrew linguistic system of this new world of Eretz-Israel in the 1880s and 1890s fell into two main blocs, a Sephardi and an Ashkenazi. For the former, the Classical and Integrated Corpora were those of communities having a Mediterranean background; for the latter, these corpora originated in the traditions and vernaculars (notably Yiddish) of Central and Eastern Europe. Whatever the variations in the Ashkenazi corpora, they were overshadowed by the differences between them and their Sephardi counterparts.

At this point, some statistics—if only close estimates—for the "Old" (pre-Zionist) Sephardi and Ashkenazi population of nineteenth century Jerusalem would be instructive. In 1847, Yehoseph Schwarz in his *Tevu'ot Ha-Aretz* estimated the city's Jewish population as 6000 Sephardim and 1500 Ashkenazim;[17] in 1867, J. F. Swift gives 4000 Sephardim and 2000 Ashkenazim,[18] whereas C. Warren's figures are 4000 and 6000 respectively.[19] A. M. Luncz claimed for 1869 that the proportions were inverse: 6000 and 4000 respectively.[20]

From the early eighties Jerusalem harbored a third, small community, whose Hebrew corpora were of older and purer vintage than the other two—the Yemenites. The Hebrew of the Yemenite immigrants in Jerusalem was a source of awed fascination to the discriminating and the linguistically informed among Jerusalem scholars. One may here cite Abraham Zvi Idelsohn, the pioneer of research into the muscial traditions of Jewish communities. In an article published in 1909, he states that Hebrew had always been spoken fluently by the Yemenites, though not "as a workaday tongue for personal needs and pleasures. This language was sacred to them and they only spoke it in the synagogue and in matters sacred, while for personal needs they used Arabic and the womenfolk know barely a word of Hebrew." Idelsohn emphatically dwells upon the potential capability of the Hebrew spoken by these Jews, conceiving it as a living language: "for every man among them can convey therein his personal desire, and it is evident that the language is not an academic one and that they are not translating their thoughts from a foreign tongue, as does the European Jew."[21]

But the Yemenite contingent was a small one, and the finely tuned sounds of the Hebrew they spoke did not find attuned ears among the rest of the Jewish population. Their Hebrew corpora would remain theirs alone.

To a great extent, the Full Return had been based on the corpora, the Classical as well as the Integrated, of the Sephardi community.[22] This was due to a number of factors—linguistic, ideological, and aesthetic. For the Sephardim, more than for the Ashkenazim, the use of Hebrew in speech was a follow-on, a continuation of some kind.[23]

Ben-Yehuda was impressed by the aesthetic qualities of the Sephardim in language as well as in appearance and behavior. He tells us of his meetings with their elders at the office of I. D. Frumkin, the editor of *Ha-Ḥavatzelet*.[24] In his own words:

> The Sephardim generally cut an attractive figure, elegant to a man in their Oriental garb. There was a charm to their behavior and they almost all conversed with the editor of *Ha-Ḥavatzelet* in Hebrew, a fluent, natural Hebrew, peppered with idioms, and with so authentic, so honeyed and Oriental an accent.[25]

His impressions of the Ashkenazi visitors he met at Frumkin's office were less positive:

> Most of the Ashkenazi visitors had an East-European[26] appearance. Only the older ones, who had come [to Palestine] when the Ashkenazim were a minority, have somewhat assimilated to the Sephardim, becoming close to them in language and custom. These older people looked less East-European. All visitors spoke Yiddish with Mr. Frumkin. Only in my honor they spoke a little Hebrew. The Hebrew of the older people was natural and fluent to an extent, their accent Sephardi. But one could immediately hear that this was no Sephardi talking.[27]

True, Ben-Yehuda does not tell us of Sephardim conversing among themselves, but of a conversation between some Sephardi dignitaries and an Ashkenazi, I. D. Frumkin. Nonetheless, this meeting proved to him that it would definitely be possible to cast the traditional Hebrew pronunciation, morphology and lexicon into a syntactic and discursive plane, i.e., to construct sentences and units of discourse.

Ben-Yehuda's words have another important implication: the said meeting between Frumkin and the Sephardi sages of Jerusalem took place days after Ben-Yehuda's arrival in the city in 1881. What we know of it provides the first testimony to the genesis of the Modern Hebrew accent, born of a blend of the Sephardi phonological system and its Ashkenazi counterpart. Of this, more later.

More important that any other factor in the process of the Full Return was the conceptual, ideological one: the urge to sever ties with the legacy of the Old World—the shtetl of Central and Eastern Europe, the *galut*. For a large portion of the immigrants who arrived in Eretz-Israel during the Second Aliyah (1903–1914), Ashkenazi Hebrew—and, needless to say, Yiddish—formed part of a semiotic system that portrayed the Old World from which they sought to escape. The feeling that such an escape was essential for establishing the new, revamped culture was deep-seated. Adopted after much debate and dispute,[28] the Sephardi pronunciation fitted in well with the new semiotic system. The adoption of the Sephardi pronunciation was a slow, gradual process. What, in fact, was created as the years went by was not a truly Sephardi pronunciation but a blend of the linguistic legacies of the two major communities, the Sephardi and the Ashkenazi.

The phonological system of this blended Sephardi pronunciation is basically *Sephardi* in its vowels (notably, no distinction between *kamatz* and *pataḥ* or *tzere* and *segol*, and the presence of *kamatz katan* identical to *ḥolam*) and its main stress patterns (final vis-à-vis pre-final stress), and *Ashkenazi* in its consonants (lack of guttural *ḥet* and *ayin,* pronunciation of *resh* as a frictionless continuant rather than as a tongued trill). Only one Ashkenazi consonantal trait failed to find acceptance (the pronunciation of the soft *tav* as *s*). Another Ashkenazi feature is the absence of salient Sephardi traits: doubled consonants (the *dagesh ḥazaq*) and the regular sounding of mobile sheva *(sheva na)* as a vowel.

To avoid confusion between the historical Sephardi pronunciation and the blended one, we shall refer to the latter as "Ashkenized-Sephardi."

Needless to say, the emergence of a phonological system which comprises Sephardi vowels and stress patterns—the Ashkenized-Sephardi pronunciation— was a result of contact between the two communities. Becoming more prevalent year by year, the use of this pronunciation was regarded as a complete rejection of the Ashkenazi pronunciation. For traditional Ashkenazi society, the acceptance of the Sephardi pronunciation was sociolinguistically a radical about-turn: a rift was created between the traditional Ashkenazi forms of Hebrew and their counterparts in the spoken language of an ever-increasing portion of the Jewish population. For the Sephardim, on the other hand, the newly-emerging pronunciation was a product of selective continuity. Since, however, a number of originally Sephardi features had thereby been abandoned, certain members of the community considered it corrupt. Be it noted, however, that in the speech of the Old Sephardi community of Eretz-Israel—and of Sephardi immigrants—several features of the historical Sephardi pronunciation, abandoned in the Ashkenized-Sephardi, were retained, above all guttural *ḥet* and *ayin* and tongued (apical) *r*.

Thus, possibly from the late eighties or early nineties, two main varieties (or speech types) of spoken Hebrew were gradually being crystallized. For lack of more appropriate terms, one is usually dubbed "General" and the other "Oriental."[29] The former is identical to our Ashkenized-Sephardi; the latter has preserved the aforementioned Sepahrdi features.[30] And owing to the social prestige of the Ashkenazi community, some speakers belonging to Sephardi families proceeded to adopt the Ashkenized-Sephardi pronunciation.

The blending of the linguistic heritage of the two communities is also evident in vocabulary, albeit to a lesser extent: Modern Hebrew has incorporated components from both the Sephardi and the Ashkenazi Integrated Corpora. Thus, for "from time immemorial," Judeo-Spanish has several expressions: *del tiempo de metushelakh* "from Methuselah's time," *del tiempo del mabul* "since the Flood," *de antiokhos zemaní* "from the time of Antiochus," and *del tiempo de mi tarapapu* "from my great-great-grandfather's time."[31] All these phrases exist in translation in Modern Hebrew: משנת תרפפו, מימי אנטיוכוס, מימי המבול, מימי מתושלח, *(mishenat tarapapu, mimei antiokhus, mimei hamabul, mimei metushelah)*.

An example deriving from the Ashkenazi heritage is לא-יוצלח *(lo yutzlaḥ,* "good-for-nothing"). This phrase, relatively little used today, was widespread in former years. In a sentence like הוא לא-יוצלח גמור *(hu lo yutzlaḥ gamur,* "he is an absolute good-for-nothing"), the phrase serves as a noun; originally, however, it consisted of a verb preceded by a negator. It came over to Hebrew from the Ashkenazi Integrated Corpus.[32]

In the first phase of its history, Modern Hebrew had naturally to contend with other languages spoken by the local Jewish population, particularly Yiddish, Judeo-Spanish, and Arabic. Mention should also be made (although information is mea-ger) of the hybrid languages—Hebrew-Yiddish, Hebrew-Arabic, Hebrew-Arabic-Yiddish or Hebrew-Arabic-Judeo-Spanish, and other combinations to boot. An interesting illustration of a hybrid comes from the son of an old Rosh-Pinah family, quoting the way his father spoke: *fi indi tsvey preydalakh yetla'u ettal'a vi tsvey feygalakh* ("I have two she-mules climbing the hill like two birds").[33] In this sentence only one word has a Hebrew base but with a Yiddish suffix *(preydalakh)*; the other words are from Arabic or Yiddish.

The most significant challenge that the incarnated language had to face was the supreme test of viability: it had to demonstrate that the Return could be achieved, against all the linguistic, ideological, and social odds. The Hebrew novelist Brenner writes despairingly in 1906:

> Maybe I should be writing this in Yiddish. Who understands Hebrew? For what or for whom does one write Hebrew? And can one write properly in a dead tongue? The masses read Yiddish ... at any rate, the Hebrew reader can read Yiddish too.[34]

Two years later, the poet Bialik declares:

> Is it not better finally to acknowledge that the prime misfortune of the Hebrew language lies not in the "effect"—its total or imaginary poverty, the lack of words or the inability to provide appropriate expressions, the shortage of readers and customers and the like—but in the "cause" itself, this cause being the fact that the majority of the people does not speak Hebrew and does not live therein and create therein its entire life with all its internal and external values?[35]

These were years of indecision, in thought and deed, of doubts, bewilderment, contorted conflict, but by sheer force of action, day in day out, Hebrew prevailed.

The extent to which things changed during the first eighteen years of the opening phase can be gauged from the words of Ahad Ha'am. Following his second visit to Eretz-Israel, in 1893, he penned the second part of his well-known article *Emet me-Eretz Yisrael* ("Truth from the Land of Israel"), in which he states:

> In the last few years, indeed, the press has managed to instill in us the belief that the schools of Eretz-Israel are the best suited to our wants, in that they give their students a national Hebrew education along with an adequate general knowledge.... At a distance, this all appears well and good, but anyone hearing for himself how teachers and pupils alike are mumbling, for want of words and expressions, will immediately feel that this kind of "speech" cannot invoke in the speaker or listener any sense of respect or affection for the reduced language; the children's tender intellect (they are generally learning French too) will sense more strongly still the artificial bonds clapped upon it by talking Hebrew.[36]

Ahad Ha'am subsequently visited the country three times, in 1900, 1907, and 1912, until settling there in 1922. In 1912, at a meeting of the Teachers' Association Center in which the activities of the Language Committee *(Va'ad Ha-Lashon)* were discussed, he came to contrast the state of Hebrew then with what he had seen of it in 1900. To quote from the minutes:

> When in Eretz-Israel twelve years ago, I found several word-coining factories, led by Ben-Yehuda's. The whole thing struck me then as ludicrous. I know not whether our language is already a living one, but the fact is that it is the language of instruction in every school and every subject, and one must therefore see to it to create one termi-

nology for all. In every school I now find a word-coining factory: Every teacher is coining with gay abandon, this one calls a certain something a so-and-so and that one a such-and-such.... Even within the same school different classes are using different words....[37]

In the same year Ahad Ha'am writes:

I saw the educational work when it began eighteen years ago, and my heart would not allow me then to believe that those few teachers who bore in their breast the great ideal of teaching Hebrew through Hebrew and who began to carry it through with such scant resources—that they would truly succeed in causing such a "revolution" of the spirit in this world of ours. Now I see that inner confidence has indeed performed miracles. "Hebrew through Hebrew" is no longer an "ideal" in Eretz-Israel but its very lifeblood, a natural phenomenon whose existence is an imperative and whose absence is now unthinkable.[38]

True, indeed, it was the labor of the teachers, a labor of love fired by a vision, that equipped the offspring of the first generation for the Hebrew that would eventually become a native language; they, and the folk of the Second Aliyah in their own circles, provided the great impetus for achieving the Full Return to Hebrew in its initial stages.

The second great phase in Modern Hebrew, the period of the British Mandate (1917–48), was the breakthrough. Historians distinguish here four aliyot: the third (1919–23), the fourth (1924–31), the fifth (1932–39), and the sixth (1939–48). When this period began, some 65,000 (or, according to another estimate, 85,000) Jews lived in Eretz-Israel; at its close, the Jewish population amounted to 600,000. The Balfour Declaration and the award of the Mandate to Britain had profound and positive consequences. It provided a framework in which the *Yishuv* (the Jewish population) could develop new political and economic systems. Social stratification underwent change, and a complex cultural activity emerged.[39]

Though the Jewish population continued to be a minority, the leadership of the Zionist movement and of the Yishuv evolved institutions geared to achieving Zionism's goals in the new circumstances, namely the creation of an autonomous political center as independent as possible of the Arab populace and the Mandatory government. The coalesence of a political, economic, and cultural center, and of course the growth in Jewish numbers, triggered a great expansion in the use of Hebrew and in its evolution—as did the well-developed educational system of the Yishuv.

Hebrew had won official status as the third official language of the Mandate, as laid down in Article 22 of the League of Nations Mandate for Palestine:

English, Arabic and Hebrew shall be the official languages of Palestine. Any statement or inscription in Arabic on stamps or money in Palestine shall be repeated in Hebrew, and any statement or inscription in Hebrew shall be repeated in Arabic.[40]

But far more important is the fact that Hebrew in this period became a native tongue for a relatively fast-growing number of people, the so-called Sabras (the native-born), and many women and men who, although non-native, had acquired a full command of the language.

The concept "native," broadly used of communication, embraces language, gesture, and proxemics (how speakers stand and sit, their mutual distance, etc.).

These systems are a clear distinguishing mark of a speech community. Briefly, the test for "native" is the absence of alien features in one's various channels of communication. With most peoples, native speakers are generally natives of the country where the language is spoken. Native Hebrew, of course, is different: it extends to the non-native born, yet leaves one in no doubt as to what it is—non-native spoken Hebrew is easily distinguishable; the slightest sound may give it away.

We have statistics for the spread of native Hebrew during this second great phase;[41] the number of those speaking Hebrew (from age two up) as "sole" or "chief" language in 1914 has been estimated at 34,000, some 40% of the Jewish populace.[42] In November 1948 it was 511,000 (75.1%).[43] And by age:

Table 13.1.

	1914 (Approx.)	Nov. 1948 (Census)[43]
Age 2–14	53.7%	75.1%
Age 15+	25.6%	69.5%

The great waves of immigration in 1919–22 and 1924–26 were mainly from Russia, Poland, and the Baltic states—with a significant proportion of pioneering youth. Later, from 1932, German immigration began arriving. These Aliyot obviously changed the communal make-up of the Yishuv.

Another major factor in the formation of Native Hebrew was the stratification of the Yishuv. Moshe Lissak has explored the structure of the Jewish elites under the Mandate, encompassing three categories: political, economic, and cultural elites.[44] Lissak shows them to have been fairly homogeneous:[45] 76% hailed from Eastern Europe, with the balance dividing up (about 10% each) between the native-born ("Sabras," some counting as Ashkenazim and some as Sephardim) and Central or Western Europeans. Over half of the members of these elites were born in the last twenty years of the nineteenth century, and if we add those born between 1900 and 1910 the figure representing these members comes to 72%. Thus Eastern Europeans, taken together with Central Europeans, made up the bulk of the elite.

During this phase, the features of the Sephardi linguistic legacy steadily declined. There was an expansion in the use of the "General" variety and a relative rejection of the "Oriental." This process, which already had its beginnings in the first phase, continued more prominently during phase two. More and more speakers of Sephardi and Yemenite origin adopted the "General" variety, by now clearly considered more prestigious. Thus, toward the end of this phase of Modern Hebrew, "Oriental" Hebrew, heir to the glorious linguistic heritage of the Sephardi population, is in retreat. Other phenomena in this social assimilation are the rejection of some Sephardi customs and the replacement of typical Sephardi family names, such as Mizrahi, by names without a Sephardi flavor.

The third phase in the history of Modern Hebrew, from the establishment of the State of Israel to the present, has seen an immense growth in the number of Hebrew speakers, due to massive waves of immigration. A high degree of literary activity has had inordinate impact on the language; several varieties of slang, abundant in vocables and highly expressive in form, have also evolved.

Native Hebrew, commonly called Israeli Hebrew, is today clearly recognizable as a well-defined layer in the history of the language and is the subject of considerable research.[46]

Notes

An earlier version of the present paper appeared as "Ha-Ivrit ha-Ḥadashah be-Hitgabshuta: Lashon be-Aspeklarya shel Ḥevrah," *Cathedra* 56 (1990):70–92.

1. On the population of Eretz-Israel in this period, see Ben-Arieh 1988.
2. See Ratzaby 1978:57.
3. See Ratzaby, ibid., p. 159.
4. See Ben-Yaakov 1985: 122.
5. See Sabar 1974: 213.
6. On Hebrew words in Judeo-Español, see Benvenisti 1985 and the great dictionary of Nehama 1977.
7. See Rabin 1986; Bar-Adon 1988.
8. *She'elah Lohatah* was the name given to the article by Ben-Yehuda himself, but Smolenskin, the editor of *Ha-Shaḥar,* altered it to *She'elah Nikhbadah.*
9. For analysis of the contents of this article of Ben-Yehuda's, see Mandel 1981 and Mandel in this volume.
10. See Morag 1959:196–97.
11. See Even-Zohar 1990: 181–82.
12. No attempt is made here at a complete treatment of this topic.
13. Compare David Yudelevitch, "Ha-Morim ha-Rishonim," in *Leqet Te'udot,* pp. 92–93.
14. This letter has been published in *Leqet Te'udot,* pp. 25–26.
15. Hebrew *góyim* (penultimately stressed), meaning "Jews who are not religiously observant."
16. A play by M. L. Lilienblum, and the first Hebrew play to be staged in the country. See *Leqet Te'udot,* p. 25 n. 2.
17. Schwarz 1900.
18. Swift 1868: 247.
19. Warren 1876: 357 on Sephardim and 359 on Ashkenazim.
20. Luncz 1910: 24. For further sources on the relative numbers of Sephardim and Ashkenazim in the nineteenth century, see Shur 1987: 657–58.
21. See Idelsohn 1909: 115; and Morag 1986, especially 161.
22. We use "community" in the singular for all Sephardi communities.
23. On the use of Hebrew as a spoken language in the years before Ben-Yehuda was active, see Parfitt 1972 and 1984, and Ornan 1984.
24. This Hebrew newspaper was first published in Jerusalem in 1863 and discontinued after about a year; it appeared again from 1870 to 1914. It was first a monthly and later a weekly.
25. Sivan 1972: 97.
26. Used pejoratively (Hebrew *galuti*—lit. "pertaining to the Diaspora").
27. Sivan, ibid.
28. Cf. Morag 1959: 195–96.
29. These terms were coined by Haim Blanc; see Blanc 1957: 164–65.
30. For a detailed description of the features differentiating the two varieties, see Morag 1959: 192–93.

31. See Schwarzwald 1986; Benvenisti 1985: 59; Bunis 1981.
32. For this and other examples of the influence on Modern Hebrew of the Hebrew component of Yiddish see Gold 1989: 104–136.
33. Radio broadcast by a member of the Schwarz family of Rosh-Pinah, 16 May 1988.
34. In *Ha-Me'orer,* 1906. See Shaked 1977: 43 and 492 n.
35. In his article *Ḥevlei Lashon,* first published in *Ha-Shiloaḥ* 18 (1908): 9–19.
36. *Leqet Te'udot,* p. 98.
37. Ibid., p. 36.
38. Ibid., p. 103.
39. See Lissak 1981: 15.
40. League of Nations Mandate for Palestine together with a note by the Secretary-General relating to its Application in the Territory known as Trans-Jordan under the provision of Article 25 presented to Parliament by Command of His Majesty; December 1922.
41. See Bachi 1956.
42. According to Bachi, the estimated Jewish population of November 1914 was 85,000.
43. Bachi gives the Jewish population of November 1948 as 650,000.
44. Lissak 1981.
45. Ibid, p. 36.
46. For bibliography, see Rosén 1977: 238–49, and Glinert 1989: 571–78.

References

BACHI, REUVEN. "A Statistical Analysis of the Revival of Hebrew." *Scripta Hierosolymitana* 3 (1956): 179–247.

BAR-ADON, AHARON. "Language Revival." In U. Ummon, N. D. Dittmar, and K. I. Mattheier, eds. *Sociolinguistics: An International Handbook of the Science of Language and Society.* Vol. II Berlin-New York: Walter de Gruyter, 1988, pp. 1688–97.

BEN-ARIEH, Y. "Ukhlusiyat Eretz-Yisra'el ve-Yishuvah Erev Mif'al ha-Hityashvut ha-Tziyoni" (The Population of Eretz-Israel and its Settlement on the Eve of the Zionist Settlement). In Y. Ben-Arieh, Y. Ben-Artsi, H. Goren, eds. *Meḥkarim be-Geografyah Historit-Yishuvit shel Eretz-Yisra'el.* Jerusalem: Yad Ben-Zvi, 1988, pp. 1–15.

BEN-YAAKOV, A. "Ivrit ve-Aramit bi-Leshon Yehudei Bavel." (Hebrew and Aramaic Spoken by the Jews of Babylonia). Jerusalem: Ben-Zvi Institute, 1985.

BENVENISTI, D. *Milim Ivriyot bi-Sefaradit-Yehudit (Hebrew Words in Judeo-Spanish).* Jerusalem: Va'ad Adat ha-Sefaradim, 1985.

BLANC, HAIM. "Hebrew in Israel: Trends and Problems." *The Middle East Journal* 11 (1957): 397–409. Reprinted in Morag 1988: 167–79.

BUNIS, D. "A Comparative Linguistic Analysis of Judezmo and Yiddish." *International Journal of the Sociology of Language* 30 (1981): 49–71.

EVEN-ZOHAR, ITAMAR. "The Emergence of a Native Hebrew Culture." In I. Even-Zohar, *Polysystem Studies* (= *Poetics Today* 11,1). Durham, N.C.: Duke University Press, 1990.

GLINERT, LEWIS. *The Grammar of Modern Hebrew.* Cambridge: Cambridge University Press, 1989.

GOLD, DAVID L. *Jewish Linguistic Studies,* I. Haifa: Association for the Study of Jewish Languages, 1989.

IDELSOHN, AVRAHAM Z. "Yehudei Teiman u-Zemiroteihem" (The Jews of Yemen and Their Songs.) *Luaḥ Eretz-Yisra'el* 14, Jerusalem: Luncz Press, 1909: 101–126.

Leqet Te'udot le-Toldot Va'ad ha-Lashon ve-ha-Akademya la-Lashon ha-Ivrit (Collected Documentation on the History of the Language Committee and the Academy of the Hebrew Language). Jerusalem: Academy of the Hebrew Langauge, 1970.

LISSAK, M. *Ha-Elitot shel ha-Yishuv ha-Yehudi be-Eretz-Yisra'el bi-Tekufat ha-Mandat* (The Elites of the Jewish Population in Mandate Palestine). Tel Aviv: Am Oved, 1981.

LUNCZ, A. M. "Yerushalayim be-Arba'im Shanah ha-Aḥaronot" (Jerusalem in the Last Forty Years). In *Luaḥ Eretz-Yisra'el* 15, Jerusalem, 1910.

MANDEL, GEORGE. "*She'elah Nikhbadah* and the Revival of Hebrew." In E. Silberschlag, ed. *Eliezer Ben-Yehuda, A Symposium.* Oxford: Oxford Centre for Postgraduate Hebrew Studies, 1981, pp. 25–39. Reprinted in Morag 1988: 32–46.

MORAG, SHELOMO. "Planned and Unplanned Development in Modern Hebrew." *Lingua* 8 (1959): 247–63. Reprinted in Morag 1988: 181–97.

———. "Ha-Ivrit ke-Lashon Ivrit shel Tarbut: Tahalikhei Gibush u-Mesirah bi-Ymei ha-Beinayim (Hebrew as a Cultural Hebrew: Processes of Crystallization and Transmission in the Middle Ages). *Peamim* 23 (1985): 9–21.

———. "Avraham Tzevi Idelsohn u-Meḥkar Mivta'eha shel ha-Ivrit" (Avraham Zevi Idelsohn and the Study of Hebrew Pronunciations). *Yuval* 5 (1986): 160–68.

———. ed. *Ha-Ivrit Bat-Zmanenu—Meḥkarim ve-Iyunim* (Studies in Contemporary Hebrew). Jerusalem: Academon, 1988.

NEHAMA, J. *Dictionnaire du Judéo-Espagnol.* (avec la collaboration de Jésus Cantera), Madrid: Consejo superior de Investigaciones Científicas, 1977.

ORNAN, UZZI. "Hebrew in Palestine Before and After 1882." *Journal of Semitic Studies* 29 (1984): 225–54.

PARFITT, TUDOR V. "The Use of Hebrew in Palestine 1880–1882." *Journal of Semitic Studies* 17 (1972): 237–52.

———. "The Contribution of the Old Yishuv to the Revival of Hebrew." *Journal of Semitic Studies* 29 (1984): 255–65.

RABIN, CHAIM. "Mahuto shel ha-Dibur ha-Ivri she-Lifnei ha-Teḥiyah" (The Nature of pre-Revival Spoken Hebrew). *Leshonenu La'am* 26 (1975): 227–33.

———. "Ma Hayetah Teḥiyat ha-Lashon?" (What was the Language Revival?). In A. Even-Shoshan et al., eds. *Sefer Shalom Sivan.* Jerusalem: Kiryat Sefer, 1980, pp. 125–40. Reprinted in Morag 1988: 16–45.

———. "Language Revival and Language Death." In J. A. Fishman et al., eds. *The Fergusonian Impact.* Vol. 2. *Sociolinguistics and the Sociology of Language.* Berlin-New York-Amsterdam: Mouton-de Gruyter: 1986, pp. 543–54. Reprinted in Morag 1988 103–114.

RATZABY, YEHUDAH. *Otzar Leshon ha-Kodesh she-li-Vnei Teyman (A Treasury of Yemenite Hebrew).* Tel Aviv, 1978.

ROSÉN, HAYYIM B. *Contemporary Hebrew.* The Hague: Mouton, 1977.

SABAR, YONAH. "Ha-Yesodot ha-Ivriyim ba-Niv ha-Arami she-be-Fi Yehudei Zakho be-Kurdistan" (The Hebrew Elements in the Aramaic Dialect Spoken by the Jews of Zakho, Kurdistan). *Leshonenu* 38 (1974): 212–13.

SCHWARZ, J. *Sefer Tevu'ot ha-Aretz.* Jerusalem: Luncz Press, 1900.

SCHWARZWALD, ORA RODRIGUE. "Ha-Madadim le-Hitukhan shel ha-Milim ha-Ivriyot ve-ha-Aramiyot ba-Sefaradit ha-Yehudit" (Indices for the Fusion of Hebrew and Aramaic Words in Judeo-Español). *Meylat (Meḥkerei ha-Universitah ha-Petuḥah be-Toldot Yisra'el u-ve-Tarbuto)* 2 (Tel Aviv 1984): 357–67.

———. "Shloshah Bituyei Avar-Raḥok ba-Ivrit ha-Meduberet" (Three Preterite Expressions in Spoken Hebrew). *Leshonenu La'am* 38 (1986): 12–15.

SHAKED, GERSHON. *Ha-Siporet ha-Ivrit 1880–1970 (Hebrew Fiction 1880–1970)*. Vol 1. Tel Aviv: Keter & Hakibbutz Hameuchad, 1977.

SHUR, N. *Toldot Yerushalayim (History of Jerusalem)*. Vol. 3. Jerusalem, 1987.

SIVAN, REUVEN. *Ha-Ḥalom ve-Shivro (The Dream and its Interpretation)*. Jerusalem: The Bialik Institute, 1972.

SWIFT, J. F. *Going to Jericho, or Sketches of Travel in Spain and the East*. New York: A. Roman, 1868.

WARREN, CHARLES. *Underground Jerusalem*. London: R. Bentley, 1876.

14

Hebrew as a Holy Tongue: Franz Rosenzweig and the Renewal of Hebrew

PAUL MENDES-FLOHR

> Hebrew is anything but a dead language. It is not dead but, as the people themselves call it, a holy language.
>
> Franz Rosenzweig[1]

I

In early December 1929, the star of *Habimah,* the nascent Hebrew theater company, Hanna Rovina, visited Franz Rosenzweig.[2] The youthful and exhuberant representative of the revival of Hebrew was beckoned to the home of the gravely ill religious thinker who had become the focus of a spiritual renaissance of German Jewry. For more than seven years Rosenzweig was confined to his small attic apartment by a paralysis that left him bereft of the ability to move his limbs, to speak, or even to smile. Yet, as Rovina recalled, he communicated emotion through his powerfully expressive eyes, and with one finger that had not utterly atrophied he laboriously and ever so painfully communicated his thoughts on a specially constructed typewriter.[3]

The visit was arranged by Eugen Meyer, a leading member of the local Jewish community which sponsored several performances of the Habimah Theater, of which Rovina was a founding member, then on a tour of Europe.[4] Upon attending one of the performances Meyer was convinced that it would give Rosenzweig deep pleasure to hear a recitation in Rovina's mellifluous Hebrew, as indeed it did.

Rovina recited a passage from *Keter David* (David's Crown), a play written by the seventeenth-century Spanish dramatist Calderon de la Braca and adapted for the Hebrew stage by the poet Yitzhak Lamdan.[5] After Rovina's passionate recitation,[6] Rosenzweig indicated on his typewriter that he would like her to read from the Hebrew Bible the passage (2 Samuel 13) concerning David's son Amnon feigning sick to have his sister Tamar feed him and grace him with affectionate attention, and upon which the play was based.[7] Deeply moved, Rosenzweig's eyes filled with tears.[8] Upon Rovina's departure, Rosenzweig wrote her a poem expressing his gratitude. The poem, written in German, appropriately opened with a Hebrew verse from The Book of Samuel:

> havi'i ha-biryah ha-ḥeder ve-evreh mi-yadekh
> ("Bring the food into the chamber that I eat of your hand."
> 2 Samuel 13:10)

The poem alludes to the tears he—and his seven-year-old son, Rafael—shed during Rovina's recitation. Rosenzweig also alludes to the Hebrew word—*biryah* ("food, refreshment")—which he also understood as meaning a purgation, a catharsis.[9] The poem reads:

> Du brachtest in die enge Stube mir
> Jene Erquickung, tragische Läuterung,
> Mit der du draussen Tausende erquickst.
> Der Vater war erschüttert und der Sohn.
> Der aber, tränenüberströmt, verliess
> In zornesflammendem Protest den Raum.
> Also erneuernd dir den Urerfolg
> Des Trauerspiels, des allerältesten:
> Des Thespis Stück "Einnahme von Milet"
> Erregte die Athensche Bürgerschaft
> So, dass—den Dichter sie in Strafe nahm.
> Urenkelkind du unsres alten Stamms,
> Urahnin du hebräischen Trauerspiels,
> Dank, dass erquickt ich ward aus deiner Hand![10]

> You have brought into my narrow room
> That refreshment, tragic catharsis,
> With which you regale thousands outside.
> The father was deeply moved and so was the son.
> But the latter, his tears streaming, left
> The room, protesting angrily.
> Thus renewing for you the triumph
> Of the most ancient of all tragedies:
> Thespis' play, The Fall of Miletus,
> So incensed the Athenian citizenry
> That it arrested the poet.
> Scion of our old race,
> Founder of Hebrew tragedy,
> Thanks for the refreshment I received at your hand.[11]

The poem was to be Rosenzweig's last creative piece of writing. Two days after having sent it to Rovina,[12] he took ill with pneumonia, dying four days later, early in the morning of December 10, 1929.

II

The emotions—the veritable catharsis—evoked by Rovina's recitation reflected Rosenzweig's deep love of Hebrew and the joy he took in the revival of his people's ancient tongue. Indeed, he regarded the revival of Hebrew—of the Jew's active knowledge of the language—as essential to the renewal of Judaism as a spiritual and religious culture. Yet Rosenzweig was no Zionist. He had profound reservations about both the political and cultural program of Zionism. Rosenzweig's affection for Hebrew reaches back to his youth. When he was a lad of eleven he brought home a stunning report card, and his duly delighted father, eager to reward his son, asked him what he would like most. The young Rosenzweig replied: "Hebrew lessons!" His somewhat puzzled father complied, and arranged a special tutor for his son.[13] At the age of twenty—seven years before his "discovery" of the spiritual power of Judaism and his momentous decision not to convert to Christianity—he renewed his study of Hebrew, this time apparently on his own. In a letter of March 1906, he announced to a friend: "I already started [studying] Hebrew several days ago, and right now I again know what I used to know."[14]

The humanistic education Rosenzweig received as a youth inculcated an appreciation of classical languages; by the time he graduated the Friedrichsgymnasium of Kassel in 1905 he had mastered Greek and Latin.[15] When he contemplated conversion to Christianity, he read the New Testament in the Koine Greek, referring to the Vulgate Latin translation of St. Jerome.[16] Rosenzweig obviously enjoyed the study of languages and had a decided knack for them.[17] As a teenager with the aid of special tutors he gained a good command of English and French.[18] Later when he studied with the philosopher Hermann Cohen the writings of Maimonides, he felt that he could not adequately understand the great medieval philosopher unless he could read him in the original Arabic.[19] So he set out to learn Arabic, which he assiduously studied. This was also true when he studied Talmud; he seems to have devoured every available Aramaic grammar. His affection for Hebrew, however, reflects more than his omnivorous appetite for languages.

Since his youth he seems to have had the strong intuition that Hebrew is the heart of Judaism, that it was the bedrock of Jewish knowledge and spirituality. Hence, when in 1918 he reversed his decision to become a Christian and resolved to remain a Jew—but a pious Jew—it was only natural that he would devote his immediate efforts to attaining full sovereignty in Hebrew in all its various expressions: biblical, talmudic, or liturgical and philosophical.[20] He was quite emphatic that the Jew qua Jew could only gain access to the spiritual universe of Judaism through Hebrew. "The Jew can understand [the Bible]," he insisted in an essay he wrote in March 1917 as a soldier on the Balkan front, "only in Hebrew." True, Rosenzweig concedes, with respect to biblical ideals and values shared with Germans, the Jew could read the Bible in German translation, but when it comes to Jewish prayer it is otherwise. "The language of Jewish prayer we may state quite categorically . . . cannot be translated."[21] Even should the Jew only have a reading knowledge of Hebrew, he explained in a letter to Gershom Scholem, "the uncomprehended Hebrew gives him more than the finest translation. There is no getting away from it. Jewish prayer means praying in Hebrew."[22]

The failure of the German Jewish community to engage the hearts and minds of its members Rosenzweig ascribed precisely to its reliance on translation and its loss of Hebrew literacy:

> How senseless and unsuitable is it . . . to send Jewish children into life knowing the primary expressions of their faith only in translation! Language and meaning are co-

related, and we underestimate the intimate relation existing, even before Luther, between Christianity and the German language, if we think that Jewish contents can be clothed in German language without admitting content that is foreign to them. This becomes worse if the memory is filled with such material.[23]

To be sure, Rosenzweig was not the first to be distressed by the sorry state of German Jewry, and the increasing failure to engender among the young Jewish passion and loyalty. The quality of contemporary Jewish education was continuously debated. Reviewing the protocol of a conference of the German Rabbinical Assembly which took place in the summer of 1916,[24] he realized that German Jewish education was in disarray not so much because of a lack of a sophisticated leadership—he was pleasingly surprised by the high level of the proceedings—but by a neglect of Hebrew. "The debate on Jewish education," he wrote his parents who sent him on the battlefront a copy of the protocol, betrayed "a nonproductive anarchy": "The attitude toward Hebrew is the sore point, far more than the debate itself brought out. For Hebrew must be pursued not as the subject of study, but as the very medium through which the entire content of [Judaism] is presented."[25]

These thoughts led to his addressing an open letter to Hermann Cohen on the subject of Jewish education, containing a proposal for a radical restructuring of Jewish instruction.[26] He entitled the essay, "It Is Time," alluding to Psalm 119:126: "It is time to work for the Lord: They have made void Thy teachings."[27] In this essay, Rosenzweig proposed a far-reaching revision of Jewish education in Germany, emphasizing the centrality of Hebrew. As in his letter to his parents, he stressed that "the study of Hebrew is not [the] aim, but rather the necessary means."[28]

In his proposed program that, adhering to a model of religious instruction then prevailing in Germany, would be integrated into the curriculum of the secular schools and follow a nine year schedule, Rosenzweig envisioned Hebrew as being learned incrementally through the study of the fundamental texts of Jewish religious life. Clearly inspired by the instruction of the *ḥeder,* the traditional Jewish primary school he observed during his sojourn as a soldier in Eastern Europe,[29] he held that the young should not be introduced to the language through vocabulary lists and grammar. "The traditional method, in spite of the drawbacks . . . has an advantage which should not be underestimated: the student is not introduced to a dead grammatical structure, but learns, by its actual use, the Holy Tongue as a living language." Hence, when the student is to be taught grammar, one may assume that he or she already possesses a certain implicit knowledge of the subject. Indeed, Rosenzweig notes, "this is just the difference between learning the grammar of one's mother language and that of a foreign tongue. . . ."[30]

Knowledge of Hebrew is thus to be acquired through an "osmotic" encounter with the literary sources of Judaism. As such, Rosenzweig contended, German Jewish youth would cease to learn *about* Judaism—an exercise which perforce entails "translating" it into, thus nervously defending it before, alien thought patterns[31]—but encounter it, so to speak, naturally as the ongoing spiritual discourse of the Jewish people. To participate in this discourse, of course, a knowledge of Hebrew is essential.[32]

Rosenzweig's program for the revamping of the education of German Jewish youth was at best only partially adopted. He himself would devote his prodigious energy to adult Jewish education. In Frankfurt-am-Main, he established in 1920 the *Freies Jüdisches Lehrhaus,* which was directed to those who failed to gain adequate Jewish religious instruction in their youth. Again his model was classical Jewish learning; indeed, *Lehrhaus*—an odd locution in German—was meant as a translation of the traditional *beit midrash,* a house of study in which all Jews, irrespective of their age or station, would study Torah. Accordingly, the focus of Rosenzweig's *Lehrhaus* would be texts, the literary sources of Judaism. Rather than passively listening to lectures dispensing predigested information about Judaism, students at the *Lehrhaus* would be actively engaged in the process of Jewish learning, allowing themselves to be personally challenged by the texts of the tradition. In the process of authentic Jewish learning, Rosenzweig underscored, knowledge of Hebrew was critical.

But Rosenzweig also realized that the prevailing circumstances required some compromise. Given the difficulties faced by adults learning languages, and their eagerness to get into the heart of things, Rosenzweig could only insist on as much Hebrew as possible.[33] Translations were used but with the Hebrew text always at hand. The *Lehrhaus* also provided more conventional courses in Hebrew-language instruction. Until his illness no longer allowed, Rosenzweig himself took charge of these courses, teaching all three levels: beginners, intermediate, and advanced.[34] The teaching of Hebrew gave him special gratification.[35] He once gleefully remarked: "In the elementary Hebrew course, you have to fight for every student."[36]

Three features of his language instruction seem noteworthy. First, his courses were based on classical texts, selected according to the level of the class.[37] Second, he seems to have believed that ultimately a sound command of Hebrew grammar was crucial for a proper knowledge of the language.[38] Third, he taught—and insisted that instructors at the *Lehrhaus* follow suit[39]—the Ashkenazi pronunciation instead of the Sephardi one sponsored by Zionism.[40]

In spite of his distance from Zionism, Rosenzweig sought to have the Hebrew poet Hayim Nahman Bialik teach a seminar on his poetry in Hebrew at the *Lehrhaus.*[41] Unfortunately, Bialik's schedule did not allow him to accept the invitation. Rosenzweig was, however, more successful in soliciting the Hebrew novelist S. Y. Agnon, who at the time resided in a suburb of Frankfurt before returning to Palestine, to teach at the *Lehrhaus* in the spring of 1922.[42] At Rosenzweig's behest Agnon conducted the course in Hebrew (presumably in a Sephardi pronunciation). Rosenzweig greatly admired Agnon's writing, especially because of his uncanny ability to weave into his emphatically modern narrative various strata of Classical Hebrew.[43] In homage to Rosenzweig, already confined to his home by an increasingly debilitating paralysis, one of the sessions was held in his attic apartment.[44] Agnon read from a collection of his stories, "The Legend of the Scribe" *(Agadat ha-Sofer),* which he subsequently discussed with the students in Hebrew. Rosenzweig was profoundly disappointed by the inability of the students to express themselves adequately in Hebrew, although they each claimed to be a Hebraist. He did acknowledge that they may have been too shy and intimidated by the august representative of modern Hebrew.[45] "Nevertheless," as one of the participants in the seminar has testified, "the contact with the living Hebrew language and with one already eminent Hebrew authority was an unforgettable event in the history of the *Lehrhaus*."⁴⁶ Rosenzweig undoubtedly shared these sentiments.

III

Rosenzweig's affirmation of the centrality of Hebrew in Jewish life was eminently more than a matter of mere sentiment, however—it had a theoretical basis born of both sociological and theological considerations. True to the Hegelian underpinnings of his thought, both these aspects—the sociological and theological (or metaphysical)—are interlaced and dialectically interrelated, conflating into a protest against all attempts to reduce Judaism to the "civil religion" of the Jews. Civil religion, of course, is a contemporary term unknown to Rosenzweig; he spoke of the danger of an "atheistic theology"—the tendency (shared with many Christians in the modern world) to remove God in all but name from one's religious consciousness, projecting onto the exalted altar formerly occupied by the Almighty the community's values, self-image, and even interests.⁴⁷ To fend off this danger, Rosenzweig advocated inter alia the reintroduction of Hebrew—qua holy tongue, it should be emphasized—as the language of Jewish imagination and passion.

The sociological considerations informing this position were most forcefully articulated in Rosenzweig's analysis of the state of Jewish religious education in Germany. It was mistaken, he held, to regard the problem of Jewish education as identical to that of religious education in general. For Christians the problem of religious education is to provide "an emotional center"⁴⁸ for the society in which the pupil lives, to lend emotional support to the values and ideas to which one is introduced through other subjects taught at school. Christian religious instruction thus serves to strengthen one's emotional bond to the society and culture in which one lives; in a word, religious instruction is in effect an educational adjunct to the prevailing "civil religion." This cannot, Rosenzweig protests, be the role of Jewish education.

Jewish education, Rosenzweig argued, must seek to introduce the Jewish pupil and student into a "Jewish sphere," a reality which, by definition, is not Christian and thus apart from, indeed, often opposed to, the surrounding society, its values and self-image. Yet, of course, since the Emancipation the Jew is intimately part of the surrounding society. It would be foolish to deny this fact, or to seek to sever the bond the Jew has with, in this case, German culture and society. How is the Jew, then, to lay claim to the contrasting Jewish world without rejecting his or her attachment to the surrounding non-Jewish reality?

Clearly, Rosenzweig argued, the whole strategy of Jewish education must be different from that of a Christian education. In devising this strategy it must also be noted that in fostering the Jew's integration into non-Jewish society the Emancipation often led to the attenuation of the Jew's tie to a specifically Jewish world. All that is left for most modern Jews is some vague affiliation to the synagogue:

> ... Those Jews with whom we are dealing have abandoned the Jewish character of
> the home [i.e, the Jewish social reality outside school] some time during the past

three generations, and therefore for them that "Jewish sphere" exists only in the synagogue. Consequently, the task of Jewish religious instruction is to re-create that emotional tie between the institutions of public worship and the individual, that is, the very tie which he has lost.[49]

The recreation of this tie requires, in the first instance, that the Jew recognize the "Jewish sphere" as being utterly apart from the world of his or her everyday, "non-Jewish" cultural and social reality.

Accordingly, Rosenzweig observed, one does not enter the Jewish world simply by acquiring Jewish knowledge, and by adding to one's library a shelf of Judaica aside the works of Goethe, Kant, and Hölderlin. For "to possess a world does not mean to possess it within another world which includes its possessor"[50]—one does not simply make room in one's existing world for Judaism. It is not a question of extending one's *Kultur* to include Jewish knowledge.

Hence, Rosenzweig warned, it would be amiss for Jewish educators and all those intent on promoting Jewish renewal to seek to smuggle Judaism into the heart and mind of the Jew through the ideal of *Bildung*—an ideal that so enchanted emancipated Jewry[51]—which encourages in the name of intellectual and spiritual cultivation a cosmopolitan—or rather a syncretistic—pluralism:

> The [cultivated] German may possess another civilization—ancient or modern—insofar as it also belongs to the spiritual world which includes him; he can therefore acquire it without leaving his own world, maybe even without understanding its language; because in any event he will understand it only as translated into the "language" of his world; and experience has always shown that knowledge of the words of a language does not necessarily imply possession of its civilization.[52]

As a world unto its own, Rosenzweig taught, Judaism has a soul of its own, "a language of its own."[53] Herein is the significance of Hebrew—but surely not in the mere technical sense. Hebrew is more than a linguistic instrument by which a given people communicate with one another: it is the vessel bearing the Jewish soul.

At this juncture, Rosenzweig's sociological argument merges with his theological considerations for asserting the centrality of Hebrew. As the bearer of Israel's "soul," he averred, Hebrew is intimately and indissolubly linked to the sacred literature of the Jews: this literature is the numinous ground that nurtures Hebrew and gives it life, but a life that is distinct from that of all of other languages. Hebrew is a holy tongue animated by the breath of eternity. And it is through Hebrew as a holy language that the Jewish people gains its life as a holy people, as an eternal people. "The language of the eternal people," Rosenzweig says somewhat cryptically in *The Star of Redemption,* "drives it back to its own life which is beyond external life, [and] which courses through the veins of its living body and is, therefore, eternal."[54]

IV

During the first year of the *Lehrhaus* Rosenzweig delivered a series of lectures in which he explored "the spirit of Hebrew" and the sources of its holiness.[55] Alas, these lectures, simply but undoubtedly for an assimilated Jewish audience disarmingly entitled "Our Language,"[56] were not published, perhaps because Rosenzweig never developed them beyond the oral presentation. Only some fragmentary notes remain, but his thesis is therein clearly stated: rather than the spirit of Hebrew, one should speak of "the spirit of God that is poured into the vessel of the language created to receive it."[57] God's revealed Torah thus "speaks in the language of human beings." Hebrew is, then, not divine speech;[58] it is not intrinsically holy—as some Kabbalists contend. Hebrew is rather sanctified by God's gracious decision to sound His word through it. Detached from the divine word, Hebrew would presumably forfeit its sanctity.

Hebrew is, nonetheless, uniquely suited to serve as the language of revelation. In meeting this task, Rosenzweig argues, Hebrew is supported by its distinctive grammatical structure, which is oriented to the "flow of time" in contrast to the Greek focus on "a point in time."[59] Thus the Greek emphasis on nature, the Jewish on history. "In nature, as in the 'scientific' chronological history [of the Greeks], everything has a place, and one asks when?, where?"[60] And this when and where, Rosenzweig observes, lend themselves "to be lifted into a Platonic realm of meta-time and meta-space."[61] In contrast, Hebrew is always concretely historical, the past is "already" was *(schon)* or "still" to come *(noch)*. "This 'no longer' *(nicht mehr)*, this 'not yet' *(noch nicht)* are the great agitators in the clock of world history. This is the language of the prophets, for whom the future is not a somewhere, but *not yet to be*...."[62]

Hebrew is thus uniquely able to project the vision of a messianic future of the unity of humankind in history. Thus while scholarly opinion no longer allows one to speak of Hebrew as "the primal language of the human race,"[63] it is the language that bears both God's revelation and prophetic promise of redemption.[64]

The holiness of Hebrew, Rosenzweig argued elsewhere, gains its dialectic fullness only with the exile of the people of Israel.[65] In dispersion, Hebrew ceased to be a language of daily life and became a language exclusively of prayer and matters of the spirit. Exile severed—or rather freed—Hebrew from its erstwhile mundane tasks, obliging the Jews to learn secular, foreign tongues in order to make their way in the world. But "the holiness of the people's own language,"[66] which remained part of their consciousness as long as they prayed, perforce estranged them from the languages they speak. Thus, "the Jew feels always he is in a foreign land, and knows that [his] home ... is in the region of the holy language, a region everyday speech can never invade."[67]

This consciousness, Rosenzweig taught, accentuates the Jews' feeling of apartness, not so much from the peoples among whom they dwell, but from mundane, secular spheres of human action and imagination. "The holiness of the people's own language ... does not allow all their feeling to be lavished on everyday life. It prevents the eternal people from ever being quite in harmony with the times."[68] This holy dissonance has a messianic significance: it rivets the Jews to a time and space beyond the temporality and divisiveness of the mundane order, and as such the Jews are the custodians of the promise of eternity and a time free from the wiles of the finite existence of peoples locked in history and secular ambition.[69]

Although sequestered from the wiles of secular time, Rosenzweig underscored, Hebrew is hardly a dead language. It is not a frozen sacerdotal language; it still flows through the soul of the Jews, informing their everyday speech, lending it expressions, and even shaping the various secular vernaculars—Yiddish, Ladino—created by the Jews during their two-millennia-long sojourn in the Diaspora. Indeed, "the holiness of the Hebrew language never signified holiness in the original sense of 'seclusion,' a meaning which has been overcome by classical Judaism."[70] Creative spiritual life of the Jews continued to unfold in Hebrew, and the language continued to grow, gaining nourishment from the languages the Jews adopted during their journeys through history.

As a holy language, Hebrew retained a distinct vitality. How to restore this vitality in an age when so many Jews have lost all knowledge of the language was what inter alia divided Rosenzweig and Zionism. New life, he conceded, may be given to Hebrew through rebirth as a secular language—but, he warned, it would be a life that would, paradoxically, ensure its ultimate death. For languages, like peoples, that seek to tie their fortune to secular destiny face the decree that is in store for all that are bound to profane existence.

V

Rosenzweig acknowledged the sincerity and depth of the Zionist commitment to revivifying Hebrew, but he was dubious whether it was possible to secularize Hebrew and even if the Zionists should succeed in rendering the holy tongue a language like all languages, whether it would at all be a Jewish language in anything but name and origin. "The Zionists," he once sarcastically observed, "get more excited about a menu in modern Hebrew than they do about all the psalms and prophets taken together...."[71]

A review of a Hebrew translation of Spinoza's *Ethics* was the occasion of Rosenzweig's most sustained reflection on the Zionist project to secularize Hebrew.[72] The translation, issued in 1925 by the Hebrew publisher Abraham Joseph Stiebel of Leipzig, was rendered by Jacob Klatzkin (1882–1948). As a proponent of Zionism as a movement restoring to the Jewish people a "normal" national existence, Klatzkin advocated the radical secularization of Jewish life and culture. Only a clear and utter break with the past and the traditional conceptions of Jewish spiritual uniqueness, he held, could assure the "normalization"—the psychic and social health—of the people. For Klatzkin, a normal or healthy national existence was defined by the purely formal attributes of land and language; the return of the Jews to their ancestral land and the revival of Hebrew as their vernacular, everyday language were thus to be solely formal acts, free of all religious and spiritual content.[73]

Rosenzweig wryly observes that in his translation Klatzkin betrays his ideology that Hebrew should be freed from its past and rendered a "normal" national language nurtured solely by contemporary, secular experience. A true master of Hebrew, Rosenzweig noted, Klatzkin drew upon the vocabulary of medieval Jewish philosophy, in accordance with his view that Spinoza was not only familiar with this terminology but had actually thought in it before presenting his thoughts in Latin. Concurring with Klatzkin on this point, Rosenzweig endorsed his claim that his Hebrew translation of the *Ethics* had the unique distinction of "being more original than the original itself."[74] Rosenzweig further observes that Klatzkin's decision to employ classical philosophical Hebrew dictated the use of other classical terms, many of which bear the theological presuppositions of traditional Judaism. Hence, Rosenzweig ironically notes, "in the very camp of the enemy, at the very heart of the 'geometric' method, the spirit of revelation . . . manages to break through."[75]

Klatzkin's translation, Rosenzweig concludes, thus serves to disclose the impossibility of a genuine secularization of the Holy Tongue. Hebrew resists being released from its spiritual moorings. Even the various hybrid languages that the Jews have devised in their exile—Yiddish, Ladino, Judeo-Arabic—"lack the essential characteristic of profane vitality: complete dedication to the present moment."[76] This is all the more so for Hebrew; hence, "one cannot simply speak Hebrew as one would like to: one must speak it as it is. And it is tied up with the past."[77] The various strata—biblical, rabbinic, medieval, modern—of the language flow into one another, forming an organic whole. One cannot read Klatzkin's Spinoza or even a Hebrew daily without tapping the varied layers of the language. "To read Hebrew implies a readiness to assume the total heritage of the language."[78]

Hebrew, according to Rosenzweig, thus has the unique characteristic that it can survive neither as a purely profane language drawing its power from the here and now, nor as a purely sacerdotal language, reserved for the liturgy and sacred texts. In "the Jewish reality," Rosenzweig comments, it is a general principle that "something holy that wants to turn its back upon everything profane is made profane, and the profane quality of the first day hastens toward the seventh which will make it holy."[79]

From these observations Rosenzweig draws a warning: "If the new Hebrew, the Hebrew spoken in Palestine, should set out to evade the law of Jewish destiny, it might indeed achieve its purpose theoretically, but it would have to bear the consequences," the demise of the Jewish people, even as a "normal" nation.[80] These same apprehensions were echoed from within the Zionist movement by Gershom Scholem (1897–1982), not insignificantly in a letter to Rosenzweig.

VI

On the occasion of Rosenzweig's fortieth birthday in December 1926, Scholem wrote a letter recording his reflections on the "actualization" of Hebrew in Palestine.[81] Having settled in Jerusalem in 1923, Scholem confirmed Rosenzweig's fears that the revival of Hebrew was "fraught with danger." Alluding to Rosenzweig's essay on Klatzkin,[82] Scholem concurs that Hebrew cannot endure secularization:

> Many believe that the language has been secularized, and the apocalyptic thorn has been pulled out. But this is not true at all. The secularization of the language is only a *façon de parler,* a phrase! It is impossible to empty out words which are filled to the breaking point with specific meanings—lest it be done at the sacrifice of the language itself!"

Yet what is evolving in Palestine, Scholem testifies, is a "ghastly gibberish," "a faceless lingo." Scholem faults those Zionist enthusiasts who initiated the attempted secularization of the Holy Tongue. They were, he contends, impelled by an utter naiveté. "That was their good fortune! Nobody with clear foresight would have mustered the demonic courage to try to utilize a language in a situation in which only an Esperanto could have been created"—that is, a purely secularized language, bereft of memory and a sacred tradition. But Hebrew, Scholem asserts, is not given to such a spiritual lobotomy; it cannot repress the "treasures" and "religious power" hidden within it. The language, Scholem assures Rosenzweig, will, therefore, turn against its speakers:

> Language is Name. In the name rests the power of language.... We have no right to conjure up the old names day by day without calling forward their hidden power. These names [with their hidden power] will appear, since we have called upon them, and undoubtedly they will with a vengeance!... Each word which is not newly created, but taken from the good old treasures, is ready to burst. A generation which accepts the most fruitful of our holy traditions—our language—cannot simply live without tradition even if it would fervently wish to.... God will not remain silent in the language in which He affirmed our life a thousand times and more.

Scholem concludes his missive to Rosenzweig with a guarded wish: "May it come to pass that the imprudence *(Leichtsinn)* that has led us on this apocalyptic road not end in ruin."

Despite his apprehensions and even misgivings about the "nihilism" of the pioneers of modern Hebrew,[83] Scholem viewed the secularization of Judaism as dialectically necessary, indeed urgent. This belief was the basis of his Zionism. Secularization—the rejuvenation of Hebrew, the return of the Jews as well as their religious sensibility to history—was exigently required in order to wrench Judaism from the deadening grip of a spiritually desiccated Orthodoxy on the one hand, and a vacuous assimilation on the other. Though fraught with danger, secularization was the only path leading to the renewal of Judaism as a compelling religious reality.

We have no record of Rosenzweig's response to Scholem's letter. He undoubtedly appreciated the subtlety of Scholem's position, if not on ideological and theological grounds, certainly emotionally. Many of his closest associates and disciples were Zionists who were clearly motivated by genuine religious concern. Hence, in his later years Rosenzweig seems to have modified his opposition to Zionism, preferring to call himself a "non-Zionist."[84] In a series of letters to Rabbi Benno Jacob, published under the title "Letters of a Non-Zionist to an Anti-Zionist," he took the liberal rabbi to task for his doctrinaire rejection of Zionism.[85] As with all other political and cultural movements, Rosenzweig argues, one must assess its merits not only according to its ideology but also, indeed, primarily, by its deeds. One should, therefore, not judge Zionism by "the standards of its extreme theoreticians. What I mean is that Zionism must not be judged by the theories of Klatzkin...."[86] When viewed in terms of its concrete achievements one must admit that Zionism has created the conditions for veritable renaissance of Jewish religious life:

> As for Tel Aviv, the "town of speculators," which most Zionists view as a questionable Zionist achievement—I cannot help being impressed by the fact that all stores there close from *kiddush* to *havdalah* [i.e., from the commencement of the Sabbath on Friday evening to its conclusion on Saturday evening], and that thus, at any rate, the mold into which the content of the Sabbath can flow is provided. Where could

we find that here [in Frankfurt]! Where could you, or one of your liberal colleagues, find so excellent an opportunity for crowded pews. And when I hear how the pupils read the Bible in the Biram School [i.e., the Hebrew secondary school founded by Arthur Biram in Haifa], a typically nationalistic institution, I shudder at the thought of the religious instruction we offer our children.[87]

Hence, in spite of his abiding theological reservations regarding Zionism, Rosenzweig manifested a tolerant, even affectionate attitude to Zionists who abandoned bourgeois aspirations and devoted themselves to the creation in Palestine of a new Hebrew culture. Typical perhaps is the tale of Ernst Simon, one of his closest disciples. When in the spring of 1928 Simon and his young wife had set the date of their aliyah (immigration to Palestine), Simon hesitated to tell Rosenzweig, knowing that it meant they would never see one another again. Finally and with great apprehension he told him. Noting Simon's perplexity, Rosenzweig sought to comfort him with his characteristic "mixture of faith and humor." He requested his typewriter, and with excruciating effort indicated the letters which his wife then dutifully combined into the following message: "Just as for sociology there is only one excuse—a knowledge of many facts—so there is but one excuse for Zionism—to go to Palestine."[88]

As a parting gift, Rosenzweig gave Simon a copy of a recently published Hebrew volume,[89] with a dedication, a poem in Hebrew.[90] The poem, apparently the only one Rosenzweig ever wrote in the Holy Tongue, refers to the Talmud lessons Simon regularly read with him during the years of his illness:

תורה וחקיה מגדיך: מקרא וסודיה עדניך:
משנה ורזיה לאחיך: תלמוד וקשיותיה לבניך:
שמאי וגם הלל חבריך: יוסי ורב אסי שכניך:

Torah and its Laws are your precious things;[91]
Scripture and its secrets are your delicacies.
Mishnah and its mysteries are your brethren;
Talmud and its secrets are your children.
Shammai and also Hillel are your companions;
Jose and Rav Issi are your neighbors.

These words of gratitude were perhaps also a gentle reminder to Simon that he should not forget the true ground of Hebrew culture as he embarked to participate in the Zionist adventure.

VII

Rosenzweig's increasingly conciliatory attitude toward Zionism seems to have been determined by his deepening attachment to Hebrew, and his realization that the Zionism could not be understood—and dismissed—in terms of its political program and nationalistic fantasies alone. The truth of Zionism, as we have noted, was for him also reflected in the deeds of its adherents.[92]

Given his fierce criticism of "translated Judaism,"[93] Rosenzweig's romance with Hebrew found paradoxical expression in his work at translation. Together with Buber he undertook a new translation of the Hebrew Scriptures, he translated the traditional Hebrew grace after meals *(Birkat Ha-Mazon),* the Friday night service, select prayers from the Hebrew liturgy, and the poetry of the medieval Spanish Hebrew poet, Judah Halevi.[94] In these translations, experimenting with various techniques, he sought to allow the distinctive voice of the original Hebrew to echo in the German, with the ultimate intent of enticing the reader to turn to the original. Translation was, then, a didactic, provisional exercise—but, as Rosenzweig once confessed, an exercise that was necessary even for one, like himself, who knew Hebrew. With respect to his translation of Judah Halevi, he wrote to a friend, "the book is . . . meant for people who know no Hebrew—which includes, as I can tell from my own experience, most of those who 'know Hebrew.' I myself understand a poem only after I have translated it. . . ."[95] As he further explained to Scholem in a letter accompanying his translation of the grace after meals, ". . . we ourselves are guests at our own table, we ourselves. I myself. So long as we speak German . . . we cannot avoid this detour that again and again leads us the hard way from what is alien back to our own. All we have is the certainty that ultimately it will lead us there. An 'ultimately' that of course can arrive at any moment. Otherwise it would surely be unbearable. . . ."[96]

Adding to the paradox was his desire to see his own work translated into Hebrew. On the 14th of July 1922, four months after his illness was diagnosed and believing his death was imminent, he wrote in his diary an addendum to his last will and testament: ". . . I am asking my wife to remember that I fervently wish to have *The Star of Redemption* translated into Hebrew. I am also asking her not to spare considerable expense if she finds a translator. . . ."[97]

Despite the prognosis of his physicians, Rosenzweig somehow lived longer than expected, and endured for close to eight years. With miraculous effort—and with the aid of his special typewriter, faithful friends, and especially the selfless devotion of his wife—he continued his creative life. During these years he also oversaw the first attempt to translate *The Star* into Hebrew. The Jerusalem Hebraist, Joseph Rivlin, at the time teaching in Frankfurt, made some sample translation which pleased Rosenzweig greatly.[98]

Alas, the project, eventually undertaken by another Jerusalem scholar, Yehoshua Amir, only came to fruition in 1970, long after Rosenzweig's death.[99] He was, however, privileged to see one of his essays in Hebrew print. Five months before he passed away, he received page proofs of a Hebrew translation of his introduction to Hermann Cohen's Jewish writings.[100] In response he wrote:

> It gives me such fiendish pleasure to see myself in the beloved twenty-two letters [of Hebrew], that nothing else seems to matter.[101]

Notes

1. Franz Rosenzweig, *The Star of Redemption,* trans. William W. Hallo (New York: Holt, Rinehart & Winston, 1970), p. 302.

2. Nahum N. Glatzer, *Franz Rosenzweig, His Life and Thought,* 2d. rev. ed. (New York: Schocken Books, 1961), p. 171.

3. Cf. interview with Hanna Rovina broadcast on the Israel State Radio in which she

reminisced about her visit to Franz Rosenzweig: "Hanna Rovina mesaparet al Franz Rosenzweig." *Kol Yisrael,* November 14, 1972. I wish to thank Mr. Rafael Rosenzweig for bringing this interview to my attention and for providing me with a tape of it.

4. Ibid. This was actually Rovina's second visit to Rosenzweig. During Habimah's tour of Germany the previous winter, and a series of performances in Frankfurt in January 1928, Eugen Meyer first arranged for Rovina to visit the ailing philosopher. See letter from Eugen Meyer to his wife, Hebe Meyer, January 22, 1928, in which he describes in detail the meeting between Rovina and Rosenzweig. I wish to thank Mr. Rafael Rosenzweig for providing me with a transcript of this letter, now deposited in the Rosenzweig family archives in the care of Mr. R. Rosenzweig, Tel Aviv. In her aforementioned interview (note 3), Rovina seems to conflate the visits of 1928 and 1929. According to Meyer's letter, written on the very night of Rovina's first visit, she recited on that occasion from *The Eternal Jew (Ha-Yehudi ha-Nizhi),* by the Russian Yiddish writer David Pinsky, and adapted for the Hebrew stage by Ezrahi-Kryszewsky. In her interview Rovina recalls having recited for Rosenzweig the passage from the play when the Messiah's young mother (played by Rovina in countless productions of the play) hears of the destruction of Jerusalem, a particularly dramatic passage in which she issues a prolonged wail. This passage is considered one of the great moments of Hebrew theater. "Many people who heard it years ago still recall the shiver that went down their spines when they heard that lament which seemed to express the suffering to come to the Jewish people in a future life of dispersion." Mendel Kohanski, *The Hebrew Theatre* (Jerusalem: Israel University Press, 1969), p. 32. Rovina recalled being so moved by the occasion that she got lost in the recitation, and when finishing, she opened her eyes and saw Rosenzweig crying. Meyer also noted how deeply moved Rosenzweig was by Rovina's stirring recitation. According to him, she also read in Hebrew from Psalm 137 ("By the rivers of Babylon"), and passages from The Song of Songs. As a spontaneous expression of gratitude, Meyer reported, Rosenzweig gave Rovina his "favorite, old Bible." In a card to Rafael Rosenzweig, dated June 15, 1972, Rovina told him that she still had the Bible his father gave her.

5. Calderon's play itself was called *The Hair of Absalom* (Los cabellos de Absalon). In his Hebrew rendition Lamdan introduced far-reaching changes, in which, inter alia, the incestuous relations between Amnon and his sister Tamar, only hinted at in Calderon's version, were central and, for the time, shockingly explicit. See Kohanski, *Hebrew Theatre,* pp. 117–18. I should like to thank Dr. Freddie Rokem of the Theater Department, Tel Aviv University, for clarifying aspects of Habimah's repertoire and tour of Germany in 1928 and 1929.

6. This is an interpolation from Rovina's interview, in which—as indicated in note 4—she apparently conflates both visits to Rosenzweig. In her radio interview (see note 3) she recalls her impassioned rendering of the dramatic monologue of the Messiah's mother from Pinsky's *The Eternal Jew* and the effect it had on Rosenzweig; this occurred during her first meeting. But Rovina also mentions in the interview, as part of the same experience, the poem (which refers to Rosenzweig and his son crying) that Rosenzweig wrote to her in response to her second visit and recitation from *Keter David.* It would seem that on both occasions Rosenzweig was brought to tears.

7. Glatzer, *Franz Rosenzweig,* p. 171.

8. Interview with Hanna Rovina (see note 3); again this is my interpolation, the basis of which I explain in note 6. The content of the poem Rosenzweig wrote to Rovina also lends credence to this interpolation.

9. Cf. Rosenzweig's letter to Buber, December 6, 1929, then a house guest of Rosenzweig's mother, that he explain to her the meaning of the poem: "I enclose the poem so that you may explain to my mother the point *biryah,* catharsis." *Rosenzweig, der Mensch und sein Werk. Gesammelte Schriften.* Part 1: *Briefe und Tagebücher,* ed. Rachel Rosenzweig and Edith Rosenzweig-Scheinmann, in collaboration with Bernhard Casper (The Hague: Martinus Nijhoff, 1979), 2:1236. This reading of the term *biryah* is novel to Rosenzweig. I wish

to thank Professor Uriel Simon, Bar Ilan University, and Dr. Ze'ev Gries, The Haifa Technion, for confirming that such an understanding of the term is found neither in rabbinical nor in post-rabbinical biblical commentaries.

10. Franz Rosenzweig to Hanna Rovina, December 4, 1929, in *Briefe und Tagebücher,* 2:1235f.

11. Translation in Glatzer, *Franz Rosenzweig,* p. 171.

12. With the poem Rosenzweig also sent her a copy of the Book of Samuel in German, presumably the translation he made together with Martin Buber and then just recently published: *Das Buch Schmuel,* verdeutscht von Martin Buber gemeinsam mit Franz Rosenzweig (Berlin: Lambert Schneider, 1928). See Rovina's card to Rafael Rosenzweig, mentioned in note 4.

13. *Briefe und Tagebücher,* 1:2. Cf. Glatzer, *Franz Rosenzweig,* p. xxxviif.

14. Letter to Hans Ehrenberg, 17 March 1906, ibid., 1:34–35; trans. in Glatzer, *Franz Rosenzweig,* p. 9.

15. According to the report of the headmaster of the Friedrichsgymnasium, for the year that Rosenzweig graduated from that institution, during the nine years one spent at the school 68 credit-hours were devoted to Greek, and 36 to Latin; by comparison, students were required to take 26 credit-hours of German, 8 credit-hours of history, 34 credit-hours of mathematics, and 10 hours of physics. See Friedrich Heussner, *Königliches Friedrichs-Gymnasium zu Cassel. Jahresbericht über das Schuljahr 1904/05 von dem Direktor* (Cassel: Friedrichs-gymnasium, 1905), p. 3. On Rosenzweig's Gymnasium studies, see Peter Adamski, ed., *Jüdische Schüler am Friedrichsgymnasium zu Cassel. Eine Dokumentation der Geschichtswerkstatt am Friedrichsgymnasium anlässlich der Franz Rosenzweig Gedenktage 1986* (Kassel: D. M. Kassel, 1986), pp. 5–6.

16. These biographical details were related by Nahum N. Glatzer in his lectures on Rosenzweig at Brandeis University, where I studied with him in the 1960s. I have, however, found no independent documentation of this report, although it is manifestly evident from Rosenzweig's correspondence, especially that of 1916 with Eugen Rosenstock-Huessy regarding Judaism and Christianity, that he was thoroughly at home in the Greek New Testament and the Vulgate. Cf. E. Rosenstock-Huessy, *Judaism Despite Christianity. The "Letters on Christianity and Judaism" Between Eugen Rosenstock-Huessy and Franz Rosenzweig* (New York: Schocken Books, 1971). It is also noteworthy that as a twenty-year-old, Rosenzweig chose to read during his summer vacation The Song of Songs in the Septuagint. See his diary note from August 23, 1906. *Briefe und Tagebücher,* 1:54. Also see his letter of May 28, 1917 to Rudolf Ehrenberg, in which he broaches a never realized plan to write a comparative study on the treatment of the Psalms in the Septuagint, the Vulgate, Luther, as well as by traditional Jewish commentators. Ibid., 1:410f.

17. Cf. "The more languages one knows, the more one is a human being. Can one know *(können)* more than one language? Our word *können* is just as flat as the French *savoir.* One lives *(lebt)* in a language." Rosenzweig, "Vom Geist der Hebräischen Sprache," in Rosenzweig, *Gesammelte Schriften,* Part 3: *Zweistromland. Kleinere Schriften zu Glauben und Denken,* ed. Reinhold Mayer and Annemarie Mayer (Dordrecht: Martinus Nijhoff, 1984), p. 719.

18. French and English were also taught at the Friedrichsgymnasium, but clearly with much less emphasis than that given to Greek and Latin. In comparison to the 68 credit-hours of Greek and 36 credit-hours of Latin, only 20 credit-hours of French were required during the course of one's studies at the school; English was optional with only four credit-hours offered. See F. Heussner, *Königliches Friedrichs-Gymnasium,* p. 3.

19. Memoir of Rosenzweig's cousin Gertrud Oppenheim, cited in *Briefe und Tagebücher,* 1:151.

20. See memoir of his friend Bertha Badt-Strauss, cited in *Briefe und Tagebücher,* 1:150.

21. Rosenzweig, "It Is Time: Concerning the Study of Judaism," in Franz Rosenzweig, *On Jewish Learning,* ed. Nahum N. Glatzer, trans. William Wolf (New York: Schocken Books, 1955), p. 30. This essay, calling for a radical revision of Jewish education in Germany, was first published in 1917 as an open letter to Hermann Cohen, whose academic prestige rendered him perhaps the most esteemed personality of German Jewry; see n. 26.

22. Letter to Gerhard (Gershom) Scholem, dated March 10, 1921, cited in Glatzer, *Franz Rosenzweig,* p. 102.

23. Rosenzweig, "It Is Time," p. 34.

24. Cf. *Verhandlungen und Beschlusse der Generalversammlung des Rabbinerverbandes in Deutschland zu Berlin* (Frankfurt-am-Main: J. Kauffmann, 1916).

25. Letter, Franz Rosenzweig to Parents, October 18, 1916, in *Briefe und Tagebücher,* 1:257.

26. Rosenzweig's proposals for a radical revision of Jewish education in Germany were addressed to Hermann Cohen, because, as Rosenzweig stated in his "open letter," "the majority of those German Jews who intend to live as Jews in Germany honor you as their intellectual leader." Rosenzweig, "It Is Time," p. 27. Significantly, when Rosenzweig wrote this essay, he was also deeply exercised by the problems of education in general, and, indeed, wrote extensively on the subject. See his essay, "Volksschule und Reichschule," which he wrote at the front in October 1916 and circulated among his friends and family. In his correspondence this essay is discussed frequently and at length. It is now published in Rosenzweig, *Zweistromland,* pp. 371-411. Not surprisingly, this essay reflects his interest in languages. Calling for a fundamental restructuring of the German educational system, he gives special attention to the study of foreign languages. He urges that the emphasis be shifted from "learning" to "understanding" languages, and to this end recommends a comparative linguistic approach. Cf. his letter to his parents, November 3, 1916, in which he elaborates this proposal with extensive examples from German, Middle High German, Greek, English, French, Italian, Latin, Bulgarian, and Russian. *Briefe und Tagebücher,* 1:266-71.

27. Because he was at the front when the essay was published (in the *Neue Jüdische Monatshefte),* Rosenzweig's parents read the proofs of the essay on his behalf. He gave them instructions to be certain that the verse from Psalm 119:26 appear in Hebrew, and "under no circumstances whatsoever should it be transliterated *et la'asot,* et cetera." Letter, Franz Rosenzweig to Parents, April 21, 1917, *Briefe und Tagebücher,* 1:396

28. Rosenzweig, "It Is Time," p. 42.

29. Cf. Rosenzweig's letters to mother, May 28, 1918, and June 4, 1918, cited in Glatzer, *Franz Rosenzweig,* pp. 74-76, 77-78.

30. Rosenzweig, "It Is Time," p. 32.

31. Rosenzweig's view of the apologetic posture inherent in "translated Judaism"—entailing as it does a transposition of Jewish teachings not only to a different linguistic but also to a different cognitive system—is discussed below in section 3 of this essay.

32. Replying to a friend who expressed appreciation of the essay, "It Is Time," and the urgency to adopt such a program set forth therein, Rosenzweig exclaimed: "One may add or subtract from [the program] almost at will. But one thing must be preserved, the central position of Hebrew." Rosenzweig to Josef Prager, September 30, 1917, *Briefe und Tagebücher,* 1:452.

33. Rosenzweig also had to compromise his opposition to lectures. The *Lehrhaus* would include public lectures and lecture courses in its curriculum. Rosenzweig, however, sought to have the lecturers adopt a "dialogical method" whereby audience participation

would be encouraged. He, nonetheless, regarded the heart of the *Lehrhaus* program to be *Arbeitsgemeinschaften*, study groups based on texts.

34. In the winter semester 1923, special courses in basic Hebrew were instituted at the *Lehrhaus* for children between the ages of 9 and 13. "These tuition-free classes were established to attract the attention of parents to the *Lehrhaus* program." Jehuda Reinharz, "The *Lehrhaus* in Frankfurt-am-Main: A Renaissance in Jewish Adult Education," *The Yavneh Review. A Student Journal of Jewish Studies* (Summer Issue, 1969), p. 23.

35. Interview with his close associate at the *Lehrhaus,* Nahum N. Glatzer, July 1984.

36. Cited in Glatzer, *Franz Rosenzweig,* p. 93.

37. For example, a beginners' course, which Rosenzweig gave in the spring semester of 1922, was based on the liturgy of the Friday evening service; an intermediate course for the same semester was based on "easy passages from Leviticus and Numbers." For a full listing of the course offerings at the *Lehrhaus,* from 1920 to 1927, see Michael Buhler, *Erziehung zur Tradition. Erziehung zur Widerstand. Ernst Simon und die jüdische Erwachsenenbildung in Deutschland* (Berlin: Institut Kirche und Judentum, 1986), pp. 49–70.

38. See Rosenzweig's letter to Ernst Simon in which he castigates his young colleague for neglecting Hebrew grammar. Simon, who was preparing for *aliyah,* apparently spoke Hebrew with many mispronunciations. These errors Rosenzweig ascribed to an inadequate knowledge of Hebrew grammar. He graciously offered to give Simon a crash course on the subject, adding, "grammar is not an esoteric science *(Geheimwissenschaft),* although one can learn it only by the Kabbalist Scholem and his disciples; it is actually the most fun thing in the world." Letter, Rosenzweig to Ernst Simon, November 28, 1924, *Briefe und Tagebücher,* 2:1005.

39. I am indebted to Professor Everett Fox of Clark University (Worcester, Massachusetts) for sharing this information gathered in an interview he conducted with a former instructor at the *Lehrhaus.*

40. The preference for the Ashkenazi pronunciation may have been prompted by sociological as much as presumably ideological considerations. For Rosenzweig the study of Hebrew was primarily intended to enable one to participate in the liturgy of the synagogue, and since in Germany the prevailing tradition was Ashkenazi, it was only natural that it should be taught in the schools. Cf. "Considering the close connection between the instruction and the synagogue, it is self-evident that the Hebrew pronunciation used in the classrooms should be the same as that used in the synagogue. . . ." Rosenzweig, "It Is Time," p. 32.

41. Learning that Bialik was in Germany for an extended visit, Rosenzweig sought through Martin Buber to solicit his participation in the *Lehrhaus.* Cf. "Will Bialik still be in Hamburg during the summer? Do you believe it possible that he would be willing to do something in the *Lehrhaus,* in Hebrew naturally?" Rosenzweig to Buber, February 5, 1923, *Briefe und Tagebücher,* 2:891. See follow-up letters, February 22, 1923; February 27, 1923; September 16, 1923; ibid, 2:894, 896, 922f.

42. Agnon's course was a seminar entitled simply, "S. J. Agnon: Aus eigenen Werken. Lekture und Erklärung.—Hebräische Kenntnisse vorausgesetzt" (S. J. Agnon: From his own works. Lecture and Explication—Knowledge of Hebrew required).

43. N. N. Glatzer, "Ha-leshonot ve-ivrit bimeyuḥad be-mishnato shel rosenzweig" (Languages and Hebrew in Particular in Rosenzweig's Thought), in *Yovel Shai. Festschrift in Honor of S. Y. Agnon,* ed. Baruch Kurzweil (Ramat Gan: Bar Ilan University, 1958), p. 229.

44. Ibid.

45. Cf. Rosenzweig's letter to Rudolf Hallo. "End of 1922," cited in Glatzer, *The Philosophy of Franz Rosenzweig,* p. 118f.

46. N. N. Glatzer, "The Frankfurt Lehrhaus." *Leo Baeck Institute Year Book* 1 (1956):

111. In time, Glatzer was to become one of the most prominent translators of Agnon into German.

47. Rosenzweig, "Atheistische Theologie," *Zweistromland:* 687–98.
48. Rosenzweig, "It Is Time," p. 28.
49. Ibid.
50. Ibid, p. 29.
51. On modern, especially German, Jewry's romance with the ideal of *Bildung,* see George Mosse, *German Jews Beyond Judaism* (Bloomington: Indiana University Press, Cincinnati: Hebrew Union College, 1985).
52. Rosenzweig, "It Is Time," p. 29f.
53. Ibid., p. 30.
54. Rosenzweig, *The Star of Redemption,* p. 302f.
55. The course, "Unsere Sprache," was given in the winter semester, January–March 1921, of the *Lehrhaus.*
56. Rosenzweig initially contemplated calling these lectures "The Spirit of the Hebrew Language." Friends objected, claiming that this title would misleadingly suggest that the lectures were only for those already knowledgeable in the subject. It was suggested that he call the lectures instead "The Jew and His Language." His wife, Edith, then recommended the title that was finally accepted, "Our Language" *(Unsere Sprache).* Letter, Rosenzweig to Margrit (Gritli) Rosenstock, December 12, 1920. Unpublished. Eugen Rosenstock-Huessy Archive, Four Well, Vermont. I wish to thank Freya von Moltke and Rafael Rosenzweig for rendering this letter available to me.
57. Rosenzweig, "Vom Geist der Hebräischen Sprache," in *Zweistromland,* 721.
58. In another essay, Rosenzweig does refer to Hebrew as "the language of God" *(die Sprache Gottes).* In this context, however, he is not employing the term in an ontological sense, but in a loose rhetorical manner to refer to Hebrew as sacred language in contrast to "the spoken [that is, secular] languages of man." Rosenzweig, "Classical and Modern Hebrew," in Glatzer, *Franz Rosenzweig,* p. 266. German: "Neuhebräisch," in Rosenzweig, *Zweistromland,* p. 726.
59. Rosenzweig, "Unsere Sprache," p. 720. He notes that this characteristic is shared by all Semitic languages.
60. Ibid.
61. Ibid.
62. Ibid.
63. Ibid., p 721
64. Rosenzweig concluded the lectures, at least according to his notes, in an exhortatory vein: "Hold yourselves and your children fast to this reservoir of power, do not let the language be extinguished in your midst so that 'the spirit of Hebrew' will not expire with it." Ibid.
65. Cf. Rosenzweig, *The Star of Redemption,* the sections entitled "The Peoples and Their Languages," and "The Holy Language," pp. 300–302.
66. Ibid., p. 302.
67. Ibid.
68. Ibid.
69. A similar tension toward the "profane" realities encountered in Exile is engendered by Israel's abiding attachment to the Holy Land and the Holy Law. Cf. *The Star of Redemption,* sections entitled "The Peoples and Their Native Soil," "The Holy Land," "The Peoples and Their Law," "The Holy Law," pp. 299–300, 303–304.
70. Rosenzweig, "Classical and Modern Hebrew," in Glatzer, *Franz Rosenzweig,* p. 266.
71. Letter, Rosenzweig to mother, February 7, 1919, *Briefe und Tagebücher,* 2:624.

72. Rosenzweig, "Classical and Modern Hebrew. A Review of a Translation into the Hebrew of Spinoza's *Ethics,*" in Glatzer, *Franz Rosenzweig,* pp. 263–71. In the original this essay bears the title, "Neuhebräisch" (Modern Hebrew). First published in *Der Morgen* 11, 1 (1926): 105–109; now in *Zweistromland,* pp. 723–29.

73. On Klatzkin with a selection of his writings, see Arthur Hertzberg, *The Zionist Idea. A Historical Analysis and Reader* (New York: Schocken Books, 1963), pp. 313–27.

74. Klatzkin, "Translator's Preface," Baruch Spinoza, *Torat Ha-Middot* (Hebrew translation of Spinoza, *Ethics*) (Leipzig: Abraham Josef Stiebel Verlag, 1925), p. xx.

75. "Classical and Modern Hebrew," p. 270.

76. Ibid., p. 268.

77. Ibid.

78. Ibid.

79. Ibid., p. 268.

80. Ibid.

81. Scholem's letter was included in a folio of greetings presented to Rosenzweig on his fortieth birthday. The folio or "Mappe" was organized by Buber with the assistance of Martin Goldner, then the secretary of *Freies Jüdisches Lehrhaus* founded by Rosenzweig. The folio of greetings by forty-six friends was given a title page: *Franz Rosenzweig: zum 25 Dezember 1926. Glueckwuensche zum 40. Geburtstag.* A facsimile of the folio was published, in a limited edition, by the Leo Baeck Institute of New York. In an accompanying volume Martin Goldner introduces the facsimile edition as well as translating into English the various contributions. The citations from Scholem's letter follow Goldner's translation, which I have altered somewhat in accordance with my understanding of the original German text.

82. Scholem does not explicitly mention Rosenzweig's review of Klatzkin's translation of Spinoza's *Ethics,* but, given the theme of Scholem's essay and the manner in which he treats the problem of Hebrew's "secularization," it is manifest that he is referring to Rosenzweig's essay. See Ephraim Broide's detailed discussion of the background to Scholem's letter in an "afterword" to a Hebrew translation of the letter in the Jerusalem literary journal, *Molad* 42 (Winter 1985/6): 119–21.

83. Scholem, "A Free Man: On J. L. Magnes (Hebrew) *Devarim be-Go* (Writings on the Jewish Heritage and Renaissance) (Tel Aviv: Am Oved, 1975), p. 489. Scholem characterizes the overall attitude of the early halutzim toward Judaism, not just Hebrew, as "nihilistic."

84. The evolution of Rosenzweig's attitude toward Zionism is discussed in Stephane Moses, "Politik und Religion. Zur Aktualität Franz Rosenzweigs," in *Der Philosoph Franz Rosenzweig.* Internationaler Kongress, Kassel 1986, ed. Wolfdietrich Schmied-Kowarzik (Freiburg and Munich: Verlag Karl Alber, 1988), 2:855–75.

85. Rosenzweig, "Briefe eines Nichtzionisten an einen Antizionisten," *Der Jude* (February 1928); these letters are now published separately in *Briefe und Tagebücher,* 2:1138, 1140f., 1143ff., 1148ff.

86. Cited in Glatzer, *Franz Rosenzweig,* p. 357f.

87. Ibid., p. 357.

88. See *Briefe und Tagebücher,* 2:1181 n. 1 to letter no. 1191. Cf. Ernst Akiva Simon, "Rosenzweig: Reflections of a Disciple," in P. Mendes-Flohr, ed., *The Philosophy of Franz Rosenzweig* (Hanover, N. H. and London: University Press of New England, 1988), p. 213. In a conversation in 1980, Simon related to me this encounter, recalling that it must have taken Rosenzweig at least fifteen minutes to "dictate" the message.

89. The volume was an edition of Nachman Krochmal's works, edited by Simon Rawidowicz and published in Berlin by Ajanoth Verlag, in 1924. I wish to thank Mrs. Toni Simon, Jerusalem, for bringing this volume, with the dedication by Rosenzweig, to my attention.

90. According to a note appended by Simon in pencil, this was "dictated by Rosenzweig during the last year of his life as a dedication to this book that he gave me as a parting gift on the eve of our aliyah before Pesach 5688 and as expression of his gratitude for studying in his presence Gemara during the days of his illness" (Hebrew). For several years Simon would come at least once a week to Rosenzweig's residence and read to him Talmud.

91. Simon appended a note to the verse, "Cf. Deuteronomy 33:13." (. . . Blessed of the Lord be his land; for the precious things of heaven, . . .")

92. Rosenzweig's biographer, Nahum N. Glatzer, discerns three distinct stages in the development of Rosenzweig's attitude toward Hebrew: from a nigh-sacerdotal view of Hebrew in *The Star of Redemption,* to an affirmation of Hebrew as the language of Jewish study and spiritual discourse, to an acknowledgment of Hebrew as being nurtured by both the religious and secular experience of the Jew. See Glatzer, *"Ha-leshonot . . . be-mishnato shel rosenzweig,"* pp. 229–36. Also see Ephraim Meir, "Franz Rosenzweig ve-gishato lalashon ha-'ivrit," *Leshonenu La–am,* (March-April 1987): 368–74.

93. Rosenzweig, "It Is Time," p. 34.

94. On Rosenzweig's translation, see Everett Fox, "Franz Rosenzweig as Translator," *Leo Baeck Institute Year Book,* 34 (1989): 371–84.

95. Letter, Rosenzweig to Margaret Susman, August 22, 1924, quoted in Glatzer, *Franz Rosenzweig,* p. 134.

96. Letter, Rosenzweig to G. Scholem, March 10, 1921, quoted in Glatzer, *Franz Rosenzweig,* p. 102.

97. Quoted in ibid., p. 116.

98. Letter, Rosenzweig to J. Rivlin, October 24, 1926, *Briefe und Tagebücher,* 2: 1109f.; also see Glatzer, *"ha-leshonot . . . be-mishnato shel rosenzweig,"* p. 236.

99. Franz Rosenzweig, *Kokhav ha-Ge'ulah,* trans. Yehoshua Amir (Jerusalem: Mosad Bialik, 1970). In his diary entry of June 9, 1922, in which he recorded his wish to have *The Star* translated into Hebrew, Rosenzweig indicated that he felt that a literal translation of the title would be incorrect—*"Kokhav ha-Ge'ulah* has the wrong ring to it"; he suggested instead "Kokhav Ya'akov"—"a Star out of Jacob"—a reference to Numbers 24:17. See Glatzer, *Franz Rosenzweig,* p. 116.

100. Rosenzweig, "Einleitung" to Hermann Cohen, *Jüdische Schriften* (Berlin: C. A. Schwetschke & Sohn, 1924), 1:xiii-lxiv. The Hebrew translation was done by Leo Rosenzweig, no relation to Franz.

101. Letter, Rosenzweig to Julius Guttmann, July 14, 1929, quoted in Glatzer, *Franz Rosenzweig,* p. 166.

15

The Status of Hebrew in Soviet Russia from the Revolution to the Gorbachev Thaw

AVRAHAM GREENBAUM

It is hard to speak about Hebrew in the former Soviet Union without saying something about Yiddish, the official language of the Jewish nationality in that country to this day. The "war of the languages" in the Russian Empire is beyond the purview of this essay, but we must not forget that such a conflict took place, and that it had a deleterious effect on the Jews' claim to be a nation like any other. Even before the revolution the fathers of the new society used the language problem as a stick with which to beat the Jews. Stalin, in his essay "Marxism and the National Question," made a point of the fact that the Jews had no single language; his Georgian origins made him aware that Yiddish was not even the common vernacular of the Jews in the Czarist empire.[1] As for Lenin, he went further, and saw inter alia in the fact that the Jews spoke a "jargon" a refutation of their claim to be called a nation.[2] Neither Lenin or Stalin, in their published writings, expressed themselves on the Jews or their languages after the revolution. But it was under Lenin's regime, in the early Soviet period, that the decision was made to recognize Yiddish as the everyday language of the large mass of Soviet Jewry; ergo, the Jewish language was Yiddish. From that time on and until at least the death of Stalin the words *evreiskii iazyk* ("Jewish language") in Soviet writings came to mean Yiddish.

We assume that this would not have happened had the Jews of Russia had a free choice in the matter. Evidence for this we see in the educational situation among the Jews of interwar Poland and the Baltic states, where we find the Hebrew networks much stronger than the competing Yiddish ones. But the people who counted in the Soviet system were not the masses but the revolutionaries, and in the case of the Jews the revolutionary camp consisted of adherents of Yiddish. We are referring to the parties of the Jewish left: The Bund (Social Democratic), Poale Zion (Socialist-Zionist) and the United Jewish Workers Party (Socialist-Territorialist). As these parties disintegrated or were driven underground, many of their members joined the Communist Party for the specific purpose of staffing its Jewish sections *(Evsektsiia)*.[3] The Evsektsiia soon became the dominant force in the evolving new Jewish culture.

At the beginning things were still in a state of flux, and the new regime had more to do than to worry about the Hebrew-Yiddish dichotomy. As a result the Hebrew-oriented institutions (schools, newspapers, publishing houses) continued to function in 1918. In that year A. J. Stybel, a well-known patron of Hebrew letters, began his project to translate world literature into Hebrew, and centered it in Moscow. That same year Saul Ginsburg, a historian and folklorist, published *he'Avar,* a Hebrew historical journal, in the new capital. But an end was put to the new journal after two issues when the Communists seized the presses, while Stybel soon moved his project to Warsaw.[4]

The downgrading of Hebrew received formal sanction in July 1919, after the advocates of Yiddish carried the day in the People's Commissariat of Education. The partisans of Hebrew, among whom the Moscow "crown rabbi" Jacob Mazeh played a leading role, did their best, and might even have won the Commissar of Education, Anatoli Lunacharskii, to their side. But the Marxist historian Mikhail Pokrovskii, Lunacharskii's assistant, was firmly in the Yiddish camp. Mazeh's memoirs depict the commissar-intellectual Lunacharskii as torn between party loyalty and a desire not to give in to cultural barbarism, but even he was not convinced by the rabbi's argument that the poor kept up Hebrew while the rich bourgeoisie assimilated.[5] The fact that Mazeh and others on the Hebrew side were well-known Zionists probably played into the hands of the Evsektsiia, who depicted Hebrew as the language of Zionism, clericalism, and counter-revolution. We quote the most important paragraph of the regulation issued by the People's Commissariat of Education in order to resolve the conflict:

> It is recognized that the Hebrew *(Ivrit)* language is not the language of discourse of the Jewish people's masses and is therefore not considered as a language of the national minorities; from the pedagogical point of view it is in the same position as a foreign tongue, not being the language of discourse of the people's masses within the borders of the Russian Soviet Federated Socialist Republic.[6]

The regulation did make it clear that Hebrew as a language of instruction in Soviet schools was illegal, and steps were soon taken to phase out the "Tarbut" network. For their part the Jewish Communists did their best to make sure that the vaguely worded concession on Hebrew as a foreign language remained a dead letter. The widespread impression that Hebrew became a "forbidden language" has no basis in Soviet law and was never completely true in practice; but Hebrew was under a cloud, so to speak, and its study and use, except in certain very limited frameworks, were strongly discouraged.

The famous exception in the early period was the Hebrew theatrical troupe "Habima," and the Soviet authorities would point to its existence to refute the charge that Hebrew was persecuted.[7] But this kind of "tokenism," which the Soviet regime liked to resort to when challenged, fooled no one, and in any case "Habima," which for a time had even enjoyed a state subsidy, left for greener pastures in 1926. Nor did it make any difference that some Jewish Communists indulged a secret love for Hebrew and Hebrew books,[8] or that someone in Soviet Asia once published a Hebrew geography textbook under government auspices after proving that Yiddish was not the local Jewish language.[9]

It was, however, not too simple to suppress the ancient tongue. For one thing, the Soviet constitution then and now guaranteed freedom of religious worship, which meant that Hebrew liturgical and related texts should be made available. On the secular plane Hebrew, as the language of an ancient civilization, was studied in universities. It would also be expected that Hebrew, as a component of Yiddish, would be of interest in advanced Yiddish courses. Modern Hebrew was, of course, the language of the Jewish settlement in Palestine, but this was precisely the reason that the Evsektsiia did its best to squelch all attempts to have Hebrew classes for adults.[10]

Finally, there was the small universe of Hebrew letters. The Hebrew "national poet," Haim Nahman Bialik, and some of his colleagues left in 1921 after becoming aware that they had no future in Russia; it is said that, upon the intervention of Maxim Gorky, who admired Bialik, Lenin himself approved the exit permits.[11] But a coterie of younger writers, who considered themselves no less dedicated to the revolution than the Evsektsiia, rejected the identification of Hebrew with Zionism and Palestinocentrism. They were convinced that the official recognition of Yiddish as the Jewish tongue was the result of a fraud perpetrated by the Evsektsiia. They had little hope that what had been done could be undone, but demanded the right to hold meetings and publish their "revolutionary" writings.

Let us see how the various elements interested in Hebrew fared in practice. It seems that the traditional Jews had the greatest success. During the period of the New Economic Policy or NEP (1921–28), when private publishing was permitted, new presses sprang up to take the place of the ones in the large cities seized by the Communists for their Yiddish publications. A number of liturgical and similar books, such as prayer books, calendars, and Passover *hagadot*, found their market. In fact, of the over fifty Hebrew books printed in the years 1918–28 in Soviet Russia, we know forty-six to have been of this type.[12] There were in this sphere some unusual occurrences, such as the permission granted to the rabbi of Leningrad to print his novellae on the Talmud in a Communist press, and a short-lived rabbinic journal.[13]

Classical Hebrew continued to be studied in the few academic institutions with a Semitological tradition,[14] but modern Hebrew was not then taught, as far as we know, at the Institute of Living Eastern Languages. Hebrew was taught, together with German, as a component of Yiddish in the pedagogical institutes and faculties which served aspiring teachers of Yiddish.

These Hebrew courses were deliberately abandoned at the end of the twenties as a symbol of increased commitment by Jewish Communists to the Soviet cause. Another symbolic step taken by them at the time was the elimination of the forms which certain Hebrew letters take at the end of a word.[15] There was no reason for this decision other than a symbolic final break with Hebrew, and indeed this practice was largely abandoned after the death of Stalin.[16] The next logical step would have been Latinization, a possibility which was considered but not adopted.

In the meantime the Hebrew writers who wanted to see their paeans to the revolution in print knocked on all possible doors, but usually found that their attempts to hold meetings or publish collections were frustrated by the official consultant on Jewish affairs, the Evsektsiia. The story of Hebrew literature in Soviet Russia has been told elsewhere by this writer and others.[17] Here we merely note that the sum total of their efforts was four books, all but one actually pamphlets, in the 1923–27 period; the only book, *Bereshit* (1926), had to be printed in Berlin. When in 1927 permission was given to print a few poems on the tenth anniversary of the revolution, no one realized that this was the end of Hebrew literature in the country for over fifty years.[18]

The increasing harshness of the period after 1928 made the first decade after the revolution look like a period of solid achievement. Not only did no one dare now to ask for a permit to publish a Hebrew literary miscellany; even religious publishing, which seemed guaranteed by the Soviet constitution, was no longer allowed. Hebrew writers either emigrated or, with few exceptions, disappeared gradually into the prison camps. In late 1948, when Stalin began to persecute Jewish culture as such, even Yiddish literature was suppressed. In Stalin's last years the Hebrew alphabet survived only on the Chinese border, where the Jewish Autonomous Province's Yiddish newspaper, *Birobidzhaner shtern,* appeared. Even Soviet Semitology was affected: we believe that the closing of the "Chair of Assyriological-Hebraistic Studies" at Leningrad University in 1950 was politically motivated.[19]

After Stalin's death there was a gradual revival of Yiddish literature, although the pre-war schools and newspapers never returned, and indeed it cannot be said that there was any great need for them in a period of accelerated linguistic assimilation of Soviet Jewry. But the authorities indicated in different ways that Yiddish was still the official language of the Jewish nationality.[20] The line against Soviet Hebrew literature was maintained, and until the eighties the writers who returned from the labor camps still smuggled their writings into Israel to be published there under pseudonyms. The harassment of those who studied modern Hebrew privately in classes and groups is too well-known to need description. Yet Hebrew now came into its own, and the fact that it was the language of a state undoubtedly had much to do with it. The change can be seen in the upswing in Hebraic studies in the scholarly journals after the first collection on "Semitic languages" was published in 1963,[21] the same year Feliks Shapiro's Hebrew-Russian dictionary came out.[22] The word *gebraistika* began to appear, modern Hebrew was taught to officials who needed it in their work, *ivrit* was adopted to designate Hebrew as such, whether ancient or modern, and it can be said that the third edition of the "Large Soviet Encyclopedia," which began in 1970, made Hebrew and Yiddish equal as Jewish languages.[23]

In 1956 there began a modest revival of religious publishing with the *Sidur ha-shalom*[24] issued that year by the Moscow Jewish Religious Society (Congregation) and reprinted in a more usable format twice since. The same year the practice of publishing small calendars of the coming Jewish year was resumed, likewise by the Moscow *kehila*.[25] These publications suffer from a chronic lack of Hebrew type and of persons with the needed skills, not to speak of the political pressures which give them their peculiar coloration.

The Gorbachev era is beyond our scope. Suffice it to say that the previously prohibited Hebrew classes were now informally and sometimes formally permitted. Such Jewish cultural activity as exists is, for obvious reasons, largely in Russian, but a small collection of Hebrew literature has been attempted. The official Jewish school, which opened in Riga in September 1989, had a strangely "Evsek" atmosphere, with Hebraists having had to struggle to introduce Hebrew into the upper grades.

Notes

1. Joseph Stalin, *Marxism and the National and Colonial Question: a Collection of Articles and Speeches* (London: M. Lawrence, 1936) repr. 1942, p. 10. The opening essay, "Marxism and the National Question," was first published in 1913.

2. V. I. Lenin, *Sochineniia,* 4th ed., (Moscow: Gos. izd. polit. lit., 1946), 7:84. The English translator, in updating or correcting the style, translated *zhargon* as "Yiddish": Lenin, *Collected Works,* 4th ed. (Moscow: Foreign Languages Pub. House, 1961), 7:100.

3. Cf. Zvi Y. Gitelman, *Jewish Nationality and Soviet Politics; the Jewish Sections of the CPSU, 1918–1930* (Princeton: Princeton University Press, 1972), pp. 149–230, for a detailed description of this process.

4. See the memoirs of the Hebrew Yiddish journalist Ben-Zion Katz in *ha-Tsefira,* March 4, 1927; and, in a variant but more accessible version, his *Zikhronot* (Tel Aviv: N. Tverski, 1963), pp. 254–58.

5. Jacob Mazeh, *Zikhronot* (Tel Aviv: Yalkut, 1936), 4:13; and cf. A. Tsentsiper, *'Eser shenot redifot* (Tel Aviv: Berit Kibuts Galuyot, 1930), pp. 33–34.

6. We quote the Yiddish version as published in the official *Kultur un bildung* 1, 24 (1920): 32. In the same issue the Yiddish education activists protest the decision as far too mild.

7. See for example the letter from Russia printed in the Palestine Hebrew literary journal *Ketuvim,* June 15, 1927. Over the years *Ketuvim* paid considerable attention to the status of Hebrew in Soviet Russia.

8. Gitelman (see note 3 above), pp. 279, 282–83.

9. M. Z. Amitin-Shapiro, *Geografya kelalit . . .* (Tashkent: ha-Komisariat le-Haskala, 1920), published by the Commissariat of Education of the Turkestan Republic. The only other official Soviet publication with a Hebrew title page known to us is the Academy of Science Library's *Kohelet Moshe* (Leningrad: ha-Akademiya le-Mada'im shel Berit ha-R.S.S., 1936), which continues the prerevolutionary catalog of the famous Friedland collection of Hebraica. The publication of the catalog was not continued further.

10. M. Levitan, then in charge of Jewish education in the Ukraine, wrote in 1922 that such courses should be permitted only under rigid safeguards, with teachers loyal to the Soviet system, since most such requests were a "cloak for Zionism" (*Emes,* June 4, 1922).

11. Ben-Zion Dinur, *Bi-yemei milḥamah u-mahapekhah* (Jerusalem: Bialik Institute, 1960), p. 464.

12. The list we are using here was sent anonymously to Palestine by the Soviet Jewish historian and litterateur Saul Borovoi, who at the time must have had a secret love for Hebrew: "ha Defus ha-'ivri be-S.S.S.R. (Rusya)." *Kiryat sefer* 5 (1928-29): 250–54. Borovoi claims to have seen nearly everything published in Hebrew in the 1920s. The Hebrew book output in the USSR has also been cataloged in the Israeli bibliography of Soviet Yiddica and Hebraica *Jewish Publications in the Soviet Union 1917–1960,* comp. Y. Y. Cohen and M. Piekarz, ed. Kh. Shmeruk (Jerusalem: The Historical Society of Israel, 1961). This bibliography, however, includes works published in 1917 before the revolution as well as those published in the Ukraine during the brief period of its independence.

13. We are referring to Rabbi David Tebele Katzenellenbogen's *Ma'yan mei neftoaḥ* (Petrograd: Printed by Krasnyi Agitator, 1923); Katzenellenbogen had unusually good con-

nections with the authorities. The rabbinic journal, which was closed by the authorities on a pretext after two issues, is *Yagdil torah,* ed. by E. Abramsky and S. J. Zevin. It appeared in Bobruisk in 1928.

14. See the survey of the subject in Konstantin Tsereteli's pamphlet *Semitics* in the series *Fifty Years of Soviet Oriental Studies (Brief Reviews),* Moscow 1968.

15. On these and other problems of Hebraisms in Yiddish see A. Greenbaum, *Jewish Scholarship and Scholarly Institutions in Soviet Russia, 1918-1953* (Jerusalem: Hebrew University Centre for Research and Documentation of East European Jewry, 1978), pp. 110-12.

16. The final letters were restored in 1961 except in the newspaper *Birobidzhaner shtern.* Soviet Yiddish has retained the unusual practice, adopted soon after the revolution, of spelling words of Hebraic origins phonetically rather than as in Hebrew or Aramaic. This practice, however, can be defended on practical and pedagogical grounds in addition to the obviously ideological.

17. A. Greenbaum, "Hebrew Literature in Soviet Russia," *Jewish Social Studies* 30 (1968): 136-48; idem, "Hebrew Literature in Soviet Russia: A Second Look," *Minority Problems in Eastern Europe Between the World Wars...,* ed. A. Greenbaum (Jerusalem: Hebrew Univ., Institute for Advanced Studies, 1988), pp. 144-48. For a different approach see Yehoshua A. Gilboa, "Hebrew Literature in the U.S.S.R.," *The Jews in Soviet Russia since 1917,* ed. L. Kochan (London: Oxford Univ. Press, 1970, repr. 1972), pp. 216-31; and more extensively in the same author's *Oktobra'im 'ivrim; toldoteha shel ashlayah* (Tel Aviv: Tel Aviv University, Diaspora Research Institute, 1974).

18. It should, however, be noted that until the mid-thirties Hebrew writers were still able to publish freely abroad.

19. Indirect evidence we see in the survey by Israel Kovelman, "Hebraistik in di rusishe lern-anshtaltn un visenshaftlekhe institutsyes," *Sovetish heymland* (1975): 3, 158-62, which shows a strange gap in Leningrad Semitics between 1950 and 1955. The break and its probable motivation was confirmed for me by the one-time Leningrad Semitics student Hayim Sheinin.

20. For example, Yiddish, as one of the languages of the Soviet peoples, was given a chapter in the collection *Iazyki narodov SSSR,* vol. 1 (Moscow: Nauka, 1966).

21. We refer to *Semitskie iazyki,* vol. 1 (Moscow: Izd. vostochnoi lit., 1963); cf. the survey by Tsereteli (note 14 above). For some reason Arabistics was distinguished from the largely Hebrew-Aramaic oriented "Semitologiia" in contemporary Soviet writing. Hebrew-Aramaic studies had earlier found a modest place in *Palestinskii sbornik,* an old Czarist journal which was revived in Soviet Russia in 1954.

22. Feliks Shapiro, *Ivrit-russkii slovar',* ed. Bentsion Grande, (Moscow: Gos. izd. innostrannykh i natsional'nykh slovarei, 1963). Shapiro's daughter, after emigrating to Israel, wrote that her father struggled long and hard to publish the dictionary, which he did not live to see in print. See *Feliks L'vovich Shapiro* (Jerusalem: Jewish Agency, 1983), pp. 7-8.

23. In the first (interwar) edition of *Bol'shaia sovetskaia entsiklopediia, evreiskii iazyk* ("Jewish language") meant Yiddish, Hebrew being subsumed under *drevneevreiskii iazyk* ("Ancient Jewish language"). In the second edition, under the more-or-less open anti-Semitism of the period around 1950, the entry "Jewish language" was eliminated; the entry on ancient Hebrew noted that it was the language of the State of Israel and the "literary language of the Jewish bourgeoisie in different countries of Europe and America." In the third edition, which began publication in 1970, "Jewish language" became a brief reference to the new articles "Idish" and "Ivrit," with the latter now including ancient Hebrew as well.

24. "Prayer Book of Peace," named after the prayer for world peace and for the welfare of the Soviet government which is the distinguishing feature of this prayer book. Edited by Rabbi Jacob Shlifer, it was reprinted in 1968 and 1980.

25. Since only few of these calendars have reached Israel's libraries, we assume but are not certain that they have been issued annually since 5717 (1956/57). In the fifties they were reproduced from handwriting; by 5729 (1968/69) they were printed, but even the more attractive and elaborate issue for 5750 (1989/90) has numerous typographical errors in Hebrew, and still shows Soviet secular holidays, such as May Day and Lenin's Birthday, but not Israel Independence Day and Jerusalem Liberation Day.

16

Language as Quasilect: Hebrew in Contemporary Anglo-Jewry

LEWIS GLINERT

Quasilects

Most studies of human language, be they linguistic, sociological, ethnographic, or whatever, have been concerned with language as a "normal" faculty with "normal" functions. By this I mean a language that (a) provides an interface between form and meaning, (b) gives free rein to the faculty for infinite production of well-formed sentences and, (c) functions to communicate meaning (Grice 1957, 1968). Whichever other semiotic functions a language may play—as a symbol of identity, as a means of exclusion and so on—it is generally with languages that *also* have a "normal" structure and function (Fishman 1979) that the language sciences have been concerned.

In recent years, however, as the study of language in its social context has burgeoned (see the preface to this volume), we have seen an awakening of interest in all manner of purportedly "marginal" functions of language. As Michael Stubbs has observed in his study of written language (Stubbs 1980), each and every type of language system merits analysis on its own terms—and while our understanding of "normal" systems is undeniably of great comparison value, it must not usurp the study of other forms and functions of language.

Particularly scant attention has been paid to systems of the type represented by Hebrew as an ethnoreligious language in nontraditionalist Western Jewish life—systems in which next to no one "knows" the language in the sense of a being able to interpret or produce an infinite number of well-formed structures and in which the communication of meaning has come to play a fairly minor role. I wish to refer to such languages as "quasilects."

A quasilect is fundamentally different from a pidgin (see, e.g., Valdman 1977) or "foreigner talk" (Clyne 1981). While these seek to play an active communicative role to varying extents, with some degree of grammatical open-endedness, the quasilect has a quite different function and is based on a corpus of fixed utterances. Nor should a quasilect be confused with the kind of "dying" systems analyzed in Dressler and Wodak-Leodolter (1977) and Dorian (1989), in which a monostylistic or pidginized variety has come about such that the elements of the dying language still, at very least, carry meaning and maintain some kind of productive potential. Even the "semi-speakers" of the dying Sutherland Gaelic described by Dorian (1977), with their gross analogical levelling and other structural reduction, were a far cry from the quasilects that I have in mind.

I wish to propose a highly tentative set of features for what constitutes a quasilect (and quasilectal use). A quasilect is used for salient cultural purposes, with the following features: (a) users are unable to use it for open-ended active linguistic communication; (b) users are unable to use it for open-ended receptive linguistic communication; and typically (c) users do not know of this variety being currently used as a normal language; (d) users know of this variety having once been used as a normal language.

Such quasilects are not to be sought wherever an uprooted speech community maintains residual links with the mother country—in most such cases, the end of meaningful and communicative functioning of the old ethnic vernacular will simply spell the end for that language's functions, witness for example immigrant language shifts in the U.S.A. (Veltman 1983). No quasilect "phase" will arise here. Rather, one must look for cases of diglossia where an ex-vernacular (and "ex" may mean many, many generations ago) plays a religious function, particularly one associated with a great classical tradition (Fishman 1972). Examples are Arabic in non-Arab Moslem communities such as in coastal Kenya (Parkin, forthcoming), Northern Ghana (Goody 1968), and Nigeria and Mali (Brenner and Last 1985), Sanskrit among Hindus, Latin among Catholics, and Classical Greek among acculturated Cypriot emigrés. As Fishman 1985 has observed, such minorities with religious classicals may maintain an ethnic vernacular too (e.g., in the U.S.A. the Amish, Hasidim, and Greeks), but it is invariably the religious classical that is more secure—despite its being a quasilect.

This study will explore the functioning of one such quasilect, Hebrew, within the present-day British Jewish community. This community is one of the last major bastions of Ashkenazidom, both phenomenologically and objectively representing a continuation of many of the institutions, practices, and values of Eastern and above all Central Europe[1] (by contrast, notably, with French Jewry which underwent decimation followed by a massive North African influx, and with U.S. Jewry which in many respects constitutes a tradition all of its own, see Liebman 1974 and Sklare and Greenblum 1979.).

I shall focus on use rather than attitude. Were phenomenological language data available, they would indeed have been welcome; at the same time, attitudinal data are not objective reality and can in fact so easily divert attention from patterns of use.

Anglo-Jewish Religion and Language

Three languages play a major part in Anglo-Jewish religious life: English, Hebrew, and Yiddish. The role of Hebrew must be seen in terms of the overall linguistic polysystem, and at the same time in terms of an overarching *semiotic* polysystem creating more abstract, symbolic levels of "meaning."

The most striking feature of this polysystem is that the overwhelming majority of British Jews are monolingual. Although no statistics have been gathered, either by census or by other survey, this is the indubitable impression that is gained. Just a small minority of British Jews has any proficiency, written or oral, in a Jewish language—Hebrew or Yiddish—as "normal" vehicles of communication. This small minority embraces (a) those who have acquired proficiency in Hebrew as a modern language (occasionally through adult education, more often by time spent in Israel), (b) those who have been educated to some sort of proficiency in Hebrew as a traditional religious medium, (c) those (largely overlapping group b) with a proficiency in Yiddish, mostly as a vernacular "home-and-hearth" language but sometimes (and increasingly, as the number of Eastern-European-born Jews declines) as a language of Ultraorthodox religious instruction, and (d) a few thousand Israeli emigrés.[2] For the overwhelming majority of British Jews, Hebrew is—to varying degrees—a quasilect.

This study will examine the function of Hebrew in the core religious activity of worship and study. The way in which the Hebrew quasilect functions can throw light on the role of religion in Anglo-Jewish life, particularly on the relationship between religious and ethnic identity, and also on ethnoreligious Jewish subgroupings. It is unfortunate that so little is known about Anglo-Jewish attitudes. As Kosmin and Levy (1983) put it, "the lack of regular communal polling and time series data on Jewish opinions . . . is in marked contrast to the situation in the U.S.A., Australia and other diaspora communities." Nor has substantive anthropological research been conducted. This study must perforce draw largely on my own observations as a participant-observer.

At this point, a brief sketch of the ethnoreligious subgroupings is essential. There are seven main groupings, in terms of synagogue membership, which can be labelled: Ultraorthodox, "middle-of-the-road" Orthodox, Sephardi Orthodox, Masorti, Reform, Liberal, and unaffiliated.[3] The Kosmin and Levy 1983 survey of the Jewish community in Redbridge was able to make do with a three-way division: Orthodox (the factor being that neither Ultraorthodox nor Sephardi Orthodox were significantly represented in Redbridge), Progressive (covering Masorti, Reform, and Liberal), and unaffiliated.

The figures for these three groups were roughly 73% Orthodox, 16% Progressive, and 11% unaffiliated.[4] A national sample of Jewish adults in 1970 yielded similar figures: 76%, 15%, and 7%. The small but rapidly growing ultra-orthodox sector counts for maybe 5% of the total.

Kosmin and Levy found that these subgroupings are often more a matter of synagogue affiliation than of any more general Jewish social network or set of beliefs, and this is a point that must be stressed. The decision as to whether to affiliate to an Ultraorthodox or a mainstream Orthodox synagogue is sometimes more a reflection of synagogue availability and social and institutional preferences, etc. than of personal ideology; so too, particularly, for the choice between mainstream Orthodox, Masorti, Reform, and Liberal synagogues.

Hebrew in Jewish Worship

Throughout the entire spectrum of Anglo-Jewish synagogues—from the Ultraorthodox through to the Reform and Liberal Movements—Hebrew is the prime medium of worship. Worship refers primarily to synagogue prayer and Torah recitation. Although tradition stipulates two or three communal services every day, the Kosmin and Levy 1983 survey of the fairly typical Redbridge community reported that just 10% of over-15s (and a somewhat larger percentage of under-15s) attended synagogue regularly, in the sense of attending at least once on most Sabbaths. Of these, 60% were male. A further 17% attended on some Sabbaths and on festivals, 33% only on festivals (amounting to perhaps ten days a year), and 30% only on very special occasions (Yom Kippur, Bar Mitzvah, weddings). Ten percent never attended.

A further, secondary, aspect of worship is the recitation of prayers in the home, e.g., grace after meals, blessings before religious acts, and prayers on going to bed. By far the most widespread and substantial use of Hebrew in the home—and thus for many Jews the most salient—is the annual recitation of the Hagadah, the Passover Story, at the family Seder Night.[5] Let us consider the various Jewish subgroups in turn.

Middle-of-the-Road Orthodox

In Middle-of-the-Road Orthodox synagogues, all regularly scheduled prayer services are conducted almost entirely in Hebrew. Most services last two to three hours and consist of a sequence of fixed texts read from a prayer book and a scroll or printed book of the Torah (Five Books of Moses). There are in practise no options or spontaneous prayers.

Some of the texts are said silently, some are recited or sung in unison (with a prayer leader or choir generally keeping time), and some are chanted by a leader while the congregants periodically respond or—in the case of the Torah recitation—silently follow from their own text. Just two texts are regularly recited aloud by individual worshippers: (a) the Blessings said by an individual "called up" to the podium for the Torah recitation, and (b) the Kaddish prayer recited by mourners. These are not to be said in English. In addition, a boy celebrating his Bar Mitzvah Sabbath is expected to read a portion of the Torah aloud in Hebrew.

How far does the service involve a use of Hebrew—given that many women and more than a few men read Hebrew with great difficulty, if at all, and that both the prayer-book and the printed Torah generally have an English translation but no English transliteration? In practise, most worshippers who do not read Hebrew will be able to sing certain Hebrew prayers by heart but will have to read the prayers recited silently or listened to quietly from the English translation, or not at all. How much this happens is unclear, though one factor tending to promote a readiness to use English quietly is that children's prayer services, held simultaneously at many synagogues, often use a mixture of Hebrew and English.

The lack of English transliteration in the standard prayer-books is noteworthy.[6] The two texts said aloud individually in public worship, the Torah Blessings and the mourner's Kaddish, are deemed extremely important; indeed many worshippers attend over many months with the express purpose of reciting the mourner's Kaddish. Clearly, the community expects its members to acquire sufficient literacy to read these two texts (they cannot readily be picked up orally) in the original. Similarly, the "Bar Mitzvah boy" is expected to spend months training to read his few Torah verses in the original, with a complex chant. This is a selective Hebrew phonic literacy. Such literacy is a counter-example to Goody's (1968:222) generalization that "in religious literacy it is more important to learn the Holy Word [orally, if necessary] than to learn to read."

The many worshippers who do read Hebrew well enough to keep up with the prayers will not, for the most part, understand much of it. (That they have learned to read without understanding is due to the phonic regularity of Hebrew.) Most will understand just a few score words.[7] Of course they have an English translation on the facing page in their books, but this will not usually have been studied intensively at religion classes or adult education classes,[8] nor does the tempo of prayer allow one to refer to the English while reciting the Hebrew. So the act of worship generally takes place just in Hebrew. Indeed, little attempt is usually made by the rabbi to explain the prayers during the service. Only during the recitation of the Torah is the gist sometimes given, although here congregants are in any case at liberty to read the English translation at their leisure—here there are no set responses requiring one to keep an eye on the Hebrew.

Why do most British Jews worship in a barely comprehensible tongue? The question of what the worshippers themselves think they are doing, intriguing though it is, is not easily addressed. Do they consider themselves engaged in an act of communication with God; and is this a receptive or an active communication or both? Do they rather see this as a communicatively undifferentiated act of phatic communication with the divine? Is there instead a sentiment that this is a "demonstration" and not an act of communication—a kind of "nonserious" language use, in the sense of Goffman (1974) and Clark and Gerrig (1990)?

Any direct study of opinions, if it exists, will itself require cautious analysis. Any evidence from Anglo-Jewish folklore would also be valuable.[9] It should immediately be observed that worshippers generally refer to the act of praying by the Yiddish verb *dáven* or *dóven,* while the Torah recitation is termed *leyning* or *layning* (neither word has other current uses that might shed light on its import). This dichotomy may have something to say about the nature of the communication; so too may the very use of Yiddish terms suggestive of traditional values (rather than, say, the English term "to pray").

Let us enumerate a number of conceivable explanations for this use of Hebrew in worship. One is that this is simply a perpetuation of the traditional Jewish philosophical-legal notion that Hebrew is intrinsically sacred and hence worship in Hebrew is preferable—and efficacious even when not comprehended (Glinert 1987, Glinert and Shilhav 1991, Loewenthal, in this volume). However, given the willingness of Middle-of-the-Road British Judaism to acculturate in such matters as style of synagogues, style of pastoral rabbis, and educational standards in general, one might have predicted a modicum of English in its services, if only to avoid an educational strain and to avoid embarrassment to the uneducated.

An alternative explanation is that Hebrew plays a key role of making synagogue different from church. Synagogue architecture, the dress of the Jewish clergy and so on are, after all, somewhat undistinctive. And although Orthodox Jewish prayers, in their talk of return to Zion, the Temple and much else, manage to be distinctively Jewish, this in itself may not be enough. Indeed, the brand of English translations available may actually have a "church-like" ring about them.[10]

But there is undoubtedly more to it than this. What makes the use of Hebrew as a quasilect in worship so highly valued is the fact that synagogue worship is so salient in the cultural system of semiobservant Jews (more so, for example, than the dietary regulations and the Passover),[11] and that Hebrew qua language is a ready symbol of ethnic identity. While ethnic minority groups do not invariably feel a need to maintain their ethnic vernacular—Yiddish is a case in point—language is undoubtedly one of the commonest ethnic features (Fishman 1980, Edwards 1985). Note that most British Jews are just three generations away from a East European society in which the vernacular itself was a Jewish one. Alongside this ethnic function come Hebrew's religious associations as original language of the Torah and the rabbis; it is noteworthy that after-school religion classes are commonly known as "Hebrew classes." (See the discussion below of Hebrew education.) Thus using Hebrew is both an act of solidarity and an act of devotion.

It is particularly revealing that the major cognitive rite of initiation into the religious and ethnic group, the Bar Mitzvah (with its ambivalently religious and nonreligious ceremonies or rituals), centers on a trial by language—of a clearly quasilectal character: no one will know or ask if the "Bar Mitzvah boy" comprehends the Torah portion he reads (save, privately, the rabbi or tutor), but he will be expected to chant and pronounce correctly, and will probably, as mentioned, have spent many months training for it.

It may even be argued that the semi-incomprehensibility of the Hebrew and the general equanimity toward its quasilectal quality themselves serve to create a religious "absolute,"[12] a "mystery"—while the side-by-side translation, present in principle but probably little used, acts as a rational "cover" balancing and "excusing" the mystery. Ironically, worship in Hebrew may work so well for the semiobservant, nominally Orthodox masses precisely because it is not a clear comprehensible language. It heads off the philosophical and literary qualms that many such readers would have with a simple, straight English version of the prayers.

Such a model of the quasilectal function of Hebrew can be given further refinement by widening the picture to take in occasional religious services, e.g., special memorial services and civic services at the synagogue, circumcisions, marriages, and funerals. Here a certain amount of English translation is often used, not because the texts are particularly unfamiliar but, arguably, because they depart from the (highly standardized) synagogue service, especially when they are held away from the synagogue and involve a personal ceremony. (The limiting case, of a personalized prayer said within the synagogue, namely the *El Male Raḥamim* Memorial Prayer for the individual, is always in Hebrew.)[13] Thus Hebrew appears to be part of a "package" or closed system of formal synagogue worship, yielding slightly at the edges to a slightly less impersonal or public use of English—"impersonal" referring to the constant emphasis on the national experiences in the Jewish prayers.

The closedness of this system to any open-ended use of language is reinforced (or perhaps, conversely, reflected) by the near-universal use of the Singer's Prayer Book and of a choice of two or three sets of festival prayer books. Although Jewish thought has put a high premium on spontaneous and personally composed outpourings of the soul—indeed, Eastern European prayer books featured all manner of popular compositions, *tekhines,* in vernacular Yiddish for women—Middle-of-the-Road Anglo-Jewry perceives worship as fixed prayers to be said on fixed occasions. Spontaneity and enthusiasm are sought within these constraints, and in this case within the constraints of the Singer's Prayer Book.

All the use of Hebrew so far discussed as worship involves an essentially phatic communion, i.e., one that "does not function as a means of transmission of thought" and "in which the ties of union are created by the mere exchange of words" (Malinowski 1935). Any communication between worshippers, i.e., the sermon and announcements, is naturally in English—with the exception of the use of Hebrew to "call up" various worshippers by name to the podium for the recitation of the Torah, a set sentence involving the Hebrew name of the respective worshipper and functioning as an integral part of the ritual.

Running like a leitmotif through the discussion has been the fixedness of the form of prayer. A variable does, however, exist: the choice of pronunciation. This has proved a matter of controversy, with implications for Hebrew as a quasilect.

A majority of synagogues, rabbis, and prayer leaders probably use what one may call "Anglo-Ashkenazi" pronunciation, a peculiarly British outgrowth of European Hebrew reading pronunciations[14] (varying according to the local English pronunciation). Until the 1960s this was the one generally taught under Orthodox auspices. However, identification with the State of Israel, plus a growing knowledge of spoken Israeli, has created pressure to introduce an Israeli-type pronunciation, both in education and in the synagogue service. (This pronunciation is known as "Sephardi" and is indeed close to that used by the small old-time Anglo-Sephardi community, all of which gives it more religious legitimacy than mere association with Israel.) The British chief rabbi, Immanuel Jakobovits, used his authority over the Middle-of-the-Road Orthodox communities to stem such change in synagogue services, at least temporarily, but reluctantly allowed it in schools and Sunday classes (Jakobovits 1984:28–30). The outcome is that an increasing proportion of worshippers, perhaps the majority in younger communities, use the Israeli-type accent.

For many of them, this may be of no more significance than praying in the older accent. But many others, making an actual switch to the Israeli-type accent or simply knowing some spoken Hebrew, will be aware of forming a bond with modern Israeli usage. This will accord with their pride in that country,[15] a pride that has a religious dimension expressed through Israel Independence Day religious services, through the fund-raising sermon for Israel commonly delivered on Yom Kippur evening at the moment when the synagogue is at its fullest, and through the prayer for Israel prominently declaimed every Sabbath. It is no coincidence that the rabbis often make a point of reading the prayer for Israel in the Israeli-type pronunciation.

The rise of this pronunciation has implications for the quasilectal status of Hebrew. While still unable and generally unconcerned to use this language like a "normal" language, British Jews are liable to associate it increasingly with the "normal" all-purpose vernacular of modern Israel. It would be revealing for models of "normal" versus quasilectal language to examine the effect of such "normality by association" upon attitudes and behavior. Are Jews more inclined to improve their proficiency in synagogue Hebrew (or indeed in spoken Hebrew) by virtue of using the same pronunciation for both? Might the stylized chant or language of synagogue Hebrew outweigh the similarities and frustrate the association? Predictions might be forthcoming from the North American experience, where the Jewish day school and Sunday school systems have emphasized spoken Hebrew for two generations, but have now—for reasons often more to do with the time and teachers available or with perceptions of Israel than with issues of "normality"—widely reverted to a concentration on "synagogue skills" (Glinert 1992). Mintz (1992) has gathered a rich variety of experiences and theorizings by American educationalists on the question of "which Hebrew?"; but sociolinguistic study of this realm remains to be done.

The Ultraorthodox

At first blush, the use of Hebrew in Ultraorthodox and Orthodox worship is almost indistinguishable. Ultraorthodox prayer services are conducted entirely in Hebrew, including the prayer for the queen and government and marriages, funerals, and other irregular services.

This small difference, however, is a reflex of a fundamentally different language attitude. The Hebrew of the ancient sources is explicitly considered the sacred tongue (and commonly called *loshn koydesh* "sacred tongue") and its use in worship a powerful numinous aid. Even as the codes of law technically allow worship in the vernacular, they dismiss it in practise as importing alien ways—and they offer assurance that lack of comprehension is no barrier to the efficacy of prayer. One expression of this value (originally a Hasidic tale with a polemically populist intent) is the widely-told tale of the child who cannot read his prayers and instead lets loose a heart-felt whistle. Another is the fact that obscure and euphuistic poems that none but the most learned can translate figure prominently in the festival prayers.

The Ultraorthodox, males and females alike, by dint of intensive education and constant repetition of prayers, generally acquire fluency in reading, some degree of comprehension skill with simple prayer book or Bible prose, and a large repertoire of memorized prayers. To this is added, typically among males, a semimemorized knowledge of many passages in the Pentateuch and Talmud. And it is here that one might expect a fundamental departure from the quasilectal model presented for Middle-of-the-Road Orthodox worship. Ultraorthodoxy sets great store by lifelong, open-ended study by its menfolk of the religious sources (Heilman 1983), in which profound comprehension rather than rote translation, let along mere memorization, is of the essence.

Implicit in this is the notion that one should strive to maximize one's comprehension of Hebrew—yet Ultraorthodox attitudes and practices appear to belie this:

schools rarely if ever teach Hebrew language as such, be it grammar or lexis; at most, they teach word lists and ad hoc grammar for the particular texts being translated or analyzed. Ultraorthodox bookstores rarely carry linguistic aids to study. Texts used in worship are accorded cursory linguistic study. More important are the so-called "mechanics" of prayer—reading fluency, familiarity with the structure of the prayer book, associated customs—and the profundities behind the literal text. Until recently, the British Ultraorthodox rarely used prayer books with an English translation; if, in the last decade, American prayer books with a modern Ultraorthodox translation and commentary have become widespread, it appears to be on account of the commentary. Rarely is Hebrew penmanship or productive writing stressed. Nor is there any attempt to import Hebrew usage per se into one's English vernacular (along the lines of the embroidery of Swahili with religious Arabic described in Parkin, forthcoming); the mark of a scholar is to import Hebrew quotations from the sources.

All this is not, however, seen as jeopardizing a knowledge of Hebrew. Hebrew is to be learned inductively, by osmosis as it were, through sheer intensiveness of textual exposure. The received wisdom is that this has always worked and will go on working.

If one is not quite satisfied with this as a functional explanation, recent history can supply a vital clue: Ultraorthodoxy is living in the after-echo of the traumatic eighteenth and nineteenth century Jewish Enlightenment, which set in train the great loss of faith and the secularization of the Jewish masses. A central feature of this Enlightenment was the elevation of Hebrew linguistic study to a supreme goal (see Shavit and Bartal, in this volume). The Ultraorthodox reaction continues to the present, usually expressed latently in the ways adumbrated above but occasionally in explicit terms too (Glinert and Shilhav 1991).

The net result is a distinctively Ultraorthodox model of the Hebrew quasilect. Hebrew is indeed to be learned and comprehended as a "normal" system—but in a manner deliberately unlike the "normal" (i.e., normal in the traditional Ultraorthodox perception) methods of learning a foreign or classical tongue. Those sufficiently advanced to wish to use Hebrew for active communicative writing (typically articles on religious themes) may do so, and will be congratulated; but with no explicit attention to matters of style. For Hebrew to be used for personal communication, e.g., letters, as it so commonly was in all religious circles, is very unusual— save where an Israeli is involved. In sum, then, it is Hebrew knowledge in the passive that takes up most energies.

Speaking Ashkenazic Hebrew is simply not on the agenda. Here too external forces may have played a negative part: the rise of Zionist-sponsored spoken Hebrew has coincided with the end of old Hasidic customs of speaking Hebrew on the Sabbath. This brings us to a further, salient feature of Ultraorthodox worship that is explicitly designed to maintain a distance between traditional *loshn koydesh* and "normalized" Hebrew (commonly dubbed *Ivrit*): an Ashkenazi form of pronunciation is the norm in all such synagogues, typically marked off from Middle-of-the-Road pronunciation by a propensity for the diphthong *oy* where the former will use *o*, thus *yoysef* for *yosef*. The virtue of tradition, of upholding "the teachings of one's mother," is often adduced as the reason for this; but it is revealing that many such synagogues prohibit an Israeli born into an Israeli accent from leading the prayers in his pronunciation—despite the fact that this pronunciation is already familiar to all.

"Progressives"

In the Reform and Liberal synagogues[16] language policy and practice has always been markedly less Hebrew-oriented—but this is widely changing. The underlying conception of Hebrew has ranged from that of an extreme quasilect with at best nominal historical value to a language worthy of religious reverence and limited study—and, recently, even to an identification of sorts with "normalized" functions of modern Hebrew.

The Progressive worship as a whole is a case of a circular interplay between values and praxis. The earlier ideologues of European and Anglo-American Progressivism, opposed to ideas and symbols of nationhood and committed to rationalism and an isomorphism with the other major faiths of Britain, wanted Hebrew worship cut back or cut out (Plaut 1963, Petuchowski 1968: chap. 5, and Meyer 1988: chap. 2).[17] The tendency of less committed and less Hebrew-literate Jews to gravitate to such synagogues reinforced this praxis, and there they and their offspring in turn received little Hebrew reinforcement.

At the same time, as Kosmin and Levy have underlined, the individual Reform Jew commonly mirrors the individual Middle-of-the-Road Jew in education and values, with substantial switching between Progressive and Middle-of-the-Road membership.

Taking Reform worship first,[18] their standard prayer book, "Forms of Prayer," gives implicit recognition to the importance of Hebrew by offering a large body of Hebrew prayers with their English translation, plus extra readings in English. There are no rubrics dictating or suggesting how much of the Hebrew should be used, and in fact congregations vary widely in their choice. (Progressive Judaism has been intrinsically laissez-faire, linguistically and otherwise.) English has tended to outweigh Hebrew, but an even balance is now emerging, a point to which I shall return.

Revealingly for the function of Hebrew, the congregation generally uses Hebrew and English for different texts, rather than using the English as a translation of the Hebrew or vice versa; Hebrew is not being presented as a language to be understood or studied in the course of worship, but as a quasilectal medium—and one that is no marginal symbol akin to the Stars of David, which a worshipper may see around him yet which make absolutely no demands upon him, but a central feature of ritual: the traditional "highlights" of worship (which the Orthodox value the highest and require to be said with the greatest concentration or while standing or the like), e.g., Shema, Amidah, Kedushah, Kaddish, are generally said in Hebrew. (Contrast this with the marginal function of Hebrew, along with most things ethnic or transcendent, in the American Reform synagogue, "Temple Shalom," studied by Furman 1987.) All singing is in Hebrew—perhaps a more appropriate medium for emotive, nonrational activity, perhaps because a hymn in English feels more un-Jewish than a piece of prose. No distinction is made between biblical and rabbinic texts.

The one activity in which Hebrew does come in tandem with its English translation (line-by-line or section-wise) is, significantly, the recitation of the Torah. This is not "prayer" but "study." As a whole, where once the reader or choir frequently read solo, today's worship tends to be responsive or collective, encouraging and expecting at least a Hebrew reading ability—transliterations are not used. Again, this is no ornamental "Star of David" phenomenon.

There is, moreover, a steady shift toward an even balance between Hebrew and English, with both rabbinic and lay support. Two factors, possibly related, are in play: first, growing identification by the Reform movement with Jewish ethnicity, with Israel and with Hebrew as its national language, embodied in the foundation of the first Reform day school, with Israeli teachers teaching Israeli Hebrew, and the growth of Israel-oriented Reform youth groups; second, a steady move back to traditionalism, illustrated by the new edition of the prayer book with its shift toward the traditional form of prayers.

As Reform synagogues have used a Sephardi, quasi-Israeli pronunciation for many years, the associativity with Israeli Hebrew is that much stronger. It cannot, however, affect the fundamentally quasilectal nature of Reform Hebrew until fulltime Jewish education becomes the norm.

By contrast, the Liberal movement (half the size of the Reform movement) is broadly more radical in practices and values, and has made much less use of Hebrew. Some Hebrew texts do feature in their official prayer book, Service of the Heart (1967); thus, it calls for Yotzer Or, the first paragraph of the Shema, and the Amidah to be recited in Hebrew, whereas Ahavah Rabbah is to be said in English. However, the fact that it opens from right to left—unlike any Hebrew book—symbolizes the marginal position of Hebrew; it seems to be more of historical than of philosophical or transcendental value.

Yet here too there is a shift toward tradition and toward greater use of Hebrew; the revised prayer book to appear in 1993 will have more traditional Hebrew wordings, without rubrics compelling the worshipper to use one language or the other. Reform and Liberal rabbis now train together, Liberal and Reform educational systems are converging, and a full merger may be less than a generation away.

The Liberal quasilect stands toward one extreme of the quasilect: a language has been "learned," in the sense of acquiring a phonic ability of sorts, but is put to little use. At the other extreme, as we have seen, some Orthodox Jews make substantial use of the language while still unable or unconcerned to acquire even merely receptive communicative ability.

Other Anglo-Jewish Uses of Hebrew

Worship aside, the only other major use of Hebrew in Anglo-Ashkenazi life is in education—to which allusion has already been made. Other, minor uses are a few dozen Hebrew-Yiddish cultural terms such as *shabbos, kosher, rosh hashono* (used as part of general communication and thus outside the quasilect), in given names, and in certain set-piece written uses: documents, written invitations and announcements, and memorial inscriptions. An exploratory analysis of these minor uses is found in Glinert (1985); here I shall dwell briefly on the quasilect in education.

Some 10 to 15 percent of Jewish children (mainly under-11) attend Jewish day school, while some 65 to 75 percent attend part-time synagogue classes, mostly for a few years leading up to Bar Mitzvah or its female equivalent and many (if not most), nominally Orthodox as well as Progressive, for just two to three hours on a Sunday morning.

In most Jewish day schools, Hebrew involves fluency reading, particularly of sacred texts, a little penmanship, and a fair amount of translation work on these texts. The predominant pronunciation is now the Israeli one; but as only a handful of primary schools use Israeli Hebrew as a teaching medium (and only for religious studies) and high-school Israeli Hebrew studies get short shrift, the result is not an active command of the modern language. For the religious language, the result is at most a part-competence in receptive communication. Although most Orthodox schools invest many hours in text study, language skills are imparted mainly by induction.

Part-time synagogue classes operate in English. Although many make elementary use of spoken Hebrew, as part of a "direct method" of teaching Hebrew reading, they are well-satisfied with semifluency in reading and a basic rote comprehension of a few basic prayers and short Bible passages by age 13. Sunday-only pupils may well spend half their total learning time wrestling with Hebrew reading, the main test being the Bar Mitzvah passage. It is not surprising that these classes are popularly referred to as "Hebrew classes." ("Are you going to Hebrew today?" one child may ask another.)

The childhood education system creates the quasilect that will continue to serve the British Jew throughout his life. With the (important) exception of the year or years spent by Ultraorthodox students at yeshivah and seminary, adult education has little impact, whether through classical or modern Hebrew study. And although there may be a trend away from weekday after-school education to either day school or Sunday school, it will not fundamentally affect the pattern of a stable Ashkenazi Hebrew quasilect.

Epilogue

This study has sought to focus attention on the existence of a noncommunicative but far from dysfunctional use of Hebrew in Ashkenazi life, as what I have termed a "quasilect."

A generation ago, it may have seemed to many that the time for such a Hebrew in Britain was past. On one side, the "normalized" Israeli Hebrew and the concept of the new Jewish state promised to occupy the center ground of the school curriculum; on the other, and partly in response, the traditional quasi-meaningful use of Hebrew in worship and study seemed bound to continue its steady decline—within the general decline of traditional Judaism.

Today, in Britain as in the U.S.A., the status of local Jewish culture in the curriculum has been bolstered, while any hopes of Israeli Hebrew becoming a second language have been chilled by the realities of the school timetable and foreign-language teaching techniques, and by the sheer physical separation of Israel from the overwhelming majority of local Jews. Within this context, the future of the Anglo-Jewish Hebrew quasilect appears a stable one.

Notes

1. On Modern British Jewry in general, little social scientific research exists. See the collections by Gould and Esh (1964), Lipman and Lipman (1981), Krausz (1969), Harris (1972), Grizzard and Raisman (1980), Glinert (1985), and above all Kosmin and Levy (1983).

2. There is a fairly substantial number of Israeli "temporary residents," who are irrelevant to this study.

3. The actual institutional groupings and the names they give themselves are somewhat more complex. The Ultraorthodox, distinguished from other Orthodox groups by a tendency toward the more stringent options offered in the Jewish codes of practice, typically with a sentimental and behavioral attachment to the traditional Eastern-European Jewish lifestyle (Friedman 1987, Glinert and Shilhav 1991), tend to call themselves *heimish* or *frum*—the latter also being used to include those members of "Middle-of-the-Road" Orthodox synagogues who are traditionally observant in practice. The Ultraorthodox world in turn divides into three fairly distinct subgroups, known by the adjectives *khasidish, litvish,* and *yekkish.* The "Middle-of-the-Road" Orthodox—the quote marks are to indicate that this is a popular rather than "official" in-group epithet—are represented for the most part by two large bodies, the United Synagogue and the Federation of Synagogues, each with its own educational and synagogue network.

4. Kosmin and Levy 1983: 7.

5. The Hagadah needs to be considered separately; in behavioral and folkloristic terms, it is arguably on the borderline between an act of worship and an altogether different kind of ritual act.

6. The *Authorized Daily Prayer Book,* edited in the last century by Simeon Singer and popularly known as "Singer's Prayer Book," has a near-monopoly. Some American prayer books do provide a transliterated Kaddish; and at the Torah-reading podium a transliteration of the blessings is sometimes provided. It is equally remarkable that even the many and varied editions of the Passover Hagadah (read by the family group in a particularly informal manner) rarely include transliteration of the Hebrew.

7. Few worshippers progress beyond a fairly basic quasilectal linguistic plateau. A prime factor is that the prayers are a mix of early rabbinic compositions, with a simple, fairly repetitive lexis and grammar, and biblical and medieval poetry posing a substantial linguistic and literary challenge.

8. Whether the quasilectal nature of the Hebrew of worship is caused by or is itself the cause of such educational policies is a moot point.

9. On the notion of folk-linguistics, see Hoenigswald (1966) and Bauman (1975). I am not aware of any British-Jewish folkloric studies.

10. Those elderly British Jews who were raised in Eastern Europe were wont to read certain prayers—private meditations—in their Yiddish vernacular. But Yiddish was a specifically Jewish language, unlike English. Indeed, the English rendition in both the first (1890) and the second (1962) edition of the oft-reprinted Singer's Prayer Book has an unabashedly archaic "King James" ring to it. Only in 1990 was a modern translation substituted.

11. This is the inference from any saliency metric invoking "hours spent at." Kosmin and Levy (1983:9) conclude from their own diverse data that "the synagogue is a central institution of Jewish life."

12. On the notion of the religious language as an "absolute," see Waardenburg (1979).

13. As an example of the extent to which English is avoided even in personalized prayers, the blessing pronounced over a synagogue donation commonly uses the word *ginis* (none other than the obsolete unit of currency known as the guinea, i.e., 21 shillings) rather than a recognizably current term like "pound."

14. See Katz (this volume). Rather than any of the Central or East European pronunciations of the *holam* vowel (au, oy, ey), all of which are found in Standard English, the Anglo-Ashkenazi reading-pronunciation has adopted the "o" vowel as used in "home," perhaps as a supra-dialectal form. So too, interestingly, have the American-Ashkenazi *and* the American-Sephardicized pronunications. Another, now obsolescent Anglo-Ashkenazi pronunciation based on earlier waves of West-Central European migration had an *ou* diphthong for stressed *kamatz* in open syllables.

15. Kosmin and Levy (1983: chap. 5) report 1970 NOP survey findings that 80% of their Jewish sample favored a Jewish state, 36% would have liked to live in Israel, and 38% would have liked their children to live in Israel. Of course, between "favoring" Israel and actually contemplating migration stretches a broad range of other positive attitudes.

16. The fledgling Masorti movement, nominally intermediate between Orthodox and Reform, has only emerged in the last decade. I have not attempted to draw a profile of it.

17. The Anglo-Sephardi influence on early British Reform Judaism may have contributed to this maintenance of Hebrew. For a brief sketch of the British Progressives, see Kershen (1990).

18. I am indebted to Michael Shire for his assessment of the Reform and Liberal movements. Rigorous quantitative or other studies have yet to be undertaken.

References

BAUMAN, RICHARD. "Quaker Folk-Linguistics and Folklore." In Dan Ben-Amos and Kenneth S. Goldstein, eds. *Folklore: Performance and Communication.* The Hague: Mouton, 1975, pp. 255–63.

BRENNER, LOUIS, and MURRAY LAST. "The Role of Language in West African Islam." *Africa* 55,4 (1985): 432–46.

CLARK, HERBERT H. and RICHARD J. GERRIG. "Quotations as Demonstrations." *Language* 66,4 (1990): 764–805.

CLYNE, M., ed. *Foreigner Talk.* International Journal of the Sociology of Language 28, 1981.

DORIAN, NANCY. "The Problem of the Semi-Speaker in Language Death." In Dressler and Wodak-Leodolter 1977: 23–32.

———, ed. *Investigating Obsolescence: Studies in Language Contraction and Death.* Cambridge: Cambridge University Press, 1989.

DRESSLER, WOLFGANG and RUTH WODAK-LEODOLTER, eds. *Language Death.* International Journal of the Sociology of Language, 12 (The Hague: Mouton, 1977).

EDWARDS, JOHN. *Language, Society and Identity.* London: Basil Blackwell, 1985.

FISHMAN, JOSHUA A. *Language and Nationalism.* Rowley, MA.: Newbury House, 1972.

———. "Yiddish and *loshn koydesh* in Traditional Ashkenaz: The Problem of Societal Allocation of Macro-functions." In Albert Verdoodt and Rolf Kjolseth, eds. *Language in Sociology.* Louvain: Peeters, 1976, pp. 39–47.

———. "The Sociolinguistic 'Normalization' of the Jewish People." In E. Polome, ed. *Archibald Hill Festschrift.* Vol. 3. The Hague: Mouton, 1979.

———. "Language Maintenance and Ethnicity." *Canadian Review of Studies in Nationalism* (1980): 229–48. Reprinted in Joshua A. Fishman, ed. *Language and Ethnicity in Minority Sociolinguistic Perspective.* Clevedon: Multilingual Matters, 1989, pp. 202–23.

———. "The Societal Basis of Intergenerational Continuity of Additional Languages." In K. R. Jankowsky, ed. *Scientific and Humanistic Dimensions of Language. Festschrift for Robert Lado.* Amsterdam: John Benjamins, 1985, pp. 551–58. Reprinted in Joshua A. Fishman, ed. *Language and Ethnicity in Minority Sociolinguistic Perspective.* Clevedon: Multilingual Matters, 1989, pp. 224–32.

FRIEDMAN, MENAHEM. "Life Tradition and Book Tradition in the Development of Ultraorthodox Judaism." In Harvey E. Goldberg, ed. *Judaism Viewed from Within and Without.* Albany: State University of New York Press, 1987, pp. 235–55.

FURMAN, FRIDA KERNER. *Beyond Yiddishkeit: The Struggle for Identity in a Reform Synagogue.* Albany: State University of New York Press, 1987.

GLINERT, LEWIS. "The Language of Anglo-Jewish Religious Life." In Lewis Glinert. *Aspects of British Judaism.* London: School of Oriental and African Studies, *Occasional Papers,* 11, 1985, pp. 7–20.

———. *Aspects of British Judaism.* London: School of Oriental and African Studies, *Occasional Papers,* 11, 1985.

———. "Hebrew." In Arthur A. Cohen and Paul Mendes-Flohr, eds. *Contemporary Jewish Religious Thought.* New York: Scribners, 1987, pp. 325–30.

———, and YOSSEPH SHILHAV. "Holy Land, Holy Language: A Study of an Ultraorthodox Jewish Ideology." *Language in Society* 20 (1991): 59–86.

———. "Hebrew Toward the Year 2000: From Symbol to Substance." In Mintz 1992.

GOFFMAN, ERVING. *Frame Analysis.* New York: Harper & Row, 1974.

GOODY, JACK. "Restricted Literacy in Northern Ghana." In Jack Goody, ed. *Literacy in Traditional Societies.* Cambridge: Cambridge University Press, 1968, pp. 199–264.

GOULD, JULIUS, and S. ESH, eds. *Jewish Life in Modern Britain.* London: Routledge & Kegan Paul, 1984.

GRICE, H. PAUL. "Meaning." *Philosophical Review* 66 (1957): 377–88.

———. "Utterer's Meaning, Sentence-Meaning, and Work-Meaning." *Foundations of Language* 4 (1968): 225–42.

GRIZZARD, NIGEL, and PAULA RAISMAN. "Inner City Jews in Leeds." *Jewish Journal of Sociology* 22 (1980): 21–33.

HARRIS, SYDNEY. "The Identity of Jews in an English City." *Jewish Journal of Sociology* 14 (1972): 63–84.

HEILMAN, SAMUEL. *The People of the Book: Drama, Fellowship, and Religion.* Chicago: University of Chicago Press, 1983.

HOENIGSWALD, HENRY M. "A Proposal for the Study of Folk-Linguistics." In William Bright, ed. *Sociolinguistics.* The Hague: Mouton, 1966, pp. 16–20.

JAKOBOVITS, IMMANUEL. *If Only My People. . . .* London: Weidenfeld & Nicolson, 1984.

KERSHEN, ANNE, ed. *150 Years of Progressive Judaism in Britain.* London: The London Museum of Jewish Life, 1990.

KOSMIN, BARRY and CAREN LEVY. *Jewish Identity in an Anglo-Jewish Community: The Findings of the 1978 Redbridge Jewish Survey.* London: Research Unit of the Board of Deputies of British Jews, 1983.

KRAUSZ, ERNST. "The Edgware Survey: Factors in Jewish Identification." *Jewish Journal of Sociology* 11 (1969): 151–63.

LIEBMAN, CHARLES. "The Religion of American Jews." In Marshall Sklare, ed. *The Jew in American Society.* New York: Behrman House, 1974.

LIPMAN, SONIA, and VIVIAN LIPMAN, eds. *Jewish Life in Britain 1962–1977.* New York: K. G. Saur, 1981.

MALINOWSKI, BRONISLAW. *Coral Gardens and Their Meaning.* London: George Allen & Unwin, 1935.

MEYER, MICHAEL. *Response to Modernity: A History of the Reform Movement in Judaism.* New York and Oxford: Oxford University Press, 1988.

MINTZ, ALAN. *Hebrew in America: Perspectives and Prospects.* Detroit: Wayne State University Press, 1992.

PARKIN, DAVID. "Language, Government and the Play on Purity and Impurity: Arabic, Swahili and the Vernaculars in Kenya." In Richard Fardon and Graham Furniss, eds. *African Languages, Development and the State.* London: Routledge. Forthcoming.

PETUCHOWSKI, JACOB J. *Prayerbook Reform in Europe: The Liturgy of European Liberal and Reform Judaism.* New York: World Union for Progressive Judaism, 1968.

PLAUT, W. GUNTHER. *The Rise of Reform Judaism.* New York: World Union for Progressive Judaism, 1963.

SKLARE, MARSHALL and J. GREENBLUM. *Jewish Identity on the Suburban Frontier.* Chicago: Chicago University Press, 1979.

STUBBS, MICHAEL. *Language and Literacy: The Sociolinguistics of Reading and Writing.* London: Routledge & Kegan Paul, 1980.

VALDMAN, A., ed. *Pidgin and Creole Linguistics.* Bloomington and London: Indiana University Press, 1977.

VELTMAN, C. *Language Shift in the United States.* Berlin: Mouton, 1983.

WAARDENBURG, JACQUES. "The Language of Religion, and the Study of Religions as Sign Systems." In Lauri Honko, ed. *Science or Religion: Studies in Methodology,* The Hague: Mouton, 1979, pp. 441–57.